DEVELOPMENT SOCIOLOGY

In this exciting and challenging work, Norman Long brings together years of work and thought in development studies to provide a key text for guiding future development research and practice.

Using case studies and empirical material mainly from Latin America, *Development Sociology* focuses on the theoretical and methodological foundations of an actor-oriented and social constructionist form of analysis. This style of analysis is opposed to the traditional structuralist/institutional analysis which is often applied in development studies.

With an accessible mix of general debate, critical literature reviews and original case-study materials this work covers a variety of key development issues. Among many important topics discussed, the author looks at commoditisation, small-scale enterprise and social capital, knowledge interfaces, networks and power, globalisation and localisation as well as policy formulation and planned intervention processes.

This book should be read for its desire to pursue a form of analysis that helps us to understand better (and more realistically) the kinds of development interventions and social transformations that have characterised the second half of the twentieth century and will no doubt continue to characterise future development studies.

Norman Long is Professor of Sociology of Development at Wageningen University in the Netherlands. He is the author of *An Introduction to the Sociology of Rural Development* (Routledge, 1977) and co-editor of *Battlefields of Knowledge* (Routledge, 1992) and *Anthropology, Development and Modernities* (Routledge, 2000).

DEVELOPMENT SOCIOLOGY

Actor perspectives

Norman Long

London and New York

First published 2001
by Routledge
2 Park Square, Milton Park, Abingdon, Oxon, OX14 4RN

Simultaneously published in the USA and Canada
by Routledge
270 Madison Ave, New York NY 10016

Routledge is an imprint of the Taylor & Francis Group

Transferred to Digital Printing 2006

© 2001 Norman Long

Typeset in Goudy by Taylor & Francis Books Ltd

British Library Cataloguing in Publication Data
A catalogue record for this book is available from the British Library

Library of Congress Cataloging-in-Publication Data
Long, Norman
Development sociology: actor perspectives
p. cm Includes bibliographical data and references
1. Rural development. 2. Community development 3. Economic development
4. Social change I. Title
HN49. C6 L66 2001
307.1'412 –dc21

ISBN 0–415–23535–9 (hbk)
ISBN 0–415–23536–7 (pbk)

Publisher's Note

The publisher has gone to great lengths to ensure the quality of this reprint
but points out that some imperfections in the original may be apparent

TO THE THREE 'A's IN MY LIFE,
ANN, ALISON AND ANDREW

CONTENTS

ILLUSTRATIONS

Tables

Figures

PREFACE AND ACKNOWLEDGEMENTS

This book sprang from the idea of Ann Long to assemble a collection of my published papers dealing with actor-oriented analysis for translation into Spanish. She had frequently witnessed the difficulties that some Latin American colleagues and post-graduates had in reading the English texts, and was equally aware of my own struggle to lecture in Spanish. Interest in my work in Latin America has grown over the past ten years, but little of this output has been translated into Spanish. She plotted with a friend and colleague, Magdalena Villarreal, who also had an interest in seeing a Spanish collection, to help put together such a volume. A further motive for the volume was their wish to present me with the Spanish version of the book as a form of celebratory surprise, rather like the normal *festschrift*, on the occasion of my retirement from the Chair at Wageningen University at the end of 2001.

However, in preparing the English text for translation, it became obvious to both of them that my help would have to be enlisted. Many of the individual chapters recommended for the book by colleagues in touch with my work, and by Magda based on her experience of teaching actor-oriented analysis to Mexican postgraduates, undoubtedly needed a good deal of updating and rewriting.

Between them the main contents and structure of the volume had largely been determined, but of course an attractive and informative Spanish version hinged crucially on the production of the new text in English. It was in this manner, then, that I became introduced and enthused into working on the English version of the present book. The rest, as the saying goes, should have been history. But life can take strange turns. The whole venture was interrupted and almost prevented from seeing the light of day due to my need for heart surgery a year ago. 'I've always had heart problems' is a comment I often make when asked about my health! But this was a bolt from the blue that kept me away from finishing the re-casting and writing of the book. Again I must thank Ann, not only for nursing me back to health through what proved to be an emotionally draining period, but for encouraging me to believe I could finish the job. Enjoying for a period thinking and reading about things other than development sociology – returning to my old interest in the British 'pastoral' composers of the first half of the twentieth century – I could avoid finishing the book. In the end, the completion of the manuscript was, as always in my life and work, due in no small measure to the unconditional support given me by my wife Ann.

The task turned out to be far bigger than either of us anticipated. The re-casting of old, and the writing of new chapters cost an inordinate amount of time and energy, which I no longer had in the same abundance. Ann assisted and at times cajoled me into focusing properly on the work at hand, cutting rambling parts of the text which I had inevitably become fond of and reluctant to dump, and straightening the argument and pulling it together.

This book, however, represents more than just a targeted joint effort, since throughout our everyday lives together we have shared and developed many common intellectual and social standpoints. Indeed my own ideas have been seamlessly shaped by Ann's own capacities and experiences working as an educational psychologist and book editor/translator. And none of this is incidental to the kind of theoretical and method-ological approach I have been struggling to build. Actor-oriented, interface and social constructionist perspectives clearly mark out a critical intellectual terrain in which the insights of sociology, anthropology and psychology converge. For example, when I first set to work on understanding 'interface' encounters, this was done in the context of Ann also struggling day-in day-out at critical interfaces with teachers, parents and their children. She had, that is, already acquired a practical and theoretical understanding of cultural and institutional interfaces. Indeed the close connection and convergence of our professional lifeworlds is itself an example of how social interfaces work. Though of course not always smoothly, we have in the end both learnt many things about how to build fulfilling interconnected lives, so important for human existence, especially in a world where personal and societal catastrophe seems always around the next corner.

My work over the last ten to fifteen years has been driven by general methodolog-ical and epistemological questions. This book, therefore, cannot claim to be a fully rounded account of the field of development sociology. It specifically addresses issues of a theoretical nature that primarily link with agency/structure questions. The book should be read for its drive to pursue analysis that helps us to understand better and more realistically the kinds of development interventions and social transformations that have characterised the second half of the twentieth century onwards and into the era of increased globalisation.

Of course, in a book of this nature, many substantive areas are missing, among them gender, environmental issues and the management of natural resources (including wildlife conservation) and humanitarian aid. There is also inadequate treatment of theories of the state and local patterns of governance, and of ideology and religion. Cultural identities in a globalising world where frontiers are no barrier to the move-ment of capital, labour or ideas, though mentioned, are likewise scantily covered.

The book tries to avoid a third-worldist vocabulary and perspective. Its scope embraces situations characteristic of the poorer, less industrialised societies, but does not exclude insights drawn from Europe and the US. The emphasis on rural contexts and rural development likewise does not exclude urban and more industrial or high-tech situations. Indeed, especially in the discussion of global/local change, it becomes impossible to carve up the world in ways that polarise the richer and poorer countries, thus treating them as quite different realities. While it is true that there are massive inequalities across the globe and that these divisions may be deepening, in order to understand the complex and diverse nature of the changing world we must do our best not to draw boundaries and counterpose what are perceived as markedly contrasting ideal types. In fact the most striking thing about the age we live in is of course that boundaries are breached all the time and political and economic borders are redrawn and constantly transgressed, as evidenced by the growing problems of illegal interna-tional migration.

As I hope this book clearly demonstrates, it has never been my intention to promote actor-oriented analysis as a fully elaborated theoretical model or toolkit of methods and techniques. Indeed to do so would run counter to the spirit of the endeavour. Instead, my interest has been in grappling conceptually with the flexibilities, ambiguities and socially constructed and self-transforming nature of social life, and to find conceptual handles for doing so. While the focus of the book is upon processes of development and social change, the approach can be useful to other fields of enquiry in social science, and undoubtedly parallel concerns arise in cultural studies and the arts. For example, as the contemporary composer, George Benjamin, concludes: 'what is really new about 20th century music is constructivism, the idea of composers inventing their own laws and composing not in a well-known and much used vernacular tradition but inventing their own world, a world of sound and a world of laws and techniques' (from Michael Oliver (ed.) (1999) *Settling the Score. A Journey Through the Music of the 20th Century.* London: Faber and Faber).

A short appendix has been added to give readers an overview of the main body of concepts used in the book and their interconnectedness. It is intended, like the constituent chapters, to be used flexibly. The reader may note some repetition of arguments and illustrations across chapters. This will make it easier for individual chapters and parts to be read independently of the full text.

Here I wish to acknowledge and thank my Wageningen colleagues Alberto Arce, Dirk van Dusseldorp, Paul Hebinck, Jos Michel, Monique Nuijten, Jan den Ouden, Sarah Southwold, Gerard Verschoor and Pieter de Vries, and many of my past and present post-graduates, who have contributed – each in their own way – to putting Wageningen rural development sociology and actor-oriented analysis on the international map.

I wish to extend a special word of gratitude to Jan den Ouden for reading and commenting on large parts of the book. He has brought a fresh and at times critical eye to the text and contributed many useful and challenging observations and suggestions for improvement of particular chapters. Throughout my twenty-year period at Wageningen, Jan and I have become close colleagues and good friends who have, shoulder-to-shoulder, braved the destructive waves of administrative reforms foisted upon us in the name of improved efficiency, rationalisation and accountability.

I owe a debt to many colleagues and friends whose ideas and work have contributed to the book. Among them I would like to mention Alberto Arce. He has taken issues of actor-oriented analysis into several adjacent (and sometimes surprising) fields of intellectual enquiry. At the core of much of his work is the centrality of knowledge processes in development, a position that I share with him, as evidenced by our jointly authored Chapter 9.

Magdalena Villarreal is an especially close friend and colleague. Apart from playing an important role in bringing this endeavour to fruition, she has, over the past ten years, worked closely with me on issues of commoditisation and globalisation, and more generally has made an invaluable contribution to the advancement of actor-oriented studies. Two chapters in the present volume originate from our joint publications.

In addition, I would like to thank Niels Röling and Cees Leeuwis of Communication and Innovation Studies for the lively interest they have shown in my work. And finally, a special word of appreciation must go to Jan Douwe van der Ploeg, once a member of my Chair group and now Professor of Rural Sociology, for the opportunity to work together with him on several key articles and chapters in books that deal with issues of social heterogeneity, planned intervention and actor perspectives. In the main body of this book, I pause several times to acknowledge the important and highly stimulating contributions that he and his group have made to the line of analysis I pursue.

Finally, the manuscript has been delivered, though a year late. Polly Osborn of Routledge, who never gave up on the project, deserves my thanks for her interest and support.

Norman Long
Bennekom, The Netherlands, February 2001

INTRODUCTION

Unlike other general works in the field of development studies, this book focuses on the theoretical and methodological foundations of an actor-oriented and social constructionist form of analysis as opposed to structural, institutional and political economy analyses. It also aims to show the usefulness of such an approach for providing new insights into critical areas of empirical enquiry. The latter cover a variety of key development issues: commoditisation and commodity values, small-scale enterprise and social capital, knowledge interfaces, networks and power, the interrelations of globalisation and localisation, as well as the dynamics of policy discourse and planned intervention. Wherever possible the arguments are elaborated and brought to life by reference to case studies and empirical materials collected during periods of fieldwork in parts of Africa and Latin America.

Following the so-called 'impasse' in development studies in the mid-1980s, considerable interest was directed towards resolving the theoretical and methodological shortcomings of existing structural and generic theories of development that espoused various forms of determinism, linearity and institutional hegemony. They were also, by and large, 'people-less' and obsessed with the conditions, contexts and 'driving forces' of social life rather than with the self-organising practices of those inhabiting, experiencing and transforming the contours and details of the social landscape. One way out of this impasse, I argued, was to adopt an actor-oriented perspective that explored how social actors (both 'local' and 'external' to particular arenas) are locked into a series of intertwined battles over resources, meanings and institutional legitimacy and control.

Much of the groundwork for this had already been laid down conceptually in a variety of interactionist and phenomenological studies undertaken by sociologists and anthropologists in the 1960s and 1970s, and ethnographic case-study methods had grown in popularity across a number of different areas of social research. It only required a little sociological imagination and a willingness to provoke, to make the next step: namely, to mount a number of strategic forays into the territory of development theory and practice, aimed at deconstructing the 'received wisdoms' of this specialised niche of knowledge production and prescription. While some of my early forays offered reasoned arguments for incorporating actor issues and analysis into existing frameworks, and thus tilting the balance towards the agency side of the structure/actor equation[1], others adopted a more combative stance, pitching a critique at the orthodoxies then prevalent within policy and planning circles.[2]

In the early 1990s, in what was evidently a more postmodernist intellectual environment, several theoretical attempts to resolve the shortcomings of existing social theories of development were offered. Some were couched in terms of post-structural Marxism and

1

were essentially 'revisionist' in tone (e.g., Corbridge 1990[3]), others drew upon Foucauldian discourse analysis to reveal the power and yet potential fragility of Western representations of 'modernity' and 'developmentalism' (e.g., Ferguson 1990, Hobart 1993 and Escobar 1995). And yet others adopted a more pragmatist point of view that affirmed the central importance of ethnographic methods and a critical assessment of 'participatory' processes, linked to the acknowledgement of the important role that local populations can make to the process of change (e.g., Pottier 1993, and Nelson and Wright 1995). Concomitant with these developments was the publication of three general theoretical overviews (Schuurman 1993, Booth 1994, and Preston 1996)[4] that explicitly take up actor-oriented analysis as a pivotal new direction in the re-orientation of research on social change and development. While each book reaches somewhat different conclusions, actor-oriented and social constructionist modes of analysis are identified as a significant advance and antidote to the excesses of structuralist and culturalist types of explanation.

A cumulative effect of this increased interest in challenging existing orthodoxies in development research and practice has been that actor-oriented analysis and issues relating to the conceptualisation of agency and processes of social change have now moved to centre stage. This holds not only for academics researching social change and development but also for policy actors and development practitioners in general. Indeed, the approach has recently been taken up[5] by national and international bodies involved in the design, implementation and evaluation of specific policies, such as the UK Department for International Development (DFID), the Nordic and Dutch aid programmes, the World Bank, UNESCO, and many development NGOs.

This book, then, provides an integrated presentation of actor-oriented theory, concepts and practice that is philosophically grounded in a social constructionist[6] view of change and continuity. My version of a constructionist perspective focuses upon the making and remaking of society through the ongoing self-transforming actions and perceptions of a diverse and interlocked world of actors. These emergent processes are complex, often ambivalent, and highly contingent upon the evolving conditions of different social arenas. They also entail networks of relations, resources and meanings at different scales of organisation. These range from small-scale interactional contexts, institutional domains in which actions, expectations and values are framed and contested, to more global scenarios that shape human choices and potentialities at a distance but which are themselves the products of the extended chains and repercussions of social action and their impacts on both human and non-human components.

Social constructionism has its historical roots in the phenomenological and sociological perspectives of Mannheim (1936), Berger and Luckmann (1967) and Schutz (1967), and owes much to the symbolic interactionist studies of Goffman (1959, 1961) and the ethnomethodology of Garfinkel (1967). Despite differences in methods of research and in the theoretical significance accorded to social meaning and practice, what these traditions have in common is the view that social phenomena are made up of a multiplicity of constructed and emergent realities. In more recent years there has been a growing interest shown by psychologists in this perspective. Their concern for language and discursive practice in everyday life has built bridges with the more sociological and anthropological traditions (see Burr 1995 for an overview).[7] The work of George Kelly, which actually dates back to 1955, has been inspirational. He developed a personal construct theory of cognition based on the basic metaphor of 'man the scientist' who continuously seeks to construe, make sense of and give order to the world of experience. As Sarbin and Kitsuse

(1994: 5) comment, had he used the concept of 'actor' rather than 'scientist' his work would have connected directly with the insights of his sociological contemporaries and would have probably had more influence on directing the way forward in psychology. More recently in psychology, as I suggest below, social constructionism has become linked – maybe too tightly linked – to the analysis of the role of discourse and language in the construction and representation of everyday life.

This close affinity of an actor approach to the tenets of social constructionism as applied to issues of development and social change is acknowledged by David Booth as being distinctive in two ways. He explains:

> One focus of special interest here is the multiple forms of social knowledge and their relations with power. Another is the diversity of outcomes of social processes that becomes visible once the constructedness and interactive character of such processes are given their due.
>
> (Booth 1994: 12)

Yet despite this concurrence of views in constructionist thinking, a number of prominent social anthropologists have recently expressed their objection to the notion of 'construction' – whether social or cultural. They argue that the concept implies the idea of 'ready-made plans' and 'blueprints' that function like musical scores or scripts (Ingold 1996: 99–146). In contradistinction to this, and drawing upon a long pedigree of constructionist research and thinking, I take the view that constructionism[8] is principally concerned with understanding the processes by which specific actors and networks of actors engage with and thus co-produce their own (inter)personal and collective social worlds. This is not simply achieved on the basis of reworking existing cultural repertoires, or language and learned behaviour, but also through the many ways in which people improvise and experiment with 'old' and 'new' elements and experiences, and react situationally and imaginatively, consciously or otherwise, to the circumstances they encounter. Hence the idea of social construction does not imply that people have a clear view of how or on what basis their perceptions of reality are formed, of why they do things in the first place, or of how their doing of things affects outcomes. All we know is that '[s]ocial life is always provisional, "work-in-progress", never completed and therefore not constructed in any ultimate way' (Ellen 1996: 103). But this is not to say that social relations, normative framing and discursive practices are not in some manner 'built' or retrospectively interpreted as resulting from coordinated modes of action and belief.

Another contentious issue is the role that language and discourse plays in the structuring of everyday social practice. Social constructionism has often been closely associated with the use of discourse or conversational analysis for understanding processes of social interaction and negotiation, the constitution of power relations, and the co-production of knowledge (see Potter and Wetherall 1987 on the interplay of 'interpretative repertoires', Gergen and Gergen 1984 on narrative accounts, Fairclough 1989 on critical discourse analysis, and Parker 1992 and Burr 1995 for accounts of discourse analysis in social psychology). However, discourse is never dependent solely on verbalisation in text, everyday talk or public rhetoric. It is equally manifest in non-verbal behaviour, bodily expressions and feelings, as well as in how people relate to specific goods, artefacts and technologies that come, as it were, already endowed with particular social meanings and valuations. An actor-oriented type of social constructionism, then, requires that we throw our net high and wide. We must encompass not only everyday social practice and language games, but also larger-scale institutional frameworks, resource fields, networks of communication and support, collective ideologies, socio-political arenas of struggle, and the beliefs and cosmologies that may shape actors' improvisations, coping behaviours and planned social actions.

Parallel to the way in which constructionism has been misconstrued as privileging cultural representation and the power of language and discourse, so actor-oriented analysis has sometimes been reduced to rational choice theory or criticised for being 'methodologically individualist' (i.e., explaining social behaviour in terms of individual motivations, intentions and interests). This view seriously distorts the aims and methods of an actor perspective, since the world of social action is never made up of a series of detached individuals and atomised decision-makers. Persons and their environments (which include other people and institutional frames) are reciprocally constituted. Moreover, they do not simply respond to the imperatives of cultural norms and values, or to the dictates of dominant discourses.

As will quickly emerge in the reading of the book, my own predilection rests with a type of actor analysis that explains how the meanings, purposes and powers associated with differential modes of human agency intersect to shape the outcomes of emergent social forms. In order to pursue and illustrate this argument, I will also need to demonstrate that agency itself is framed and hedged in by various cross-cutting discourses, institutional constraints and processes of 'objectification', though these very same processes also permit or promote certain modes of social agency. A further implication of this is that it becomes essential to question or deconstruct certain conventional abstractions such as planned intervention, commoditisation, exchange value, the hegemony of the state, and the dichotomy between so-called expert and local knowledge, in order to replace them by more nuanced, actor-defined conceptions. I also eschew all forms of essentialism and determinism that assume simple cause-and-effect happenings or those that are built upon the logic of universal laws or central tendencies. Such formulations run counter to the actor-oriented premise that it is the complex interlocking of actors' 'projects' and practices, and their intended and unintended outcomes, that compose the constraining and enabling frameworks of social action.

The book is divided into three parts. Part 1 deals with general theoretical and methodological issues. The first chapter spells out the theoretical foundations for an actor-oriented analysis, giving special attention to questions of lived experience, agency, issues of knowledge and power, and to the need for developing 'theory from below'. This is followed by a critical assessment (Chapter 2) of policy and implementation models and practices. It challenges orthodox assumptions concerning the efficacy of planned intervention and argues the necessity of viewing intervention as an ongoing socially-constructed and negotiated process that goes beyond the time/space frames of intervention programmes. It also provides a brief evaluation of theories of state intervention. Chapter 3 provides an overview of the key concepts and methodology entailed in carrying out empirical research within an actor/social constructionist perspective. Having already delineated the main elements of an interface analysis, Chapter 4 explores its usefulness for understanding three contrasting Mexican interface situations.

Part 2 is devoted to issues concerning commoditisation processes, social value, entrepreneurship and small-scale enterprise. It opens with a critical discussion (Chapter 5) of the merits and shortcomings of commoditisation models of social change, highlighting the importance of the social construction of value and meaning within economic processes. The next chapter (Chapter 6) deals with the significance of money and social currencies in cross-border commodity networks, illustrated through a detailed Mexican–US case-study. The third element of Part 2 focuses on the nature and dynamics of economic enterprise. Chapter 7 is a case-study of a multiple, family-based enterprise from the highlands of Peru. It shows how social networks, information sources and family organisation shape the development and later demise of the enterprise.

Part 3 is devoted to knowledge interfaces, power and globalisation. Chapter 8 discusses the significance of knowledge questions for development research. It highlights the central importance of social networks, social representations and power relations for examining development interfaces. Chapter 9 shows interfaces at work. It analyses a Mexican case-study involving encounters between government officials and local rural actors. The emphasis is on the interplay of different lifeworlds and bodies of knowledge, and the dilemmas faced by one frontline agricultural officer who is caught between the demands of his peasant clients and those of his administrative superiors. The final chapter (Chapter 10) develops an interpretation of the main features of global change at the turn of the twenty-first century, focusing on processes of globalisation and localisation. It also characterises the changing nature of rural/global relations and space, and concludes by identifying some priority areas for future development research.

Part I

THEORETICAL AND METHODOLOGICAL ISSUES

1

THE CASE FOR AN ACTOR-ORIENTED SOCIOLOGY OF DEVELOPMENT[1]

This chapter lays the foundations for an actor perspective on development intervention and social change. It opens with a brief critical overview of the paradigmatic character of structural versus actor approaches, followed by a delineation of the theoretical and episte-mological advantages of adopting an actor-oriented analysis. In the second half of the chapter I trace my own struggle with theory and practice during the course of my Latin American work in Peru and Mexico. And in the conclusion I return to the issue of paradigm change and the prospects for a revitalised sociology of development.[2]

The paradigmatic world of research

When considering the rise and decline of paradigms one could not do better than to begin with Cynthia Hewitt de Alcántara's (1982) interesting treatment of anthropological paradigms in post-revolutionary Mexico. She provides a detailed history of anthropolog-ical schools of thought and research practice dealing with Mexican rural life and agrarian problems. Hewitt draws her concept of paradigm from Kuhn's (1962) original work on the character and succession of contrasting paradigms or worldviews in the development of science. Modifying Kuhn's simple unilinear picture of paradigm development, Hewitt (following Masterman 1970: 74; see also de Mey 1982: 223) suggests that social science has always been composed of a multiplicity of paradigms, of which none has so far achieved the hegemonic status of a central theory or universal paradigm.[3] Hence, although for certain periods particular theories or images of society may be considered more credible than others, due to the support they receive from scholars and academic institutions, the winds of change are always round the corner. This arises principally because general sociological theories and metaphors are mostly rooted in contrasting, if not incompatible, epistemologies; that is, they conceive of the nature of social phenomena and explanation quite differently.

Nevertheless, as Hewitt's study beautifully demonstrates, it is possible to plot the waxing and waning of particular paradigms over time and to identify periods during which certain images and types of analysis have predominated over others. Few scholars would challenge, for instance, the observation that the general course of debates and interpreta-tions on development since the Second World War has been from perspectives based upon the concept of modernisation (in the mid-1950s), to dependency (in the mid-1960s), to political economy (in the mid-1970s), to some kind of ill-defined postmodernism of the mid-1980s onwards. This latest postmodernist phase is depicted in many quarters – even among certain die-hard structural Marxists – as entailing the deconstruction of previous orthodoxies,[4] or perhaps even as a form of theoretical agnosticism which some scholars would regard as verging on empiricism.[5]

A glance at the extensive post-war literature on development and social change immediately throws up a sharp divide between, on the one hand, work that deals with aggregate or large scale structures and trends (often described as 'macro') and studies that characterise the nature of changes at the level of operating or acting units (often depicted as 'micro').[6] The former generally frame their analyses in terms of concepts drawn from modernisation theory or they adopt a structural or institutionalist perspective based on some variety of political economy analysis. The latter, while they may also highlight dimensions relevant to these same general theories, are more likely to provide detailed accounts of differential responses to structural conditions and to explore the livelihood strategies and cultural dispositions of the social actors involved. At one level, this difference in analysis coincides crudely with the division between economics, political science and macro-sociology, as against anthropology and history; or more accurately between scholars concerned with the testing of general structural models and those interested in depicting the ways in which people manage the dilemmas of their everyday lives. Some remarkable studies have of course managed to combine these levels reasonably successfully, but on the whole these have been few and far between.[7] A principal reason why it has been difficult to integrate structural and actor perspectives is that their theoretical and epistemological assumptions diverge, although this is not to say that it is impossible to combine them within a single study.

The convergence of structural models of development

Despite obvious differences in ideology and theoretical trappings, two structural models have until relatively recently occupied centre stage in the sociology of development – modernisation theory and political economy. And both evince certain paradigmatic similarities and common analytical weaknesses.

Modernisation theory visualises development in terms of a progressive movement towards technologically and institutionally more complex and integrated forms of 'modern' society. This process is set in motion and maintained through increasing involvement in commodity markets and through a series of interventions involving the transfer of technology, knowledge, resources and organisational forms from the more 'developed' world or sector of a country to the less 'developed' parts. In this way, 'traditional' society is propelled into the modern world, and gradually, though not without some institutional hiccups (i.e. what are often designated 'social and cultural obstacles to change'), its economy and social patterns acquire the accoutrements of 'modernity'.

On the other hand, Marxist and neo-Marxist theories of political economy stress the exploitative nature of these processes, attributing them to the inherent expansionist tendency of world capitalism and to its constant need to open up new markets, increase the level of surplus extraction and accumulate capital. Here the image is that of capitalist interests, foreign and national, subordinating (and probably in the long run undermining) non-capitalist modes and relations of production and integrating them into an uneven web of economic and political relations. Although the timing and degree of integration of countries into the world political economy has varied, the outcome is structurally similar: they are forced to join the brotherhood of nations on terms not determined by themselves but by their more wealthy and politically powerful 'partners'. Although this type of theory contains within it a variety of schools of thought, in essence the central message remains much the same, namely, that patterns of development and underdevelopment are best explained within a generic model of capitalist development on a world scale.[8]

These two macro perspectives represent opposite positions ideologically – the former espousing a so-called 'liberal' standpoint and ultimately believing in the benefits of gradualism and the 'trickle-down' effect, and the latter taking a 'radical' stance and viewing 'development' as an inherently unequal process involving the continued exploitation of 'peripheral' societies and 'marginalised' populations. Yet, on another level, the two models are similar in that both see development and social change emanating primarily from external centres of power via interventions by the state or international bodies, and following some broadly determined developmental path, signposted by 'stages of development' or the succession of different regimes of capitalism. These so-called 'external' forces encapsulate the lives of people, reducing their autonomy and in the end undermining local or endogenous forms of cooperation and solidarity, resulting in increased socio-economic differentiation and greater centralised control by powerful economic and political groups, institutions and enterprises. In this respect it does not seem to matter much whether the hegemony of the state is based upon a capitalist or socialist ideology, since both entail tendencies towards increased incorporation and centralisation.

Both models therefore are tainted by determinist, linear and externalist views of social change.[9] My summaries of their viewpoints simplify and perhaps caricature their arguments, but a careful reading of the literature will, I believe, bear out the conclusion that they do in fact share a common set of paradigmatic beliefs. This contention is also supported by the existence of similar assumptions that underpin the commercialisation (i.e. modernisation) and commoditisation approaches to agrarian development (see Vandergeest 1988, and Long and van der Ploeg 1988).

A brief view of recent structural analysis

While the shortcomings of these earlier structural models – especially their failure to explain adequately the sources and dynamics of social heterogeneity – are now widely acknowledged by political economists and sociologists alike, much current social theory remains wedded to universalism, linearity and binary oppositions (Alexander 1995: 6–64). This not only applies to the analysis of development processes (see Chapter 2 for a detailed critique of notions of planned intervention) but also more generally to theoretical interpretations of contemporary socio-cultural change (see Chapter 10). For example, many writers on postmodernity succumb to a 'stages theory' of history when they write of the transition from 'Fordist' to 'post-Fordist' forms of production (i.e. from mass production to flexible specialisation) as if this were a simple unidirectional process in tune with other socio-cultural changes. Implicit here is an ideal typical view of what it is to be 'postmodern'. One example of this is Don Slater's (1997: 174–209) use of a postmodernist lens for looking at the 'new times' in which we are living. Slater's interpretation pivots on the somewhat dubious assumption that the movement to post-Fordist patterns of organisation is congruent with other dimensions and representations of change, such as the shift from 'organised' to 'disorganised' modes of capitalism, from commodity 'exchange-value' to the increasing importance of 'sign-value', and from social identities based on criteria of work and citizenship to those based on global lifestyles.[10] One is left wondering whether at this level of abstraction the empirical complexities and variabilities of contemporary life can ever be adequately addressed.

What clearly is missing in this is the attempt to analyse in depth the intricate and varied ways in which new and old forms of production, consumption, livelihoods and identity are intertwined and generate heterogeneous patterns of economic and cultural change. Two different though equally challenging attempts to offer such an analytical framework are Marsden *et al.*'s (1993) re-conceptualisation of rural changes in the UK (*Constructing the Countryside*), and Smith's (1999: 131–191) analysis of processes of socio-economic restructuring in regions of Spain and Italy in his book *Confronting the Present*.

Other contemporary theorists have focused on reformulating structural analysis in order to take more explicit account of globalisation. For example, Preston (1996: 273–93) distinguishes three ways in which the global system has been theorised: (1) from a post-modernist market-oriented, knowledge-based and global consumption/lifestyles point of view; (2) through the application of Marxist/dependency theory to explain shifts in the global patterns of capitalism and changes in the fortunes of particular economic and political power blocs (such as the demise of the Soviet system and the rise and later vicissitudes of the East Asian countries); and (3) through an attempt to develop new interpretations of structural change by identifying what he designates 'a logic of ever greater global inter-dependence' between groups occupying specific niches in the global scene that aim to identify common problems (such as those relating to global environmental and/or world trade issues) and press for the establishment of negotiated global agreements and regula-tory frameworks (Preston 1996: 292).

On the other hand, other scholars have concerned themselves with the 'declining coherence of national...economies and national regulatory states' (Buttel 1994: 14). The proponents of this line of analysis argue that new capitalist 'regimes of accumulation' and 'modes of regulation' are generated when internal contradictions, technological develop-ments and the global political economy threaten existing national and local institutional frameworks as well as the viability of the prevailing economic and political order. In these critical situations, it is argued, new modes of organising capital accumulation and social reproduction develop.[11]

As several authors (e.g. Jessop 1988: 151, and Gouveria 1997) point out, these processes of restructuring should not be viewed as disembodied from social action, since they are a product of past and present social struggles. But, by and large, the principal protagonists identified in these struggles are those representing individual nation-states and transnational bodies such as the International Monetary Fund (IMF), the World Bank or the World Trade Organisation (WTO). These latter types of institutional actors seek to give order to the global economy and to manage any turbulence that may arise. In so doing they attempt to steer national government policies away from the 'developmentalist project' of the past towards a more 'robust' neo-liberal economic regime (for a fuller account of this process, see McMichael 1994).[12] Such a perspective, of course, fails to give significant attention to the multiplicity of other social actors and interests involved in such restructuring processes. Nor does it appreciate the extent to which, under certain circumstances, so-called less 'powerful' actors can make their voices heard and dramati-cally change the course of events, as was witnessed at the recent 1999 Seattle meeting of the WTO when hundreds of people took to the streets and successfully blocked the assembly's unequivocal acceptance of the principle of free trade.

Preston's appraisal of structural analysis leads him to a similar conclusion: namely, that what we need is a move away from structural explanations in favour of a more 'agent' or 'actor'-focused analysis. It is here that his argument (Preston 1996: 301–3) coincides with my own longstanding advocacy of such a perspective (Long 1977a, 1984b and 1992). The next section elaborates on the implications of such a theoretical shift.

An actor-oriented approach

Although less well articulated in the literature on development until relatively late in the twentieth century, there has always been a kind of counterpoint to structural analysis in development sociology. This is what I have called the 'actor-oriented approach'. Nourishing (either explicitly or implicitly) this interest in social actors is the conviction that, although it may be true that important structural changes result from the impact of outside forces (due to encroachment by the market, state or international bodies), it is theoretically unsatisfactory to base one's analysis on the concept of external determination. All forms of external intervention necessarily enter the existing lifeworlds of the individuals and social groups affected, and in this way they are mediated and transformed by these same actors and structures. Also, to the extent that large-scale and 'remote' social forces do alter the life-chances and behaviour of individuals, they can only do so through shaping, directly or indirectly, the everyday life experiences and perceptions of the individuals and groups concerned. Hence, as James Scott expresses it:

> Only by capturing the experience in something like its fullness will we be able to say anything meaningful about how a given economic system influences those who constitute it and maintain or supersede it. And, of course, if this is true for the peasantry or the proletariat, it is surely true for the bourgeoisie, the petite bourgeoisie, and even the lumpen proletariat.
>
> (Scott 1985: 2)

A more dynamic approach to the understanding of social change is therefore needed which stresses the interplay and mutual determination of 'internal' and 'external' factors and relationships,[13] and which recognises the central role played by human action and consciousness.

One way of doing this is through the application of actor-oriented types of analysis, which were popular in sociology and anthropology around the late 1960s and early 1970s. These approaches range from transactional and decision-making models to symbolic interactionist and phenomenological analysis. One advantage of the actor approach is that one begins with an interest in explaining differential responses to similar structural circumstances, even if the conditions appear relatively homogeneous. Thus one assumes that the differential patterns that arise are in part the joint creation of the actors themselves. Social actors, however, must not be depicted as simply disembodied social categories (based on class or some other classificatory criteria) or passive recipients of intervention, but as active participants who process information and strategise in their dealings with various local actors as well as with outside institutions and personnel. The precise paths of change and their significance for those involved cannot be imposed from outside, nor can they be explained in terms of the working out of some inexorable structural logic, such as implied in de Janvry's (1981) model of the 'disarticulated periphery'.[14] The different patterns of social organisation that emerge result from the interactions, negotiations and social struggles that take place between several kinds of actor, not only those present in given face-to-face encounters but also those who are absent yet nevertheless influence the situation, affecting actions and outcomes.

Having said this, however, it is necessary to underline the shortcomings of several kinds of actor-oriented approach promoted in the 1960s and 1970s, especially by anthropologists (see Long 1977a: 105–43). In an attempt to combat simple culturalist and structuralist views of social change, these studies concentrated upon the innovative behaviour of entrepreneurs and economic brokers, on individual decision-making processes, or on the ways in which individuals mobilised resources through the building of social networks (see Chapter 7 of this book). Yet many such studies fell short because of a tendency to adopt a voluntaristic view of decision-making and to stress the transactional nature of actor strategies which gives insufficient attention to examining how individual choices are shaped by larger frames of meaning and action (i.e. by cultural dispositions, or what Bourdieu (1981: 305) calls *habitus* or 'embodied history', and by the distribution of power and resources in the wider arena). And some studies foundered by adopting an extreme form of methodological individualism that sought to explain social behaviour primarily in terms of individual motivations, intentions and interests.[15]

Another brand of actor-oriented research (especially prevalent among political scientists and economists, but also taken up by some economic anthropologists such as Schneider (1974) is that which uses a generalised model of rational choice based on a limited number of axioms, such as the maximisation of preferences or utility. While the former types of actor analysis tend to treat social life and especially social change as essentially reducible to the constitutive actions of individuals, the rational choice approach proposes a 'universal' model whose 'core features encode the fundamental properties of human behaviour' (Gudeman 1986: 31, who criticises this approach).[16] The principal objection to this, of course, is that it offers an ethnocentric 'Western' model of social behaviour based upon the individualism of 'utilitarian man' that rides roughshod over the specificities of culture and context.

The central significance of starting from 'lived experience'

In contrast to these types of actor approach, Unni Wikan (1990) presents a fascinating interpretation of everyday Balinese social practice. Her ethnography is remarkable for the way in which it unmasks the conventions and contrivances of Balinese public cultural displays and ritual performances – so often the object of anthropological interest – to reveal a rich and versatile repertoire of ways of coping with the crises, hardships and heartaches of daily living. She concludes that '[u]nless this composite and complex nature of social order is also represented in our anthropological accounts, we risk depicting Balinese as engrossed in public spectacle, as people without hearts and without compelling personal concerns' (Wikan 1990: 35).

The same critical observation is pertinent to the field of development, where we also need to get behind the myths, models and poses of development policy and institutions, as well as the reifications of local culture and knowledge, to uncover 'the particulars of people's "lived-in worlds"'. That is, we need to document the ways in which people steer or muddle their ways through difficult scenarios, turning 'bad' into 'less bad' circumstances. As Wright Mills (1953) once commented in a slightly different context, sociological explanation requires addressing both 'public concerns' and 'private dilemmas'.

The advantage of an actor-oriented approach is that it aims to grasp precisely these issues through a systematic ethnographic understanding of the 'social life' of development projects – from conception to realisation – as well as the responses and lived experiences of the variously located and affected social actors (cf. a similar formulation by Olivier de Sardan 1995: 50–4). Central elements of this ethnographic endeavour focus on the elucidation of internally-generated strategies and processes of change, the links between the 'small' worlds of local actors and the larger-scale 'global' phenomena and actors, and the critical role played by diverse and often conflicting forms of human action and social consciousness in the making of development.

'Compelling personal concerns' and the straw man of methodological individualism

While most writers dealing with questions of development intervention and changing livelihoods readily recognise the importance of what Wikan (1990) describes as 'compelling personal concerns', these are often transposed into simple structural statements about the vulnerabilities of the 'lower classes' and the pay-offs of the 'wealthy or advantaged', or alternatively they are cast within a rational choice model of behaviour based on universal axioms such as the maximisation of preferences of utility and the principle of strategic intentionality. Neither formulation accords satisfactorily with the broader implications of the concepts of lived experience, livelihoods and everyday social practices of actor-oriented analysis. This issue is further compounded by the fact that several commentators (see, e.g., Alavi 1973, Harriss 1982, Vanclay 1994 and Gould 1997) accuse actor-oriented researchers of centring their explanations too much on the agency and instrumental rationality of individuals.

As a rebuff to these criticisms, Lockie – who summarises well my position – argues:

> Although I think it would be fair to say that studies informed by the actor perspective tend to emphasise the discursive rationality of actors at the expense of practical consciousness, theoretically I do not think this assertion is a justifiable criticism. Rationality is not, according to Long (1992), a property of individuals, but is drawn from the stock of available discourses that form part of the cultural milieux of social practice. Referring again to the construction of agency, it follows that conceptions of rationality, power and knowledge are also culturally variable, and cannot be separated from the social practices of actors.
>
> (Lockie 1996: 45–6)

As this quotation amply underlines, actor-oriented concepts aim to find room for a multiplicity of rationalities, desires, capacities and practices, including of course those also associated with various modes of instrumentalism. The relative importance of these various ideas, sentiments and ways of acting for shaping social arrangements and for bringing about change, can only be assessed contextually and will depend upon a host of interconnected social, cultural, technical and resource components. The complexity and dynamism implied in this calls for research methodologies (see Chapter 3) that reach beyond simple interactionist or individualist modes of enquiry and explanation.

It is for these reasons, then, that the charge of 'methodological individualism' – which seeks to study and explain social phenomena through understanding individuals' motivations, intentions and interests – is misplaced. That is, it acts, that is, as no more than a straw man for all those theorists who wish to fault actor analysis for devoting too much attention to the everyday predicaments, subjectivities and social trajectories of individual actors who, in cooperation or conflict with other acting persons, make up the fabric of social life.

Agency, knowledge and power

In 1977, I published *An Introduction to the Sociology of Rural Development*. At the time the sociology of development was at a crossroads theoretically and one could not be sure in which direction analysis and debate would move. One important motive for writing the book was to encourage a more open discussion between scholars of differing theoretical persuasions and to argue the case for combining actor and historical-structural approaches. Since then many things have happened, including the explosion of postmodernist writings and the emergence of less doctrinaire 'post-structuralist' forms of political economy (now sometimes labelled 'the new political economy'[17]) which have opened up space for the consideration of actor issues and perspectives. Nevertheless, these efforts are likely to abort unless certain key conceptual and methodological issues are squarely tackled, of which the issue of agency is central.

In an attempt to improve on earlier formulations, many writers have turned back to reconsider the essential nature and importance of 'human agency'. This meta-theoretical notion lies at the heart of any revitalised social actor paradigm and forms the pivot around which discussions aimed at reconciling notions of structure and actor revolve. But before recounting these discussions, it is important to stress that the question of agency has not simply been confined to a circle of sociological and anthropological theorists and their audiences. It has also penetrated empirical work in political science (Scott 1985), policy analysis (Elwert and Bierschenk 1988), communication studies (Leeuwis 1993, Engel 1995 and Engel and Saloman 1997) and history (Stern 1987).

In general terms, the notion of agency attributes to the individual actor the capacity to process social experience and to devise ways of coping with life, even under the most extreme forms of coercion. Within the limits of information, uncertainty and other constraints (e.g. physical, normative or politico-economic) that exist, social actors possess 'knowledgeability' and 'capability'. They attempt to solve problems, learn how to intervene in the flow of social events around them, and to a degree they monitor their own actions, observing how others react to their behaviour and taking note of the various contingent circumstances (Giddens 1984: 1–16).[18]

Yet, while the quintessence of human agency may seem to be embodied in the individual person, single individuals are not the only entities that reach decisions, act accordingly and monitor outcomes. 'Capitalist enterprises, state agencies, political parties and church organisations are examples of social actors: they all have means of reaching and formulating decisions and of acting on at least some of them' (Hindess 1986: 115). But, as Hindess goes on to stress, the concept of actor should *not* be used to refer to collectivities, agglomerates or social categories that have no discernible way of formulating or carrying out decisions. To suggest, for example, that 'society' in the global sense of the term, or classes and other social categories based on ethnicity or gender, make decisions and attempt to implement them is to attribute mistakenly to them the quality of agency.[19] It also tends towards the reification of classificatory schemata (based on generalised notions of social identity, roles, statuses and hierarchies) that form part of an individual's or organisation's conceptual apparatus for processing the social world around them and upon which action takes place. Thus we should avoid types of analysis that reduce questions of social action to the performance of pre-determined social roles or to the exigencies of symbolic-normative orders or social hierarchies (Crespi 1992: 48).[20] While the potentials for social action are undoubtedly in part shaped by such dimensions, a critical component consists of those processes by which social arrangements or 'structures' are constructed, reproduced and changed. This implies the notion of organising processes and practices, and ongoing contestations over meanings and values. It also points to the variability of action with respect to meanings, norms and the attribution of intentionality, since social actors can engage with, distance themselves from, or adopt an ambiguous stance towards certain codified rules and interpretations (cf. Crespi 1992: 60).

Hence agency – which we may recognise when particular actions make a difference to a pre-existing state of affairs or course of events – is embodied in social relations and can only be effective through them. It is not simply the result of possessing certain persuasive powers or forms of charisma. The ability to influence others or to pass on a command (e.g. to get them to accept a particular message) rests fundamentally on 'the actions of a chain of agents each of whom "translates" it in accordance with his/her own projects' – and 'power is composed here and now by enrolling many actors in a given political and social scheme' (Latour 1986: 264). In other words, agency (and power) depend crucially upon the emergence of a network of actors who become partially, though hardly ever completely, enrolled in the 'project' of some other person or persons. Agency then entails the generation and use or manipulation of networks of social relations and the chan-nelling of specific items (such as claims, orders, goods, instruments and information) through certain nodal points of interpretation and interaction. Hence, it is essential to take account of the ways in which social actors engage in or are locked into struggles over the attribution of social meanings to particular events, actions and ideas.

Looked at from this point of view, development intervention models (or policy measures and rhetoric) become strategic weapons in the hands of those charged with promoting them. Yet the battle never ends, since all actors exercise some kind of 'power', leverage or room for manoeuvre, even those in highly subordinate positions. As Giddens (1984: 16) puts it, '[a]ll forms of dependence offer some resources whereby those who are subordinate can influence the activities of their superiors'. And in these ways they actively engage (though not always at the level of discursive consciousness) in the construction of their own social worlds and experiential lives, even though, as Marx (1962 [1852]: 252) cautions us, the circumstances they encounter are not simply of their own making.

Considering the relation of actor and structure, Giddens argues that the constitution of social structures, which have both a constraining and an enabling affect on social behaviour, cannot be comprehended without allowing for human agency. He writes:

> In following the routines of my day-to-day life I help reproduce social institutions that I played no part in bringing into being. They are more than merely the envi-ronment of my action since...they enter constitutively into what it is I do as agent. Similarly, my actions constitute and reconstitute the institutional condi-tions of actions of others, just as their actions do mine...My activities are thus embedded within, and are constitutive elements of, structured properties of insti-tutions stretching well beyond myself in time and space.
>
> (Giddens 1987: 11)

While Giddens's general point is well taken, this embeddedness of action within insti-tutional structures and processes should not, of course, imply that behavioural choice is replaced by an unchanging routine, or that an actor 'follows a pre-given ideological script' (Dissanayake 1996: 8) or is 'a carrier of dispositions [*habitus* or "system of generative schemes" à la Bourdieu] which are themselves the conduits of interests' (Turner 1992: 91). Indeed as Turner and others (e.g. Wikan 1990) have persuasively argued, a theoretical interpretation of social action must go beyond a consideration of knowledgeability, consciousness and intentions to embrace also 'feelings, emotions, perceptions, identities and the continuity of agents [persons] across space and time' (Turner 1992: 91).[21] Moreover, 'it is a necessary feature of action that, at any point in time, the actors "could have acted otherwise": either positively in terms of attempted intervention in the process of "events in the world", or negatively in terms of forbearance' (Giddens 1979: 56). Also we must assume that actors are capable (even within severely restricted social and personal space) of processing (self-consciously or otherwise) their lived experiences and acting upon them.

Hindess (1986: 117–19) takes the argument one step farther by pointing out that the reaching of decisions, or social positioning vis-à-vis other actors, entails the explicit or implicit use of 'discursive means' in the formulation of goals, pursuit of interests and fulfilment of desires, and in presenting arguments or rationalisations for the actions undertaken. These discursive means or types of discourse (i.e. cultural constructions implied in expressing, either verbally or through social practice, points of view or value perspectives)[22] vary and are not simply inherent features of the actors themselves: they form a part of the differentiated stocks of knowledge and resources available to actors of different types. Since social life is never so unitary as to be built upon one single type of discourse, it follows that, however restricted their choices, actors always face some alternative ways of formulating their objectives, deploying specific modes of action and giving reasons for their behaviour.

It is important here to point out that the recognition of alternative discourses used by or available to actors, challenges on the one hand the notion that rationality is an intrinsic property of the individual actor, and on the other that it simply reflects the actor's structural location in society. All societies contain within them a repertoire of different lifestyles, cultural forms and rationalities which members utilise in their search for order and meaning, and which they themselves play (wittingly or unwittingly) a part in affirming or restructuring. Hence the strategies and cultural constructions employed by individuals do not arise out of the blue but are drawn from a stock of available discourses (verbal and non-verbal) that are to some degree shared with other individuals, contemporaries and maybe predecessors. It is at this point that the individual is, as it were, transmuted metaphorically into the *social actor*, which signifies the fact that the term is a social construction rather than simply a synonym for the individual or a member of *Homo sapiens*. One needs also to distinguish between two different kinds of social construction associated with the concept of social actor: first, that which is culturally endogenous in that it is based upon the kinds of representations characteristic of the culture in which the particular individual or network of individuals is embedded; and second, that which arises from the researcher's or analyst's own predispositions and theoretical orientation (also of course essentially cultural in that they are probably associated with a particular school of thought and community of scholars).

This social construction of actors touches crucially upon the issue of agency. Although we might think that we know perfectly well what we mean by 'knowledgeability' and 'capability' – the two principal elements of agency identified by Giddens – these concepts must be translated culturally if they are to be fully meaningful. One should not, therefore, presume (even if one can muster evidence of increasing Westernisation or globalisation) a constant, universal interpretation of agency across all cultures. It is bound to vary in its cultural make-up and rationale. Because of this we need to reveal what Marilyn Strathern (1985: 65) calls the 'indigenous theory of agency'. Drawing upon African and Melanesian examples, Strathern shows how notions of agency are constructed differently in different cultures. She argues that attributes such as knowledge, power and prestige are attached differently to the concept of 'person'. In Africa the notion of personhood is predominantly tied to the idea of 'office', i.e. people 'occupy' certain statuses, 'play' certain roles, undergo rites of initiation and installation on assuming these, and are viewed as influencing others by virtue of their positional relationship to them. In contrast, status and other personal attributes in Melanesia are viewed as less permanently attached to individuals or defined in relation to a given matrix of positions; instead they are continually being transacted, negotiated or contested. One might draw similar contrasts between cultural theories of power and influence as they exist in different segments of Latin American societies, for example among peasants and urban populations, or within the bureaucracy, church and army.

Such differences underline the importance of examining how notions of personhood and thus of agency (knowledgeability/capability) are differently constituted culturally and affect the management of interpersonal relations and the kinds of control that actors can pursue vis-à-vis each other.[23] In the field of development, this means analysing how differential conceptions of power, influence, knowledge and efficacy may shape the responses and strategies of the different actors (e.g. peasants, development workers, landlords and local government officers). One should also address the question of how far notions of agency, which differ according to the type of policy being promoted, can be imposed on local groups. Here I have in mind, for example, the application of concepts such as 'stakeholder' analysis, 'popular participation', 'targeting the poor' or 'the role of the progressive farmer' in planned development.[24]

Moreover, if we take the view that we are dealing not only with a multiplicity of social actors but also with 'multiple realities', which imply potentially conflicting social and normative interests, and diverse and discontinuous configurations of knowledge, then we must look closely at the issue of just whose interpretations or models (e.g. those of agricultural scientists, politicians, farmers or extensionists) prevail over those of others and in what circumstances. Furthermore, knowledge processes are embedded in social processes that imply aspects of power, authority and legitimation, and thus they are just as likely to reflect and contribute to the conflict between social groups as they are to lead to the establishment of common perceptions, interests and intentionalities.

This interweaving of processes of knowledge and power constitutes a central focus of Part 3 of this book. It will suffice here to highlight certain parallel processes. Like power, knowledge is not simply something that is possessed and accumulated (Foucault, in Gordon 1980). Nor can it be measured precisely in terms of some notion of quantity or quality. It emerges out of processes of social interaction and is essentially a joint product of the encounter and fusion of horizons. It must therefore, like power, be looked at relationally and not treated as if it could be depleted or used up. Someone having power or knowledge does not entail – like the zero-sum model – that others are without. Nevertheless both power and knowledge may become reified in social life: we often think of them as being real material things possessed by actors and we tend to regard them as unquestioned 'givens'. This process of reification or 'blackboxing' (Latour 1993) is, of course, an essential part of the ongoing struggles over meanings and images, and over the control of strategic relationships and resources. Knowledge encounters involve struggles between actors who aim to enrol others in their 'projects', getting them to accept particular frames of meaning and winning them over to their points of view. If they succeed, then other parties 'delegate' power to them. These struggles focus around the fixing of key points that have a controlling influence over the exchanges and attributions of meaning (including the acceptance of reified notions such as authority).

The foregoing discussion has, I hope, clarified why the concept of agency is of central theoretical importance. An actor-oriented approach begins with the simple idea that different social forms develop under the same or similar structural circumstances. Such differences reflect variations in the ways in which actors attempt to come to grips, cognitively, emotionally and organisationally, with the situations they face. Therefore an understanding of differential patterns of social behaviour must be grounded in terms of 'knowing/feeling, active subjects' (cf. Knorr-Cetina 1981b: 4, who stresses the 'knowing' or social cognitive dimension), and not merely viewed as due to the differential impact of broad social forces (such as ecological change, demographic pressure, or incorporation into world capitalism). A main task for analysis, then, is to identify and characterise differing actor practices, strategies and rationales, the conditions under which they arise, how they interlock, their viability or effectiveness for solving specific problems, and their wider social ramifications. The latter aspect raises two further theoretical issues which I reserve for detailed treatment in Chapter 3: the significance of small-scale interactional settings and organising practices and their importance for understanding so-called macro phenomena; and the need for some notion of 'emergent' structures and contexts which come into existence as the combined result of the intended and unintended consequences of social action.

The theoretical challenge of research in highland Peru

In an attempt to make more concrete this theoretical discussion, let me now link this to my own previous struggles with theory and practice in the context of Latin America.[25] This, I believe, provides a useful reflective backcloth against which to place my theoretical argument.

The year 1971 found my wife Ann and I in the Mantaro Valley of central Peru, where I worked together with Bryan Roberts on issues of regional development, migration, small-scale enterprise and rural/urban social change (Long and Roberts 1978 and 1984). Coming from Africa I was struck by both the similarities and the differences in social process. Like those Zambian villagers with whom I had lived and worked in the 1960s, the peasant labour force in the Mantaro Valley was integrated through temporary migration into a mining sector, and some of its savings were invested back in the village, mostly in small-scale entrepreneurial activities. The wives or widows of miners ran several of the small shops in the village we lived in. The big difference, however, was that central Peru had been commoditised for centuries since the coming of the Spanish settlers. It therefore manifested a complex, diversified and market-oriented economy spanning agriculture, commerce, transport, small-scale industry and mining. Land ownership was highly fragmented and to a large degree privatised. This was a population driven by the spirit of capitalism. Many of the rural entrepreneurs I had known in Zambia were 'smart' (Long 1968), but the local people of the Mantaro Valley had the opportunities to be smarter.

I was also struck by the high geographical mobility of people. Everybody seemed to be on the move, taking care of their little plots of land here and there, their sheep somewhere else in the higher-altitude pastures, and their small investments in housing and education outside the village. There was an incredible flow of produce through local markets, but a lot more moved directly from the villages to Lima and the mining towns. These various economic and social patterns were enmeshed in a rich cultural life consisting of family events, patron saint fiestas, regional clubs, and informal networks of friends and *compadres*.

This new field situation presented a challenge analytically. My background as a social anthropologist gave me the wherewithal to describe and analyse micro processes, but it did not provide much of a theoretical framework for dealing with the ways in which these processes were locked into larger economic and political systems. So I turned for help to the existing Latin American literature on development. This was my first encounter with dependency theory. As I picked my way through the variations on this theme, I gained some new insights, but, in the end, dependency models did not seem to explain some of the more interesting aspects of the Mantaro situation. The most striking issue to come to grips with was that, despite being heavily influenced by the presence of a foreign-owned mining enclave, the hinterland was characterised by a dynamic peasant and small-scale entrepreneurial sector within which significant capital accumulation was occurring. This appeared to run counter to the assumptions of enclave theories. Another theoretical difficulty was that there was no obvious chain or hierarchy of dependency tying village to provincial centre to regional capital to the metropolis. This also cast doubt on dependency formulations.

The Mantaro data presented a mountain of complexities. One of these was how to analyse a region, taking into account not only economic and administrative criteria but also the cultural and socio-political dimensions. Another was how to develop an analysis of the interrelations of capitalist and non-capitalist labour processes and patterns of economic organisation. We also had to work out ways of analysing the impact of government intervention that would give sufficient weight to how the organisation and activities of local and provincial actors shaped the outcomes of development at regional, and even national, level.

In grappling with these and similar problems, I turned to the work of the French neo-Marxists who had reformulated the issue of underdevelopment in terms of an analysis of the articulation of capitalist and non-capitalist modes of production (see Meillassoux 1972, Terray 1972 and Rey 1975 for West African cases, and Cotler 1967–8, 1970 and Montoya 1970 for highland Peru). One of the attractions of their approach was that it did not assume that non-capitalist institutions and relations were automatically eliminated under capitalism. Rather, the 'survival' of certain non-capitalist forms was considered functional for capitalist expansion itself.

Again, some of the insights gained were useful, but the approach was limited in several respects. In the first place, it tended to exaggerate the autonomy and internal coherence of different forms or modes of production, attributing to them different economic logics. Second, it failed to deal with the question of differential responses under structurally similar circumstances: why, for example, did some villages or groups within a village become closely integrated into the mining sector and others not? And why did some become more differentiated or more diversified than others? There was also the problem of the lack of attention given to actor strategies and rationalities.

These shortcomings of mode of production analysis served to reinforce my conviction that the main theoretical challenge facing us was in fact to explain how heterogeneity was generated and contained within a single politico-economic structure, or even within the same economic unit, such as the household unit or the family farm. An approach was needed that stressed the importance of analysing the interrelations and interpenetration of different labour processes, including those based on non-capitalist principles of organisation within capitalist formations. So I attempted to develop such an approach by means of a series of case-studies dealing with different types of small-scale enterprise – commercial farms, trading and transport businesses, as well as multiple enterprises and confederations of households spanning several economic branches. Some of my findings are detailed in Chapter 7.[26]

This question of variance and heterogeneity within economic systems and how to handle it theoretically has remained a central concern of mine and is reflected in two debates I later took up: namely the relationship of wage and non-wage forms of labour within the household and/or farm enterprise (Long 1984a); and the nature and differential impact of commoditisation processes on agrarian populations (Long et al. 1986, and Chapter 5 of the present book). In the former I stressed the importance of considering cultural and situational definitions of 'work' in the social estimation (what Marxists might call 'the valorisation') of labour (Long 1984a: 16–17). In the latter, I made a strong plea for viewing commoditisation and institutionalisation from an actor perspective, since these processes 'only become real in their consequences when introduced and translated by specific actors (including here not only farmers but also others such as traders, bureaucrats and politicians)' (Long and van der Ploeg 1989: 238).

By the 1980s, the dependency and neo-Marxist bubble had burst. Political economists and others interested in problems of underdevelopment were struggling to return to a more grounded empirical and genuinely historical approach to problems. As David Booth (1985) pointed out, the 'new' Marxist-inspired development sociology that emerged in the early 1970s was, by the end of the decade, at an impasse. The main reason for this was that it had become wedded to demonstrating the *necessity* of particular patterns of change instead of explaining how they actually came about. The source of such determinism was the prior commitment to showing how the capitalist mode of production structured development, when evidently the complexities and variabilities of structural change under capitalism could not simply be reduced to the working out of capitalist principles of accumulation and exploitation. The notion of articulating modes of production, or arguments about 'formal' versus 'real' subsumption of labour, could not solve this problem either, since theoretical primacy still rested with the 'laws' of capitalist development.

Developing theory from below

An Introduction to the Sociology of Rural Development (Long 1977a) grew out of the Peruvian research and the debates that it generated. In retrospect, the main theoretical contributions of our work in central Peru can be summarised as follows.

First, it challenges enclave theories of development that suggest that integration into the international economy entails relative stagnation for the hinterland economy. On the contrary, the Mantaro case shows that capitalist expansion can generate significant growth and diversification for the non-enclave sector, leading to an intricate pattern of socio-economic adaptations that make it possible for certain local groups to feed off the enclave and put their savings to good use in regional or village-based enterprise, although this was mostly in trade and transport rather than agriculture. As one reviewer of our work put it, this was 'less a matter of achieving a low step on the escalator of growth than of continually inventing income strategies that insure[d] a modest economic lot' (Walton 1985: 471). And in some parts of the regional hinterland there emerged significant processes of small-scale capital accumulation.

Second, we trace the effects that these various strategies 'from below' have on the evolution of the enclave sector itself, showing how over time a network of interrelations between mine production, trade, transport, peasant agriculture and the provincial urban economy was consolidated. This we designated the mine-based 'regional system of production', a shorthand for the complex system of capital, labour and socio-political linkages that developed historically between various economic sectors and activities, and between the social classes that were spawned by them. This system of linkages was dynamic and not simply determined by the actions of the enclave sector. It also looked different from different parts of the social landscape and at different historical junctures. It was continually being remoulded by the struggles that emerged between different individuals and social groups, and was of course affected by the ways in which outside interests and arenas impinged upon it.

Third, an important dimension of our work concerned regional power structures. The Mantaro study showed that the regional system of production did not produce a consolidated wealthy business or agricultural class that monopolised control over crucial regional resources, or that rallied the necessary political support to pursue its interests nationally, as has often been assumed for regions of this type. The absence of such a politically powerful class gave petty entrepreneurs and village politicians plenty of room for manoeuvre vis-à-vis intervening organisations of the central government. The 1969–1975 Land Reform, for example, like many previous programmes of rural development, ran into serious difficulties in some parts of the region when peasants and small-scale entrepreneurs successfully outwitted government agencies and officials responsible for its implementation (Long and Roberts 1984: 248–55).

Fourth, our case studies of small-scale traders and transporters showed that interactional data on the types of social networks and normative frameworks utilised by these individuals, together with observational studies on cooperation and conflict within the farming villages and towns of the region, often provided better insight into the dynamics and complexity of power relations and idioms of subordination than any form of 'aggregated' structural analysis could achieve. The latter framework allows little room for local actors' views on their situation or for variation in organisation and response within so-called hegemonic structures.

These observations bring out the important point that much of our theoretical argumentation developed out of the way in which the study was formulated and carried out in the field. Instead of defining the region to be studied in terms of administrative, ecological or cultural criteria, we started by sampling the lives of different segments of the population living in the vicinity of the mines and the Mantaro river that flows close by. We did not begin, as other researchers had done, with the mining enterprises themselves or with macro-economic data on foreign investment and capital and labour flows. Our work commenced by selecting a number of contrasting social locations (e.g. certain agricultural and livestock villages, the regional capital of Huancayo, and the smelter town of La Oroya) within which we studied in depth the lifeworlds of different social groups (e.g. peasant farmers, shopkeepers, market traders, craftsmen, unskilled miners, mine employees, transporters and professionals). This entailed developing a series of detailed ethnographies using qualitative research methods such as social situational and network analysis, and life history and enterprise studies. These observations and interviews provided a window on certain important structural processes and allowed us to identify the important, but often inadequately handled, differential patterns of change. Later, once we had some understanding of the different activity fields and life experiences of the main protagonists and other participants in this ongoing regional scenario, we sought to collect more quantitative and aggregated data (both historical and contemporary) so as to give body to our analysis of the dynamic system of linkages. In this way we sought to combine an actor-oriented with a historical–structural approach, thus bringing together a concern for the broad historical changes taking place in the regional and national arenas, with a careful documentation of the micro histories, strategies and personal predicaments of peasant householders, miners and entrepreneurs (see Chapter 3 for an account of further methodological implications).

This approach centres upon the notion of human agency, since it locates individuals in the specific lifeworlds in which they manage their everyday affairs. It also means recognising that, within the limits of the information and resources they have and the uncertainties they face, individuals and social groups are 'knowledgeable' and 'capable'; that is, they devise ways of solving, or if possible avoiding, 'problematic situations', and thus actively engage in constructing their own social worlds, even if this means being 'active accomplices' to their own subordination (Burawoy 1985: 23). Hence the lifeworlds of individuals are not preordained for them by the logic of capital or by the intervention of the state, as is sometimes implied in theories of development. Social structures (including regional systems), as Giddens explains, are 'both constituted by human agency, and yet at the same time the very medium of this constitution' (Giddens 1976: 121). Every act of production is at the same time an act of reproduction: 'the structures that render an action possible are, in the performance of that action, reproduced. Even action which disrupts the social order…is mediated by structures which are reconstituted by the action, albeit in a modified form' (Thompson 1990: 150–1).

Our Peruvian research makes abundantly clear the need to give proper weight to both human agency and emergent structures. The data show the complex ways in which the strategies pursued by different interest groups – peasants, miners, entrepreneurs, company managers and state bureaucrats – have contributed importantly to the evolution of the regional system. In this way we question the assumptions of many models of development that interpret the restructuring of economic systems as resulting from the impact (or the 'logic') of external economic and political forces and which continue to adhere to a 'stages' theory of history.

Drawing the threads together, we can say that my Peruvian research experience buttressed my belief that no sociological or historical study of change could be complete without: (1) a concern for the ways in which different social actors manage and interpret new elements in their lifeworlds (2) an analysis of how particular groups or individuals attempt to create space for themselves in order to pursue their own 'projects' that may run parallel to, or perhaps challenge, government programmes or the interests of other intervening parties; and (3) an attempt to show how these organisational, strategic and interpretive processes can influence (and themselves be influenced by) the broader context of power and social action.

Deconstructing 'planned intervention'

The above theoretical concerns – reinforced by my arrival in Wageningen where the relationship between theory and practice has always been hotly debated – led in the early 1980s to my taking a keener interest in issues of policy and planned development. Like the dominant theoretical paradigms of the 1960s and 1970s, much policy analysis still seemed to cling to a rather mechanical or systems model of the relationship between policy, implementation and outcomes. The tendency in many studies was to conceptualise this as essentially linear in nature, implying some kind of step-by-step process whereby policy was formulated, implemented and then followed by certain results, after which one could evaluate the process in order to establish how far the original objectives had been achieved. Yet, as my own field research on the Peruvian Land Reform programme had shown – and enlightened planners and development workers will readily appreciate – this separation of 'policy', 'implementation' and 'outcomes' is a gross oversimplification of a much more complicated set of processes which involve the reinterpretation or transformation of policy during the implementation process, such that there is no straight line from policy to outcomes. Also, 'outcomes' often result from factors which cannot be directly linked to the implementation of a particular development programme. Moreover, issues of policy implementation should not be restricted to the study of top-down, planned interventions by governments, development agencies and private institutions, since local groups actively formulate and pursue their own 'projects of development', which may clash with the interests of central authorities.

There was already a growing recognition of these deficiencies among policy analysts who sought new ways of conceptualising policy formulation and implementation. For example, it was suggested that implementation should be viewed as a transactional process involving negotiation over goals and means between parties with conflicting or diverging interests (Warwick 1982). This was paralleled by new forms of organisational analysis that looked at the dynamics of administrative action in policy implementation (Batley 1983). There were also a few interesting anthropological studies that examined the social and cultural interfaces between bureaucratic agencies and their clients (Handelman and Leyton 1978).

These new directions coincided with my own growing interest in intervention issues. My experiences in Zambia and Peru had taught me that farmers and their households organise themselves individually and collectively in a variety of ways when faced with planned intervention by government and other outside bodies. The discursive and organisational strategies they devise and the types of interactions that evolve between them and the intervening parties necessarily give shape to the ongoing nature and outcomes of such intervention. The problem for analysis, therefore, is to understand the processes by which external interventions enter the lifeworlds of the individuals and groups affected and thus come to form part of the resources and constraints of the social strategies and interpretive frames they develop. In this way, so-called 'external' factors become 'internalised' and often come to signify quite different things to different interest groups or to the different individual actors, whether implementers, clients or bystanders. The concept of intervention, then, needs *deconstructing* so that it is seen for what it is – an ongoing, socially-constructed, negotiated, experiential and meaning-creating process, not simply the execution of an already-specified plan of action with expected behavioural outcomes. One should also not assume a top-down process as is usually implied, since initiatives may come from 'below' as much as they do from 'above'. It is important, then, to focus upon intervention practices as shaped by the interaction among the various participants, rather than simply upon intervention *models*, by which we mean the ideal typical representations that planners or their clients have about the process. Using the notion of intervention *practices* allows one to focus on the emergent forms of interaction, procedures, practical strategies and types of discourse, cultural categories and sentiments present in specific contexts.

Thinking through these issues led me to the view that a more sophisticated analysis of intervention processes was called for, which hopefully would also have positive spin-offs for planners and development practitioners as well as for local groups pursuing their own values and interests. Hence rethinking intervention was as urgent for those directly involved in the process as for the researcher.

Exploring intervention processes in western Mexico

In 1986, I initiated new field research in order to explore further these intervention issues. The research focused upon irrigation organisation, actor strategies and planned intervention in western Mexico, where access to water for irrigated agriculture and other purposes was central to the economic and livelihood problems of the rural population, and where both government and private companies attempted to control water and other production inputs for sugar production for the national market and for fruit and vegetables destined for the United States. In carrying out this research, we aimed to contribute to several fields of practical and theoretical interest: the development of an *interface* approach that analyses the encounters between the different groups and individuals involved in the processes of planned intervention; the study of peasant-based development initiatives and the ways in which local actors (including 'frontline' government personnel) attempt to create room for manoeuvre in pursuit of their own 'projects'; and the development of an actor-oriented, social constructionist approach to the study of irrigation and water management problems.

The project was a coordinated team effort, requiring detailed field investigations in different localities and arenas of action.[27] In order to research these themes in an integrated manner, we adopted an actor-oriented methodology. This had certain implications for how we conceptualised the central analytical issues. In the first place, we started with an interest in irrigation *organisation*, not irrigation *systems*. This implied a concern for how various actors or parties organise themselves around the problems of water management and distribution. This goes beyond the analysis of the physical and technical properties of the different systems of irrigation to consider how different interests, often in conflict, attempt to control water distribution or to secure access to it and to other necessary inputs for irrigated agriculture. Irrigation organisation therefore emerges as a set of social arrangements worked out between the parties concerned, rather than simply 'dictated' by the physical layout and technical design, or even by the 'controlling' authorities who built and now manage the system. Hence irrigation organisation should not be represented as an organisational chart or organigram, but rather as being made up of a complex set of social practices and normative and conceptual models, both formal and informal.

The second dimension was the question of actor *strategies*. This concept was central to our research because we aimed to interpret agricultural and social change as an outcome of the struggles and negotiations that take place between individuals and groups with differing and often conflicting social interests and experiences. Strategy is important at the level of how producers and other rural inhabitants attempt to resolve their livelihood problems and organise their resources. It entails that producers and householders actively construct, within the limits they face, their own patterns of farm and household organisation and their own ways of dealing with intervening agencies. The same is true of government bureaucrats or company brokers – they, too, attempt to come to grips organisationally and cognitively with the changing world around them by devising strategies for pursuing various personal and institutional goals and likewise the day labourers, even if their choices are much more restricted. Focusing upon strategies in this way might appear to give too much emphasis to processes of rational calculation and decision-making, but throughout the fieldwork we sought to anchor our research questions, observations and analysis to actors' lived experiences, desires, understandings and self-defined problematic situations, while at the same time trying not to impose our own categories of interpretation.

The third issue concerned *planned intervention*. This embraced both formally organised state intervention as well as that of the transnational and national companies and family enterprises that attempted to organise and control production and commercialisation of the key products. As I have indicated, the project stressed the importance of looking at this problem in terms of the interactions that evolved between local groups and intervening actors. Intervention is an on-going transformational process that is constantly re-shaped by its own internal organisational and political dynamic and by the specific conditions it encounters or itself creates, including the responses and strategies of local and regional groups who may struggle to define and defend their own social spaces, cultural boundaries and positions within the wider power field. Our research was especially oriented towards identifying the types of organising practices, socio-political interfaces and configurations of knowledge and power that developed out of these complex processes of negotiation.

This type of intervention study entails some understanding of wider structural phenomena, since many of the choices perceived and strategies pursued by individuals or groups will have been shaped by processes outside the immediate arenas of interaction. One way of achieving this, we suggested, was through adopting a modified political economy perspective, which would analyse how labour processes and the organisation of production and related economic activities were structured by the larger arenas of economic and political power relations, including the ways in which the state attempted to control and manage the outcomes of local-level development (Bates 1983: 134–47). Such an approach would also give attention to analysing the social, cultural and ideological mechanisms by which particular economic systems and types of 'production regime' (Burawoy 1985: 7–8) are reproduced. We argued that, providing one avoided the shortcomings of certain types of political economy (e.g. the tendency to accord theoretical primacy to the capitalist mode of production and its 'laws' of development, and to class categories and hierarchies of dominance), then such a perspective could offer a useful framework for examining how structural factors (such as changing markets and international conditions, shifts in government development policy or in the power exercised by particular groups at national or regional level) affected farmer organisation and strategy, including the commitment to specific types of production such as irrigated export agriculture.

Thus an actor-oriented approach, with its emphasis on the detailed analysis of the life-worlds, struggles and exchanges within and between specific social groups and networks of individuals, is not, as some writers have suggested (Alavi 1973, and Harriss 1982: 27), antithetical to such structural issues, since it is important also to take full account of the conditions that constrain choice and strategy. At the same time, however, we must accept the implication that combining structural and actor perspectives and issues necessitates the critical rethinking of certain key concepts of political economy, such as commoditisation, state hegemony, 'subsumption' of the peasantry, the primacy of the 'laws' of capitalist development, and perhaps even the concept of the market itself. Several chapters in the present book address these and related theoretical problems. On the other hand, actor-oriented analysis has to learn how to handle better the issues of 'structure' and 'structural constraints', while continuing to accord sufficient room to the central role played by diverse forms of human action and social consciousness in the making of development.

Although a major challenge, it seemed possible to weave these differing strands into a single framework of analysis. The above-described Mexican research has in large part succeeded in doing so through focusing upon processes of intervention and heterogeneity within different social arenas. The kinds of complex struggles and outcomes covered included, for example, the negotiated deals struck by private companies for the renting of peasant holdings for the production and commercialisation of export crops; the efforts of agricultural technicians struggling to implement or in some cases subvert government irrigation policy; the battles at the interfaces between different categories of sugar producers, their leaders and the sugar mill; the preservation of social and cultural space by agricultural labourers in the face of highly regulated and at times coercive production regimes; and the vicissitudes of women's groups which at times invite and at others resist intervention by outside authorities.

Concluding reflections on paradigm change

It is now time to return to the question of theoretical paradigms discussed at the beginning of the chapter, where I argued that the social sciences have in fact always been characterised by a multiplicity of paradigms. The reasons for this seem to relate, first, to the sheer variety and complexity of social phenomena that invites alternative visions and modes of analysis, and second, to the difficulty of establishing a common epistemology for grounding research methods and findings. According to Giddens (1987: 19), this is compounded by the fact that 'there is no way of keeping the conceptual apparatus of the observer...from appropriation by lay actors', which makes the distinction between 'the researched' and 'the researcher' ever more blurred.

The existence of multiple paradigms does not of course exclude the possibility of some of them becoming prominent at particular historical junctures and being promoted by particular groups of scholars and institutions, as Hewitt's study demonstrates for Mexican anthropology. It would be wrong, however, to expect the rise and fall of paradigms to conform to a neat 'stages' theory of intellectual development whereby new conceptions and findings lead to progressively more sophisticated modes of theoretical understanding. In fact one might even turn the argument around and say that dramatic shifts in theory and paradigm often signal the introduction of new simplifying conceptions or gimmicky ideas that close off certain existing areas of inquiry in favour of new ones. While this sometimes results in stimulating new insights, it may also produce increasingly sterile and inward-looking research, such as some of the work associated with Althuserian structuralism and with extreme forms of postmodernism. Furthermore, although it might be possible to identify specific periods when certain orthodoxies or 'schools of thought' have occupied the centre stage, a more fine-grained analysis would almost certainly reveal other scholars (professional and lay) operating outside the 'mainstream'. Some of the latter might later be accredited with seminal contributions and their own band of devotees. Also, like all other intellectual and professional fields, development sociology is full of politicking for control over institutional resources, networking to secure the support of a wide constituency of colleagues, and the manipulation of the sources and legitimacy of knowledge and reputation.[28]

These comments on multiple paradigms and communities of scholars lead me to consider briefly the contemporary situation of development sociology and, by implication, other areas of social science. If, as I have argued, this multiplicity is based on important differences of epistemology (between, say, structuralist versus phenomenological views), then it is hardly likely to disappear. Furthermore, as Kuhn's early work clearly underlines, while certain historical periods may be characterised by the predominance of a particular worldview or the growing clash of opposing theoretical paradigms, others may manifest a kaleidoscope of possibilities and combinations. Although for some the latter may seem disconcerting due to the absence of a clear blueprint for doing research and a lack of fixed principles for legitimising research work and conclusions, this scenario, I believe, is much more conducive to the development of new explorative and innovative types of research. This is the situation in which we find ourselves at the beginning of the twenty-first century. We are at a critical and exciting turning-point when old orthodoxies have largely given way to (or at least allowed room for) new modes of conceptualising the complexities and dynamics of social life. Development sociology is on the brink of making major theoretical advances, not least of which is the development of a more integrated analysis of how agency, institutions, knowledge and power interrelate in the new global age.

2

DEMYTHOLOGISING PLANNED
INTERVENTION[1]

As the previous chapter suggested, a critical analysis of policy and intervention processes[2] requires demythologising notions of planned development. That is, it is important to challenge the time–space definitions, normative assumptions and praxeology implied in orthodox intervention models, and to expose the limitations of certain theoretical conceptions that underpin them, giving particular attention to the theorisation of commoditisation, institutional incorporation and the interrelations of state and civil society. This chapter offers such a critique and proposes as an alternative that we view intervention as a 'multiple reality' made up of differing cultural perceptions and social interests, and constituted by the ongoing social and political struggles that take place between the various social actors involved.

From the outset we must distinguish between *theoretical models* aimed at understanding processes of social change and development and *policy models* that set out the ways in which development[3] should be promoted. This distinction is important but not absolute, since policy models are explicitly or implicitly based upon theoretical assumptions and interpretations that are supposed to explain how change takes place or how objectives are to be achieved.[4] Theoretical models may address themselves to specific dimensions (e.g. rural or urban development, or the transformation of the state apparatus and macro-economic frameworks) and some aim to characterise the essential elements of policy-making and implementation itself. Hence we have 'rational' models which are based upon the belief that, by bringing more information, thought and analysis into the policy-making process, policies will become more effective; 'disjointed incrementalism' which regards policy-making as the science of 'muddling through' whereby policy-makers consider a narrow range of alternatives and respond to political contingencies as and when they arise (Lindbolm 1980); and various models that treat policy-making and implementation as inherently political processes involving bargaining and transactions between different interest groups (Warwick 1982, Palumbo 1987).[5]

The interrelations of theoretical and policy models are, however, often left unexplicated and therefore unclear. It becomes important then to focus on intervention *practices* as they evolve and are shaped by the struggles between the various participants, rather than simply on intervention *models*, by which we mean the ideal-typical constructions that planners, implementers or clients may have about the process. Focusing upon intervention practices allows one to take account of emergent forms of interaction, procedures, practical strategies, types of discourse, cultural categories and the 'stakeholders' (Palumbo 1987: 32) involved in specific contexts, and to reformulate questions of state intervention and development from a more thoroughgoing actor perspective.

The need to deconstruct the concept of intervention

The dominant theoretical paradigms of planned intervention in the 1960s and 1970s espoused a rather mechanical model of the relationship between policy, implementation and outcomes. A tendency in many studies (which still lingers on in certain policy discourses) was to conceptualise the process as essentially linear in nature, implying some kind of step-by-step progression from policy formulation to implementation to outcomes, after which one could make an *ex post facto* evaluation to establish how far the original objectives had been achieved. Yet, as any experienced planner or development worker will readily appreciate, this separation of 'policy', 'implementation' and 'outcomes' is a gross over-simplification of a much more complicated set of processes which involves the reinterpretation or transformation of policy during the implementation process itself, such that there is in fact no straight line from policy to outcomes. Also, outcomes may result from factors not directly linked to the implementation of a particular development programme. Moreover, issues of policy implementation should not be restricted to the case of top-down, planned interventions by governments, development agencies and private institutions, since local groups actively formulate and pursue their own 'development projects' that often clash with the interests of central authority (Long 1984b: 177–9, van der Ploeg 1987).

By the early 1980s, there was a growing recognition of such deficiencies among policy analysts who sought new ways of conceptualising policy formulation and implementation (see Grindle 1980, and Clay and Schaffer 1984). It was argued, for example, that implementation should be viewed as a transactional process involving negotiation over goals and means between parties with conflicting or diverging interests, and not simply as the execution of a particular policy (Warwick 1982). This was paralleled by new forms of organisational analysis that looked at the dynamics of administrative action in policy implementation (Batley 1983); by anthropologists who addressed themselves to questions concerning the nature of planning as an ideology and social activity (Robertson 1984); and by others interested in examining how public services are allocated through the interactions that take place between 'front-line' agency personnel and their clients (see Schaffer and Lamb 1976, Lipsky 1980, Handelman and Leyton 1978; see also Rees 1978, who focuses on the cultural perceptions and social management strategies of agents and clients).

These new directions coincided with a growing awareness of the diverse ways in which individuals and their households organise themselves individually and collectively in the face of planned intervention by government or other bodies. The strategies they devise and the types of interaction that evolve between them and the intervening parties shape the nature and outcomes of such intervention (see Long 1984b, Long and Long 1992, and de Vries 1992, 1997). A central problem for analysis, therefore, is to understand the processes by which interventions enter the lifeworlds of the individuals and groups affected and thus come to form part of the resources and constraints of the social strategies they develop. In this way so-called external factors become 'internalised' and come to mean different things to different interest groups or to the different individual actors involved, whether they be implementers, clients or bystanders.

These considerations lead to the conclusion that the concept of intervention needs deconstructing so that we recognise it for what it fundamentally is, namely, an ongoing, socially constructed and negotiated process, not simply the execution of an already-specified plan of action with expected outcomes. The usual 'assumption is that decision makers, before they act, identify goals, specify alternative ways of getting there, assess the

31

alternatives against a standard such as costs and benefits, and then select the best alternative'. However, as Palumbo and Nachmias go on to point out, policy-makers often 'are not looking for the best way or most efficient alternative for solving a problem. They are instead searching for support for action already taken, and for support that serves the interests of various components of the policy shaping community' (Palumbo and Nachmias 1983: 9–11). It is not enough, then, to modify or seek refinements of orthodox views on planned intervention. Instead one must break with conventional models, images and reasoning.[6]

The image of intervention as a discrete 'project' in time and space

Despite these critical observations, development intervention is still often visualised as a discrete set of activities that takes place within a defined time–space setting involving the interaction between 'intervening' parties and 'target' or 'recipient' groups. Such an image isolates intervention from the continuous flow of social life and ongoing relations that evolve between the various social actors, including of course – though not exclusively – the manifold ways in which local actors (both on- and off-stage) interrelate with state institutions and officials. Thus conceptualising intervention as a discrete and clearly localised activity[7] obscures the theoretically important point that intervention never is a 'project' with sharp boundaries in time and space as defined by the institutional apparatus of the state or implementing agency. Interventions are always part of a chain or flow of events located within the broader framework of the activities of the state and/or international bodies, and the actions of different interest groups operative in civil society. Moreover, interventions are linked to previous interventions (in policy models through 'evaluation studies'), have consequences for future ones, and more often than not are a focus for inter-institutional struggles or represent arenas where battles over perceived goals, administrative competencies, resource allocation and institutional boundaries are fought out.

Consequently a critical analysis of intervention seen both as ideology and practice must go beyond the time and space definitions contained within conventional policy models. Intervention is not confined to the specific 'space' as delimited by the identification of the target group or population. Nor do the people on the receiving end of policies, or those responsible for managing implementation, reduce or limit their perceptions of reality and its problems to those defined by the intervening agency as constituting the 'project' or 'programme'. People process their own experiences of 'projects' and 'intervention'. They construct their own memory of these experiences, as well as taking into account the experiences of other groups within their socio-spatial networks. That is, they may learn from the differential responses, strategies and experiences of others outside the target population or specific action programme. Hence intervention is not a discrete phenomenon in space and time. In practice it has no clear beginning, demarcated by the definition of goals and means, nor a final cut-off point, the 'end' of the project as defined by the writing of the evaluation report.

This boxing-in of space and time (and therefore also of strategies and options) characteristic of development project thinking, is underpinned by various kinds of interventionist discourse which are essentially 'diagnostic and prescriptive' in nature (Apthorpe 1984: 128), and which promote the idea that problems are best tackled by dividing up empirical complexity into 'a series of independently given realities' based on 'sectoral' criteria (i.e. by designing policies specifically focused upon agriculture, health, housing etc.). According to

Schaffer (1984: 143), such policy discourse also encourages the misconception that policy comprises verbal and voluntaristic decisions and authoritative documents, after which something else quite different, called implementation, takes place.

This image of policy and intervention processes is reinforced by the notion of the 'project cycle' that arranges various activities (such as setting the policy agenda, defining the problem, formulating alternatives, designing the policy, implementing it and evaluating the results) sequentially in a linear and logical order (see Clay and Schaffer 1984: 3–5, and Palumbo 1987: 38–41). This encourages the view that project preparation and implementation takes the form of a 'rational' problem-solving process which involves experts (either alone or in consultation with their clients) 'in becoming aware of symptoms, in formulating the problem, in identifying the causes (diagnosis), in generating alternative solutions and in choosing and implementing an appropriate one...[and] finally, help[ing] evaluate the results' (Röling 1988: 57).[8]

If, however, we stand back from these ideal-typical, time–space conceptions and instead concentrate upon understanding planned intervention as a complex set of evolving social practices and struggles, then time and space can be reintroduced as elements of specific historical processes, which become distorted when confined to the time–space grid of the project model. There is, for example, on the side of the 'intervened', the accumulated knowledge of previous experiences of interventions of various sorts, not only those organised by the state or the agency in question. These experiences constitute a kind of historical imprint and template which is both collective, in the sense that it is shared as a legacy by a particular group of people, and individual, in that the biographies of particular actors contain within them specific 'intervention' experiences. And the same holds for those groups and institutions described as the 'intervening' parties, such as government development agencies or individual bureaucrats. Specific intervention processes must therefore be viewed in relation to collective and individual memories (what Bourdieu 1981: 305–6 has called 'objectified' and 'embodied' history) of state–civic society relations, local initiatives and inter-institutional struggles.

Intervention then implies the confrontation or interpenetration of different lifeworlds and socio-political experiences, which may be significant for generating new forms of social practice and ideology. Looked at from this point of view, the time–space conceptions contained within orthodox intervention models become a strategic weapon in the hands of intervening agencies.[9] By adopting the notion that intervention consists of spatially and temporally discrete projects, one – as it were – takes out history, thus implying that memory and learning from the past are in fact superfluous.[10] This attitude is reinforced by the assumption that, whatever the difficulties of the past and however entrenched the patterns of underdevelopment, a well-designed and well-targeted programme of intervention can make the break with the dead weight of 'traditional' modes of existence, thus stimulating or inaugurating 'development', whatever its specific features.

The 'cargo' image of intervention

The specific terminology used in intervention discourse, including the description of the direct encounters between intervening parties and farmers, is coloured by the notion that there is a traffic of presents or gifts which come from the outside and have supreme qualities which cannot be produced within the local situation itself. This is illustrated graphically by the idea of 'miracle' seeds, 'improved' varieties, 'the message of extension', and 'the benefits of privileged receivers'. These metaphors reproduce the image of an all powerful 'outside' and an inferior 'inside'. Several such terms also carry a magico-religious connotation, which can be compared with the idea of 'cargo' found in the cargo cults of Melanesia. Adherents of such cults believed that if they followed the right moral and ritual procedures and honoured the spirits then they would be rewarded with the sudden and miraculous arrival, by ship or aircraft, of a cargo of highly valued commodities from overseas. How and where these commodities (e.g. tins of corned beef, matches and other manufactured items) were produced was unknown to the Melanesians, and so they assumed that the whites who brought them had privileged access to forms of esoteric knowledge which the Melanesians themselves had lost. Adhering strictly to the ethical code of the cult in anticipation of the arrival of the cargo was itself regarded as an act of redemption.[11]

Equally strategic in intervention ideology is the clear separation of 'internal' and 'external' factors, of 'inside' and 'outside'. Although interventions do not really possess an 'inside' and an 'outside', since intervention practices consist (and can only consist) of the intermingling of differing flows of events and interests, from which intervention as a socially-negotiated process itself emerges, this separation of 'inside' and 'outside' is nevertheless omnipresent and central to standard policy models.

The separation of inside from outside is, it seems, indispensable for the related image that intervention consists of the delivery of some kind of material or organisational input or 'package' from outside (or the 'world beyond') which is designed to stimulate the emergence of certain 'internal' activities geared towards the achievement of higher levels of production, income-generation, economic 'efficiency' or the better utilisation of existing resources and the 'human factor'. Even those programmes (often promoted by NGOs rather than the state) that do not have tangible material packages to offer but instead deal in less tangible items, such as organisation or knowhow, are based on the idea of transferring to target groups those capabilities or types of knowledge that it is assumed they lack. Hence the argument runs: target groups need organisational skills and the help of intermediate persons, 'facilitators' or brokers in order to obtain access to outside institutions and resources; without such inputs they are simply incapable of managing their own life circumstances and solving the problematic situations they face.

Linked to this 'cargo' image is the underlying belief that local situations, lifeworlds or ways of organising social life are somehow ill-founded or no longer valid and inappropriate, and hence need restructuring or perhaps even eliminating altogether, if development is to take place. The proposed 'cargo' is designed to resolve this by establishing new and more appropriate ways of doing things. Thus intervention becomes a way of reshaping existing social practice and knowledge and of introducing new elements (for instance, 'miracle seeds') that either replace or accord new meanings to already established ways of doing things (van der Ploeg 1989: 154, 161). The ideological underpinning of this is the belief that the injection of external inputs will provide a better solution to problems than those means that already exist, thereby opening up new opportunities and improving people's living conditions and welfare.

In synthesis, one might say that intervention is both perceived and legitimated as the continuous production of discontinuities. If development is supposed to come about through intervention and the restructuring of existing social forms, then development implies discontinuity, not continuity, with the past. The situation chosen for intervention is deemed inadequate or needing change; thus local bodies of knowledge, organisational forms and resources are implicitly (and sometimes quite explicitly) de-legitimised; and consequently external inputs are assessed as necessary and indispensable. It is in this way that the normative framework and technical instruments of planned development are validated by interventionists. This suggests that intervention should not be seen solely or perhaps even primarily as consisting of material and organisational inputs, but rather as involving a kind of 'trade in images'[12] which seeks to redefine the nature of state–civic society relations through the promotion of certain normative standards of what development is and should entail. Here one should recognise the central role played by technology in promoting new social values and ways of organising society (see, e.g., Galtung 1982, and Latour 1983).

The construction of these images is sustained by a process of 'labelling' which functions to promote or impose certain interpretative schemata concerned with the diagnosis and solution of 'development problems'. As Wood (1985) argues, labelling is common to all forms of social communication, and therefore is characteristic of development policy discourse. The latter contains classificatory devices for identifying problems for solution, for describing the nature of the population to be affected and the context, and for arriving at 'solutions'. This is illustrated by the ways in which policy makers use simple notions (1) to depict the 'obstacles' to development (e.g. the assumed dualism of large estates and peasant communities in Latin America, or the 'conservative' nature of 'traditional' values), (2) to identify the 'target' population (e.g. 'the landless', 'poorest of the poor' or 'peasant women'), and (3) to put forward the means by which to solve the problems identified (e.g. 'land reform', 'basic needs' programmes, or the introduction of new technological and/or organisational packages aimed at farmers with 'development potential' or who are considered to be 'receptive to change'). Labelling therefore legitimises the diagnostic and therapeutic measures undertaken by public bodies. It also attempts to establish the parameters and superiority of the discourse of planned intervention itself, drawing for example upon concepts such as 'efficiency', 'the collective good', 'social equity' and 'means–ends' rationality.[13] Where material inputs are introduced they are organised strictly along the lines of the initial schemata of classification (i.e. according to certain 'labelling' criteria). Thus, for example, farmers with 'development potential' or who are considered to be 'receptive to change' will receive the lion's share of credit, livestock or technology, and even if many of them 'fail' to utilise these benefits strictly in accordance with recommended practice, the programme will nevertheless continue to reaffirm its initial goals. For example, in locations where means of transport are scarce, trained oxen might be valued more for the transportation of goods and persons than for ploughing, the original reason given for their introduction. The same holds for technological packages that are 'unpacked' by the farmers themselves in order to deal with problems which the original programme had not addressed or foreseen. In this respect it is interesting to recall that farmers who divert credit earmarked for specific purposes into alternative investment channels (even if into sound income-generating activities) are usually designated 'delinquents'.[14] Labelling them in this way serves, of course, to reinforce the original goals and normative values of the programme. Hence, paradoxically, any shortfalls or perceived 'failures' in the programme will simply lead to increased efforts or renewed proselytisation by agency staff in order to attain their targets next time round.[15]

Hence the activities of development agencies and their personnel cannot simply be interpreted in terms of material and organisational inputs, since they entail above all the introduction of normative and evaluative concepts that define the problems, solutions and means. Although the interpretative strategies developed by agency personnel for carrying out their tasks will vary in accordance with their own individual interests and cultural understandings, their repertoires will be broadly similar since the ways in which they allocate resources or explain and legitimise plans will reflect the images and priorities of development promoted by the particular institution for which they work. Also, given their commitment to externalist solutions, intervening agencies will normally aim to supplant or subsume local conceptions and strategies of development. This disregard for local knowledge and local development capabilities is further reinforced by the argument that experts of various kinds are needed to facilitate an understanding of the problems for solution and to design and implement a smooth and efficient transfer of skills, information, technology and resources. Thus, as Edwards has commented in a trenchant critique entitled 'The irrelevance of development studies',

> The natural consequence of a concern for technical interpretations of reality is that knowledge, and the power to control it, become concentrated in the hands of those with the technical skills necessary to understand the language and methods being used....The logical corollary of a world-view, which sees development as a series of technical transfers mediated by experts, is that, given a sufficient number of situations, or projects, in which these transfers are made, 'development' will occur. But, as Sithembiso Nyoni [Zimbabwean Director of Organisation of Rural Associations for Progress] has pointed out, no country in the world has ever developed itself through projects; development results from a long process of experiment and innovation through which people build up the skills, knowledge and self-confidence necessary to shape their environment in ways which foster progress toward goals such as economic growth, equity in income distribution, and political freedom.
>
> (Edwards 1989: 118–20)

Even the increased interest in learning about local knowledge and practice (now heavily subsidised by UN development agencies and championed by applied social scientists such as Chambers (1983), Rhoades (1984), and Richards (1985) becomes trapped by the limitations which it places upon itself. I have in mind here the various so-called 'participatory' research methods aimed at learning about farmer practice and knowledge. Although geared towards the design of more appropriate and 'sustainable' technological packages and modes of organisation, most of these approaches remain in the hands of the 'experts'. Consistent with this situation is the burgeoning interest in issues of 'participation' and 'participatory' research shown by international development agencies (Nelson and Wright 1995), whose commitment is undoubtedly inspired by the belief that participation will help to reduce infrastructural costs, organisational burdens and improve the accuracy of the research they carry out.

All this suggests that inherent to the process of planned intervention is a contest over the dominance and legitimacy of competing images of development. But we must not simplify this by assuming that the contest merely involves the clash between intervening agencies and local interests. It also entails struggles within and between the development agencies themselves.

Evaluation as the moment of objectification[16]

Exploring the normative dimensions of planned intervention raises a further crucial element. This concerns the idea of the 'evaluation' of projects or programmes that is required to take place periodically during their lifespan. Justification for the continuance or disbanding of a particular project or programme must, it is argued, be based upon a systematic retrospective overview of the project, its original objectives and its achievements. Normally a project is not deemed 'successful' unless it is shown to have reached some of its stated objectives and to have achieved these without incurring too great a cost to the organisation responsible or to the target population itself. Yet even if measured a 'failure' by these criteria, an evaluation may nevertheless provide the rationale for reformulating the programme and trying once again to achieve these same goals.[17] Since it is seldom the case that evaluations question the whole idea of planned intervention and the rationality of planning, it is usually the farmers, environmental factors or the mysteries of distant commodity markets that are blamed for failure, not the package or the activities of the agency itself. In this way evaluation comes to play a useful role in confirming the self-fulfilling prophecy that interventionist policies are indeed viable and ideologically sound, even if moderated or buttressed by the hidden forces of the so-called free market.

A critical analysis of intervention practices necessitates that we go beyond the simple statement of the policy functions of evaluation studies. Evaluation must be analysed in the first place as a mechanism interlinking different interventions through time; and second, as an important factor in the systematic production of ideologies legitimating the role of intervening agencies and thus also the implied power relations between these agencies and target groups.[18]

Moreover, a critical analysis should avoid the temptation of using evaluation studies simply to denounce the unfulfilled goals of particular policies. A critique that merely focuses on the 'failures' produced is beside the point. 'Failure' is seldom a reason (at best it is one of the pretexts) to halt a particular intervention policy. Normally 'failures' are the starting point for the elaboration of the next round of interventions. One could even argue that a certain degree of 'failure' is strategic in the reproduction of intervention itself. Irrigation schemes, integrated rural development programmes or extension programmes can in fact go on for decennia, since every four years (or whatever time span is planned for periodic evaluation) it may be concluded that the established goals have 'not yet' been reached, or that 'new problems', such as salinisation or a decline in the demand for particular products, have arisen (see Bolhuis and van der Ploeg 1985: 322).

As the latter example underscores, intervention is big business, not only for firms and consultancy bureaux but also for the government agencies or NGOs involved. For all of them, 'development' is a commodity with a calculable exchange value that reproduces and legitimises particular intervention practices and interests. Consequently, the rules of the game called 'evaluation' are conditioned more by the social interests of those involved in manufacturing, promoting, selling and utilising a particular commodity than by the functions it is assumed to fulfil in the intervention model.

Beyond policy models: theorising planned intervention

So far I have argued for the deconstruction of linear and cyclical models of planned intervention. Such models and strategies of intervention, however, are underpinned (explicitly or implicitly) by general theoretical suppositions and interpretations. It is therefore time I expressed my misgivings about these more general sociological models. I cannot here attempt a full critique of existing relevant frameworks. Instead I limit the discussion to three crucial areas of analysis: the issue of agrarian development and agency, processes of institutionalisation, and the conceptualisation of the state and state action.

Agrarian development, heterogeneity and agency

Planning and intervention are in the end about 'development'. At least that is what is claimed and what legitimises intervention practices. Limiting the discussion, for the sake of brevity, to the question of agrarian development, there are three essentials for developing a methodological and theoretical approach that avoids the myopia of interventionist thinking.

In the first place, we must recognise that the claim that intervention is the key to agrarian development is not only false but also, if we consider the possible implications of such a claim, part of the problem of development itself. Most dominant theories somehow assume that development has to be 'induced' (see Hayami and Ruttan 1985 on 'induced technical and institutional change'); that is, external interventions are considered necessary in order to trigger off the process. And, although probably no one would maintain that no development whatsoever takes place outside the domain of intervention, it is none the less a widely shared opinion that 'substantial' or 'adequate' development depends critically upon intervention: in other words, on the introduction of packages consisting of various combinations of expertise, capital, technology and effective modes of organisation. The logical converse of this, of course, is that outside this realm of the 'cargo cult' there is 'ignorance', 'incapacity', 'poor resources', 'backward' forms of technology and 'powerlessness'; that is, those very features normally reproduced through the labelling processes outlined earlier, and which one should especially combat during the initial stages of intervention.

Even a brief acquaintance with the literature on agrarian history, economics and sociology, however, would show conclusively that the bulk of evidence runs counter to this dichotomised view. Agrarian development is not limited to intervention practices. It is potentially omnipresent in the countryside, and where it does not manifest itself as a relatively autonomous, diversified and dynamic process, this is probably because it has become impeded or obstructed in some way, and one of the mechanisms by which this occurs (and here we enter the real problem) is through intervention itself. Thus, behind the claim that intervention is the trigger or driving force of development is the fact that intervention practices more often than not aim to control the pattern of local economic and political development. Policy interventions seek to bring the dynamic of local initiative into line with the interests and perspectives of public authorities, and to reproduce the image of the state (or its agencies) as being the key to development. This intent to increase outside control may affect the effectiveness of, and the meanings accorded to, local development activities. Especially when the establishment of new forms of control consists of the externalisation of particular parts of the farm labour process to outside (market) institutions, or when a massive and abrupt scientification of agriculture is involved, the overall effect might well become a major obstacle to locally-spurred development. Indeed much historical evidence documents the counterpart process; namely, that a reduction in control by central state authorities often stimulates a sudden revitalisation and proliferation of local development activities. For example, the rise of the independent farmer (or rancher) in the central highlands of Peru at the turn of the twentieth century was spurred by the development of new forms of *local* political control and jurisdiction *vis-à-vis* the dominant centres of power located in the towns of the region. Spahr van der Hoek and Postma (1952) provide a similar account for the agrarian history of Friesland, focusing upon the impact of farmers' struggles for 'the plenitude of power' within their own farmers' organisations; and Hayami and Ruttan (1985) likewise link Japanese agricultural development to various local initiatives.

This relates to the second point. As I have argued elsewhere, 'agricultural development is many-sided, complex and often contradictory in nature. It involves different sets of social forces originating from international, national, regional and local arenas. The interplay of these various forces generates specific forms, directions and rhythms of agricultural change' (Long and van der Ploeg 1988: 37). Heterogeneity is thus a structural feature of agrarian development. It does not emerge casually nor can it easily be engineered. Rather it must be seen as the outcome of processes that are designed and realised from 'below' in a diversity of local settings (van der Ploeg 1986). This 'manufacturing' of diverse forms of local knowledge – which results from the detailed and socially-mediated translation of local resources, constraints and conditions into action – is fundamental to the production and reproduction of this heterogeneity. Externally designed and planned interventions that work with 'tested' and standardised solutions are simply unable to build upon local knowledge and experience. And so, in the end, they possess very little mastery over these highly diverse local situations.

The third important point is that the study of intervention should be inserted into an appreciation of the wider (now increasingly 'global') context, and thus embrace both the dominant tendencies of development and their counter-tendencies (see Arce and Long 2000). Depending on the circumstances, particular actors and organisations may be strategically spurred on by specific interventions, while others may find their interests, strategies and livelihoods impeded or completely blocked. It is important therefore to explore the effects of particular project interventions not only on 'target groups' and other defined 'stakeholders' but also more broadly on 'hinterland' actors, livelihoods and institutions. One must also identify the patterns of interaction and accommodation that take place between the different groups of actors, and analyse the ways in which their particular histories, collective memories and time–space conceptions shape the reception and outcomes of particular policy measures. Such studies differ from standard project evaluation procedures. Whereas the latter address the 'fictitious' question of whether or not original goals have been reached, the former – based on a broad social impact approach – conceptualises intervention as a part (and perhaps only a minor part) of a wider complex of social practices built upon the interlocking of various actors' strategies and intentionalities (see also Olivier de Sardan 1995: 173–5). Only by throwing the net wide in this way can we examine the consequences of specific interventions for the already existing 'autonomous' or 'endogenous' modes of development and organisation (for further discussion, see Long 1984b, Cernea 1985, Long and van der Ploeg 1994).

Agrarian structures and processes of institutionalisation

Some concept of 'agrarian structure' is necessary in order to identify and classify the types of agricultural development patterns, the forms of interaction between differently located social actors (agrarian and non-agrarian) and the intersection of institutional frames and contrasting economic and political arenas. In this respect it is crucial to explore the relevant operational or management units, and the patterns of resource allocation, exchange and communication that interconnect them. Here I do not only have in mind production units (such as the peasant household, cooperative, hacienda or plantation) but also those institutions that are interlinked with them through existing social divisions of labour (Benvenuti 1987). In this way production units are articulated with other institutions and markets through a network of commodity as well as technico-administrative relations which have an important impact on the organisation of the farm labour process (van der Ploeg 1986, 1990). Using such an approach, the notion of agrarian structure can be operationalised as composed of a set of interlinked human agencies involved in the 'everyday negotiation of the role-definition and role-enactment of farmers' (Benvenuti 1985: 225) and forming part of a wider regional constellation which, following Long and Roberts (1984), one might call 'a regionalised system of production'. The latter is shorthand for the complex system of capital, labour and socio-political linkages that develops historically between various economic sectors and activities and between the social classes and groups that are spawned by them. This system of linkages is dynamic and not simply determined by the actions of one dominant sector. It is continually being remoulded by the struggles that go on between different individuals and social groups, and is of course affected by the ways in which outside forces impinge upon it (cf. Long 1984b: 175–7). Only in this way can the reification implicit in conventional definitions of agrarian structure be avoided.

If we adopt this actor approach to the analysis of intervention processes, identifying the types of arenas, interface struggles, negotiations and transformations that take place, then evidently the actors involved, their identities and their subjective interests and perspectives must be considered independently of intervention rhetoric. In so doing, of course, one runs counter to modernisation as well as Marxist theories, since both are geared towards the understanding of the 'integration' or 'submission' of the rural world and its actors within the global framework of capitalism. There is in fact a remarkable convergence between both these schools of thought (see Vandergeest 1988, and Long and van der Ploeg 1988). In both, centralist and determinist tendencies prevail and are reified, thus obscuring the nature and potential of individual and/or collective strategies and responses (Long 1984b and 1988).

An actor-oriented approach to agrarian structure allows for the recognition of commoditisation and institutional incorporation (or bureaucratisation) as basic trends in contemporary rural history, without attributing to them deterministic effects (which, among other things, depict farmers and other actors in the local arena as increasingly 'powerless'). From an actor perspective, commoditisation and institutionalisation only become real in their consequences when given meaning by specific actors (including here not only farmers but also others such as traders, bureaucrats and politicians). Integration into new markets or the introduction of a new technology can only be mediated and translated by the specific strategies and understandings of the actors involved: they are not disembodied processes. A further consequence is that certain forms of heterogeneity emerge as the logical accompaniment of commoditisation and institutionalisation, requiring theorisation. It is not enough, as Bernstein (1986: 19) suggests, to treat heterogeneity simply as a matter of empirical diversity.

This implies that such trends do not necessarily undermine power relations within the local situation, nor do they eliminate an active role for the farmers involved. What they do result in is a shift in the basis of power relations, and also a shift in the various definitions of farmers' roles and their interrelations. At the same time, increasing commoditisation and institutionalisation often result in the emergence of new structural discontinuities, and hence in the creation of new points of leverage and space for manoeuvre which may become crucial in the interaction with various intervening agencies (Long 1989).

The above points of course relate directly to the discussion on planned intervention. Intervention practices often do result in abrupt and massive increases in commoditisation and institutionalisation, and these processes are often seen as the primary vehicles of development.[19] But even so, one should not deduce from this that local actors are simply 'expropriated' and reduced to being powerless. While the tendencies towards such forms of expropriation might be strong, we will find within the same arena certain counter-tendencies where new points of leverage and new power relations will emerge. I have already described intervention practices as political struggles over access to, and distribution of, certain critical resources and, above all, as normative struggles over the definition of development and the role of the different actors. These processes will be all the more significant if commoditisation and institutionalisation constitute important components of intervention practice. Thus, rather than eliminating social and normative struggles, intervention practices are likely to radicalise them, introducing new discontinuities and heightening confrontations between differing interests and values.

Images and theoretical interpretations of the state

A final critical issue underpinning much interventionist thinking is the conception of the state. Here we can distinguish between several interpretations.[20] The first is what is called the 'logic of capital' model based upon Marxist theories of development that interpret the actions of the capitalist state in terms of the imperatives and intrinsic 'logic' of capitalist development (de Janvry 1981). It stresses how state power holders and institutions function to secure the long-term survival of capitalist forms of accumulation, thus safeguarding the interests of the dominant class or class alliance. This process is complicated by the fact that capital accumulation on a global scale is subject to periodical crises that require corrective measures by the state. The state may also institute policies that have negative consequences for certain segments of the dominant class or class alliance, and that offer concessions to subordinate groups such as peasant producers or workers. It is at such historical junctures that the state is said to acquire some measure of independent action or 'relative autonomy' vis-à-vis the dominant class, although in the end the 'objective power of capital' and the shoring up of the system work to the benefit of capitalist interests, national and foreign.

One unresolved issue in this line of reasoning is the question of 'state autonomy' (see Hamilton 1982: 8–13, and Skocpol 1985). Since analysis is essentially directed towards revealing the underlying structure and laws of capitalism, it becomes difficult on general theoretical grounds to allow much room for independent action by the state (its agencies and associated organisations), if by this we mean action against the interests of the dominant class, which can ultimately result in fundamental changes in the existing capitalist mode of production. In order to resolve this, one needs to define more precisely the sets of social forces impinging upon state power holders and institutions and to determine the means and extent of political control exercised by powerful interest groups, including the dominant national and foreign classes (see Milliband 1969, for a discussion of the mechanisms used by the dominant class, e.g. in obtaining positions in state institutions, membership of key committees, lobbying, campaigning and controlling the media).

One draws the conclusion, then, that the logic of capital approach to state intervention does not differentiate sufficiently between what one might call the 'imperatives' and the 'actualities' of capitalist development as they work out in differing social contexts. There is also the tendency to reify state institutions and actions, and consequently to neglect the importance of such processes as inter-agency, inter-ministry or inter-group struggles in the determination and execution of policy programmes. In fact these actions and struggles largely shape and reproduce the set of collectivities concerned with the institutionalised organisation of political power.

A second analytical approach focuses on the process of institutional incorporation whereby farmers/peasants or other local groups become integrated into the wider technico-administrative environment consisting of various state and non-state organisations (Benvenuti 1975, Benvenuti and Mommaas 1985). Incorporation is depicted in terms of three interconnected processes: 'externalisation', which describes how production tasks are increasingly taken over by external bodies; 'scientification', which identifies the growing importance of modern technology; and increased 'centralisation' by the state. The latter process functions to coordinate the interrelations between the various institutions and assists in resolving conflicts that might arise between the different interest groups, such as farmers, peasants, extensionists, bankers and farmers' organisations or cooperatives.

The institutional incorporation model is essentially Weberian in its stress on the significance of modern forms of organisation, technology and rationality. However, unlike Weber, it is more concerned with the nature of the institutional environment surrounding the producers than with the characteristics of bureaucratic institutions *per se*. It aims to show how integration into an external network of institutions, which develops its own 'coordinated rationality', undermines independent forms of production and decision-making, highlighting, for example, the increasing role played by special agencies set up by the state to promote integrated rural development programmes and to establish quality-controlled production for export. Transnationals and agri-businesses also increasingly assume an important role in the organisation, processing and 'internationalisation' of agricultural production, as Sanderson (1986) documents for Mexico in the mid-1980s. This pattern of development marginalises the farmer even more, since private companies or state enterprises introduce contract farming and rental systems in order to have firmer control over farm planning and the execution of production tasks. Frequently, cooperatives and farmers' organisations perform similar functions. This institutional complex, it is argued, develops a high degree of consensus among participating organisations over the diagnosis and solution of problems faced by the farmer, and in terms of a commitment towards promoting technological development and commercial production. The process is accompanied by increased centralisation by the state and is therefore common to both capitalist and socialist economies.

Although the concept of the state remains underdeveloped, the implication seems to be that modernisation entails increasing forms of 'corporatism', whereby central government makes a pact with various socio-economic interest groups to bring them into processes of policy planning, sometimes even allowing them considerable space to determine their own affairs. The institutional system encompassing the farmer becomes part of 'the extended state' which integrates socio-economic producer groups into the governmental system through a system of organised representations; in just the same way as labour unions and employers' associations become 'governing institutions' (Winkler 1976). Benvenuti's line of argument therefore seems to attribute considerable coordinating power to the state bureaucracy: only the state it seems is in a position to determine the rules of the game and establish the working relations between the parties concerned. Although Benvenuti's scheme is interesting for the emphasis it places on organisational dimensions, it fails in fact to examine in any depth the nature of bureaucratic organisation and relationships and thus makes the unwarranted assumption that the institutions and development agencies involved in constructing the farmers' institutional and technological environment fit together coherently and present a concerted attack on the autonomy of the farm enterprise. There is no appreciation of the importance of inter-agency conflict or of the struggles that take place between farmers' organisations and government or private institutions. A related problem is the failure to locate the discussion within an analysis of existing power structures at either regional or national level. Unlike Marxist approaches that interpret state actions and policies as fundamentally derivative of either class relationships and struggles or of the logic of capitalist development, this perspective defines the state as essentially made up of a complex set of organisations backed by executive political power, which effectively controls territory and people. Hence it is the enduring executive and administrative apparatus that makes authoritative decisions that is 'the basis of state power as such' (Skocpol 1979: 29).

The two foregoing models of agrarian development and the state present alternative ways of conceptualising the increasing encapsulation of farming populations: the first focusing upon the expansion of commodity markets and capital penetration, and the second on the impact of various rural institutions set up to serve the farmer by organising production inputs and outputs. Although both approaches mention the important role played by state agencies and other organisations, neither approach attempts to analyse the types of interactions and negotiations that occur between the representatives of the various organisations and the farmers themselves. When they do refer to encounters between the state and local groups, no room is allowed for the ways in which farmers or peasants themselves attempt to structure the interfaces they are drawn into. Thus the image one receives is that of a passive rural population faced by overwhelming external forces. Moreover, since both these theoretical interpretations assign little importance to the role of local forms of organisation and knowledge in development, they tend to reinforce the image and efficacy of conventional top-down planning and intervention policies.

They likewise show no interest in or sensitivity towards the ways in which the representatives of encapsulating institutions interpret their mandates and define their work tasks vis-à-vis their client populations. Benvenuti tends to assume that a common rationality and normative definition develops among implementers and organisational representatives, be they technicians or administrators. Bernstein writes rather simply about state policy and actions and the ways in which they facilitate capitalist expansion; and de Janvry follows a more structuralist line, arguing that the state (and therefore those that represent it) will generally act in the interests of capital accumulation, even if it means opposing the short-term interests of a dominant class or class alliance. Hence the bureaucrat or policy-maker is allocated an equally passive role.

All three writers would of course claim that they are making simplifying assumptions in order to develop coherent models. Nevertheless, it is my contention that in order to explain the differences that may arise, both within a defined population and between contrasting situations, it becomes necessary to look more closely at the sets of relationships that evolve between intervening agencies and local groups, and to make this a point of theorisation. Only then will we be able to establish more precisely the degrees of capital subsumption or institutional control exercised by the state or other external institutions *vis-à-vis* different categories of actors, enterprises and households. It will also help to give flesh and blood to the somewhat disembodied structures assumed to be generic to capitalist modes of organisation and to institutional incorporation more generally.

Farmer responses and strategies from an actor perspective

Returning now more specifically to the issues of agrarian change, it is my view that an actor-oriented analysis can go some way to meeting these criticisms. Based as it is on the idea of differential responses to changing circumstances, it assumes that there always exist variations within agricultural systems such that we can expect different patterns of response and change. These different forms are in part created by the farmers themselves: farmers are not simply to be seen as passive recipients, but as actively strategising in terms of their own projects and interacting with outside institutions and personnel. The understanding of agrarian change is therefore complex and requires working from the very beginning with the concept of heterogeneity. Farmers and other local actors shape the outcomes of change. Change is not simply imposed on them and different social patterns develop within the same structural circumstances. For instance, Bolhuis and van der Ploeg (1985) have drawn the contrast between 'intensification' and 'extensification' strategies that coexist within the same farming population in both Peru and Italy. These differences show how farmers cope differently with processes of commoditisation and institutional incorporation. Another example is my own study (Long 1968) of small-scale commercial farmers in Zambia that exhibited differences in the mobilisation and organisation of labour which, I suggest, affects the long-term trajectory and viability of their farm enterprises. These differences among them were traced to a division within the community between Jehovah's Witnesses and non-Witness farmers. The former adhered to a stricter and more ascetic social code and were able to build upon a network of social ties based upon church membership and restructured kinship relations, and were thus able to develop more stable strategies for organising farm inputs and for accessing agricultural extension and credit facilities.

Another example is that of Bennett (1981) who analyses differences in farm management styles among Canadian farmers. Bennett depicts the folk categories which farmers themselves use to describe differences in farm enterprise development and from this he shows that the 'best' manager from the point of view of local culture is not the farmer who follows economically ideal, maximising, management styles but the one who adapts these standards to his own operations. The latter are influenced by the stage of development of the farm enterprise, and by the constraints of the larger system.

Bennett shows that the management criteria used by the farmers are multiple, including farmer qualities such as perseverance, sincerity, ability to juggle conflicting objectives, or possessing particular kinds of knowledge and skill, as well as estimates of production, income, and the conditions of the farm machinery, fields, fences, or stock. He is then able to show that some of these differences in styles and strategies are reflected quantitatively in different outcomes of production and farm development. He concludes that the extent that producers respond to the 'right' signals [i.e. in accord with the economist's market incentive models], in order to provide desired production magnitudes, is a rough measure of the extent to which they have assimilated the very frames of reference and types of discourse used by the economic analysts of the agricultural market. However, this response is never perfect, and often it varies widely.

(Bennett 1981: 234)

In fact farm strategies are affected by many factors besides simple market incentives. Strategies vary according to stage of farm development and in rhythm with the family life-cycle. For example, although the area is considered highly suitable for specialised wheat production, farmers attempting to establish their farms frequently mix different types of production on a small scale in order to realise the benefits of diversification, while others in the same position opt for the more risky strategy of land acquisition and speculation. According to local folk terminology, the former are designated 'scramblers' and the latter 'land grabbers'. Similarly, bursts of investment in farm machinery and infrastructural improvement seem to be a feature of the point at which the transfer of the farm to the new generation is imminent.

Bennett's study, then, indicates the need to look more closely than either commoditisation or institutional models do at the ways in which farmers manage, not only their on-farm resources, but the sets of external relationships, institutions and policy regimes that impinge upon them. Variations in the pattern of farm development could be further illustrated by reference to 'centralised' versus 'coordinated' patterns of organisation (Long and Richardson 1978: 191–200), 'multiple enterprise', combining agricultural and non-agricultural activities (see Chapter 7), long-term versus short-term production strategies (Ortiz 1973), and increasing heterogeneity in farming styles and strategies in relation to the mobilisation of labour (see den Ouden 1995 for West African villages in Benin, and Cheater 1984 for Zimbabwe).

The study of agrarian change requires that we theorise the question of structural variance and differential responses to change. Change should not be assumed to be linear, step-by-step, or to converge towards some predetermined form or end-point. In fact, it is highly heterogeneous and often divergent, and sometimes reverts to earlier modes of organisation or is cyclical, depending upon the particular historical and contextual circumstances.

Actor perspectives on state policy and intervention

Applying an actor-oriented approach to questions of state intervention entails an entirely different way of formulating the problem from that of the two previous theoretical perspectives. All forms of external intervention necessarily enter the lifeworlds of the individuals and groups affected and thus, as it were, come to form part of the resources and constraints of the social strategies they develop. In this way so-called external factors are internalised and may come to mean quite different things to different interest groups or actors. Externally originating factors are therefore mediated, incorporated and often substantially transformed by local organisational and cognitive structures. They are also shaped by the ongoing exchanges and negotiations that take place between farmers or other local actors and intervening agents. Close attention must therefore be given to understanding how particular interventions (e.g. a new agricultural technology or a land reform programme) become modified or even completely transformed through the interplay of local and extra-local structures and processes.

Grindle's (1985) book on agrarian development represents an interesting attempt to tackle questions of state intervention from a fairly explicit actor perspective. However, she concerns herself primarily with state elites and bureaucrats rather than with local producers or peasant groups. One theme she is interested in is the role and variable autonomy of state elites in the formulation and implementation of public policy. She shows that the executive and bureaucratic apparatus may pursue national development in opposition to the interests of particular powerful groups or class coalitions or alliances. She argues that giving more emphasis to the 'public managers' enables one to focus on the development belief systems and ideologies of policy-makers and planners, on the formulation and implementation of specific decisions, and on the skills and influence of particular political leaders.

This leads to an analysis of the extent to which technocrats and public managers form an 'independent state' and allocate resources in a way that expands their own power and wealth. Emphasising these dimensions, she claims, helps account for the expansion of the state apparatus itself. She does not assume the state to be either autonomous or monolithic. Rather, she is interested in the question of relative degrees of autonomy over time and across policy sectors and ministries. This does not ignore the fact that state elites are constrained by wider political and economic realities. State development policies may at any given time coincide with the interests of dominant groups, but it is difficult to infer the domination of the state simply from the content or impact of the policy itself. Thus Grindle argues against de Janvry by suggesting that policies to promote agrarian capitalism or land reform, for example, do not consistently result from the clear domination of the state by specific class interests (foreign and national). They are also influenced by the development ideologies adopted by state elites, by the leadership of particular individuals, and by the political accommodations and bargains struck between state elites and other groups (especially in the private sector).

In her earlier study of CONASUPO, the Mexican government staple food marketing and service agency, Grindle (1977) uses an exchange model to analyse the ways in which bureaucrats develop strategies for pursuing both public and personal goals. She shows that informal exchanges tend to evolve into longer-term commitments between individuals of different hierarchical levels and to pyramid into networks of exchange alliance, resembling the patron–client pattern often described by anthropologists and political scientists for Latin America (see, e.g., the account of the Brazilian political patronage system by Leeds 1964; for a more sophisticated treatment of Mexican political networks and processes, see Carlos and Anderson 1981 and de la Peña 1986). She documents the patterns of career mobility and the problems that arise because of the insecurity of job tenure produced by the Mexican *sexenio* (six-year period) electoral system. She looks at the methods used for obtaining employment and the ways in which office chiefs, departmental heads and others set about recruiting local subordinates and using their public positions to enhance the power of the government agency and its top administrators. She then examines how personal political alliances affect or are mobilised to bring about policy change.

Another aspect concerns policy implementation, primarily at provincial state level. In line with Martinez (1983), Grindle shows how central government policy is diluted or redefined at the state level as a result of the pressure from powerful local groups and because of the exigencies of responding to immediate situations of conflict and competition. Those states where CONASUPO offices were staffed by individuals directly dependent upon central office leadership for continued career mobility opportunities were those in which the most effective implementation of central policy took place.

Finally, she looks at the delivery of the rural development programme at local level. Public officials working at grassroots level became intermediaries between the low-income clients of the agency and the institution itself, in order to achieve a more rapid and adequate delivery of services. Again personal alliance structures were critical for the effectiveness of these brokers at local level. In the same way that 'successful' field officers formed part of the personal followings of their superiors, so did their peasant clients serve them. Grindle elucidates the dilemmas of the field officer but gives much less attention to analysing peasant responses and strategies. Indeed the bottom end of the process is largely assumed rather than fully described and analysed. There is, for example, no adequate analysis of power relations and organisational resources and social expectations at the level of the agricultural producers. In fact the study virtually stops at the point of direct interface with them.

A later study of the interaction between government field officers (tecnicos) and peasants in an area of rural Mexico (Arce 1986 and Chapter 9 of this volume) fills a number of these gaps. It shows, for example, how tecnicos are often caught between two systems of knowledge (that of the administrator/technician and that of peasant villager) and that it becomes impossible for them to bridge these worlds, not least because the administrative unit to which the tecnicos belong develops its own accommodations (through the influence of the boss and his network of support) to the situation. Arce's study provides a fuller picture of the way lower-level, front-line government officials operate, their worldviews and development perspectives, their networks of influence and the mechanisms for retaining control which include sending troublemakers (grillosos) to remote areas called 'punishment zones' (areas de castigo) when they do not conform to the working rules set by the administrative boss.

Complementary to this type of study of the lower echelon of government institutions[21] are studies of the everyday life and culture of state formation. These works focus upon exploring, as Nuijten (1998: 10) puts it, 'the practices of representation and interpretation which characterise the relation between people and the state bureaucracy and through which the idea of the state is constructed'. Nuijten illustrates this by analysing how local peasant leaders and villagers process and interpret official acts, projects, speeches and documents put out by government ministries, and in so doing develop a representation of the culture of state institutions in Mexico. This cultural construction reflects both an optimism and a pessimism vis-à-vis the state. On the one hand central government is depicted as a 'hope-generating machine', while on the other, it is characterised by 'opacity, distrust and conspiracy, which always surrounds conflicts, negotiations and dealings with the bureaucracy' (ibid.).[22]

Grindle has a distinctive view of the nature of state authority. She first argues against simple notions of an alliance of domestic and foreign capital dominating the state and prescribing the nature and direction of state policy. She points out that reformist policies occasionally impinge upon dominant class interests, sometimes even curbing the operations of foreign capital, and at other times they might incorporate non-elite groups. A second important point is that state policies are not all that consistent and often not easily identifiable. While a given policy may benefit a specific group, others may infringe directly on the same group's interests. There are also unintended consequences of policy and many policies are adopted but never in fact implemented. Hence linking policy content and policy-making by a state elite with control exercised by domestic or international capitalist class interests poses difficult conceptual problems. In many respects state policy is an outcome of competing and conflicting interests among bureaucratic entities of the state itself, although, as Grindle is quick to acknowledge, this process is also influenced by the impact of wider economic and political forces.

In this respect her work combines a 'pluralist' approach (see Dahl 1961) that emphasises how government agencies and officials act as one set of pressure groups among many others, with an interest in examining the interaction between the bureaucratic elite and other elite groups in terms of their influence over state resources and policy. Such an approach has the advantage of focusing attention upon the ongoing processes of political bargaining that shape the formulation and implementation of policy.

A more explicit actor-oriented perspective than Grindle's would bring out the significance of building into the analysis a better appreciation of human agency. This entails, as already suggested in the discussion of agrarian change and development, both the idea of how individuals or groups – not solely class bound – develop social strategies on the basis of existing knowledge, resources and capabilities, and the idea of emergent organisational forms that both enable and constrain their actions. Hence, the execution of political power and policy becomes an active and ongoing transformation process (often with unforeseen outcomes), involving both cooperation and conflict among the various parties involved. It takes place within specific historical and institutional contexts which are themselves continuously being shaped and transformed by the actions of constituent groups and individuals.

We must, then, go beyond the notion of intervening parties 'acting on behalf of' the state or some other 'superior authority' or 'class interest'. Individual personnel and development agencies differentially interpret and act upon the policies they are required to implement, and their behaviour is influenced not only by their administrative experiences but also by their experiences in other domains (e.g. in the family, the political arena, in interaction with fellow professionals, ex-students, etc.). In this way biographies and experiences drawn from different social contexts feed into and shape the actions of state officials as well as their 'clients' (Arce 1993). Agency is therefore as crucial for them as it is among so-called 'target' groups.

Applying this theoretical perspective to questions of the state and state policy leads one to a fuller appreciation of the complexities of intervention practices and processes. It emphasises the theoretical importance of considering differential responses to and outcomes of intervention, and thus exposes the limitations of highly generalised models. It criticises planning models that assume a simple linear or cyclical process of policy formulation, implementation and outcomes, and points to the need to examine how policy programmes are transformed during the process of implementation. It posits that state policy is not only determined by major structural factors, such as trends in capital accumulation on a global and national scale, international markets, and the assumed importance of class struggle, but also by the social interests, ideologies and administrative styles of the state's political and bureaucratic elite. In addition, it points to the value of undertaking comparative studies of the social impact and dynamics of particular forms of state intervention at regional and local levels, and of the more 'autonomous' processes taking place off-stage or in the interstices of formal politico-administrative frameworks. This approach affords a better understanding of the practices of intervention and their ongoing transformations.

3

BUILDING A CONCEPTUAL AND
INTERPRETATIVE FRAMEWORK[1]

As I have made clear in Chapter 1, it is not my aim to formulate a generic theory of society or social change based on universal principles that govern how social orders are constituted and transformed. Instead I seek to understand the processes by which particular social forms or arrangements emerge and are consolidated or reworked in the everyday lives of people. I am interested, that is, in analysing the heterogeneous social and discursive practices[2] enacted and interpreted by social actors in the making and remaking of their lives and those of others. An actor-oriented perspective offers valuable insights into these processes of social construction and reconstruction. It also enables one to conceptualise how small-scale interactional settings or locales interlock with wider frameworks, resource fields and networks of relations, thus facilitating a re-thinking of key concepts such as 'constraints', 'structure' and 'micro–macro' relations.

The intention of this chapter, then, is to clarify the conceptual and methodological foundations of an actor-oriented approach. It does this through elucidating certain critical concepts and analytical procedures. I hope in this way to convey to readers the usefulness of such a methodology for exploring issues of change and continuity, and not only to those concerned directly with questions of 'development'. But, first, let me synthesise the cornerstones of the approach.

Cornerstones of an actor-oriented approach

These can be summarised as follows:

1 Social life is heterogeneous. It comprises a wide diversity of social forms and cultural repertoires, even under seemingly homogeneous circumstances.
2 It is necessary to study how such differences are produced, reproduced, consolidated and transformed, and to identify the social processes involved, not merely the structural outcomes.
3 Such a perspective requires a theory of agency based upon the capacity of actors to process their and others' experiences and to act upon them. Agency implies both a certain knowledgeability, whereby experiences and desires are reflexively interpreted and internalised (consciously or otherwise), and the capability to command relevant skills, access to material and non-material resources and engage in particular organising practices.
4 Social action is never an individual ego-centred pursuit. It takes place within networks of relations (involving human and non-human components), is shaped by both routine

49

and explorative organising practices, and is bounded by certain social conventions, values and power relations.

5 But it would be misleading to assume that such social and institutional constraints can be reduced to general sociological categories and hierarchies based on class, gender, status, ethnicity, etc. Social action and interpretation are context-specific and contextually generated. Boundary markers are specific to particular domains, arenas and fields of social action and should not be prejudged analytically.

6 Meanings, values and interpretations are culturally constructed but they are differentially applied and reinterpreted in accordance with existing behavioural possibilities or changed circumstances, sometimes generating 'new' cultural 'standards'.

7 Related to these processes is the question of scale, by which I refer to the ways in which 'micro-scale' interactional settings and localised arenas are connected to wider 'macro-scale' phenomena and vice versa. Rather than seeing the 'local' as shaped by the 'global' or the 'global' as an aggregation of the 'local', an actor perspective aims to elucidate the precise sets of interlocking relationships, actor 'projects' and social practices that interpenetrate various social, symbolic and geographical spaces.

8 In order to examine these interrelations it is useful to work with the concept of 'social interface' which explores how discrepancies of social interest, cultural interpretation, knowledge and power are mediated and perpetuated or transformed at critical points of linkage or confrontation. These interfaces need to be identified ethnographically, not presumed on the basis of predetermined categories.

9 Thus the major challenge is to delineate the contours and contents of diverse social forms, explain their genesis and trace out their implications for strategic action and modes of consciousness. That is, we need to understand how these forms take shape under specific conditions and in relation to past configurations, with a view to examining their viability, self-generating capacities and wider ramifications.

Actors' perceptions, cultural representations and discourses

The approach begins with actor-defined issues or problematic situations, whether defined by policy-makers, researchers, intervening private or public agents or local actors, and whatever the spatial, cultural, institutional and power domains, arenas and fields implicated. Such issues or situations are, of course, often perceived, and their implications interpreted, very differently by the various parties/actors involved. Hence, from the outset one faces the dilemma of how to represent problematic situations when confronted with multiple voices and contested realities. A social arena or field is of course discursively constructed and delimited practically by the language use and strategic actions of the various actors. How far consensus is achieved over the definition of situations requires empirical evidence. One should not assume a shared vision. Actors must work towards such a common interpretation or accommodation of views and there are always possibilities for dissenting from it.

All actors operate – mostly implicitly rather than explicitly – with beliefs about agency; that is, they articulate notions about relevant acting units and the kinds of knowledgeability and capability they have *vis-à-vis* the world they live in. This raises the question of how people's perceptions of the actions and agency of others shape their own behaviour. For example, local farmers may have reified views about 'the state' or 'the market' as actors, which, irrespective of their dealings with individual government officials or market traders, can influence their expectations of the outcomes of particular interventions. The same applies to the attribution of motives to authoritative local actors, such as political bosses and village leaders. The central issue is how actors struggle to give meaning to their experiences through an array of representations, images, cognitive understandings and emotional responses. Though the repertoire of 'sense-making' filters and antennae will vary considerably, such processes are to a degree framed by 'shared' cultural perceptions, which are subject to reconstitution or transformation. Locally situated cultures are always put to the test as they encounter the less familiar or the strange. Analysis must therefore address itself to the intricacies and dynamics of relations between differing lifeworlds, and to processes of cultural construction. In this way one aims to understand the production of heterogeneous cultural phenomena and the outcomes of the interplay between different representational and discursive domains, thus mapping out what we might describe as a cartography of cultural difference, power and authority.

But, since social life is composed of 'multiple realities', which are, as it were, constructed and confirmed primarily through experience, this interest in culture must be grounded methodologically in the detailed study of everyday life, in which actors seek to grapple cognitively, emotionally and organisationally with the problematic situations they face. Hence social perceptions, cultural dispositions, values and classifications must be analysed in relation to interlocking experiences and social practices, not at the level of general cultural schema or value abstractions. For example, the production of commodities for global markets implies a whole range of value transformations, not only in regard to the commodity chain itself (i.e. the analysis of 'added value' at the points of product trans-formation, commercialisation and consumption) but also in terms of how such commoditisation impacts on the social values attributed to other goods, relationships, livelihood activities and forms of knowledge. In this way involvement in commodity chains may set off (but not determine) a number of significant cultural transformations.

In order to analyse these dimensions we must reject a homogeneous or unitary concept of 'culture' (often implied when labelling certain behaviour and sentiments as 'tradition' or 'modernity') and embrace theoretically the central issues of cultural repertoires, hetero-geneity and hybridity. The concept of cultural repertoires points to the ways in which various cultural elements (value notions, types and fragments of discourses, organisational ideas, symbols and ritualised procedures) are used and recombined in social practice, consciously or otherwise. Heterogeneity points to the generation and co-existence of multiple social forms within the same context or same scenario of problem-solving, which offer alternative solutions to similar problems, thus underlining that living cultures are necessarily multiple in the way in which they are enacted (cf. the concept of polymorphic structures in the biological sciences[3]). And hybridity refers to the mixed end products that arise out of the combining of different cultural ingredients and repertoires. Of course there are certain inherent difficulties in the use of the term 'hybridity' to characterise contem-porary patterns of change since, like *bricolage*, it suggests the sticking together or strategic combining of cultural fragments rather than the active self-transforming nature of socio-cultural practice. In a recent, deliberately provocative book, Alberto Arce and I have suggested instead the term 'social mutation' for such internally generated and transforming processes (Arce and Long 2000: 17–18, 159–83).

A useful way of exploring the significance of particular cultural repertoires and how they interact and interpenetrate situationally is discourse analysis. By 'discourse' is meant a set of meanings embodied in metaphors, representations, images, narratives and statements that advance a particular version of 'the truth' about objects, persons, events and the relations between them. Discourses produce texts – written and spoken – and even non-verbal 'texts' such as the meanings embedded in architectural styles or dress fashions.

Discourses frame our understanding of life experiences by providing representations of 'reality' (often taken-for-granted), and shape or constitute what we consider to be the significant or essential objects, persons and events of our world. It is of course possible to have different or conflicting versions of the same discourse, or incompatible discourses relating to the same phenomena. For example, discourse on development varies considerably depending upon the political or ideological position of the institution or actor concerned. Nevertheless, as Escobar (1995) shows in his account of the term, 'development' has its roots in the post-Enlightenment obsession for 'progress', 'social evolution' and the pursuit of 'modernity'. Following the Second World War, the idea of development as a form of social engineering, geared to designing and actively transforming so-called 'traditional' societies through the injection of capital, technology, and forms of bureaucratic organisation, was added to the vocabulary of progress. This marked the beginnings of the period of massive state and international intervention in the 'developing countries'. Development thus became synonymous with development aid and the aid industry. As Escobar points out:

> From this perspective, development can be best described as an apparatus that links forms of knowledge about the Third World with the deployment of forms of power and intervention, resulting in the mapping and production of Third World societies. Development constructs the contemporary Third World, silently, without our noticing it. By means of this discourse, individuals, governments and communities are seen as 'underdeveloped' and treated as such.
>
> Needless to say, the peoples of Asia, Africa and Latin America did not always see themselves in terms of 'development'. This unifying vision goes back only to the post-war period, when the apparatuses of Western knowledge production and intervention (such as the World Bank, the United Nations, and bilateral development agencies) were globalised and established their new political economy of truth...To examine development as discourse requires an analysis of why they came to see themselves as underdeveloped, how the achievement of 'development' came to be seen as a fundamental problem, and how it was made real through the deployment of a myriad of strategies and programmes.
>
> (Escobar 1995: 213)

Embodied in this history of development intervention were powerful narratives and images that represented the world in a particular way, offering a diagnosis of problems and their solutions. Although the general outcome was the widespread dissemination of 'Western' ideals and technology, resulting in post-colonial modes of exploitation, it also laid the seeds for the emergence of counter-discourses 'from below', which challenged established views and advanced 'alternatives to development'. This text from Escobar clearly hints at the existence of such countervailing discourses among subordinate groups, and thus points to the significance of the interplay of multiple discourses in any particular context.

It is important to unravel the discourses utilised in specific arenas of struggle, especially where actors vie with each other for control over resources in pursuit of their own livelihood concerns. Here it is essential to recognise that discourses are not separate from social practice – hence the use of the phrase 'discursive practice' in the writings of Foucault (1972, 1981). Another point is that discourses co-exist and intersect with each other but are seldom fully elaborated as abstract arguments. More often bits and pieces of discursive text are brought together in innovative ways or in strange combinations in specific situations to advance specific points of view or contention. Indeed the multiplicity and fragmentation of discourse is more evident than a coherence worldview or system of beliefs (I take up these issues again in Chapters 8 and 9, in relation to knowledge processes).

I argue therefore that the promotion of any particular discourse depends on the situational use of other discourses. For example, neoliberal policy, with its stress on 'letting the market do its job', is often accompanied by discourses that emphasise issues of 'equity', 'participation' and the problems of 'marginalisation'. Indeed structural adjustment measures have in turn given rise to 'social compensation' policies aimed at protecting the poorer and weaker social sectors. The World Bank and various national governments were obliged to introduce the latter to counterbalance the increased levels of poverty among certain groups that resulted from such measures.

This brings out the point that shifts in discourse are not simply prompted by the challenge of alternative discourses, but often by critical events that reveal the discrepancies between existing orthodoxy and actual social circumstances. Escobar gives the example of the new social movements that now act globally as a vanguard for change using elaborate counter-discourses against hegemonic institutions.

How does the concern for discourse relate to actor-oriented analysis?

A first observation is that discourses may 'belong' to institutions such as the state, the World Bank or the local community, but it is actors (individuals or institutional representatives) who use them, manipulate them and transform them. Or perhaps we should say that it is the encounter between, or confrontation of, actors (such as peasant farmers, extensionists, agricultural scientists, traders and international development experts) and their ideas and values that perpetuate or transform dominant discourses. Adopting an actor-oriented approach is, I believe, a good way to understand these processes, since it places emphasis on *situated* social practice and provides a methodology for analysing discursive practice and development interface situations (discussed later in this chapter and illustrated in Chapter 4).

According to Escobar, the power of dominant representations of development is grounded in the way in which '[T]hird World reality is inscribed with precision and persistence by the discourses and practices of economists, planners, nutritionists, demographers and the like, making it difficult for people to define their own interests in their own terms – in many cases actually disabling them from doing so' (Escobar 1995: 216). Nevertheless there is ample evidence that – with respect to specific issues such as sustainability, human rights and pollution – many groups (local and global) now contest expert views and in so doing they create new discursive and political space. Actor-oriented analysis is especially appropriate for disentangling the complexities of these struggles.

Lifeworlds, livelihoods and organising practices

Situated social action, then, implies issues of both social practice and meaning. One way of tackling this problem is to draw upon Schutz's phenomenological view that an understanding of social life should centre on the notion of lifeworlds. *Lifeworld* is the term used by Schutz (1962) to depict the 'lived-in' and 'taken-for-granted' world of the social actor. It entails practical action shaped by a background of intentionality and values, and is therefore essentially actor-defined (see Schutz and Luckmann 1973 for a fuller explication).[4] Everyday life is experienced as some kind of ordered reality, shared with others (i.e. it is inter-subjective). This 'order' appears both in the ways in which people manage their social relationships and in how they problematise their situations. Even a brief conversation with an individual quickly reveals some aspects of his/her effective or meaningful network of social relations and at the same time a glimpse of the personal constructs with which the person categorises, codes, processes and imputes meaning to his or her experiences (past and present).

Inter-individual action encompasses both face-to-face and more 'distanced' relationships. The types of social relationships range from interpersonal links based upon dyadic ties (such as patron–client relations and involvement in various types of transactions – buyer–seller, producer–money lender, and client–ritual specialist, farmer–extensionist, etc.) to social and exchange networks, to more formally constituted groups and organisations (such as farmers' organisations, cooperatives, village councils, churches, etc.) where legal prescriptions, bureaucratic legitimacy and authority and defined membership criteria assume greater significance.

Central to the idea of inter-individual networks is the concept of 'livelihood'. Livelihood best expresses the idea of individuals and groups striving to make a living, attempting to meet their various consumption and economic necessities, coping with uncertainties, responding to new opportunities, and choosing between different value positions.[5] Studying livelihoods also entails identifying the relevant social units and fields of activity: one should not prejudge the issue, as many studies do, by fixing upon the more conventional anchorage points for an analysis of economic life such as 'the household', 'the local community', 'the production sector' or 'the commodity chain'. Indeed in many situations confederations of households and wide-ranging interpersonal networks embracing a variety of activities and crosscutting rural and urban contexts, as well as national frontiers, constitute the social fabric upon which livelihoods and commodity flows are interwoven. In addition, we need to take account of the normative and cultural dimensions of livelihoods; that is, we need to explore the issue of lifestyles and the factors that shape them.

In this regard, Sandra Wallman (in her studies of households in Wandsworth, London) makes an interesting contribution. She writes:

> Livelihood is never just a matter of finding or making shelter, transacting money, getting food to put on the family table or to exchange on the market place. It is equally a matter of ownership and circulation of information, the management of skills and relationships, and the affirmation of personal significance [involving issues of self-esteem] and group identity. The tasks of meeting obligations, of security, identity and status, and organising time are as crucial to livelihood as bread and shelter.
>
> (Wallman 1982: 5)

Wallman does not, then, focus solely on material or economic resources but also on less materially tangible dimensions which include perceptions, skills, symbolic forms and organisational strategies. Hence she adds to the three conventional categories – material resources, labour and capital – three additional critical elements, namely 'time', 'informa-tion' and 'identity'. The emphasis on the latter brings us to an important, often neglected element, namely, the identity-constructing processes inherent in the pursuit of liveli-hoods. This is especially relevant since livelihood strategies entail the building of relationships with others whose lifeworlds and statuses may differ markedly.

Livelihood therefore implies more than making a living (i.e. economic strategies at household or inter-household levels). It encompasses ways and styles of life/living, and thus also value choice, status, and a sense of identity *vis-à-vis* other persons. It implies both a synchronic pattern of relationships existing among a delimited number of persons for solving livelihood problems or sustaining certain types of livelihoods, as well as diachronic processes. The latter covers actors' livelihood trajectories during their life courses, the types of choices they identify and take, and the switches they make between livelihood options.

Livelihoods are both individually and jointly constructed and represent patterns of inter-dependencies between the needs, interests and values of particular sets of individuals or groups. Analysis of the types of inter-dependencies that exist has led, for example, to the recognition of what Gavin Smith (1984) terms 'confederations of households'. The latter consist of networks of ties between a number of residentially discrete households based upon and sustained by a pattern of exchanges and complimentarities of livelihood. These confederations may manifest 'coordinated' or 'centralised' networks of social relations (or both), and are likely to change over time due to divergence of interests and activities. Some will decompose and regroup, and new memberships and configurations will emerge (see below, and Chapter 7 of this volume for a Peruvian illustration of this point).

Network configurations

Starting with actors' problematic livelihood situations leads to a consideration of the ways in which they develop social strategies to cope with them. These situated practices involve the management and coordination of sets of social relations that carry with them various normative expectations and commitments, as well as the deployment of technolo-gies, resources, discourses and texts in the form of documents that likewise embody wider sets of meanings and social relations.[6]

Social networks are composed of sets of direct and indirect relationships and exchanges. The nodes in a network may be individuals or organised groups – for example, family enterprises or business firms. Their morphological characteristics are related to content and structure; that is, the individual relationships can be depicted in terms of their normative contents and frequency of interaction which shape specific exchanges, while the overall configuration of connecting links can be characterised in terms of span, density and clusters. Networks evolve and transform themselves over time, and different types of networks are crucial for pursuing particular ends and engaging in certain forms of action. For example, information and resource mobilisation networks are more effective when they are open-ended and span a large universe of options, whereas networks required for carrying out specific collective actions (such as mounting strikes and demonstrations, and maintaining terraces or irrigation works) are usually close-knit with high levels of shared interests and agreed norms of practice. A further important point is that, though much of the literature on social networks depicts networks as made up of relatively balanced and dense sets of relations based on principles of reciprocity, in fact most social networks are composed of uneven and partial sets of relations that strain towards patterns of centralisation and hierarchy.

The analysis of formally constituted groups and legally recognised organisations raises issues concerning institutional frameworks, hierarchies of authority and mechanisms of control and regulation. All social scenarios involve a diverse range of institutional forms. While much organisational analysis focuses on formal rules and administrative procedures, highlighting for example the ways in which government, private company and development agency rules and regulations shape the workings of organisations, an actor perspective concentrates on delineating actors' everyday organising and symbolising practices and the interlocking of their 'projects'. This reflects a concern for emergent forms of interaction, practical strategies and types of discourse and cultural construction, rather than for administrative models and ideal-typical constructions.

In analysing different types of social arrangements within organisations, it becomes useful to identify certain ordering principles (see Law 1994). According to John Law, ordering principles are built upon strategic interests and representations of self and other. They should not be seen as fixed institutional frames or normative criteria, but rather as flexible or contestable interpretative modes that give some order to the flux of social life. Such ordering principles are often embodied in networks that criss-cross different domains and the fuzzy administrative-cum-managerial boundaries of formal organisations, and they may also provide a rationale for the ways in which competing firms or associations interrelate within a given organisational field.

The issue of 'collective actors'

At certain points in the above discussion I have hinted at the significance of 'collective' actors, resources and symbols. It is now time we clarified the term 'collective' with respect to three distinct connotations, each relevant to the understanding of social practice.

The first sense is that of a coalition of actors who, at least at a given moment, share some common definition of a situation, or similar goals, interests or values, and who agree, tacitly or explicitly, to pursue certain courses of social action. Such a social actor or entity (e.g., networks of actors or some sort of enterprise) can meaningfully be attributed with the power of agency, that is the capacity to process experience, make decisions and to act upon them. Collective actors of this type may be informally or formally constituted and spontaneously or strategically organised. Furthermore, as Adams (1975) has argued, such operating units fall, broadly speaking, under one of two contrasting forms: those that are characterised by a *coordinate* pattern of relations as against those that are *centralised*. In the former, there is no central figure of authority, since the individuals grant reciprocal rights to each other, while retaining the prerogative to withdraw from the particular exchange relationships at their will. Here networks are generally symmetrical in form but often have ambiguous and shifting boundaries. On the other hand, in the centralised case, there are imbalances in the exchanges, differences in access to strategic resources, and a degree of centralised control and decision-making exercised by an authoritative body or persons (and sometimes backed by 'higher' authorities) who claim to 'represent' the collectivity in its dealings with external actors.

The second sense of collective actor (or rather *collectif*) is that of an assemblage of human, social, material, technological and textual elements that make up what Latour (1994) and Callon and Law (1995) designate a heterogeneous 'actor-network'. This usage attempts to dissolve the 'commonsense' distinction between 'things' and 'people' by arguing that 'purposeful action and intentionality are not properties of objects, but neither are they properties of human actors. Rather, they are properties of institutions, of *collectifs*' (Verschoor 1997: 27). That is, they are emergent effects generated by the interaction of numerous human and non-human components, not by a group of individuals who decide to join together to undertake some common endeavour. Hence attempts to define collective social action without acknowledging the constitutive role played by materials, texts and technologies fall short analytically because they assume that collective social arrangements are simply the aggregated outcome of the effective agencies and interests of the participating individuals. The merit of this second interpretation of collective, then, is twofold: it stresses the heterogeneous make-up of organising practices founded upon enrolment strategies; and it warns against individualist/reductionist interpretations of collective forms.

The third meaning of collective actor recognises that social life is replete with images, representations and categorisations of things, people and institutions that are assumed or pictured as somehow constituting a unitary whole. For example, entities such as the state, the market and the community are often endowed with generalised (or collective) modes of agency, and in this sense, they shape actors' orientations and actions. But it would be wrong analytically to adopt particular actors' representations of these institutional entities as the primary grid for analysing their interactions with these collective 'others'. The principal reason for this is that representations and categorisations are embedded in the pragmatics and semiotics of everyday life from which they acquire their social significance, and they should not therefore be disconnected from social practice. Indeed, a major advantage of actor-oriented analysis is that it aims to problematise such conceptions and interpretations through an ethnographic study of how specific actors deal with the problematic situations they encounter.

All three kinds of collective actors – notwithstanding the probable epistemological objections and reservations of Latour – have a place in a social actor-oriented analysis.

Social fields, domains and arenas

So far the discussion of social action has tended to focus on self-organising processes, thus emphasising the ways in which social arrangements are socially constructed through the interlocking of actor strategies and interpretations. But now we need to shift the optic to consider the processes by which actions, desires and decisions are framed, enclosed or contained within wider fields of action. It becomes necessary, that is, to develop concepts for dealing with the constraining and enabling processes of social similarity and difference.

Rather than adopt an approach that identifies certain institutional orders which normatively frame different areas of social life, and that places too much emphasis on normative consistency and hegemonic relations between different social strata, I propose to deploy the concepts of social 'fields', 'domains', and 'arenas'. All three concepts address the issue of the bounding of social spaces and how they are constituted or transformed.

The notion of social field conjures up a picture of open spaces: an irregular landscape with ill-defined limits, composed of distributions of different elements – resources, information, technological capacities, fragments of discourse, institutional components, individuals, groups and physical structures – and where no single ordering principle frames the whole scene. Whatever configurations of elements and relationships make up the field, these are essentially the product of human and non-human interventions, both local and global, as well as the result of both cooperative and competitive processes. Depending on the analytical focus, the composition of a social field can be depicted in terms of the distributional patterns of natural resources, types of production and economic enterprise, demography, politico-administrative institutions, transport and communication flows, marketplaces, infrastructural features, and cultural and ethnic groupings, etc., and further specified by reference to the prevailing sets of interests and activities characteristic of the field (e.g. political, educational, environmental or agricultural concerns). One might also describe a social field in terms of the relative coherence or fragmentation of its component parts.

The idea of the social field appeared first in the early writings of the Manchester School (see Barnes 1954, and Epstein 1958) where emphasis was placed on the complex sets of overlapping social relationships between distinct areas of social life; and later, in my own Zambian study (Long 1968), where I argue that

> the idea of a *field* of activity is much wider than what we normally mean by an economic or political *structure* for it refers not only to those institutional arrangements specifically designed to attain certain economic or political ends, but also takes account of other kinds of relationships and values that may be utilised for the same purpose.
>
> (Long 1968: 9)

In other words, the concept addresses the heterogeneous character of social action resulting from the intersection of different social domains.

Bourdieu's (1977, and Bourdieu and Wacquant 1992: 94–115) impressive attempt to establish a theory of social practice also builds upon the notion of social field, but his formulation adopts a more structural view than the one I wish to advance. Throughout his discussion he draws upon the analogy of the 'game' (like a sporting activity that takes place in a stadium with admission fees, etc.: see Bourdieu and Wacquant 1992: 98–100, 107–8) with its logic, rules and regularities, and he emphasises the importance of social positions within the field and the need for certain properties of 'capital' (economic, social, cultural, symbolic) in order to compete successfully for the stakes of the field. Hence, for Bourdieu, the notion of field is a central organising concept for the analysis of power and status, and for establishing the distribution of material and symbolic forms of capital.

In contrast, I argue for the elaboration of two additional concepts – social domain and arena. While social field sets the scenario in terms of the availability and distribution of specific resources, technologies, institutions, discourses, values and potential social allies or enemies, it is the notions of domain and arena that permit the analysis of the processes of ordering, regulating and contesting social values, relations, resource utilisation, authority and power. The composition and decomposition of particular social fields depends on the strategic use of, and interconnections between, different social domains. It also requires a careful analysis of the dynamics of social arenas in which struggles over resources and meanings are explicitly fought out.

Here I use 'domains'[7] to identify areas of social life that are organised by reference to a central core or cluster of values which, even if they are not perceived in exactly the same way by all those involved, are nevertheless recognised as a locus of certain rules, norms and values implying a degree of social commitment (cf. Villarreal 1994: 58–65). Examples include the domains of family, market, state, community, production and consumption, although, depending upon the situation, particular domains will differ in their prominence, pervasiveness or social significance. In this way domains are central to understanding how social ordering works, and to analysing how social and symbolic boundaries are created and defended. The values and interests associated with particular domains become especially visible and defined at points where domains are seen to impinge on each other or come into conflict. Hence domains, together with the notion of arena – and how they are delimited – give us an analytical handle on the kinds of constraints and enabling elements that shape actors' choices and room for manoeuvre. Domains should *not* be conceptualised *a priori* as cultural givens but as produced and transformed through the shared experiences and struggles which take place between actors of various sorts. Like the notion of 'symbolic boundaries' enunciated by Cohen (1987: 16), domains represent for people a set of shared values that 'absolves them from the need to explain themselves to each other – [but] leaves them free to attach their own meanings to them'.

'Arenas' are social locations or situations in which contests over issues, resources, values, and representations take place (cf. Olivier de Sardan 1995: 178–9). That is, they are social and spatial locations where actors confront each other, mobilise social relations and deploy discursive and other cultural means for the attainment of specific ends, including that of perhaps simply remaining in the game. In the process, actors may draw on particular domains to support their interests, aims and dispositions. Arenas therefore are either spaces in which contestation associated with different practices and values of different domains takes place or they are spaces within a single domain where attempts are made to resolve discrepancies in value interpretations and incompatibilities between actor interests.

The concept of arena is especially important for identifying the actors and mapping out the issues, resources and discourses entailed in particular situations of disagreement or dispute. While the idea of arena has an affinity to that of 'forum', the latter carries with it the implication that the rules for debate are, in a sense, already agreed upon, whereas contestation in an arena usually denotes discontinuities of values, norms and practices. Arena is an especially useful notion when analysing development projects and programmes, since intervention processes consist of a complex set of interlocking arenas of struggle, each characterised by specific constraints and possibilities of manoeuvre (see Elwert and Bierschenk 1988).

While in general parlance the idea of an arena conjures up the picture of a fight or struggle taking place in some clearly demarcated local setting, we should not assume that arenas primarily involve face-to-face confrontations and only local interests, values and contests. On the contrary, external and geographically distant actors, contexts and institutional frames shape the social processes, strategies and actions that take place in these localised settings. Furthermore, local situations, struggles or networks are, as it were, often stretched out or projected spatially as well as temporally to connect up with other distant social worlds. Very few social arenas in fact are self-contained and separate from other arenas and areas of social life. The impact of modern communication and information technologies has been crucial here, since these allow for much more spontaneous, technology-mediated interactions of global proportions, thereby underlining the importance of developing analyses of interlocking arenas that go beyond earlier territorialised conceptions of social space based on dichotomies such as 'rural–urban', 'centre–periphery', and 'national–international orders'.

From social drama to critical event analysis

In the 1950s Victor Turner introduced the concept of 'social drama' to depict social situations where the disruption of an existing set of social relations or breach of norms occasions efforts to repair the damage and restore social order or institute some new, negotiated social arrangements. As Turner graphically puts it, focusing upon social dramas attempts to make transparent 'the crucial principles of social structure in their operation, and their relative dominance at successive points in time' (Turner 1957: 93). This, he argues, enables one to analyse the realignments in power relations consequent upon the struggles that take place between specific individuals and groups (p. 131). He documents the ongoing relationships and situational interests of those who are directly party to the conflict and its mode of resolution. In this way, his study is limited to localised issues pertaining to contests over local leadership and does not much explore the broader political and cultural implications.

Social dramas that are more complex in scale and ramification can be looked at using a similar approach, though we will need to go beyond the scope of situational analysis.[8] This is evident, for example, when we attempt to analyse social dramas such as the 1994 Zapatista uprising in Chiapas, southern Mexico, and its aftermath, where information technology such as e-mail and Skylink were used to propagate Zapatista views to win wider national and international support and influence the negotiations taking place between Zapatista leaders and government spokesmen. This drama, which is only now close to being resolved in January 2001, also generated a series of dramas involving struggles in other social sectors of the Mexican population for better political representation, or aimed at countering the detrimental effects of neoliberal policies.[9] The use of the internet links together many spatially dispersed actors who may never meet face-to-face but who constitute 'virtual communities' that clearly exert influence over their members and play an increasingly crucial role in the definition, representation and symbolisation of complex dramas or critical events. International news correspondents who descended upon Chiapas, and their network of colleagues via portable satellite connections throughout the world, played an important role in profiling the conflict, and developed ploys to keep the story on the front pages. One intriguing case of this was the craze for Zapatista paraphernalia that erupted: journalists wrote about the Zapatista dolls that had appeared, and the pens, T-shirts and other souvenirs. And it is said (Oppenheimer 1996: 29–30) that it was the correspondent for the Spanish daily La Vanguardia who had suggested to an Indian street hawker selling traditionally dressed dolls that she should produce dolls dressed as Zapatistas. Two days later the hawker turned up with the new merchandise, complete with black ski masks like the Zapatistas themselves! Soon afterwards the wearing of the black mask took on a wider comico-political significance throughout Mexico as a general, unspoken symbol of protest against government.

Another instructive critical event concerns the explosion at the Union Carbide chemical plant in Bhopal, India, in 1984, which affected many thousands of people who had nothing to do directly with the industry or the Union Carbide company, and who received none of the industry's benefits. The explosion and what followed over the short and longer term enrolled a whole range of actors – spanning local, national and international arenas – around a number of moral, humanitarian, legal and political issues. Thus heated debates and protracted negotiations ensued over the rights of the local labour force, the levels of environmental impact, quality control standards, the freedom of transnationals to flout national and international agreements, the allocation of blame and accountability, the rights and levels of compensation for affected workers, town and village residents, and so on. The political and moral ramifications were enormous since the Indian State, regional government, international bodies, Union Carbide, and the legal profession itself were all, as it were, put 'on trial'.

In a perceptive analysis of the Bhopal disaster, Veena Das (1995) highlights the dynamic interplay of bureaucratic, scientific and judicial discourses and images around the symbolisation of pain, victimisation, healing and compensation. She argues that this type of social drama can be considered as a 'critical event', because people were seriously confronted with the limitations of existing institutions and practices available for dealing with the many problems that Bhopal raised. Such events often result from institutional breakdowns, administrative impotence and/or a lack of political will to manage problematic or critical situations, be they famine, ecological degradation, the risks of modern technology, or ethnic conflicts that result in the breakdown of the state and civil order.

Interlocking projects and the concept of 'structure'

These various social and organisational processes function as a nexus of micro and macro relations and representations. They often involve the development of interlocking actor 'projects', lifeworlds and circumstances that give rise to situations where self-reflexive strategies mesh to produce a measure of accommodation between the actors concerned. Interlocking projects are therefore crucial for understanding the articulation and management of actor interests and lifeworlds, as well as for the resolution of conflicts. They constitute, that is, a 'new' or 're-established' field of enablement, constraints and mutual sanctioning within which new embodiments of agency and social action take shape (for further discussion of the concept of interlocking projects and practices, see N. Long and van der Ploeg 1994 and A. Long and van der Ploeg 1995).

Actors' projects are realised within specific arenas and fields of action. Each project is articulated with other actors' projects, interests and perspectives. This articulation might be regarded as strategic – conscious or otherwise – in that the actors involved will attempt to anticipate the reactions and possible moves of the other actors and organisations. The setting up of coalitions and/or distantiation of particular actors *vis-à-vis* others is an intrinsic part of such action. For example, the various arenas in which farming interests are pursued contain what Benvenuti (1991) characterises as 'quasi-structures', such as, for example, a centrally regulated chain of commodity relations or particular networks of state agencies commanding authoritative and allocative power. The point, however, is that these 'structures', as they are often called, are not disembodied entities, nor do they have a unilinear and uniform structuring effect on social practice or actors' choices. They link together, around a common rationale or set of interests, a number of participating social actors.

In social science there is a strong tendency to equate the notion of structure with that of the *explanans*, so that structures are conceptualised as specific sets of driving forces that, it is postulated, explain certain phenomena. Such a procedure is justified by positing some notion of a generic mode of things or set of 'normal conditions' that are ideally assumed to exist somewhere. For reasons clearly spelt out in Chapter 1, this supposition is basically inadequate, even more so in times of turmoil and change. What is required is a thorough deconstruction of the notion of structure. This entails building upon the notions of agency (i.e., actors and their projects) and social heterogeneity, and bidding farewell to structure understood as *explanans*. This is especially urgent where 'structure' is visualised as a set of external forces or conditions that delineate and/or regulate specific modes of action, thought to be required or necessary, while other modes are defined as impossible rather than improbable (it is here that determinism is rooted). The same applies to historical approaches that search for simple causal/structural explanations situated in the past. History never relates in a unilinear or uniform way to the present and future. As Kosik (1976) has made clear, their relation is essentially dialectical, involving both elements of the possible and the real. That is, history always contains more than one possibility, where the present is the realisation of only one of these; and the same holds for the interrelations between the present and the future. What is decisive for Kosik is *praxis*, or in my terms the process by which actors' projects and practices interlock and interact to produce emergent forms or properties. In the process certain possibilities are excluded and others are made possible or realised.

One argument against actor-oriented methodology is that it dwells on individual agency, neglecting the significance of the way actions are embedded in wider social relations and structural settings. By now it should be clear that this is not my position. What I object to is the notion of structure as *explanans*, which results in a reification of central normative or statistical tendencies. As soon as heterogeneity is introduced into the analysis then this kind of structuralism no longer provides a sufficient explanation. On the other hand, it is important to emphasise that this critique does not wish to dispense with the idea of structure altogether, since the question of how specific social relations are constructed, reproduced and transformed remains central to the analysis. In more substantive terms, structure can be characterised as an extremely fluid set of emergent properties that, on the one hand, are a product of the interlocking and/or the distantiation of various actors' projects, while on the other, they constitute an important set of reference points and constraining/enabling possiblities that feed into the further elaboration, negotiation and confrontation of actors' projects.

Understanding structure in this way – as a product of the ongoing interplay and mutual transformation of actors' 'projects' – is not to imply that structure should be conceptualised simply as the aggregation of micro-episodes, situations or projects. It would clearly be nonsensical to argue, for example, that the operation of commodity markets or capitalist economic institutions generally could be meaningfully described or accounted for *solely* by observing the behaviour of individual buyers and sellers, or capitalists and international financiers taken individually. Marx rightly emphasises the existence of certain structural conditions that make possible the processes of capitalist production and exchange. However, it would be equally nonsensical to claim that the operation of such commodity markets and institutions is based on a logic or set of governing principles that are independent of the dispositions and agency of the actors involved. In fact, it is only through the interlocking of specific actors' projects (e.g., their simultaneous agreements to buy and sell specific goods, capital stocks or services) that commodity markets as such can emerge and be reproduced. Hence, what might at first sight appear to be relatively stable structural features linked to the characteristics of particular commodities and their market potential can be better understood as highly specific, self-transforming configurations of actor projects and practice.

Actors' projects and practices are not simply embedded in structural settings defined by commodity circuits. Instead, it is through the ways in which they interlock that they create, reproduce and transform particular 'structures'. Market relations are at least mediated, if not actively sought after and constructed by the actors themselves. Some farmers actively distance their labour from the market, others engage in what Ranger (1985) has termed 'self-commoditisation' – that is, the so-called causal links with the market are actively constructed in such a way as to allow people to fit these into their own preferred lifestyles or livelihood concerns. Thus the explanation of specific social practices and cultural styles inevitably returns us to consider further how these practices are themselves linked to or distantiated from those of other actors. Social practice, then, does not have a clearly distinguishable *explanandum*, nor does it in itself constitute a simple *explanans*. In farming at least, the two fuse: a style of farming is, in the end, its own *explanans*. It is a socially constructed *modus operandi* and, simultaneously, the *opus operatum*. And the same holds for technological and institutional designs. Introduced technology can serve as a blueprint for an ongoing reorganisation of farming so that the latter corresponds with the assumptions and requirements built into the technological design. But it can equally be deconstructed in order to be combined selectively with other, more local elements, so as to fit better with existing styles of farming (instead of reorganising farming so as to fit better with the new technology).

Here one should re-emphasise that the foregoing discussion should not be taken to imply that markets, state institutions, technology, ecology and other 'externalities' are irrelevant to social practice and heterogeneity. The point is simply that such factors should not be seen as determinants that entail self-evident limits beyond which action is judged to be inconceivable, but rather as boundary markers that become targets for negotiation, reconsideration, sabotage and/or change, i.e. as barriers to be removed or transformed (Bourdieu 1984: 480). A major complication is that farm enterprise development is increasingly the object of interventions aimed at representing these external parameters as indeed self-evident. That is, they are objectified and represented as guiding, if not coercive, structures that form part of the game and that are linked (directly or indirectly) to specific interests and actions. In this context, these so-called causal links are themselves actively constructed by the actors themselves to comprise interlocking configurations.

Small-scale interactional settings and their significance for understanding macro phenomena

Let me now consider more explicitly the issue of how to integrate theoretically the analysis of small-scale interactional settings with that of larger institutional or social structures. Like the issue of structure and causality reviewed above, this remains a thorny problem in research, and a number of solutions have been proposed (for an excellent overview of micro and macro theory and methodology, see Knorr-Cetina and Cicourel 1981). A radical solution is proposed by Randall Collins (1981), who argues for the reconstitution of macro sociology on the basis of its necessary micro foundations. According to him, what is needed is a systematic programme of 'micro translation' of the principal concepts of macro sociology. This entails the 'unpacking' of macro sociological metaphors:

for instance, the notion of 'centralisation of authority' can be reduced to (a) a series of statements about micro situations in which certain actors exert authority over others, and (b) a description of 'the links in the chain of command', i.e. an account of who passes orders to whom. In Collins's view, the only genuine macro variables in any such unpacking of concepts are those concerning time, number and space. 'All social reality, then, is micro experience; but there are temporal, numerical, and spatial aggregations of these experiences which constitute a macro-level of analysis' (Collins 1981: 99).

According to this argument, it follows that sociology should focus its attention on the systematic analysis of micro situations and thus avoid working with macro concepts that are not properly grounded in everyday social life. Hence, for example, concepts of class and class relations only become meaningful once they are shown to be characteristic of particular lifeworlds made up of certain shared experiences involving struggles over differential livelihood chances (often, but not exclusively, centring upon the workplace and access to the basic means of production). Foucault (in Gordon 1980: 102) takes a similar point of view when he outlines his approach to the study of power relations. He argues that, although power may seem remote and tied up with 'juridical sovereignty and State institutions' and thus beyond the arena of everyday social interaction, it actually manifests and reproduces or transforms itself in the workplaces, families and other organisational settings of everyday life (see Foucault 1981: 94).

The importance of 'emergent structures'

These arguments suggest that, in order to avoid reification of macro concepts, we should build our understanding of society 'from below'; that is, by documenting everyday micro situations and situated social practice. However this cannot succeed unless we challenge Collins's reasoning in one important respect. Macro structures should not simply be conceptualised as aggregations of micro episodes or situations, since many of them come into existence as the result of the unintended consequences of social action. Thus, as Giddens has insisted throughout his writings, the properties of social institutions[10] and of certain global structures (such as Wallerstein's notion of 'the world system') are emergent forms that are neither explicable (nor fully describable) in terms of micro events. Whilst it is true that institutional forms do not strictly speaking have a 'life of their own' – somehow beyond the reach of human agency – and are deeply engrained in everyday social practice, they do nevertheless possess characteristics that cannot be fully comprehended by merely dissecting the minutiae of social encounters.

It would, for example, be nonsensical to argue that the operation of commodity markets and capitalist economic institutions can be meaningfully described or accounted for *solely* by observing the behaviour of individual capitalists, international financiers, stockbrokers, etc., or by studying in depth only the social encounters and struggles that take place between the owners or managers of capital and workers. Marx was right to emphasise the existence of certain structural conditions (such as those facilitating the formation of a 'free' labour force or the realisation of exchange-value and profit) that make possible the processes of capitalist production and exchange. He also argued that the various actors involved in capitalist production have a limited and to a degree distorted comprehension of the nature of the system as a whole.[11]

Macro structures are in part the result of the unintended consequences of numerous social acts and interactions which, as Giddens (1984: 8–14) explains, become the enabling and constraining conditions of social action itself. A run on a bank resulting from heavy withdrawal by creditors (set off by rumours that the bank is unable to meet its financial obligations) generates further withdrawals due to increasing lack of public confidence, perhaps in the end leading to its eventual collapse. The actions taken by the individual customers and by the bank officials would, of course, have contributed to this deteriorating situation, but they were hardly likely to have intended the outcome. A pertinent agrarian example is a land settlement programme aimed at promoting the economic independence of peasant family farmers which, after a number of years, resulted in these farmers becoming indebted to moneylenders to the extent that they could no longer make their own decisions as to which crops they would grow (Siriwardena 1989). In this case, neither the government planners nor the peasants themselves intended or really foresaw this eventuality. It resulted principally from the types of relationships that gradually evolved between the key actors involved (peasants, moneylenders, traders and government officials).

These examples are relatively simple for us to understand and to trace out the chain of effects. Most sociological cases are in fact much more complex and it is often difficult to disentangle the numerous consequences of particular social actions as well as their feedback effects. Nevertheless, carefully focused research can document the ways in which particular social interactions and decisions have a ripple effect on more distant social arenas, or over time create emergent sets of relations that form larger-scale systems or fields of action. It is therefore important that we have ways of characterising and analysing these more 'global systems'. Collins's insistence, then, on the study of micro situations and micro translation should not be interpreted to mean that we can simply do away with concepts for dealing with more macro phenomena. We should also not conceptualise the macro level as solely made up of the aggregation of micro situations or micro processes, since we must give attention too to emergent properties which manifest themselves in qualitatively distinctive modes of organisation.[12]

I cannot here expand much upon this important issue of emergent structures and their feedback effects on choice and social behaviour. Suffice it to point out that emergent forms range from relatively small-scale interpersonal networks, to institutional arrangements for organising people and territory (e.g., as shown by the pattern of activities and interrelations of state agencies in particular local settings), to large-scale political and economic systems. These different scales of emergent phenomena are of course often intricately interrelated, as the example from the central highlands of Peru in Chapter 1 illustrates.

The interface problematic for research and policy issues

It is at this point that the notion of social interface becomes relevant as a way of exploring and understanding issues of social heterogeneity, cultural diversity and the conflicts inherent in processes involving external interventions. Interfaces typically occur at points where different, and often conflicting, lifeworlds or social fields intersect, or more concretely, in social situations or arenas in which interactions become oriented around problems of bridging, accommodating, segregating or contesting social, evaluative and cognitive standpoints. Social interface analysis aims to elucidate the types and sources of social discontinuity and linkage present in such situations and to identify the organisational and cultural means of reproducing or transforming them. It can also help to develop a more adequate analysis of policy transformation processes since it enables us to understand more fully the differential responses by local groups (including both 'target' and 'non-target' populations) to planned interventions. It may likewise assist in forging a theoretical middle ground between so-called micro and macro theories of social change by showing how the interactions between 'intervening' parties and 'local' actors shape the outcomes of particular intervention policies, often with repercussions on the patterns of change at regional, national and even international levels.

Although the word 'interface' tends to convey the image of some kind of two-sided articulation or face-to-face confrontation, social interface situations are more complex and multiple in nature, containing within them many different interests, relationships and modes of rationality and power. While the analysis focuses on points of confrontation and social difference, it must situate these within broader institutional and knowledge/power domains. In addition, it requires a methodology that counterpoises the voices, experiences and practices of all the relevant social actors involved, including the experiential 'learning curves' of policy practitioners and researchers.

Precursors to the concept of interface

An early attempt to analyse the problems associated with the intersection of different normative and politico-administrative orders is that by Gluckman, Mitchell and Barnes (1949) who describe what they call 'the intercalary position' of the African village headman created by the establishment of British colonial rule. They argue that the role of the headman was potentially fraught with conflict and ambivalence since he was pulled in two opposite directions at once: loyalty to his kinsmen and village, and loyalty to the chief and the colonial administration.

Although at the time this offered a useful insight into some of the inherent problems of the British colonial policy of 'indirect rule', Gluckman et al.'s formulation differs from my own in that it leans heavily upon a role model that conveys a somewhat static and dichotomised picture, implying that despite conflict the structural relations between the two social orders remained more or less well equilibrated and unchanged. There is also no attention given to documenting the precise strategies adopted by village headmen for steering a middle course between these conflicting demands, nor any account of how colonial officers accommodated themselves to the situation. These shortcomings are consistent with Gluckman's commitment to an institutional and equilibrium model of social change (Gluckman 1958, 1968; Long 1968: 6–9).

A completely different and much more recent attempt to deal theoretically with issues of social discontinuity in local settings is Cohen's (1985) *The Symbolic Construction of Community*. Cohen links the problem to the need for a new perspective on 'community', which he applies to both local residential and ethnic groups. The approach, he suggests, focuses upon the exploration of how such groups construct boundaries around themselves in order to mark themselves off from others. This process simultaneously involves shared symbolic elements that broadly define community boundaries (i.e., marking out the distinctions between 'us' and 'them'), thus creating a 'sense of belongingness', as well as forms of strategic interaction between particular individuals (sometimes called 'cultural brokers') who, as it were, establish the parameters and conceptions of 'self' and 'other' relevant to particular interactional contexts and confrontations with 'outsiders'.

Cohen develops his standpoint through critically reviewing existing approaches to the study of 'community' and through presenting a series of ethnographic vignettes selected to make the case for a symbolic anthropology of community. By concentrating upon the processes by which 'people become aware of their culture when they stand at its boundaries', Cohen's (1985: 69) discussion comes close to some of the conceptual and theoretical issues raised under the rubric 'interface'. A major difference lies, however, in its heavy emphasis on cultural constructions and symbolic defence of 'community', at the expense of considering in more depth the strategic deployment of organisational and political resources. A further limitation is that the study concentrates upon the 'communities' of local groups, giving scant attention to the strategies and 'symbolic communities' of the intervening parties, such as government officials, missionaries or traders.[13]

These shortcomings are in fact largely overcome in an earlier symbolic interactionist study by Handelman (1978), who argues that 'insufficient attention has been given to the clash between the ways in which supra-local institutions conceive of administrative territories and the ways in which territorially based populations conceive of themselves as communities'. He then goes on to identify 'the official/client interface as the crucial point of articulation wherein such discrepancies of connection and communication are most likely to be evident, and hence as a likely *node through which to expose the coercion and fragility of structures of power*' (Handelman 1978: 5–6).

This methodological point, of course, coincides with the case I wish to make for interface analysis. Handelman develops his theoretical point of view through detailed studies of social security in Israel (1976) and child care in Newfoundland (1978). He demonstrates that government officials dealing directly with the public do not simply allocate benefits to individuals in a mechanical, 'according to the book', fashion. Instead they are active contributors to the production of decisions, using their own discretion and evolving their own *modus operandi*. Underlying and providing a rationale for the administrative and allocative practices they adopt, are certain worldviews that have crystallised out of the many interactions and decision-making processes in which they have been involved previously, with both clients and colleagues (see Rees 1978 for a similar account of differential worldviews among social workers in Britain). He also shows how 'client cases' are constructed by officials on the basis of ways of typifying persons and behaviours that are consistent with the stock of knowledge and ideology of the lifeworld of the organisation in which they work. Hence official/client interfaces are simultaneously shaped by organisational 'imperatives' and by the particular organisational experiences of the official in question. As Arce (1989: 48–9) points out, one important lacuna in Handelman's approach (see also Handelman 1976) is his lack of attention to the ways in which an official's 'worldview' and strategies are affected by past and present experiences *outside* the bureaucratic context.

A different approach to this question of the allocation of public services or benefits (or even penalties) is illustrated by the work of the late Bernard Schaffer and his colleagues at Sussex University's Institute of Development Studies (Schaffer and Lamb 1976), on the subject of 'access theory'. Their main aim was to develop an analytical framework for the analysis of bureaucratic transactions with clients involving the administrative allocation of goods and services in non-market-distributed systems, where factors other than income determine allocation. Their empirical work is concentrated upon documenting the factors affecting access to particular public goods and services, such as housing, social security and agricultural credit, by different categories of client.

Their approach to the problem can be illustrated with an agricultural example. A given cultivator – placed at the base of the access pyramid – may be eager and defined as eligible for one or more services such as agricultural extension, credit and technical inputs, but he may still not get what he wants or is legally entitled to. The reason for this is that there operate a number of informal, spoken or unspoken, rules governing his exclusion. Such a cultivator usually finds himself at some point standing in a queue before a counter across which the service he seeks is expected to be delivered. Yet the counter is more than a physical barrier or location where official transactions take place. It functions as a medium for reconciling the interests of applicants and allocators and for defining precisely who will and will not receive access to the goods or services 'on offer'. Behind the counter is an administrator who is, at one and the same time, maintaining the service, serving his own private or group interests, and waiting in a queue himself for the service to be approved by his administrative superior. He is therefore part of an administrative hierarchy or bureaucracy. The passing down of goods and services depends not only on simple allocative efficiency or upon the individual behavioural characteristics of the farmers or allocators but also on regulations governing the eligibility of recipients, queue discipline, and the characteristics of superior and inferior administrative levels in the allocative hierarchy. It will also depend upon the existence of alternative channels for the service (what Schaffer calls *exit*) and on the susceptibility of the different systems of access to client manipulation (what is called *voice*).

This image provides Schaffer and colleagues with the basis for developing a descriptive model for depicting the various factors and processes affecting allocative decisions and for defining the type and level of access accorded to different clientele. The approach has been applied to a number of third world situations. For example, Barbara Harris (1978) uses access language to analyse the organisation of multipurpose cooperatives in Sri Lanka. She concludes that access concepts are indeed a fruitful way of identifying the factors that account for variations in the organisation and provision of services between cooperative unions, between them and their branches, between branches, and within the cooperative hierarchy. She shows in fact how the organisational structure encourages the use of both exit and voice strategies, which militate against the achievement of equity among members or between branches, and how the outside entrepreneurial interests of managers affect this also.

A major difficulty with this type of analysis, however, is that one cannot always easily identify counters and queues. The analogy of obtaining goods and services across the counter goes too far and can operate only when there exist clearly defined tangible items for allocation. In contrast, many interface situations involve a series of encounters between implementers and clients that cannot be bundled up into discrete packages of goods and services. Extension officers may regularly visit farmers in their areas but it would be difficult to regard each visit as entailing some clearly defined benefit for the farmer. The interaction between extensionist and farmer is composed of a number of different, and often diffuse, elements, of which only some could be seen as entailing questions of access. Furthermore, client interfaces are not one-off affairs: they imply interactions over time during which the actors' perceptions may change and their goals may be deflected or redefined. Also the client may become interested in acquiring new sorts of services, pieces of information or social contacts (even to the extent of breaking off the initial relationship all together). Or farmers may decide to focus their efforts on obtaining political favours for the future – accumulating 'good will' rather than seeking access to new forms of agricultural knowledge and technology. And this is further compounded when dealing with large and complex forms of state intervention (e.g., land reform programmes), since one is faced with such a plethora of types of counters and interfaces (formal and informal) relating to allocation processes that it becomes almost impossible to know which ones to study in depth. Add to this the existence of so many interface workers and so many potential sources of interpretation and manipulation, with the high probability that actors will misread information or play games of bluff with each other and so forth, and it becomes doubly difficult to apply access concepts.

In order to come to grips with these complexities, one would need to specify the types of interactional arenas and situations one wished to deal with and, like Handelman, collect detailed extended case studies documenting how not only material goods but also social meanings are transacted and negotiated at particular interfaces by the actors involved.[14] Access theory, whose conceptual framework derives from the image of making deals across the counter, seems ill suited to exploring these important social and cognitive interface dimensions.

Key elements of an interface perspective

Interface as an organised entity of interlocking relationships and intentionalities

Interface analysis focuses on the linkages and networks that develop between individuals or parties rather than on individual or group strategies. Continued interaction encourages the development of boundaries and shared expectations that shape the interaction of the participants so that over time the interface itself becomes an organised entity of interlocking relationships and intentionalities. For example, the interface between management and workers in a factory or between landlord and tenants persists in an organised way over time with rules, sanctions, procedures, and 'proven' practices for handling conflicting interests and perceptions. The former is framed through the roles accorded to trade union officials, workers' representatives, management personnel and independent arbitrators, and the latter through a hierarchy of personalised ties based upon patron–client and friendship relations. The same organising capacity holds for interfaces involving government officials and local peasant or farmer leaders, or for those occurring between less formally constituted groups that differ from each other on religious, ethnic or other grounds. As small group studies have shown, even the most informal networks of individuals and families will tend to evolve standardised modes of relating to non-members and outsiders. The establishment of such normative middle ground may be endogenously and/or exogenously negotiated, and may involve contestation between state, private and civic organisations and interests that aim to influence or control the rules of engagement.

Interface as a site for conflict, incompatibility and negotiation

Although interface interactions presuppose some degree of common interest, they also have a propensity to generate conflict due to contradictory interests and objectives or to unequal power relations. Negotiations at the interface are sometimes carried out by individuals who represent particular constituencies, groups or organisations. Their position is inevitably ambivalent since they must respond to the demands of their own groups as well as to the expectations of those with whom they must negotiate. This, of course, is the dilemma of the village leader, workshop foreman or the student representative on a university board; indeed of anyone occupying an intercalary position between different social domains or hierarchical levels. Those who become skilled in managing such ambivalent positions are able to deploy them to their personal or political advantage, and sometimes they act as intermediaries or brokers.

In analysing the sources and dynamics of contradiction and ambivalence in interface situations, it is important not to prejudge the case by assuming that certain divisions or loyalties (such as those based on class, ethnicity or gender) are more fundamental than others. One should also not assume that, because a particular person 'represents' a specific group or institution, he or she necessarily acts in the interests or on behalf of his/her fellows. The link between representatives and constituencies (with their differentiated memberships) must be empirically established, not taken for granted.

Interface and the clash of cultural paradigms

The concept of interface helps us to focus on the production and transformation of differences in worldviews or cultural paradigms. Interface situations often provide the means by which individuals or groups come to define their own cultural or ideological positions vis-à-vis those espousing or typifying opposing views. For example, opinions on agricultural development expressed by technical experts, extension workers and farmers seldom completely coincide; and the same is true for those working for a single government department with a defined policy mandate. Hence agronomists, community development workers, credit officers, irrigation engineers and the like often disagree on the problems and priorities of agricultural development. These differences cannot be reduced to personal idiosyncrasies but reflect differences laid down by differential patterns of socialisation and professionalisation, which often lead to miscommunication or a clash of rationalities (Chambers 1983, Box 1984). The process is further compounded by the coexistence of several different cultural models or organising principles within a single population or administrative organisation (Law 1994) which creates room for manoeuvre in the interpretation and utilisation of these cultural values or standpoints.

Interface identifies the nature of contests (explicit or implicit) over the dominance and legitimacy of particular socio-cultural paradigms or representations of modernity; although, at the same time, it is important to recognise that commitments to specific normative or ideological frames, and types of discourse and rhetoric, are usually situation-specific. That is, for the actors involved they do not remain constant across all social contexts. It becomes necessary, therefore, to identify the conditions under which particular definitions of reality and visions of the future are upheld, to analyse the interplay of cultural and ideological oppositions, and to map out the ways in which bridging or distancing actions and ideologies make it possible for certain types of interface to reproduce or transform themselves.

The centrality of knowledge processes

Linked to the last point is the importance of knowledge processes. Knowledge is a cognitive and social construction that results from and is constantly shaped by the experiences, encounters and discontinuities that emerge at the points of intersection between different actors' lifeworlds. Various types of knowledge, including ideas about oneself, other people and the context and social institutions, are important in understanding social interfaces. Knowledge is present in all social situations and is often entangled with power relations and the distribution of resources. But in intervention situations it assumes special significance since it entails the interplay or confrontation of 'expert' versus 'lay' forms of knowledge, beliefs and values, and struggles over their legitimation, segregation and communication.

An interface approach, then, depicts knowledge as arising from 'an encounter of horizons'. The incorporation of new information and new discursive or cultural frames can only take place on the basis of already-existing knowledge frames and evaluative modes, which are themselves re-shaped through the communicative process. Hence knowledge emerges as a product of interaction, dialogue, reflexivity and contests of meaning, and involves aspects of control, authority and power.

Power as the outcome of struggles over meanings and strategic relationships

Like knowledge, power is not simply possessed, accumulated and unproblematically exercised (Foucault, in Gordon 1980: 78–108). Power implies much more than how hierarchies and hegemonic control demarcate social positions and opportunities, and restrict access to resources. It is the outcome of complex struggles and negotiations over authority, status, reputation and resources, and necessitates the enrolment of networks of actors and constituencies (Latour 1994, Callon and Law 1995). Such struggles are founded upon the extent to which specific actors perceive themselves capable of manoeuvring within particular situations and developing effective strategies for doing so. Creating room for manoeuvre implies a degree of consent, a degree of negotiation and thus a degree of power, as manifested in the possibility of exerting some control, prerogative, authority and capacity for action, be it frontstage or backstage, for flickering moments or for more sustained periods (Villarreal 1992: 256). Thus, as Scott (1985) points out, power inevitably generates resistance, accommodation and strategic compliance as regular components of the politics of everyday life.

Interface as composed of multiple discourses

Interface analysis enables us to comprehend how 'dominant' discourses are endorsed, transformed or challenged. Dominant discourses are characteristically replete with reifications (often of a 'naturalistic' kind) that assume the existence and significance of certain social traits and groupings, pertaining, for example, to 'communities', 'hierarchical' or 'egalitarian' structures, and cultural constructions of ethnicity, gender and class. Such discourses serve to promote particular political, cultural or moral standpoints, and they are often mobilised in struggles over social meanings and strategic resources. Yet, while some actors 'vernacularise' dominant discourses in order to legitimate their claims upon the state and other authoritative bodies, others choose to reject them by deploying and defending countervailing or 'demotic' (lit. 'of the people') discourses that offer alternative, more locally-rooted points of view.[15]

A major task of interface analysis is to spell out the knowledge and power implications of this interplay and the blending or segregation of opposing discourses. Discursive practices and competencies develop primarily within the circumstances of everyday social life and become especially salient at critical points of discontinuity between actors' life-worlds. It is through the lens of interface that these processes can best be captured conceptually.

Interface and planned intervention

Drawing upon the above insights, it becomes clear that interface analysis can make a useful contribution to an understanding of how processes of planned intervention enter the lifeworlds of the individuals and groups affected and come to form part of the resources and constraints of the social strategies they develop. Thus, so-called 'external' factors become 'internalised' and come to mean quite different things to different interest groups or to the different individual actors, whether they be implementers, clients or bystanders. In this way interface analysis helps to deconstruct the concept of planned intervention so that it is seen for what it is – namely, an on-going, socially constructed and negotiated process, not simply the execution of an already-specified plan of action with expected outcomes. It also shows that policy implementation is not simply a top-down process, as is often implied, since initiatives may come as much from below as from above (see Chapter 2, and Long 1992: 19; also Long and van der Ploeg 1989).

Hence it is important to focus upon intervention practices as shaped by the interactions among the various participants, rather than simply on intervention models, by which is meant the ideal-typical constructions that planners, implementers or their clients have about the process. The concern for intervention practices allows one to focus on the emergent forms of interaction, procedures, practical strategies and types of discourse and cultural categories present in specific contexts. It also enables one to take full account of the 'multiple realities' of development projects (by which we mean the different meanings and interpretations of means and ends attributed by the different actors), as well as the struggles that arise out of these differential perceptions and expectations.

From this point of view, then, planned intervention is a transformational process that is constantly re-shaped by its own internal organisational, cultural and political dynamic and by the specific conditions it encounters or itself creates, including the responses and strategies of local groups who may struggle to define and defend their own social spaces, cultural boundaries and positions within the wider power field.

The interactions between government or outside agencies involved in implementing particular development programmes and so-called recipient populations cannot be adequately understood through the use of generalised conceptions such as 'state–citizen relations' or by resorting to normative concepts such as 'local participation'. These interactions must be analysed as part of the ongoing processes of negotiation, adaptation and transformation of meaning that takes place between specific actors. Interface analysis, which concentrates upon analysing critical junctures or arenas involving differences of normative value and social interest, entails not only understanding the struggles and power differentials taking place between the parties involved, but also an attempt to reveal the dynamics of cultural accommodation that make it possible for the various worldviews to interact. This is a difficult research topic but one which is central to understanding the intended and unintended results of planned intervention carried out by public authorities or development agencies, or initiated from below by diverse local interests. The following chapter illustrates how interface analysis can be applied to three contrasting Mexican cases.

4

ENCOUNTERS AT THE INTERFACE

Social and cultural discontinuities in development and change

I now endeavour, through selected case material from Mexico, to show the usefulness of the idea of interface for depicting organising practices and processes of knowledge/power construction.[1] I first concentrate on rural development situations, using data collected in the late 1980s and early 1990s. This is then followed by a recent study of street children in Mexico City which utilises an interface perspective to explore the contradictory dynamics of interventions designed to get them off the streets.

Water guards, the interface brokers of a large irrigation scheme in western Mexico

The Autlán–El Grullo irrigation scheme (consisting of 9,000 hectares) located in western Jalisco was constructed in the 1950s and formed part of the Mexican government's drive to promote rapid increases in agricultural production, especially of sugar cane and horticultural crops for export. The operation of the scheme required the active cooperation of a whole gamut of people (farmers, engineers, canal maintenance personnel and water guards) with distinct and sometimes conflicting interests. From the beginning, the local office of the Ministry of Agriculture and Hydraulic Resources (SARH) was made formally responsible for the overall operation of the system, including of course the work of the water guards. Later, in 1989, a water users' association acquired responsibility for canal maintenance and eventually it played a more active role in water distribution. These changes presaged the introduction of a national policy shift geared to handing over these operational tasks to local user groups.

At the time of Pieter van der Zaag's field study (1987–89), water distribution had evolved into a complex pattern that was not simply governed by the rules and procedures implemented by the SARH district office, but was mostly improvised by frontline water guards (canaleros) in interaction with local plot holders. Since the latter were free to choose which crops they cultivated (sugar cane, maize or vegetables) and to set the sowing dates, neighbouring farmers had at some stage to agree on the arrangements and cooperate with the water guards, who would schedule the water flows to their plots. This made the work of the water guards one of delicate, judicious and often irksome negotiation. The scheme employed six water guards, each managing an area of 1,500 hectares divided into 300 fields requiring irrigation turns, with about 250 water users. Each water guard controlled the gates and sluices of some 30 to 40 kilometres of lined canals; and where there was another water distribution block below theirs, they would then have to make sure sufficient water was left for their colleague to meet the demands of this block as well. This added an extra potential problem, since those managing blocks lower down the system were ever ready to accuse those higher up of misappropriating water destined for downstream. The water guards operated the weirs and sluices, and worked out (in their heads, not on paper) the water distribution programmes, thus translating and to a degree re-writing the annual irrigation plan drawn up by the district engineers. In this way the water scheduling arrangements were negotiated and renegotiated (as the irrigation season progressed) with the various user groups.

At the same time as coping with the problems involved in organising at field and canal level, the water guards had also to retain good relations with the chief irrigation engineer and his assistants stationed in the nearby district town, with whom they communicated daily. Being frontline workers, water guards were responsible for the translation of technical guidelines and administrative orders from above, which they adapted to meet the varying needs, constraints and pressures generated at farm, field and block levels. And, in some instances, they would align themselves with specific farmer groups and give voice to farmers' views and preferences vis-à-vis irrigation policy and the position taken by the engineers. Water guards were located then at several critical points of intersection in the management of the irrigation system.

The intersecting lifeworlds of water guards and farmers

A water guard works some sixty hours per week, covering between 50 and 80 kilometres on a motorbike, overviewing all the irrigation turns in operation, checking and adjusting gates, and talking to farmers, their labourers or their sharecroppers. Water distribution is worked out on an *ad hoc* basis according to crop needs, individual requests for irrigation turns and the options available within the canal infrastructure. An official who records water pressures and deficiencies within the canal network sometimes accompanies the water guard. Water requirements vary considerably, since horticultural crops need water every seven to fifteen days, maize every two to three weeks, sugar cane every three to four weeks; and sandy soils require water more frequently than clays.

The intricate, demanding nature of water management practices produces specific locally-rooted knowledge, which in turn gives water guards a degree of authority and some freedom of decision-making. They need their freedom of action to do the job properly; but they also use it for their own benefit. Thus they will favour farmer friends and irrigate their own sharecropped plot more frequently than is formally permitted. Both water guards and farmers are thus drawn into each other's worlds and often share the same experiences – some sharing the same origins as the farming families of the area. This was especially the case with the small-scale *ejidatarios*.[2] Working with smaller farmers is, as one water guard put it,

> almost like social work…You have to be there, in the field because you will always find water users there, if only to ask you a question. To me it may seem a stupid question but for them it is very important. For instance, have you seen somebody who can buy my maize?…or whatever. For them, you are like a life buoy (*tablita de salvación*), a moment of distraction, and it also serves you well.
>
> (van der Zaag 1992: 88)

Different relationships develop with the more prosperous farmers who have large water requirements. One particularly rich and influential farmer had plots in three different zones and communicated by radio with the three water guards responsible. The latter would always jump to his orders, since, as they explained, they did not want their boss later passing on identical instructions. Another had close ties with an employee of the agricultural bank who arranged cheap credit and insurance for the water guard's own crops. In exchange the farmer expected favours in respect to irrigation turns. Another example was a large-scale tomato producer who rented vast amounts of land. In this case, the water guard hardly ever met with the farmer but instead had to deal on a regular basis with his farm administrators. But when the tomato producer urgently needed water, he communicated directly with the chief irrigation engineer, who would then send instructions to the water guard.

Interactions between water guards and engineers

Every afternoon, the water guards meet with the engineers at the district office. The two water measurers and the irrigation supervisor are also present at the meeting. Of the engineers, it is usually the head of the operations department and/or his deputy who attends. The atmosphere during these meetings is relaxed. Usually, conflicts between water guards and engineers are covert. Before the meeting, the guards gather under the big tree in front of the district office. There they joke and gossip. It seems that this is the moment of the day when they can air the tensions built up during a hard day's work in the field. It is the only occasion where they are among equals and can share experiences.

During the office meeting, the discharges flowing into each zone are evaluated, and each guard has the opportunity to request a change in water quantity, and will raise any problems encountered. Then every second day they have to write a report listing the plots that have finished their irrigation turn. Only occasionally do conflicts surface, since water guards prefer to safeguard their arena of operations and preserve as much autonomy as possible to resolve problems.

Sugar refinery reports detailing which sugar cane plots have been ordered to suspend irrigation are also presented. This list is difficult to decipher because the refinery does not use plot numbers to identify the areas affected but instead uses its own list of plot holders or users expressed in six digit figures. The engineers in the office cannot comprehend this information, because they work with plot numbers; and this is further complicated by the fact that the refinery works with areas under production, and not with total land areas. Only the water guards can translate these data. The speed at which they do so is staggering. It is the water guards, then, who become the effective link between the refinery and the district irrigation administration.

On the other side, the refinery staff are unable to enforce their requests to suspend irrigation. They have to rely on the guards, who convey the order to the farmers affected who, in turn, usually dispute it or procrastinate, since an extra irrigation turn before harvesting increases the gross weight of the cane and maximises their payments. Although the guards carry out the refinery's orders, they often express some bitterness at the end of the year when they receive rumours that the refinery is donating bags of sugar to all the personnel working in the refinery but giving none to them.

Another problem left for the guards to solve concerns silted up tail-end sections of the irrigation system. Clearing the silt usually requires the use of the district's hydraulic extractor, which is often unserviceable. So, in the end, it is the water guard and the users who have to improvise a solution. On one such occasion, a water guard who complained about this at the engineers' meeting was advised by his fellows not to worry if the water overflowed and the canal broke down! It was simply not his responsibility.

While the engineer sits in an office on the first floor, overseeing the arena, the field personnel must get their boots muddy and struggle with the vicissitudes of day-to-day water management problems. Hence there is a huge divide separating the engineers and the field staff, not only in terms of educational and cultural levels, but also practically and cognitively. In short there is a marked discontinuity between what the engineer observes and how he[3] interprets things, and the perspective of the water guard. Those at the lower end of the hierarchy are confronted with great variety and complexity, while the engineers deal in abstract designs based on simplified assumptions and incomplete data. Every day the engineers update the graph on the wall that plots the relation between expected and actual volumes of irrigation water released from the reservoir. On the basis of this, the head engineer devises appropriate strategies and issues instructions to the water guards to act accordingly. In this way he complies with his formal mandate which, in the end, boils down to making proper use of the stored water in the reservoir. He knows that his superiors in Guadalajara will not complain if this is seen to be satisfactory.

All this he does without having to leave his office, where he gathers together the information, summarises it and generates the documents required by his superiors. Having interpreted all the data at hand, he devises new procedures if necessary, instructs staff and mobilises people in the field, and all this while hardly moving beyond the confines of the district office.

Strategic management in the face of farmer discontent

One day in March 1988, van der Zaag visited the fields of one lateral, where he knew there were problems with irrigation due to the limited capacity of the inlet. Miguel, the water guard, had told him that he was fed up with the situation, because he could not meet the requests for water from the users. Van der Zaag records:

> I come across Miguel. We stop and chat. I see that he looks tired. Immediately he starts to tell me of all the discussions he has had with the farmers of this canal. I realise I function as a kind of sounding board for him: he airs his frustration. He says he had expected these problems and that two years ago he had told his superior that he should press the maintenance department to construct a new inlet with a diameter of 24 inches. But nothing was done. And when, at the beginning of this irrigation season, a further 50 hectares of sugar cane were planted along this canal, he got angry with the engineer, and said he would not be responsible for the problems this would cause. Miguel concluded: 'now it is me who is facing the problems…We are like bullfighters: we fight the bulls, and the bosses are way up in the stand, yelling *olé, olé*' [paraphrased].
>
> (van der Zaag 1992: 91)

Miguel went on to explain that that morning he had come across two water users from the tail end of the canal who had accused him of purposely denying them irrigation water. He had tried to explain the situation to them; that because of the small inlet no more water could enter the lateral. 'But they did not believe me,' he sighed, 'because they had seen that the lateral upstream was completely filled with water.' They thought Miguel was favouring other water users. 'I tried to explain to them that the lateral was indeed full of water because the level was set high in order to feed a sublateral, but that all that water was "dead water" (*agua muerta*), that it was only being stored in the canal.' But he could not convince them without taking them to the spot and opening the sluice that was backing up the water. Only a small stream of water emerged and they were finally convinced.

This incident, like the situations *vis-à-vis* the refinery and the engineers, underlines the fact that the water guard must manage a complex body of local social knowledge as well as a practical technical understanding of the workings of the irrigation system and the peculiarities of his operational area. He needs to be able to draw upon and communicate this knowledge at various interfaces.

Another dimension that shapes distribution is the water guards' own interests and those of their superiors. It is not unusual for water guards to be given gifts by water users as tokens of gratitude for their services, probably with the hope of favours in return. A small share of a farmer's harvest, a sack of fertiliser, a tyre for his motorbike, a bottle of liquor, or some present at Christmas – these are useful additions to his wage. The guards are sometimes loaned the use of a farmer's agricultural labourers to help on their own plot. Or they may receive an interest-free cash loan.[4] Moreover, it is not unknown for guards to actively stimulate 'gratitude' from farmers by creating (unnecessary) 'water scarcity' in their zone. Rich farmers (those, say, with over 20 hectares of irrigated land) who never give presents are considered '*codo*' (avaricious). The water guard is cautious about accepting gifts (especially money) and will try to keep it quiet. Hence there is a critical limit to the scale and extent of giving favours to certain water users, especially if the livelihoods of other farmers become prejudiced by it. There is always, of course, the possibility that they may complain to the head engineer.

Group culture and practice

El grupo de canaleros, as the group describe themselves, consists of the six water guards, two water measurers – normally ex-water guards, and the supervisor (also an ex-water guard) who also stands in for any guard who falls ill. The group as such is most visible when they gather outside the district office every afternoon. The rest of the district personnel (some eighty persons) acknowledge them as a 'closed' group that expresses solidarity when pressing for higher wages or better conditions. Occasionally the district engineers will invite the water guards to attend their social gatherings, and may themselves receive an invitation to the water guards' annual 'closing of the gate' celebration, which marks the completion of the irrigation season.

Whenever it is necessary to reach a broad consensus and pursue common strategies, the guards assemble as a group. Regular contact and discussions encourage the sharing of experiences, knowledge and solutions, and facilitate the development of shared cultural understandings and priorities. They are all exposed to a similar work situation that requires the creative application of numerous working rules and the processing of social and technical information. Accumulated local knowledge is passed on from the older to the younger generation, and some is of course also conveyed to new guards joining the scheme.

When a new water guard is appointed (invariably a man), he will be initiated into the job by one of the water guards and expected to shadow him for at least a month. In this way the newcomer acquires a working knowledge of the many technical rules of thumb (e.g., lowering a particular shutter-gate by ten screw-threads leads to a reduced discharge of 200 litres per second). He receives advice on how to deal with both farmers and engineers, and learns the need for solidarity and caution when one of their number is accused of malpractice or corruption. One frequently-stated recommendation is: 'if you don't want trouble, never accept money from water users. A safe present would be something in kind, such as tyres for the motorbike.'

Concluding comments

Like other similar frontline workers, water guards are confronted with a technical infrastructure and institutional reality that frames their activities and responsibilities, but most crucial of all is their active engagement in the ongoing social dynamics of the irrigation system. As far as the institutional aspect is concerned, the case of the water guard neatly illustrates how low-ranking field personnel come to play an important role in scheduling and allocating services to farmers. It is the water guards who emerge as key actors in facilitating the running of the whole system. The head of the operations department would often say that 'they simply distribute the water, and we do the rest'. The water guards themselves hold the view that it is they who are 'the movers of everything'.

Although it would be exaggerated to suggest that it is the water guards who are the sole driving force in this scheme, it is certainly valid to conclude that the engineers in their offices can only have a limited view on what actually happens in the field. This allows the water guards the room to create their own autonomous fields of action. And although there have been several administrative reorganisations in the district over the last ten years, including the delegation of more responsibilities to farmers themselves, these changes have had little impact on the way in which water guards do their job. Engineers, farmers and field personnel alike express the common view that in fact it is the water guards who have been the only constant factor in the district.

The guard's technical competence is directly related to the type of infrastructure (characterised by adjustable gates and intakes), and this makes his position crucial. But within these limits he has a certain flexibility in meeting the varying demands for water. As van der Zaag puts it, 'what is flexible in the system is thus the water guard'. His flexibility lies in the fact that he cannot strictly conform to the policy dictates laid down by the district, since these can never cover all the ongoing contingencies and variables in the field. In effect, he is the multiple interface manager: he links farmers to the district irrigation office; the district office with the sugar refinery; and also, as we have seen, creates linkages between farmers. As far as the technical guidelines received from the district engineers are concerned, these are far too broad to be operational. Indeed, if water guards rigidly adhered to them, they would encounter a multitude of problems with farmers in difficult circumstances where there is water scarcity and where they are in direct conflict with others. In such circumstances, the water guard attempts to solve problems pragmatically and not through the application of formal rules.

To some extent, the situation is surrealistic in that there is very little match between the formal irrigation plans, statistics, charts and maps and the actualities of everyday water management. But the myth of convergence persists because water guards, and perhaps even the engineers and others aware of the complexity on the ground, find it in their interests to pay lip service to and comply bureaucratically with the ideal-typical model presented to them. The case shows that lower-level field personnel are more than simply employees or subordinates of government or other agencies. They are also implementers, consciously transforming broad guidelines into specific forms of practice. In some instances they may even act to organise and stimulate farmers into joining forces and taking initiatives themselves directly against the governing authority.

The remaking of development intervention from within

The following examples, also drawn from western Mexico, focus more on processes of knowledge/power construction.

Promoting and transforming women's enterprise: the interweaving of domains and identities

The first example concerns a group of women living in an *ejido*[5] village close to El Grullo, a small market town located on the margins of the irrigation scheme described earlier. Following the initiative of the Mexican Ministry of Agriculture and Water Resources (SARH) in the late 1980s to promote women's projects aimed at encouraging peasant women to become involved in market-oriented production, the group opted to set up a collectively organised bee-keeping business. Government assisted by providing credit to acquire the necessary technology and other inputs, technical advice and the opportunity to obtain a plot of land for siting the beehives and a storehouse for processing the honey and holding meetings. The original group consisted of some sixteen members, the majority of whom were already related through kinship, affinal and friendship ties.

The central challenge of the study (Villarreal 1994) was to analyse the social interfaces generated by this type of intervention, focusing on the socio-political spaces opened up by the interaction between the women and different social groups within the village and among the women themselves. Such spaces are characterised by the creation of new relations and identities, in which discontinuities of power based on existing and newly formulated interests and values are generated. At the heart of this process is the issue of 'subordination' which, as the title of Villareal's study, *Wielding and Yielding*, conveys, entails a detailed understanding of the everyday manifestations of power, in which the wielding of power simultaneously presupposes yielding to it. Thus, rather than simply assuming the existence of relations of domination/subordination based on cultural mores and differential access to critical resources (material, social and ideological), Villarreal sets out to explore the ongoing processes by which power relations emerge out of the interplay of elements of compliance, conformity and submission, as well as resistance, defiance and opposition. As she argues (1994: 263), 'subordination...implies both an action imposed from "outside" and a self-inflicted condition'. This interweaving of processes, especially as they relate to gender issues, shaped the women's modes of engagement with the project and its outcomes.

The bee-keeping project offered a methodological entry point for exploring the encounters between women beneficiaries and various state and village-level authorities, as well as for addressing the broader question of how women's strategic interests and changing identities knit into, and yet also challenge, the prevailing ethos and practices of the male-dominated worlds of the family and *ejido*. While the project itself was originally designed to promote women's agro-industrial activity, different members of the group developed their own conceptions of the meaning and value of the project to them. Although as a group they adhered to the idea of group solidarity and shared benefits, individual members differed in their self-definitions as beekeepers. Some readily took on the label of the entrepreneurial peasant woman and wished to maximise their economic returns; others saw their participation as entailing no more than a supplement to household income and were therefore less committed to industrialising the product for outside markets. Yet others saw it primarily as a recreational activity that gave them a break from the chores and tedium of household domesticity. Most were inclined to switch between these differing representations as and when they saw fit.

Over time, their battles with visiting government officials and technicians about funding, training and technology options, and their struggles with village authorities, husbands and families and opposing social groups over access to land and participation in local decision-making, strengthened their resolve to make some kind of success of their endeavours. Gradually they became adept at manipulating outsiders and contesting or silencing moves to undermine their position. They achieved this to different degrees, both individually and as a group. By general standards their gains might be judged meagre, but they were able to create space for manoeuvre and they learnt how to find their way around and extract benefits from *ejido* and municipal authorities, even if this meant complying with local cultural norms or at least paying lip service to them. As women, they often yielded to male authority, but in so doing they devised methods of shoring up their own new-found identity as a group with specific interests. This was principally achieved through enlisting male authority to speak for them. Not all sixteen women were able to remain fully committed to the enterprise and a few were edged out of membership, or were driven by their family circumstances to give priority to other activities and relationships.

Villarreal charts the history and changing dynamics of the project and the livelihood vicissitudes of the different women and their families, thus highlighting how particular domains of social life intersect to reproduce and reconfigure social asymmetries and solidarities. Using the concept of social domain, Villarreal emphasises that

> [a]ctivities within domains involve a heterogeneity of relationships...and intertwine power relations that draw upon diverse normative frames. In specific domains, 'rules of the game' are negotiated and defined, authorities recognised, and relations to institutions, to other villagers and with the environment, are [at least provisionally] 'fixed'. Interaction within a domain entails distinct organising practices, [and] criteria with which to evaluate and shape others' behaviour and ways of securing resources.
>
> (Villarreal 1994: 264, see also 58–63)

The bee-keeping project became such a domain of interaction, organised around certain interlocking practices and values. The identities adopted by the women at different stages and contexts of the project were not simply self-generated. They were coloured by a range of social expectations, images of hierarchy and boundaries for social action that derived from other domains of social experience, in particular their household/family set-ups, their social positions in and knowledge of village and *ejido* affairs, and their links with the 'outside world' through experience of town life, market relations and migration. Hence the boundaries that the women set for their undertakings and ambitions, as well as the struggles they were prepared to undergo (either individually or collectively) in defence of their own space *vis-à-vis* state and *ejido* authorities were shaped by a diverse network of relations and perceptions drawn from a wide range of social experiences. This made the project a blending of often-diverging self-images, interests and objectives. In a later stage of the enterprise, government and other outside agencies, impressed by their success, tried to steer the project towards becoming a fully fledged small industry, producing honey as a branded product for sale in wider markets. However, this transition to industrial production demanded a more consistent and heavier commitment from the members than they could muster as a group, and so the women opted to remain small-scale producers.

The critical experiences and learning opportunities for these women took place mainly through their interface encounters and dealings with other domains, both within the village and beyond. They learned how to use and manipulate the discourses appropriate to these different 'authoritative' domains and took on new identifications – as entrepreneurial women, as peasant women seeking access to resources of the *ejido*, as new-style wives and mothers, and as members of a newly crystallised social group with some clout. In short, perhaps the most striking outcome of this government project was how women were able to appropriate it and fashion it to meet their own conceptions of the already ongoing changes in the status of women. In so doing, they acquired new forms of knowledge, skills, networks and organising practices upon which new identities could be built. These changes provided a platform for a broader debate in which both women and men sought to realign and re-conceptualise their relationships in the context of changing dimensions of power and authority.

A técnico tries to bridge the gap between government and peasant livelihoods and knowledge[6]

The second example (Arce and Long 1987) concerns the dilemmas of Roberto, a *técnico* (agricultural extension worker) who tries to bridge the gap between the interests and cultural orientations of peasant producers and a government agricultural programme. As a *técnico*, Roberto was a frontline implementer of SAM (Mexican Food System, 1980–86), a national initiative that aimed to promote the production of basic staples, especially maize, for national markets. He was expected to build close ties with his clients, but was formally accountable to his SAM superiors and required to follow certain administrative procedures in the implementation of the programme. Given his pivotal position, he was well placed to acquire much experience in dealing with both the demands of the administrative system and those of his peasant clients.

Like fellow *técnicos*, Roberto's entanglements with these two contrasting – and often conflicting – social worlds produced a body of knowledge based upon personal experience, through which he devised his own strategies of intervention in both the village and official administrative arenas. Although it might be assumed that such strategies would be highly idiosyncratic – being based upon a chronology of experiences of a particular individual – in fact they were shaped by the possibilities for manoeuvre and discourse that already existed within the two arenas and by the dynamics of the institutional locales within which the actors interacted. The case shows how the different actors developed their own everyday understandings or models for action that originated from and acquired their potency and legitimation through the interplay of opposing views and contrasting forms of organisation. It also shows how *técnicos* cannot simply escape these influences and constraints by attempting to ignore their existence, and that if they try to do so, they stand to lose professional legitimacy in the eyes of both peasants and bureaucrats.

The story starts with the posting of Roberto to a remote rain-fed district of Zapopan, located to the northwest of Guadalajara. The area is mainly devoted to livestock production, supplemented by agriculture and independent, small-scale opal mining carried out by local peasants. In the past the location was renowned for its robber bands that raided gold from the Zacatecas mines. Today the area retains this image of being associated with illegal activities, due to the production of marijuana and livestock for sale in a network of illegal markets. The arrival of SAM was designed to encourage the modernisation of agriculture through the introduction of a technological package of hybrid maize with inputs of fertilisers and insecticides. Accompanying this was an *ejido* tractorisation unit whose tractor and implements were eventually sold off to two local farmers and a shopkeeper. Roberto's main task was to revitalise the production of maize and improve the take-up of agricultural credit.

His first activities involved undertaking a general diagnostic study, but this proved difficult and misleading. Producers exaggerated the inputs they invested in production and underestimated the number of cattle they managed. Maize production was high but much of it was fed to cattle or marketed outside official state-controlled channels. Also it was impossible to determine the profits deriving from the sale of livestock in unregistered slaughterhouses and from marijuana traded through migrant networks. Attempting to probe these matters further and at the same time to establish bonds of friendship and trust, Roberto entered into a frank criticism of his SAM colleagues and of government. He admitted that many SAM officials acted irresponsibly by failing to deliver fertiliser loads, which they explained in terms of spillage on the road, or by claiming a 20 per cent share of subsidies and loans secured. The paradox, he said, was that these very same officials were often treated to meals and drinks, or given gifts of local produce, as a reward for their efforts. In turn, the peasants gave examples of how they themselves had tricked government officials with inaccurate information or blatant lies: for example, one year when 50 per cent of their maize crop failed they claimed full exemption from repayment of their agricultural loans.

This sharing of information about malpractice drew the conclusion that deceit and counter-trickery were endemic in the relations between officials and local people, giving rise to a strong element of mutual distrust in their everyday lives. It also provided a platform from which Roberto, in consultation with local farmers, could identify potential new strategies for local development. Given the central importance of livestock, the scarcity of good pasturage and fodder, and the need for increased maize in national markets, one obvious possibility was the acquisition of a baler for cutting and preparing improved pasture and fodder for cattle. This would also have the spin-off effect of perhaps persuading farmers to commercialise their maize through government outlets. A second idea concerned the planting of orchards for the production of various fruits. Both ideas were originally put forward by prominent local people and quickly taken up by Roberto, who insisted that they would have to lobby the local population and deliver to his boss lists of signatures in support of these new projects; if successful, government credit would be forthcoming. The signatures took time, a lot of haggling and many tots of tequila to obtain. But, finally, Roberto set off, armed with project documents and signatures, to seek the approval of his superiors.

At this point, Roberto radiated optimism. At last he had identified an alternative local development strategy, backed by plenty of local support, that he could believe in. He went straight to the unit head to explain the ideas and to present his plans. However, he had not proceeded very far before the head intervened, pointing out that the policy of the Ministry was not to support livestock activities but rather the production of maize. Roberto was then told to go back to the village to explain the Ministry's policy and to make clear that they could not have a baler!

Roberto replied that he could not do that because this was the first petition he had managed to get from them. It was a sign that producers wanted Ministry assistance. Therefore, like it or not, he could not fail the producers. He would now take the case to the district head. At this point the unit head attempted to grab the documents, but Roberto said he would himself pass them on to the district head. This infuriated the unit head who tried (unsuccessfully) to prevent them arriving. He had become especially angry because he regarded Roberto's action as one of insubordination, as a challenge to his authority. He argued that Roberto had taken on responsibilities that were not approved by the unit head; and he made it known that this would cost Roberto dearly.

Roberto bitterly recalls that, after this, the unit head eventually went to the district head to ask him to withdraw the documents: mysteriously, the papers 'disappeared'. He further comments: 'The unit head knew that he was creating a problem for me by this action, because I then had to explain to the producers why the petition did not receive attention.' Roberto concluded that this was a standard practice among bureaucrats who sought to discredit the innovative work of *técnicos*.

The end result was that he was labelled a 'troublemaker' (*un grilloso*) and sent to join a special 'troublemakers unit' for remedial treatment in an even more remote part of the country. His lack of success in persuading his administrative boss to accept his solution for bridging the gap between peasant and government interests had the further repercussion that the peasants could now use his case (like those of his predecessors) to confirm and reinforce their existing negative evaluation of government practice and personnel. Their experience with this particular *técnico* refurbished their beliefs about how the state works, although this same set of events will later no doubt also be used to justify further attempts by local actors to restructure the interface between them and government agencies. This situation thus became an important factor in the reproduction of local livelihood strategies, which peasants effectively concealed from government, and in the reproduction of local representations of development intervention. The combined effect of these processes was to keep the social worlds of peasants and bureaucrats apart. This separation resulted in the mutual generation of socially constructed systems of ignorance.

Relations with and images of the state

As the foregoing cases show, interface studies reveal concretely the nature of the relations between state and local actors and organisations. They help to identify how much political space exists for local initiatives aimed at changing the pattern of resource distribution or at improving the benefits received by local groups, and in this way they facilitate an understanding of the character and significance of specific types of policy intervention processes. Theoretical interpretations of planned intervention often operate at a high level of abstraction and tend towards the reification of policy scenarios and the actions of 'implementing' and 'receiving' institutions and actors. In contrast, an interface approach aims to explore how various forms of state and non-state power are constituted and reconstituted in the settings and practices of everyday life. The approach also highlights the processes by which the relatively 'powerless' appropriate, manipulate and subvert outside authority in their struggles to defend and promote their own interests and projects.

Another revealing example of this process is Monique Nuijten's (1998) recent anthropological study of the interfaces between local peasant groups, government agencies, lawyers and entrepreneurs. Making full use of an actor-oriented interface approach, Nuijten prises open the 'black box' of state–peasant relations to show how a repertoire of symbolic practices and strategic manoeuvres centring on 'the idea of the state' is jointly constructed through the encounters that take place between peasants, bureaucrats, lawyers and politicians. While this idea of the state may from time to time shift in content, in line with actors' changing experiences and imagined possibilities of achieving their goals and desires, the end result is a culture of the state (partially shared by the various protagonists) which continually leaves open the possibility of claimants and intermediaries successfully resolving their problems and, at the same time, making some individual gains. As Nuijten (p. 347) comments, 'One peculiarity of the Mexican bureaucracy is precisely its ability, at certain points and in certain circumstances, to overcome people's scepticism and, indeed, entice them to start fantasising again about new projects, hence recommencing a never-ending cycle of high expectations followed by disillusion and ironic laughter'. This is what she calls the Mexican 'hope-generating machine'. In reaching this conclusion, the study documents carefully the multi-dimensional livelihoods of peasants and other actors, and traces meticulously the ways in which this idea of the state is localised and objectivised in maps, documents and legal texts which, over several decades, become a bone of contention between the various protagonists who continuously engage in mobilising support, developing new networks and designing new initiatives. In short, the analysis provides a much-needed and refreshing appraisal of the images, character and workings of the Mexican state: a picture which gives plenty of room for the agency of the many players involved.

The methodological significance of critical events

A further dimension raised by the above studies concerns how interface situations articulate with wider institutional frameworks and domains of activity. This involves two crucial observations. The first concerns the fact that interface phenomena are often embedded in critical events that tie together a number of spatially distant, institutionally complex and culturally distinct activities. This holds especially for interventions organised by outside bodies involved in the construction of large-scale infrastructural development programmes such as hydroelectric, irrigation or settlement schemes, as well as for unanticipated man-made disasters, such as the explosion of the Bhopal chemical plant in India and its aftermath or the results of 'natural' disasters such as the frequent devastating floods of Bangladesh. In each case, interventions were designed and implemented that entailed the emergence of a series of new (or transformed 'old') interfaces embracing a multiplicity of actors and institutions drawn from local, regional, national and international arenas. These situations offer a major challenge to interface analysis in that they necessitate a systematic understanding of how many heterogeneous elements – social, ecological, economic, technological, cultural and ethical – become knitted together through the interlocking of diverse actors' interests, modes of organising, resource management practices, and political and cultural aspirations and rationalisations.

The second observation relates to the fact that interfaces contain within them many of the social properties and cultural propensities said to be embedded in 'society-at-large'. That is to say, they are constituted by, as well as generative of, domains, divisions, discourses and cultural practices found more generally within the social scene, but requiring detailed interface analysis in order to reveal their crucial social mechanisms. Having said this, we must of course heed Collins's (1981) warning that macro sociological concepts must always be unpacked so as to identify their micro-foundations in everyday life settings; otherwise they are emptied of any significant meaning at the level of social practice. Foucault (1981: 94) makes the same point when he argues that, although power may seem remote and tied up with juridical sovereignty and state institutions and thus beyond the arena of everyday social life, it is actually manifested and reproduced or transformed in the workplaces, families and other organisational settings of everyday life.

Street children in Mexico City: the interface between service-providers and unwilling clients

My last example concerns a study of street children and youths whose environs constitute the spaces around the South Bus Terminal in Mexico City. Though not totally estranged from their families – whom they visit from time to time – these youngsters live on the streets, sleeping rough in the parks and sometimes in nearby charity hostels, and they survive by begging, odd-jobbing and acting as porters for taxis at the Terminal. At any one time some twenty or more youngsters occupy the area immediately adjacent to the bus and underground train stations. From an outsider's perspective, they are scruffy and reputed to be addicted to sniffing paint thinners and other solvents. While they are mostly boisterous rather than aggressive, outsiders tend to steer clear of them.

In the mid-1990s, a group of students from the Metropolitan University in Mexico City, supervised by Bernardo Turnbull (1998), undertook fieldwork among them. The project started from the assumption – common among organisations seeking to help them – that street children and youths are unfortunates who are unable to help themselves and meet their basic needs for shelter, food and clothing. They therefore cannot easily be re-integrated into mainstream society without support from charities or government agencies. The research was primarily geared to identifying the kinds of organisations and help programmes best suited to achieving these goals. However, the researchers soon discovered that there was no shortage of shelters, hostels and soup kitchens, although the children used them strategically, and only occasionally. They preferred the streets, where they were in control and free to organise their own way of life, doing odd jobs, begging or stealing to obtain enough money to feed their drug habits and for other necessities.

Consistent with the researchers' own starting point was the media's and general public's depiction of street children and youths as 'unhappy tragedies' – victims of circumstance and their own inadequacies. Poverty, social injustice and family dysfunction were accepted as sufficient causes for their behaviour and conditions. There was little attempt to examine how they actually managed to cope with life on the streets. Hence this became the main challenge of the research.

Why were outside offers of help so regularly rejected? Perhaps a participatory approach that would listen to and take account of the children's views would be successful in addressing their needs and redesigning the help programmes. The researchers assumed that the children would have views about themselves and their way of life and would be able and willing to articulate them. So, on the basis of this, it was decided to devise a series of exercises aimed at encouraging the children to define their own problems and suggest possible solutions.

The results produced a sketch of their ideal hostel, a matrix of services and hostels available, and charts drawn on the pavement to profile their time spent on the streets; and they identified the services they used around the bus station. The researchers then invited them to join the weekly research analysis meetings and to read the field notes the research students had compiled. But, despite all of this, the children showed relatively little interest. Like other similar efforts, the researchers met with a wall of disinterest, defensiveness and resistance when they tried to elicit views and information through interviewing and interacting with them. Even though they were able to establish some rapport with individual children through playing board games or sports with them, the conversations rarely went 'beyond their immediate needs, such as food, money and clothing' (Turnbull 1998: 72).

The children never fully engaged with any of these externally planned or improvised exercises. Even when one was lucky enough to strike up a casual conversation with one of them, this would almost certainly be interrupted for some reason or other. Indeed, '[t]he inclusion of any third person in these conversations normally inhibited them and very frequently terminated [the conversations] totally…They would not come to our meetings either. They did not feel curious about them, they just asked if they would be too long because they did not want to be bored' (Turnbull 1998: 76).

These experiences led Turnbull (p. 73) to reflect more deeply on the methodological and epistemological implications of this and similar research. The goal of extracting information (even using a supposedly participatory mode) would, he concluded, have to be substituted by a more dialogical and interactive method, in which knowledge is perceived as the joint product of the ongoing relations between the researcher and actor, and not as something the researcher obtains from his/her informant. The participatory and learning exercises, predefined by the researchers, took no account of the fact that the children were well accustomed to dealing with a wide array of outside groups and institutions that sought unsuccessfully to enrol them in particular projects. It was essential therefore to reorient the research around the *relationships* between researchers and children, since only then could they begin to grapple with the complex interface issues involved. Repositioning the 'research object' in this manner provided a new epistemological slant on how street children and interveners jointly construct the social life of street living. Interestingly, this point of reflection was only reached some two years into the research, when the senior researcher first became aware of social interface analysis, and for this reason the study lacks a strong ethnographic foundation. Nevertheless, its broad contours of analysis are clear and instructive.

Drawing upon this more interpretative or phenomenological point of view, the study goes on to argue that the main concern of outside agencies, such as the police, social workers and charitable bodies, tends to focus on what the children are *missing*, because of what they are *not* doing, and not on what they actually do and why. Agency staff assumed that the children would know and want what was missing. The fact that the youngsters perceived and experienced a *different* reality went unrecognised, although, as the researchers came to realise, it was not simply a question of their living under different circumstances but rather of how others located them and their desires within outsider realities. For example, when the children rejected the offer of free housing and regular food, there was much amazement among government and charity personnel.

What was required, then, was a theory that addressed the role of such discrepancies in understandings and their connections with other experiences and contexts. With its emphasis on the interplay of different lifeworlds and knowledge constructions, the interface approach seemed a likely candidate, since it could show how preconceived notions and power differentials interfered with the learning process and the building of mutual trust. The children's failure to meet outsider expectations could then be explained by reference to the way in which the children had developed an elaborate set of techniques for accessing resources and maintaining some relations with outsiders, without becoming ensnared and enrolled in the latter's visions of how to solve their problems. The approach was also able to reveal the strength of prevailing external stereotypes that stressed the 'victimisation' and 'passivity' of street children, thus denying them the capacity to respond effectively to their own life circumstances.

Pursuing these interpretative lines of enquiry gave proper weight to the capabilities and powers, or agency, exercised by the street children themselves. Outsiders were not programmed to expect or accept this, since they assumed that those living rough lacked the resources to act in any other way than circumstances dictated. Yet what was deemed to be a lack of power was in fact a particular use of it based on a different appreciation of the situations they encountered. The police sometimes caught the children, but not because they could not evade capture. The children, in fact, considered cooperation with or submission to the police and other authorities as, in some instances, convenient. Even the researchers did not expect the degree of control that street children exercised over their daily lives. This unexpectedness, of course, derived from the researchers' own taken-for-granted ways of perceiving reality and the nature of choice. A re-appraisal of the nature and relations of knowledge/power in respect to the actors' behavioural responses was critical.

The study revealed a degree of accommodation taking place between the strategies of street children and outside agencies. According to agency workers and officials, the children did not stay in hostels for as long as they should; whereas, from the children's point of view, they were simply using the help programmes instrumentally to match their immediate needs (though not necessarily rationalising it as such). This was not seen positively by outside authorities. It was considered an abuse of services and an ungrateful waste of outsider generosity and commitment. Moreover, when programmes 'failed', remedial changes were introduced that seldom questioned the underlying principles of the intervention model itself. It was simply assumed that the children would eventually follow established agency precepts and 'get off the streets'. The children, on the other hand, quickly incorporated any changes in programmes into their own knowledge of the possible, again using the facilities in ways that fitted their own perceived needs.

In this way the two worldviews remained intact and apart. Outsiders concentrated their power in the formal control of the programme and thus missed the opportunity of using the children's own knowledge and experience to transform it in a meaningful way. On the other hand, the children focused on spaces for manoeuvre within the normativity of the programme but aimed to keep outsiders from taking over what control they already had of their own lives. Hence, in these various ways, the relationship between the two worlds was not dissolved or transformed. Its end result was uneasy co-existence.

However, street children's strategies and perspectives should never be considered as totally separate from hegemonic labelling and the images given to them by outsiders. Wittingly or unwittingly, the children worked with and adopted external identifications –

as 'waifs and strays' or as 'dissolute characters'. Sometimes they even lived up to the worst expectations of outsiders by behaving in a disorderly manner and creating a rumpus so that they would eventually be taken into custody by the police and given food and shelter at a police station or hostel. Likewise, their attempts to defend or expand their sphere of operations were unlikely to succeed if they attempted to empower themselves through group action rather than by adopting more individualised strategies. Indeed, external authorities and charitable organisations probably looked more favourably on them if they presented themselves as being in search of personal salvation from the evils and degeneracy of street life than if they joined together as street children demanding certain rights.

Turnbull's study, then, provides a close-up study of the arduous life circumstances and livelihood strategies of street children. It accords them the respect and tolerance they deserve, and calls for a fuller appreciation of street children's lifeworlds, knowledge and social practices. In addition, it highlights how external ideology and authority interferes with children's own capacities to learn how to improve their own life circumstances through engagement with these other resource-rich lifeworlds. In fact, a central finding of the study is that, despite the growing number of charities and help programmes serving street children, the interventions themselves have paradoxically contributed to increasing and maintaining the number of children on the streets. The study also argues that researchers should not behave as social gatekeepers or function as facilitators who decide what is good for both groups of people, or what they are supposed to know about each other, but simply as actors that open up spaces for dialogue between these contrasting modes of knowledge construction built upon different life experiences, expectations and identities.

Issues of participation and empowerment

As shown in all four examples outlined above, interface analysis grapples with 'multiple realities' made up of potentially conflicting social and normative interests, and diverse and contested bodies of knowledge. It becomes imperative, then, to look closely at the question of whose interpretations or models (e.g., those of politicians, scientists, practitioners or citizens) prevail in given scenarios and how and why they do so. Intervention processes are embedded in, and generate, social processes that imply aspects of power, authority and legitimation; and they are more likely to reflect and exacerbate cultural differences and conflict between social groups than they are to lead to the establishment of common perceptions and shared values. And, if this is the normal state of affairs, then it becomes unrealistic and foolhardy to imagine that facilitators can gently nudge or induce people and organisations towards more 'participatory' and equitable modes of integration and coordination. This is the paradox of neo-populist discourses and participatory methods aimed at empowering local people.

Although such neo-populist measures emphasise 'listening to the people', understanding the 'reasoning behind local knowledge', strengthening 'local organisational capacity' and promoting 'alternative development strategies', they nevertheless carry with them the connotation of power being injected from outside in order to shift the balance of forces towards forms of local self-determination. In other words, they imply the idea of empowering people through strategic intervention by 'enlightened experts' who make use of 'people's science' (Richards 1985) and 'local intermediate organisations' (Esman and Uphoff 1984; Korten 1987) to promote development 'from below'. While acknowledging the need to take serious account of local people's solutions to the problems they face, the issues are often presented as involving the substitution of 'blueprint' by 'learning' approaches to the planning and management of projects (Korten 1987), or in terms of 'new' for 'old' style professionalism geared to promoting participatory management and participatory research and evaluation methods (Chambers 1993).[7]

Such formulations do not escape the managerialist and interventionist undertones inherent in the idea of 'development'. That is, they tend to evoke the image of more knowledgeable and powerful outsiders helping the powerless and less discerning local folk. Of course, many field practitioners, who face the everyday problems of project implementation, show an acute awareness of this paradox of participatory strategies. Yet no matter how firm the commitment to good intentions, the notion of 'powerful outsiders' assisting 'powerless insiders' is constantly smuggled in. This is the central dilemma of planning and designing the means for engineering change in the first place. It is not removed by stressing the goals of participation and empowerment.

The contribution of an interface perspective

It is at this point that an actor-oriented interface perspective is significant, since it provides a systematic conceptual and methodological framework for analysing the interlocking of lifeworlds and actors' 'projects'. The field of enquiry should not, of course, be restricted only to those actors and elements identified in the discourses and practices of development institutions and personnel. It must also embrace the narratives, interests, cultural repertoires, strategic actions and livelihood concerns of all actors (whether implementers, stakeholders, activists or bystanders) directly or indirectly involved in the making and remaking of development scenarios and their outcomes. Central to this is the issue of human agency; that is, the ways in which people (i.e., development practitioners as well as local actors) deal with and manipulate certain constraining and enabling elements, through the use of discursive and organising practices, in an effort to enrol each other in their various endeavours or 'life-projects'. This implies ongoing contestations and negotiations over meanings, values and intentionalities, since social actors may engage with, distance themselves from, or adopt an ambiguous stance towards certain codified rules and cultural frames (cf. Crespi 1992: 60; Arce 1999: 5). Networks become key elements in these processes for gathering information, forming opinions, legitimising one's standpoint, mobilising resources, and for bridging, defending or creating social and political space within or transcending specific institutional domains.

This struggle for space or room for manoeuvre – at once a battle over images, relationships and resources – and the social transformations and ramifications it entails, can, I believe, best be captured through an interface perspective. The notion of interface provides a heuristic device for identifying the sites of social discontinuity, ambiguity and cultural difference. It sensitises the researcher and practitioner to 'the importance of exploring how discrepancies of social interest, cultural interpretation, knowledge and power are mediated and perpetuated or transformed at critical points of confrontation and linkage. Such discrepancies arise in all kinds of social context. For example, in a village they may entail struggles between peasant and non-peasant interests and lifeworlds; in a bureaucracy, the intersection of political groupings, differing ideologies or authority levels; or in a broader arena, they may involve the interplay of "worlds of knowledge" (or what Knorr-Cetina, 1981, calls "epistemic communities"), such as those of the farmer, extensionist and agricultural scientist' (Long 1989: 221–2).

In order to get to grips with these contradictory and discontinuous processes, the practitioner or researcher needs to access and learn lessons from the 'autonomous' settings in which people cope with their own problems, irrespective of whether or not the foci of concern or parameters of action can be linked with outside intervention. This requires the adoption of an ethnographic stance rather than the use of experimental method. One must go to where people are already engaged in interactions, problem-solving activities or routine social practice and negotiate a role or combination of roles for oneself, as participant observer, active collaborator, adviser, etc. As argued in previous chapters, a fundamental principle of actor-oriented research is that it must be based on actor-defined issues or problematic situations, whether defined by policy-makers, researchers, intervening private or public agents or local actors, and whatever the spatial, cultural, institutional and power arenas involved. Such issues or situations are, of course, often perceived, and their implications interpreted, very differently by the various parties/actors involved. Hence, from the outset one faces the dilemma of how to represent problematic situations when confronted with multiple voices and contested 'realities'. A social arena is of course discursively constructed and delimited practically by the language use and strategic actions of the various actors. How far consensus is achieved over the definition of the situation requires empirical evidence. One should not assume a shared vision or common negotiating platform. Actors must work towards such joint commitments and there are always possibilities for opting out or 'free riding'.

All actors operate – mostly implicitly – with beliefs about agency; that is, they articulate notions about relevant acting units and the kinds of 'knowledgeability' and 'capability' they have *vis-à-vis* other social entities. This raises the question of how people's perceptions of the actions and agency of others shape their own behaviour. For example, local farmers may have reified views about 'the state' or 'the market' as actors, which, irrespective of their dealings with individual government officials or market traders, can influence their expectations of the outcomes of particular interventions. The same applies to the attribution of motives to authoritative local actors, such as political bosses and village leaders. The central issue here is how actors struggle to give meaning to their experiences through an array of representations, images, cognitive understandings, and emotional responses. Though the repertoire of 'sense-making' filters and antennae will vary considerably, such processes are to a degree framed by 'shared' cultural perceptions, which are subject to reconstitution or transformation. Local cultures are always, 'put to the test' as it were, as they encounter the less familiar or the strange. Analysis must therefore address itself to the intricacies and dynamics of relations between differing lifeworlds, and to processes of cultural construction. In this way one aims to understand the production of heterogeneous cultural phenomena and the outcomes of the interplay of different representational and discursive domains, thus mapping out what I described earlier as a cartography of cultural difference, power and authority.

But, since social life is composed of multiple realities which are constructed and confirmed primarily through experience, this interest in culture must be grounded methodologically in the detailed study of everyday life, in which actors seek to grapple cognitively and organisationally with the problematic situations they face. Hence social perceptions, values and classifications must be analysed in relation to interlocking experiences and social practices, not at the level of general cultural schema or value abstractions.

In analysing these dimensions, we must reject a homogeneous concept of 'culture' (often implied when labelling certain behaviour and sentiments as 'customary' or 'traditional') and instead embrace theoretically the central issues of cultural repertoires, heterogeneity and 'hybridity'. The concept of cultural repertoires points to the ways in which various cultural elements (value notions, types and fragments of discourses, organisational ideas, symbols and ritualised procedures) are used and recombined in social practice, consciously or otherwise. Heterogeneity points to the generation and co-existence of multiple social forms within the same context or scenario of problem-solving that offer alternative solutions to similar problems, thus stressing that living cultures are necessarily multiple in the ways in which they are enacted. And hybridity refers to the mixed end-products that arise out of the combining of different cultural ingredients and repertoires. Of course there are certain inherent difficulties in the use of the term 'hybridity' to characterise contemporary patterns of change, since it suggests the sticking together or strategic combining of cultural fragments rather than the active self-transforming, inter-subjective nature of socio-cultural practice. In a recent, deliberately provocative argument, Alberto Arce and I have suggested instead the term 'social mutation' for such internally generated and self-transforming processes (Arce and Long 2000).

Conclusion: a comment on policy practice

This interface framework of analysis has a direct bearing on how one looks at policy processes. Policy debates, including policy formulation, implementation and evaluation, are permeated by interface discontinuities and struggles. Indeed the whole process consists of an intricate series of socially constructed and negotiated transformations relating to different institutional domains and differentially affecting a variety of actors. Hence an awareness of the dynamics of interface encounters and how they shape events and actor interests and identities is critical. The cases outlined in this chapter illustrate the kinds of critical dimensions involved.

Whatever the precise policy issues and implementing structures, it is essential to avoid framing problems and looking for solutions from within a framework of formal-logical models and rationalistic procedures (Gasper 1997). Such approaches accord far too much weight to external expert systems and undervalue the practical knowledge and organising capacities that develop among field-level practitioners and local actors. After all it is the day-to-day decisions, routines and strategies devised for coping with uncertainties, conflicts of interest and cultural difference that make or break policy. Indeed Lipsky (1980) has argued that it is precisely at such implementation interfaces that *de facto* policy is created.

In order to understand these 'autonomous' fields of action and the pressures impinging on them, research practitioners must devise ways of entering the everyday lifeworlds of these actors (frontline personnel and locals) to learn how these latter deal with the complexities of implementer–client relationships. This requires field strategies based not only on observing and teasing out the meanings of other people's lifeworlds but also on the willingness of practitioners to share their experiences and to put them to the test. Hence we must develop types of reflexive ethnography that explore the relationship between actors' everyday and researchers' theoretical understandings of problematic situations. The added value of this approach is that it enables us to consider the practitioner (both researcher and field officer) as part of the web of powers, constraints, opportunities and potentialities of specific intervention situations. Interface analysis offers a useful conceptual framework for achieving this (Long 1992 and Grammig 2001).

In building a picture of everyday encounters and modes of organisation and knowledge, we must be careful not to reify cultural phenomena, even if local people and policy-makers do so themselves by using labelling or classificatory devices. The latter create simplifications or 'black boxes', like the idea of society being neatly divided into 'ethnic communities' or 'class categories', or planners' visions of needy 'target groups' or 'stakeholder categories', that obscure rather than throw light on the diversity and complexity of social and cultural arrangements. Moreover such reifications enter into the very process of defining problems for solution, and in this way they may perpetuate existing ideal-typical models of so-called 'normal' and 'pathological' conditions. Instead we must give close attention to the heterogeneity of social practice by focusing on the differential social responses to apparently similar structural conditions: for only in this way can we explain the significance of certain types of strategic agency and knowledge–power constructions. Examples of interface encounters should not then be cited merely to illustrate general principles of cultural polarity, organisational dualism or hierarchy. Rather, they should be visualised as providing a methodological entry point for examining the dynamics and transformation of intercultural and inter-institutional relationships and values.

As I have elaborated in this chapter, the types of interfaces associated with development intervention provide a rich field for exploring these issues, since they throw into sharp relief all the ambivalences and complexities of cultural diversity and conflict. They also reveal the paradoxical nature of planned intervention of all kinds – even that promoting 'participatory' programmes – which simultaneously opens up space for negotiation and initiative for some groups, while blocking the interests, ambitions and political agency of others. What we now urgently need is to convince policy-makers and development practitioners, in search of better project designs and management techniques, to reflect upon and share with us their first-hand experiences of 'struggling at the interface'. In this way the conceptual and methodological framework could be further developed in relation to specific policy practices.

Part II

COMMODITISATION, SOCIAL VALUES AND SMALL-SCALE ENTERPRISE

5

COMMODITISATION AND ISSUES OF SOCIAL VALUE[1]

A recurrent and central issue in development sociology has been the role that commoditisation plays in more general processes of social transformation. A good deal of energy and paper has been expended struggling with how the market and its institutions intervene in everyday social life and reconfigure existing politico-economic and cultural domains. In the 1970s and 1980s, the debate centred on the theoretical interpretation of 'exchange value', and the issue of the 'survival' or 'destruction' of peasant forms of organisation in the context of proletarianisation and urbanisation. By the 1990s, the focus had shifted to the exploration of commodity relations and the negotiation of social values within increasingly global scenarios. This chapter then maps out the broad trajectory of this continuing debate and indicates how these issues have been tackled from an actor perspective.

The 1980s commoditisation debate

Some years ago I edited a collection entitled *The Commoditisation Debate* (Long et al. 1986). The main purpose of the volume was to challenge existing structural analyses of commoditisation,[2] giving particular attention to works that attempted to interpret the transformation of peasantries within a simple commodity model (Bernstein 1977, 1979 and 1986; see also Friedmann 1981, and Goodman and Redclift 1985). The theme of the collection, however, extended to consider more generally the shortcomings of political economy perspectives and to argue the case for an actor-oriented approach.

The central issue in the analysis of commoditisation processes among peasant populations concerns the impact of increasing commercialisation and integration of farming enterprises and households into the wider capitalist economy. The commoditisation approach represented a reaction to two earlier contrasting interpretations: the Leninist 'differentiation' model, which emphasised the inevitable destruction of peasant forms of production leading to the emergence of a polarised class structure made up of an agrarian bourgeoisie and a rural proletariat; and the Chayanovian position which stressed the viability, internal logic and dynamic persistence of peasant forms of organisation despite capitalist encroachment. Commoditisation theory sought to find a way out of this apparent dilemma by arguing that the debate is essentially false, since simple or petty commodity production is an integral part of any capitalist social formation. Thus labour processes and units of production that exhibit 'peasant' or 'pre-capitalist' features are not to be seen either as intrinsically 'transitional' and doomed to eventual extinction, or as self-perpetuating and sealed off from the influence of the capitalist economy. Instead they must be examined closely to establish the precise ways in which commodity exchange and market mechanisms shape and reproduce these specific forms of production.

In the same way, commoditisation theory claimed to go beyond dualistic formulations such as that of the articulation of the capitalist mode of production with other modes, which were assumed to have their own internal logic of production and reproduction. It also aimed to resolve the theoretical inadequacies of dependency models that reduced the workings of the capitalist economy to principles of circulation and exchange rather than relations of production. Furthermore, it was viewed as replacing earlier, broad and largely descriptive accounts of change based upon the concept of 'incorporation', with a more theoretical treatment fed by ideas from political economy.

In so far as commoditisation theory corrected the deficiencies of these various formulations, it promised to provide a more solid analysis of agrarian transitions and of social and economic change in general. However, a closer examination of the tenets of commoditisation theory reveals a number of fundamental shortcomings. These centre on the lack of attention given to the active role played by peasants, farmers and small-scale entrepreneurs in the process of commoditisation itself. Indeed, one might even say that commoditisation theory avoids the principal issue of why precisely do farmers and others submit themselves to the fate that this theory assigns them to, namely to the condition of being controlled 'by definite and precise forms of capitalist regulation which act as the absolute limits of their activity' (Gibbon and Neocosmos 1985: 165).

Following this line of reasoning, one can make a number of specific criticisms of commoditisation theory. First, there is the tendency to stress external determination, which, despite attempts to stand apart from Leninist notions, tends towards a linear view of development. Second, as indicated above, it is necessary to bring farmers and simple commodity producers back into the picture in order to explore what commoditisation means in the everyday lives of those it affects. Adopting this perspective directs one towards the study of diversity and variation in social process, which, in this case, highlights such critical aspects as farmer and/or household strategies and the management of labour processes. It also has the additional advantage that one is forced to take note of the basic 'operational' units (e.g., households, cooperatives, water-user associations, etc.) that in part shape the responses of individual peasants, farmers or entrepreneurs to outside market or state intervention. Commoditisation theory remains at the level of a generic model of capitalist expansion and simply fails to deal satisfactorily with variations in the responses of different farmers or groups to these processes of incorporation. Third, it also fails to investigate the nature of the various intermediate structures that mediate between the farmer or entrepreneur and the wider economic and institutional environment in which he or she is embedded. The nearest commoditisation literature gets to this problem is the discussion of the family household as a basic unit of socio-economic organisation, and an occasional nod in the direction of patterns of reciprocal exchange among neighbours or kinsmen. Clearly, then, it is crucially important to examine more systematically the types of relationships that exist between the farm, household or enterprise and various external structures. Although, as some writers put it, externalisation (i.e., the delegation of production and reproduction functions to external bodies) may undermine independent decision-making and the autonomy of the enterprise, these outcomes are by no means automatic or uniform (van der Ploeg 1990). Furthermore, differences in the degree of externalisation within a given farming population are likely to be reflected in differences in the scales of production, levels of capitalisation and styles of farm management. Such differences, however, should not, as Bernstein (1986: 19) suggests, simply be regarded as a matter of empirical diversity requiring 'concrete investigation'. Their explanation should be part and parcel of a theory of commoditisation and the differential patterns and forms it takes.

A further issue is the extent to which individuals or groups resist the inroads of commoditisation. This again involves the question of people organising themselves rather than being organised. Whatever the degree of commoditisation and state control over production or over the functioning of the enterprises, there remains some space for manoeuvre for organising 'counter-development'. Commoditisation theory largely ignores these processes and simply assumes that the 'agents' of commoditisation (private and public) are far too powerful to be affected much by struggles from below.

The concepts of commodity and commoditisation

The commoditisation model has its origins in Marx's discussion of the notion of commodities and how they come into existence. As Marx explains:

> Commodities come into the world in the form of use-values or material goods, such as iron, linen, corn, etc. This is their plain homely, natural form. However, they are only commodities because they have a dual nature, because they are at the same time objects of utility and bearers of value.
>
> (Marx 1867: 138)

Commodities therefore reveal their amount of value when they are exchanged with each other, whether in their 'simple form' or in terms of a 'universal form' of value. Although in principle any commodity can serve as a general equivalent for measuring exchange value, money normally emerges as the socially accepted form.

Commoditisation is the historical process by which exchange-value comes to assume an increasingly important role in economies. This normally implies monetisation, since the development of commodity exchange leads to the necessity to fix a universal form of value representing the general social estimation of particular commodities. The measurement of value is achieved through the market, where commodities exchange with each other in definite quantitative proportions, such that each commodity can be considered as containing a certain amount of 'exchange value'. The expansion of commodity exchange leads eventually to what Marx calls 'generalised commodity production'.

Marx opens his analysis of capitalism by examining the nature of commodities and commodity exchange, precisely because, in his view, the wealth of capitalist societies rests upon the 'immense accumulation of commodities'. He argues, however, that one should not make the mistake of assuming that, because commodities are exchanged, their relationship rests simply on that between things. Commodity exchange in fact conceals the more fundamental social relationships essential to their production, which in a capitalist economy are 'typically' based on the appropriation of the 'surplus-value' of workers by a capitalist owner class. Thus the relationships between various goods circulating in a market must be analysed not simply in terms of the ratios at which they exchange with each other, but in terms of the amount of labour embodied in their production and the social relationships entailed. This tendency to see the products of human labour as 'things' – 'as an independent and uncontrolled reality apart from the people who have created them' – Marx calls 'the fetishism of commodities'. This notion constitutes the bedrock of Marx's analytical critique of capitalism. The reason for this, as Rubin (1973: 6) so clearly indicates, is that 'Marx did not only show that human relations were veiled by relations between things, but rather that, in the commodity economy, social production relations inevitably took the form of things and could not be expressed except through things'. This latter remark underlines the importance of elucidating the forms of social consciousness that arise within commodity economies that serve to mask the exploitative nature of the relations of capital to labour. Burawoy (1985: 32–5) has re-addressed this issue through a comparative analysis of different 'production regimes' and forms of consciousness or ideology whose effect is, at one and the same time, to 'obscure' and yet 'secure' surplus value.

Marx's study of commodity relations, then, ties together an analysis of macro-economic phenomena, labour process and exploitation, and forms of social consciousness or ideology. In the discussion that follows I will limit myself mainly to examining the significance of commoditisation processes for agrarian populations and peasant enterprise, and only briefly look at other dimensions.

The impact of commoditisation

The development of commodity relations within agrarian settings is said to be significant for the following reasons.

The reproductive cycle of the peasant household becomes tied intimately to the market, transforming (but perhaps not totally destroying) the nature of peasant enterprise. Bernstein (1979) has talked about the 'reproduction squeeze' in Africa to characterise this process, and research in highland Peru has shown the heavy dependence on cash income for the functioning of even the poorest of peasant households (Figueroa 1982, 1984). An increasing percentage of households are unable to meet their basic consumption requirements without recourse to commodity exchange (i.e., without marketing agricultural or other commodities, or without selling their own labour either within or outside agriculture). This increasing 'hunger for cash' can be measured by calculating the minimal cash element necessary for the consumption basket of household budgets. Commoditisation, therefore, tells us something about the relative balance between subsistence and market-embedded activities; and from this we can make some estimate of the level of commoditisation of the household economy. Such data have been used as a proxy for establishing how far the household economy is based on a peasant 'subsistence' as against a 'simple commodity' or 'semi-proletarian' economic strategy.

A related issue concerns the extent to which, in areas of growing commercialisation of agriculture, production inputs come to depend upon the availability of capital or credit (e.g., for the purchase of fertilisers, insecticides, hybrid seeds, or for the hiring of machinery and labour) and how far farming strategies (e.g., in relation to cropping and labour patterns) are crucially determined by market factors and external stimuli. The commoditisation model nominally assumes that increased commercial production binds the farmer more and more to external economic forces and institutional structures, leading to less and less independent farm decision-making. Thus, although farmers may nominally be independent in terms of their control over land and labour, capital (backed by the state and international interests) exercises a substantial influence over the internal operations of the farm and household. The extreme is reached, as Sanderson (1986: 25) shows, when agricultural production has become thoroughly 'internationalised' through 'a whole new mode of industrial integration', frequently introduced by transnational companies, covering 'production contracting, technological "packaging" for whole industries, and non-equity forms of international control'.

The commoditisation model also predicts that capital penetration will lead to increased socio-economic differentiation among agrarian populations with the likelihood that, over time, this will crystallise into new class structures based on differential access to the means of production (e.g., land, water and technology) and influenced by the diversification of sources of income or wealth consequent upon integration into the wider economic arena. According to Leninist interpretations (see Lenin 1899, Patnaik 1979, Njonjo 1981), economic differentiation eventually generates a tendency towards polarisation of classes: between, on the one hand, a relatively small capitalist land-owning class and, on the other, an increasingly numerous mass of agricultural proletarians and marginalised peasants. Other views, while rejecting Chayanov's notion of a partially commoditised but self-contained peasant economy (Chayanov 1925), suggest that small-scale peasant and simple commodity forms of production often survive in the face of economic differentiation and come to play a central role in capital accumulation in agriculture (see Friedmann 1980, Long and Roberts 1984, Gibbon and Neocosmos 1985, Kitching 1985).

Bernstein (1985) has stressed the importance of considering a number of other issues relating to commoditisation, which we can enlarge upon in the following manner. In the first place, he mentions the need to take full account of differences in the history of capitalist expansion. The analysis of commoditisation shows differences in historical context and timing. Commoditisation does not occur at the same time or in the same way everywhere. For example, compared to the other continents, colonialism came late to Africa. Africa experienced a long history of indirect involvement in the world economy (note the centuries-old network of trading contacts and the effects of the Caribbean and American slave trade), but systematic incorporation leading to generalised commoditisation only began in the last quarter of the nineteenth century. On the other hand, Latin America became integrated much earlier into commodity markets through Spanish and Portuguese colonial rule, dating from the mid-sixteenth century onwards. Indeed, during the very early days of the colonial period, there was a rapid expansion of commodity relations, including the recruitment of peasants for wage labour in the mine-based regional economies of the Andes and Mexico (see, for the Andes, Assadourian 1982, and Larson 1988; and for Mexico, Chapa 1978–79).

Another point Bernstein raises is that so-called peripheral economies should be considered as 'generalised commodity' economies, not 'pre-capitalist' or peasant societies located on the margins of capitalist markets and economic forces. However, the notion of a 'generalised commodity' economy can be interpreted in two ways (for a fuller discussion of these theoretical alternatives, see Bernstein 1986). First, it can be used in the classic sense in which all the conditions of production, exchange and distribution are commoditised (Friedmann's 1981 ideal-typical model of simple commodity production under capitalism makes this assumption). According to Bernstein, it is difficult to sustain this view (even for so-called advanced economies), since we need to take account of forms of non-wage work, such as domestic labour, unpaid inter-household exchange and various types of informal work that are evidently an integral and persisting element of capitalist economies (see Long 1984a, and Pahl 1984: 339, for an interesting case-study of a contemporary household 'getting by' through combining various forms of non-wage and casual work).

The 'domestic labour' debate (Fox 1980; Redclift 1985), which has underscored the major contribution of domestic 'reproductive' tasks to capitalist production and accumulation, also calls into question this classic formulation.

Alternatively, one can talk about generalised commodity economies without necessarily implying that all elements are fully commoditised or that the capital/wage labour relationship predominates throughout the organisation of production. By this, one means that individuals or households cannot reproduce themselves without some involvement in commodity circuits, and that the general 'logic' governing economic life and livelihood strategies is that of capitalism. Thus, even if the forces of production remain at a low level of development, this does not imply that peasant or simple commodity forms fall outside the capitalist domain. This latter view, it seems, fits more closely the empirical situation of contemporary lesser-developed (and also advanced) economies. It also presents a theoretical challenge to those political economists who attempt to resolve the heterogeneity of 'third-world' economies by inventing such strange sociological categories as 'disguised proletarians', 'potential capitalists' and 'wage-labour equivalents' (see Gibbon and Neocosmos 1985: 169).

Bernstein's third issue concerns the fact that processes of commoditisation are often differentiated and uneven in their regional effects. Though affected by similar types of economic change, social and ecological systems vary greatly. This, together with the different forms that capitalist penetration may take, has produced a pattern of regionalised production, which has had its political effects as well (cf. Long and Roberts 1984: 235–57, for an account of the development of Latin American regions specialising in the production of specific export commodities, such as minerals, wool, cotton and coffee). Hence some regions become labour-exporting areas, others combine subsistence-based production with the marketing of surplus, and yet others become highly commercialised and responsive to changing international demand.

Such regional economic systems are not always contained within national boundaries. On the contrary, there are numerous examples of groups maintaining exchanges across international borders. One particularly interesting case is that of the Mambwe of Zambia who, from about the 1920s onwards, became heavily involved in supplying migrant labour to the Copperbelt mines (Watson 1958). By the late 1980s, urban recession had forced many of these Mambwe workers back to their homeland, where they have developed a dynamic 'informal' economy based partly on 'transterritorial' barter exchange with Tanzanian counterparts. These exchanges, involving finger millet and beans, are non-commoditised (although whenever the need arises they can be sold) and are operated by women. The system has developed to take advantage of the differential exchange value of these items on either side of the border, and is built upon a network of pre-existing marriage and kinship ties that stretches deep into Tanzania (Pottier 1988).

Bernstein's fourth point emphasises the necessity of considering the role of the state in promoting commoditisation, a theme he has explored previously (Bernstein 1977 and 1981). The establishment of the colonial state and the introduction or consolidation of commodity exchange took place at about the same time. The colonial state played an important role in furthering commoditisation through introducing European currencies or standardised forms of exchange value, through taxation, forced wage labour systems and forced purchase of goods from private company or state-run stores. The precise mechanisms varied, but throughout Spanish, Portuguese, Dutch, British and French colonies similar efforts were made to bind rural economies to the workings of the commodity economy and to promote the production of primary products for European markets. Later on, colonial governments took a more developmentalist direction, giving attention to welfare and education, although at the same time they sought to make their colonies financially self-sufficient. This led, for example in British Africa, to the setting up of small-scale peasant farmer development programmes producing a surplus for the market (see Seur 1992).

At the end of the colonial era in Africa and Asia, the World Bank and other international agencies moved in to assist. They have remained a dominant factor shaping the patterns of agricultural and national development ever since. Political independence merely reaffirmed commitment to national development through increased integration into international commodity and capital markets. The new developmentalist states needed accumulation. This was to be achieved through export production and through stimulating internal demand for consumer commodities. Self-provisioning subsistence production and exchange were thus discouraged: 'production for the market' and 'growth strategies' were the catch phrases.

Yet market incorporation led in many cases to increased precariousness in terms of agricultural livelihoods. Many cultivators continued to use simple technology and were dependent on the delivery of inputs organised by government agencies. When these inputs, such as fertilisers and pesticides or credit, could not be provided or did not arrive on time, then the whole production process was jeopardised. In addition, there was uncertainty and vulnerability in terms of market prices.

These varying processes, it is argued, have contributed to the transformation of subsistence-oriented, non-commoditised forms of household production and exchange, leading to a more commoditised pattern based upon a cycle of reproduction dependent on the functioning of the market and on processes of capital subsumption. In a study of a remote region of the Peruvian rain forest, Chevalier (1982: 117–22) takes the argument to its logical conclusion by suggesting that even those items directly appropriated by the worker, such as land, labour-power and subsistence goods that do not pass through the market, may nevertheless be said to be 'commoditised' (i.e., to have realised their exchange value) since their 'calculable value' is transferred to other products which are sold on the market. This argument proposes the same solution to the problem of the apparent persistence of non-commoditised forms within capitalist structures, as has been suggested for non-wage domestic labour (see Bennholdt-Thomsen 1981; and my critique of this position in Long, 1984a: 8–17).

Bernstein broadly predicts three types of social outcome of commoditisation in the poorer nations. In the first place, the peasant household becomes more individualised in terms of processes of production and reproduction; that is, the operations of the household and family farm acquire a degree of independence from larger social groupings (such as the lineage or local community) and take charge of their own economic decision-making. At the same time, however, the life-chances of the household are shaped more and more by extra-local economic and institutional arenas in which other similar social units compete for economic benefits. This interpretation is similar to Friedmann's (1981) model of simple commodity production, which stresses the process by which producers are brought into direct competition with each other in the market. In a dynamic market situation this will normally lead to more specialised types of production.

The second probable outcome is, as already suggested, increased economic differentiation among producers. Although the circuits of capital accumulation in poorer economies are severely restricted, commoditisation tends to generate differences of access to productive and other resources that engender social divisions within local society. These divisions are sometimes reinforced by the use that local entrepreneurs make of 'customary' institutions. However, due to the relatively low level of capital accumulation possible and to the high-risk circumstances characteristic of these economies, it is unlikely that this pattern of economic differentiation will consolidate itself in the short term into a firmly established class structure. Classes are important, but their membership is ambiguous, insecure and changing.

These considerations suggest a third outcome for some peasant households, namely the development of diversified economic strategies combining farm and off-farm work. These diversified strategies acquire increasing significance for households whose agricultural production is insufficient to meet their basic needs in terms of self-provisioning or marketing for sale. On the other hand, diversification also often forms a critical element in the entrepreneurial strategies of the richer peasant classes (for an analysis of this process among Peruvian rural entrepreneurs, see Chapters 7 of this volume).

Critical comments on the commoditisation approach

The foregoing exposition has attempted to convey the richness of the commoditisation approach to agrarian change. Its major theoretical achievement has been to locate the study of peasant and simple commodity production within the framework of an analysis of capitalist economic processes of accumulation, thus showing the shortcomings of both the Chayanovian peasant household economy model and neo-Marxist formulations based upon the articulation of modes of production. Empirically, commoditisation studies have demonstrated the ways in which rural economies have become increasingly affected by market incorporation and processes of capital subsumption, leading to the increasing dependence of peasant households on cash income (from the sale of products and from wage labour) and on purchased goods. They have also shown the effects of different types and combinations of commoditisation at regional level and the impact of specific types of state development programmes on commoditisation, as well as the latter's effect on welfare levels. This type of research has been particularly important in view of the 'food crisis' of the 1980s and 1990s when many poorer countries became net importers of basic foodstuffs that they once exported in considerable volume.

So much for the merits of the commoditisation approach. What about its theoretical and empirical limitations? A strong tendency in much commoditisation literature is to posit the destruction of the 'autonomy' of the peasant family household. This is frequently expressed by documenting the great extent to which economic decisions (e.g., which crops to grow, whether to recruit hired hands, whether to migrate for work, etc.) are 'determined' or shaped by external market factors. Another line of analysis has been to show how capital and outside institutions 'penetrate' the farm, gradually taking control of production processes and decisions. This process may, as Lacroix (1981) and van der Ploeg (1990) have shown for commercial producers, take the extreme form of delegating most of the reproduction (e.g., breeding and seed selection, and soil improvement) and a large part of the production process to external institutions. This is what is called 'externalisation' (for the many ramifications of this process see Benvenuti 1985).

Another frequent assumption in commoditisation studies is that integration into the wider economic and institutional system leads to the 'individualisation' of the household unit, placing the newly-commoditised household into direct competition with other similar units that make up the atomistic world assumed to be characteristic of simple commodity production (Friedmann 1981).

Although each of these observations can be partly confirmed through empirical data, the issues are in fact much more complex and far more interesting analytically. Is the independent decision-making of the household or family farm as inexorably undermined as suggested? Does 'individualisation' neatly follow? And are these two tendencies not at odds with each other?

In order to explore these questions, closer attention needs to be given to the management of the operational units involved. Commoditisation models often fail to identify precisely the nature of the operational units within which individuals or social groups make decisions regarding livelihood and labour. Although people normally live in households and family groupings, the composition and functions vary enormously. It is essential therefore to identify the major types of such units (e.g., nuclear or extended family households, or multi-family or community groupings), and to examine how various commoditised and non-commoditised elements interrelate. There exist major differences in the composition and functions of operational units between peasant agriculturalists and pastoralists (for African cases, see Guyer 1981, and for the Andes, see Orlove and Custred 1980), and considerable difficulties in defining the concept of 'household', which has been used variously to refer to co-residential domestic groups, income-pooling units, property units, or resource-management units (see Wall 1983). Such structural differences relating to units of production, consumption and exchange will undoubtedly affect the process and degree of commoditisation.

On the other hand, we increasingly encounter situations in which farmers form an integral part of operational units that extend well beyond household or family groupings to compose horizontally or vertically integrated systems of production based on farmers' cooperatives, state collectives, contract farming, or a network of formal economic institutions such as banks and private firms (see Benvenuti and Mommaas 1985, for an account of the system of relationships that envelops the farmer). However, although integration into markets and external institutional structures may reduce the range of economic alternatives available to farmers, the availability of non-wage household/family labour and resources, coupled with the maintenance of local networks based on kinship, friendship or patronage, allows farmers to continue to resolve certain of their livelihood and consumption problems outside the market. As Smith (1986: 101) has stressed, commodity-producing peasants obtain many important factors of production (such as land, labour and farming knowledge) via non-commoditised relationships. It is this non-commoditised side of farming practice and household decision-making that often remains inadequately dealt with in commoditisation studies (for an exception see Glavanis 1984, which provides a detailed account of the system of borrowing tools, household utensils, animals for ploughing, plots of land, and short-term credit among Egyptian peasant farmers; also Bennett 1968, on informal exchanges among Canadian farmers, and Sik 1984, for similar patterns in Hungary).

A related issue concerns the need to look at the responses of producers from an active rather than a passive point of view: the market and other 'external' forces enter the lifeworlds of peasant households, opening up or restricting economic choice, but all such new factors are, of course, processed by people; that is, they integrate them into their own farming strategies, and in this sense they retain a degree of independent decision-making.

This 'relative autonomy' is largely possible because they continue to control how they organise their own labour and how they draw upon various non-commoditised factors of production. Somewhat paradoxically, therefore, one can argue that the actual strength and viability of market-oriented production among peasants and simple commodity producers rests in fact upon a set of non-commoditised relationships (at household, inter-household and possibly supra-household levels). In contrast, the concept of 'individualisation' projects a totally different image: that of 'atomisation', which runs counter to the bulk of empirical evidence. Looking at the active responses of peasants also raises the important issue of peasant resistance to incorporation. Bernstein has described how African cultivators resisted being incorporated into the market economy of colonial rule in certain parts of Africa, but we must acknowledge that African communities and households, almost on a daily basis, still protect certain types of social relationships, especially the family, from becoming contaminated with commodity values. This process often takes the form of sealing off specific fields of relationships symbolically so that certain social commitments are reinforced or particular resources conserved. For example, in a study of a highland village in Peru, Skar (1982: 215) shows that there existed a strong cultural norm against selling basic staples, such as maize and potatoes, which formed the core of an inter-household system of exchanges, whereas no such prescription existed for livestock, which was regularly sold to visiting traders. Men of the village also undertook wage labour outside. The latter provided the necessary extra cash with which to purchase items that peasants could not produce themselves. The 'subsistence' and 'monetary' spheres of the economy were so intertwined that money earned on wage labour might later be used to hire daily wage workers to work in the workers' own maize fields, although payment, it seems, was used more to secure reciprocity at some later date than to offer a fixed reward for the tasks performed.

This and similar examples stress the importance of examining how non-capitalist institutions and cultural forms may mediate the effects of commoditisation. In fact, in the Peruvian example, one can argue that 'non-capitalist institutions act to restructure the monetary elements introduced into the system, and [that] so long as peasants retain a relatively independent basis for the operation of their economic affairs, then capitalist relations and principles will not prevail' (Long 1984a: 13–14).

This discussion of the interrelations between commoditised and non-commoditised relationships raises, as the above example clearly shows, the much more tricky problem of the role of actors' interpretations and cultural models. Is the fact that bride payments in Africa are now paid in cash an indication that their social meaning – or that of marriage – has changed? This is a difficult question, since it requires an analysis of existing social practices (including the explanations and cultural justifications offered by the actors themselves) entailed in the total process of arranging, paying and experiencing the consequences of bride payments. One would also need to explore how the 'commoditisation' of bride payments was related to, or could be compared with, other 'commoditised' forms.

Marx argued that the notion of commodity exchange was on one level a mystification of underlying patterns of social exploitation; that is, the latter were masked by the ideology of commodity fetishism. A similar point has been made with respect to the development of commodity relations among peasant producers. A few studies (e.g., Parkin 1972, and Taussig 1980) have explored these ideological dimensions – not always from a Marxist standpoint – showing how so-called 'traditional' customs or re-interpreted religious notions may conceal the existence of deepening contradictions between classes and thus facilitate the process of capitalist exploitation. At the same time, of course, it is possible to argue that the very persistence of non-capitalist ideologies offers a seedbed for resistance to capitalism itself. It is the co-existence of these contradictory tendencies – mystification versus ideological resistance – that provides the dialectic of commoditisation.

In order to pursue these types of issue it is essential to rid the commoditisation model of its implicit ethnocentrism. Marx's original analysis of commodity forms and capitalist development was based upon nineteenth-century industrial capitalism. He and later writers (such as E.P. Thompson and Eric Hobsbawm) have demonstrated convincingly that the individuals (workers and capitalists) who experienced this industrial system 'experienced' it in ways that were compatible with the propositions of Marx's general model; but one should not assume that his theoretical conclusions could simply be transferred to other cultural and historical contexts. Moreover, Marx never adequately theorised about the contribution of non-commoditised labour and relationships to the process of capital accumulation. Nor did he give sufficient weight to the ways in which non-capitalist forms may resist the penetration of commodity values.

An analysis of commoditisation processes among peasant populations requires, then, that we give close attention to documenting and explaining the heterogeneous nature of economic and cultural change. Many commoditisation theorists have leaned far too heavily on a linear view of change. Furthermore, even though they may qualify their discussions by talking about the unevenness of local and regional diversity, they fail to go one important step further to acknowledge that local organising practices and institutions are sometimes so resilient that they shape significantly the ways in which capitalist expansion itself evolves. Hence local processes become an important source of variation in the development of commodity relations; that is, external forces are in effect always mediated by local structures (see Long 1984b) since individuals (e.g., peasants and workers) must themselves come to terms with these new elements in their lifeworlds and naturally they do this on the basis of existing worldviews, experiences and institutional forms.

The role of local organisation was in fact much better analysed in the literature on the articulation of modes of production (e.g., van Binsbergen and Geschiere 1985). Despite the evident theoretical inadequacies of mode-of-production analysis (especially its tendency towards functional dualism and its neglect of actor concepts), it nevertheless has the merit of paying serious attention to the persistence of non-commoditised labour processes and relationships, and of trying to understand how far these are transformed by, or may themselves shape, the impact of the commodity economy. Mode-of-production analysis allowed for the existence of what Moore (1973) has called 'semi-autonomous' fields of action and for the co-existence and interpenetration of different types of relations of production. Used sensitively it may enable one to understand better the precise ways in which commoditised and non-commoditised forms interrelate.

Summarising what I judge to be the main limitations of the commoditisation approach, we can draw attention to the following:

- Its view of structural change is one-sided since it accords little room for manoeuvre on the part of those being commoditised;
- It therefore gives analytical priority to the capitalist side of the equation, reducing local and regional responses to a matter of empirical circumstance and cultural or historical diversity. It fails, that is, to theorise the question of structural variance and differential responses to change;

- It takes a structural–historical approach to analysis and makes no attempt to integrate into this an actor perspective which would allow for a more dynamic understanding of the interrelations between commoditised and non-commoditised relationships;
- It does not give adequate attention to 'operational' units and processes. If it did, then the significance of non-commoditised forms, especially the central role played by non-wage labour, in peasant and simple commodity enterprise would be accorded more analytical weight;
- The failure to appreciate the theoretical importance of non-commoditised relationships for commodity relations leads to a too-ready rejection of Chayanovian types of explanation;
- Although the significance of ideology and cultural dimensions is central to Marx's treatment of commoditisation, most commoditisation studies give little attention to these aspects;
- A final consequence of these various limitations is that there is a tendency in much of the literature to deny the peasantry a strategic and active role in the process of commoditisation itself. As Burawoy (1985: 10), commenting on his own experiences as a factory worker, so graphically puts it: 'objectification of work, if that is what we were experiencing, is very much a subjective process – it cannot be reduced to some inexorable laws of capitalism. We participated in and strategised our own subordination. We were active accomplices in our own exploitation.' The same must be said of peasants experiencing commoditisation.

A view of commoditisation from the 1990s, the age of neo-liberalism

The debates of the 1980s brought to light the inherent epistemological and theoretical incompatibilities of structural versus actor explanations, and pointed to the need for a new theorisation of commodity relations and social value that would give proper attention to the analysis of globalising tendencies, while at the same time allowing for an understanding of how commodity forms are 'mediated and translated by the specific strategies and understandings of the actors involved' (Long and van der Ploeg 1989: 238).

Yet, despite the various attempts to take up this challenge, it seems we are still far from achieving a satisfactory theoretical synthesis. Indeed, in hindsight, one might conclude that the effort to grapple with these problems was doomed to failure from the start, precisely because scholars assumed that the transformation of economic life and the meaning of goods (both material and symbolic) could be reduced, following Marx's theory of value, to an analysis of the interplay of 'commodity' (exchange) and 'non-commodity' (use) values and relations.

The problem with this formulation is, in the first place, that it posits the existence of two distinctive modes of value and practice: that dependent upon market rationalities and the conversion of 'use' into 'exchange' value, and that governed by non-market principles and social reciprocities. Of course, as a caveat, most writers would acknowledge that reality is considerably more messy and that this distinction is drawn solely for heuristic reasons. Nevertheless, casting the analysis primarily in terms of commodity versus non-commodity forms – which clearly owes a lot to anthropological discussions of 'exchange' relations versus 'gift-giving' (Gregory 1982 and Strathern 1988) – shifts attention away from the more intriguing problems of the co-existence and multiplicity of social values and of how, when and by whom commodity values, as against other types of value, are judged central to the definition of particular social relationships and to the status of specific goods.

While much has since been written on this issue, only recently have discussions achieved a degree of theoretical sophistication through, for example, the analysis of the significance of trust and other types of social commitment in the development and reproduction of commodity relations and economic contracts (see Granovetter 1985, Alexander 1992 and Perri 6 1994, for interesting contributions). It has also been persuasively demonstrated that many relationships involving the movement of goods between social actors are best understood as prestations or 'recursive works that juxta-pose and valorise' the different social entities involved, and not strictly as 'transactions' expressing the relation between the things exchanged (Thomas 1991: 32, and Strathern 1988). A third area of new research concerns the question of how contrasting discourses – dealing for instance with 'the community', 'the state', 'nature' and 'the moral order' – intersect in the processes by which commodity relations are formed and valorised. Somewhat paradoxically, but not surprisingly, these non-market dimensions have emerged as critically important in an era of neo-liberal discourse, where increasingly it has become evident that the 'advancement of the market' and the 'logic of free enterprise' depend crucially upon certain non-market relations, beliefs and commitments.

An actor perspective on commodities and value

What was needed in the 1980s – and still remains a challenge – is a more thoroughgoing treatment of the processes by which commodity and other social values shape social prac-tice. The field of agricultural development and food systems offers an especially interesting area of enquiry because it inherently throws up a complex mixture of social values – some based upon notions of 'modernised' farming, family and farm property commitments, or the centrality of cost–benefit calculations, and others on questions of taste, cultural habits and the idea of simply clinging to 'what we know'. Other issues concern the purity of organically- as against chemically-produced food, or arise out of struggles that occur between different interest groups within the food chain over food quality, quotas, princi-ples of fair trade, etc. The range of actors involved is wide: consumers, supermarkets, transnational companies, governments, private entrepreneurs and agricultural producers and labourers.

As a self-critique, one might argue that The Commoditisation Debate (Long et al. 1986) clung too closely to established categories of analysis – mainly those of political economy and peasant studies – and sought to create space from within for actor and cultural perspectives. Instead it should perhaps have adopted a more robust position, arguing for an analysis that addressed itself more directly to the social construction of economic life and social value. This would have allowed for the exploration of a number of critical issues, later taken up in Battlefields of Knowledge (Long and Long 1992), concerning the inter-locking of actor 'projects', multiple discourses, and power and knowledge domains (see especially the chapters dealing with commodity issues by Andrew Long and Gerard Verschoor). This would have facilitated a better appreciation of the ways in which commodity relations and values are generated, and challenged, through the active strate-gising, network building and knowledge construction of particular producers, retailers, consumers and other relevant actors.

Such a perspective underlines the important point that commoditisation is promoted, defined or contested by the actions of specific actors. It is not a disembodied process with its own 'laws of motion', nor can it be reduced to some abstract notion of 'market forces' that propel people into gainful economic action or impoverish them. Rather, commoditisation processes take shape through the actions of a diverse set of interlinked social actors and are composed of specific constellations of interests, values and resources. Commoditisation has no given and necessary trajectory, except that negotiated by the parties involved, and as a process it is never 'complete'. It constitutes a label we apply to ongoing processes that involve social and discursive struggles over livelihoods, economic values and images of 'the market'. In fact it is more a way of looking at things than a clearly defined special category of things. As Kopytoff (1986) and Appadurai (1986) have insightfully observed, things, like people, have biographies composed of diverse sets of circumstances, in which at some points or in some arenas they are accorded the status of commodities (i.e., attributed with exchange value, either potential or realised), whilst in other contexts they are not. In this way things are seen to move in and out of the status of being considered a commodity or are viewed by the same or different persons as simultaneously embodying both commodity and non-commodity values. Also, within any given social context, the interpretation and significance of exchange value as against other kinds of value will vary or be contested. Thus, while present policy discourse mostly accords a positive image to market mechanisms, free enterprise and commodity forms, the argument can quickly be turned around. For example, as Taussig (1980) has demonstrated in his analysis of proletarianisation processes among peasants in the Andes, the notion of commoditisation may also form the basis for a critique by local actors of capitalist relations, in a similar manner to Marx's own exposure of the mystification and 'evils' of commodity fetishism.

So far my argument has mostly concentrated on examples at the commodity end of the spectrum of values, but similar issues arise when non-commoditised goods or personal relationships are contested strategically to demonstrate the 'added value' of treating them as commodities (see, e.g., Radin's (1996) riveting analysis of the moral controversies associated with the commoditisation of body parts, babies, sex, etc., in a free market era). Being enshrined in modern state law and economic practice, the commodity form – so it is argued – is likely to carry greater clout and legitimacy. Yet how far market language and institutions undermine the discursive and moral basis of non-commodity values and commitments remains to be seen. For example, market arguments for the privatisation of *ejido* land (state-owned peasant holdings) in Mexico have met with some resistance, due mainly to the existence of peasant solidarities of one kind or another that aim to promote a sense of community and egalitarianism. It is easy enough to declare the privatisation of community resources, but it is another thing to persuade peasants to put aside community or *ejido* interests and values in favour of neoliberal attitudes. On the other hand, certain groups of *ejidatarios* and *comuneros* (community members) may welcome privatisation and increased market involvement as a way of helping them to consolidate their entrepreneurial ambitions; and there will be yet others who will no doubt hedge their bets.[3]

Commodity and non-commodity issues, then, are matters of contention: they involve actors' differential interpretations of the social significance of particular people, things and relationships. Hence we must recognise the multiplicity of social values held and the co-existence of different and competing 'theories' of social value. An actor-oriented approach focuses, therefore, on the elucidation of alternative actor theories of social value and how they interrelate, rather than on the search for a single 'new' theory of value. From this point of view there can never be a single theory of social value – whether Marxist or non-Marxist; we can only have actor-generated value notions that form part of the 'mental' and 'moral' maps of individual and collective actors, and which crystallise within the encounters and negotiations that take place between them.

Exploring social value

On the basis of this, a number of critical issues arise which constitute the central concern of a number of ethnographies on agrarian change and planned intervention produced by social researchers at Wageningen University over recent years.[4] How are social values negotiated, when evidently there exists a multiplicity of values attached to particular goods and relationships? How do particular people/interest groups promote their points of view, their valorisations? How do certain discourses gain pre-eminence and enrol others? What are the situational components that shape the negotiation process? How do the qualities (intrinsic and extrinsic) of particular products affect the meanings that people give to them? Is the fixing of value predominantly related to production, exchange or consumption? What is the relative weighting of the various sets of interests involved?

Whereas neo-classical theories give priority to consumers in the fixing of value (through their demand for particular qualities and quantities of products), Marxist theory stresses the role of production, in particular the way in which the input of labour–time generates value which is then converted from use value into exchange value through the market; environmentalist 'green' theory stresses the importance of the retention of stocks of natural resources or 'capital' (i.e., 'sustainable' resources) in the attribution of value; and community and family interests propound other values such as the importance of making presentations for consolidating social relations and guaranteeing reciprocal help in times of distress. Even inputs such as paid labour may not be evaluated simply in terms of commoditised value, since they may not be given with the intention of receiving benefits of a material or monetary kind, but rather in order to reproduce certain social arrangements regarded as essential for the well-being of the group or community as a whole.

Sarah Skar (1984) neatly illustrates the latter point in a study of an Indian community in highland Peru. Having described the network of non-wage labour exchanges that reinforces village solidarity and the strongly-held attitudes against offering wages or claiming wage benefits for working in the maize fields with neighbours or kinsmen, she goes on to address the question of the occasional instance when labour is in fact hired for a daily cash wage. Yet even here it seems that the money handed over functions principally to oblige the worker to reciprocate at a later date: 'In reality the same money, bills and coins, are often paid back and forth, and it seems that the money is rather kept as a security than as a currency for buying and selling' (H. O. Skar 1982: 215). Continuing for a moment with the same ethnographic context, one might also note that coins figure prominently in Andean marriage ritual and are often believed to give off a powerful vapour which derives from mysterious buried treasures called *waris*. The newly-wed couple is advised to keep these coins safely as a guarantee of prosperity (Isbell 1978: 121–2).

These examples bring out the co-existence of several seemingly incompatible interpretations of social value within the same set of social relations which people nevertheless quite easily live with, until of course certain events precipitate the need to clear up the ambiguities in order to negotiate an agreed point of view or simply to agree to differ. This concern for the fixing of value occurs, for example, at junctures in certain political processes where value incompatibilities and social discontinuities – often reflected in the emergence of markedly divergent lifestyles – reach a peak and begin to generate schisms within the group or network of relations. At this point explicit struggles may occur over the attribution of social meanings and value, access to resources, and in relation to issues and differences of social identity. This process is a regular feature of the ways in which class or status divisions become consolidated or are disputed within a community or social group. Examples might be taken from whatever society. Religious fiestas in Latin America, for example, often become

> ...the organisational vehicles [and public occasions] for reaffirming, reconsti-
> tuting or reordering social relationships and networks. This process is intimately
> tied to the expression and possible reformulation of the symbolic and material
> value of certain relationships and groupings...Yet, [fiestas] do more than this,
> they constitute arenas within which new patterns of differentiation and opposi-
> tion or cooperation/collaboration are generated. They do not merely mirror wider
> structural processes; they too have generative power. They may 'bring to the
> surface' the facts of social differentiation and class struggle. Participating in a
> fiesta may, thus, increase the consciousness of structural change and thereby
> promote it (e.g. increasing integration into wider fields of relationships spanning
> rural and urban scenarios which connect the village to the mine or city)...
>
> (Laite and Long 1987: 28)

In other words, the study of fiestas and other public rituals offers interesting insights into the processes of value affirmation, confrontation and re-configuration. This is espe-cially true during periods of major social change, when value and attitudes may become more polarised and at the same time increasingly slippery and ambiguous.[5]

Struggles and apparent inconsistencies over social value – in this case relating to job status – can further be illustrated by an incident that occurred within a Mexican tomato company producing for the US market (see Torres 1994: 144–73). The inci-dent concerned the relative value of local skills and knowledge versus professionalised expertise. It involved the demotion and subsequent loss of salary of a long-serving skilled worker, who had acquired an immense amount of practical know-how on the job and had risen to take charge of the greenhouse where the tomato seedlings were matured into plants. He was replaced by a recent graduate in agronomy who, before completing her university training, had worked as a secretary for the company manager.

The dismissal had been partly provoked by the worker's resistance to implementing cultivation measures that he considered ill-advised, and partly by the manager's commit-ment to 'modernising' the organisation of the company. However, after three catastrophic agricultural seasons – attributed in some way to the ineptness of the new agronomist – the skilled worker was recalled to take over the running of the greenhouse. For his part, the worker made it a condition of his reinstatement that he receive the same salary as that of the agronomist! Although the manager attempted to reinforce the worker's dependent position in the hierarchy of farm tasks and responsibilities, stressing that his original contract should be adhered to, after negotiations the company had no option but to accede to his demand. In this way the worker's widely-acclaimed status as a 'knowledgeable' tomato worker led to a re-evaluation of his worth in the eyes of the company manager, resulting in his receiving the status and salary to go with it. This example brings out the importance of examining the sets of social relations and discursive strategies involved in attempts to fix values and develop modes of accommodation between opposing moralities or interests.

An analysis of these processes shows how diverging values and interests are knitted together to construct workable social arrangements. As Callon (1986) and Callon and Law (1995) have shown, this often involves both an appeal to 'higher' authorities and the use of discursive and practical strategies for enrolling others and thus mobilising support from a wider network. According to them, enrolment entails translating roles, values and resources in such a way as to draw interests together in the resolution of a 'problematic' situation. The actor-network that results is composed of ongoing chains of commitments and understandings made up of people, things and representations, and lasts only as long as the arrangements remain unchallenged by members of the network.

This image of actor-networks captures well the dynamics of enrolment processes, but it is difficult to apply to large-scale and highly heterogeneous forms of social organisation. For example, 'translating' the values and interests of all those involved in a particular food chain – encompassing peasant producers, large landowners, agricultural middlemen, agro-export companies, supermarkets and other retail outlets, and the primary consumers – into some coherent whole would seem a mammoth task for any set or coalition of actors to attempt and successfully accomplish. While it seems food chains are often assumed to generate unproblematically an international system of linkages geared to the production, processing and marketing of a specific product or products, and thus to define a common interest in a single type of product or range of products with a given value or values, this global picture obscures a much more complicated and ambiguous set of relations and values. For example, bananas grown and exported by the United Fruit Company in Central America contain within them a host of different qualities, as perceived and defined by the various actors involved, and thus function as a repository of values and conflicting interests associated with modern plantation production. It would be quite wrong to treat this network of production, commercialisation and consumption relations as an integrated and coherent commodity chain or system built upon a common framework of values and objectives.

Contests of value: organising practices and globalisation of commodities

This leads us to consider the organising practices associated with commoditisation. Here I am interested in the processes by which strategies and discursive means are used to define and allocate value, or, to put it more concretely, how people attempt to adapt to changing livelihood and normative conditions.

People are driven by images and symbols as much as by the search for material or instrumental gains. Indeed, as Verschoor (1997) argues in his study of small-scale mezcal[6] entrepreneurs in Mexico, the expansion of distribution networks (including the large population of migrant consumers in the US) entails 'identity-constructing' processes whereby entrepreneurs develop representations (i.e., images and normative schemata) of the social and economic world in which they operate and use them to secure the commitments of producers and consumers.

Central to the study is an understanding of the difficulties faced by middlemen in establishing and organising a loyal network of consumers. To achieve this, on each trip middlemen engage in a number of interface situations involving both their *mezcal* suppliers and their potential customers. What is at stake in these interfaces is the identity of consumers and producers of *mezcal* (as well, of course, as their own identity). Does a consumer know the price range of *mezcal*? Does he know the differences in quality? Middlemen negotiate these and other questions *in situ*. At the interface with consumers, for instance, they bring a number of production elements to bear on the situation: the type and origin of *agaves* that are utilised for a specific *mezcal*, the character of the competitor's product, the 'oiliness' of the liquor, the material from which the bottles are made, the quality of the barrels in which the *mezcal* is aged, and so on. The effect of these negotiations is a temporary, 'working' definition of the identity of the consumer through the definition of the identity of the producer. As Verschoor puts it, both identities are inscribed in the form of a bottle of *mezcal* passing hands, which in some instances can entice the consumer to buy a bottle of 'inferior quality' *mezcal* for an astronomical price.

Likewise, at the interface between producers and middlemen, negotiations go on as to the disposition of the producer: is he willing to expand his production? Does he know the preferences of clients? Will he give a larger credit margin on the next trip? Middlemen translate these and other questions by mobilising different elements from the 'consumer' domain, such as the preference for the taste of specific types of *agaves* coming from specific localities, choice from among competing suppliers, consumer perception that good *mezcal* (like whisky) should be 'oily', consumers' preference for certain kinds of bottles or stickers, approval or disapproval of the taste of *mezcal* aged in oak barrels, and so on. The effect of this translation is that, if a producer accepts the identity attributed to him by the middleman, then he in turn will have to take on board the characterisation of the different consumers. Thus taste, colour and presentation of a *mezcal* bottle reflects, in effect, the identities of both producer and consumer: in the end, the social and technical organisation of the production process is also inscribed in a bottle of *mezcal*.

Running an enterprise, then, entails entering or creating arenas of struggle that involve not only resources, markets and information but also concessions as to taste, cultural values and moral views and principles. In this way relationships shaped by notions of commodity – which are themselves often ambiguous and conflictive in terms of the specific rights and obligations implied – become hedged around by many other social and symbolic elements.

In order therefore to talk about contests of value, we must go beyond the elucidation of the moral and cultural underpinnings of general value positions to isolate the particular organising strategies employed to accommodate to, dispute or ignore other actors' interests, desires and interpretations. This leads us into a detailed exploration of issues of agency; that is, how actors acquire and sustain appropriate forms of knowledgeability and capability in carrying out their social actions; and how they enrol others in the projects they develop. And this, of course, brings us to the heart of a genuinely sociological view of commoditisation processes.

At this juncture it is important to recall that when we talk about agency we mean more than merely the capacity of particular individuals to monitor, evaluate and come to grips cognitively with their social worlds. The capacity to act also involves the willingness of others to support, comply with, or at least go along with particular modes of action. Hence, as I stressed in Chapter 1, agency entails a complex set of social rela-tionships, similar to Callon and Latour's (in Law 1986) 'actor-networks', made up not only of face-to-face participants but also of components acting at a distance that include individuals, organisations, relevant technologies, financial and material resources, and media-generated discourses and symbols. Organising capacity – whether at the level of the individual peasant or frontline development worker, or in terms of the coordinated actions carried out by a consortium of transnationals – necessarily involves these disparate elements. How they are cemented together is what counts in the end.

As I have implied above, many of the key actors are spatially and culturally remote, yet they have a significant impact through global networks of communication and infor-mation. This is an element of considerable importance for understanding how large-scale agricultural production and food systems are developed and reproduced. Indeed the spread of modern technology, new consumer demands for a wide variety of 'wholesome' products, and the promotion of an ideology of 'competition' and 'compara-tive advantage' – all targeted to specific production zones – owe much to developments in communication and information technology. In this manner, certain symbols and images transmitted by communication media (especially TV and videos) become central to transformations taking place in contemporary cultural repertoires throughout the world, including the constantly changing representations of the nature and value of particular commodities.

How these messages are received and processed by particular audiences dispersed in time and space throughout the world varies considerably, since local understandings and knowledge have a filtering effect on externally generated communication. Nevertheless, new communication technology creates and reinforces new types of 'technically mediated' social relations that link individuals to various 'imagined communities' throughout the world (Anderson 1989, Thompson 1990). As Lash and Urry (1994: 307) comment, these 'imagined worlds' are made up of 'historically situ-ated imaginations of persons and groups spread across the globe [and] are fluid and irregularly shaped'. To be a member of an imagined world is of course to belong to a world inhabited by non-existent persons, in the sense that there are no persons that exactly match the qualities or profiles of those who are conceived of as being members. This does not, however, reduce the impact (or agency) of such imagined worlds: consider, for example, the enormous influence that the imagined worlds of commodity markets – and how they work – have on agricultural producers, consumers and financiers. Underlying these phenomena are complex sets of interlocking processes which involve the strategic interests, alliances and lobbying capabilities of the various actors. This, once again, challenges us to develop a theoretical under-standing of agency. We have become accustomed to visualising organising practices in terms of the functioning of formal organisations or the operation of interpersonal social networks, but, as this example shows, organised response occurs not only vis-à-vis identifiable persons, via the named representatives of organisations, or collectively when, for instance, peasant producers come together to take action against some local landlord or the personnel of a state agency. It may also happen in response to more diffuse influences such as rumours of growing resistance to neoliberal measures and critiques, developed through the 'anonymous' media, to mounting environmental problems.

Concluding remarks

The dimensions explored earlier raise critical issues as to the ways in which certain events, goods and relationships are valorised, and by whom. The discussion has focused on how commodity values are mediated, appropriated and contested.

Given the complexities entailed, I have argued that it is unlikely that we will arrive at a satisfactory understanding of issues of social value through any general theory of value – whether based on neoliberal, Marxist, or the newer 'green' versions. But, as I have argued above, contests over social values are central to a better analysis of economic change, and essential for the development of a new agenda of research on commoditisation. In developing this agenda we should no longer feel trapped by the constraining categories of political economy, neoliberalism or the new institutional varieties of neo-classical economics. Instead we should forge a new way forward which accords due emphasis to what Thomas (1991: 9) has called 'the appropriation and recontextualization' of 'culturally specific forms of value and objectification'. In other words, we need to explore the ways in which 'external' notions and 'conditionalities' are translated into localised meanings and action. This challenges belief in the universality and uniformity of commodity values, whatever their cultural context, offering instead an analysis of the interweaving of social values, power and agency.

In addition to the importance of the local embedding of commodity values, we also need to address ourselves to the wider institutional frameworks within which commoditisation takes place. Here we must give thought to how we might develop a more thorough analysis of the 'externalisation' of production and product transformation processes and of the process of 'scientification' that accompanies this[7] (see Benvenuti 1975, and van der Ploeg 1990). Such a task could, I believe, provide new insights into the nature and functioning of larger institutional structures which so far have tended to elude actor-oriented types of analysis.

Finally, I wish to underline that the main focus of this part of the book – namely a reconsideration of commoditisation processes – lies at the very heart of grappling with and understanding contemporary change. Commodity values constitute the bedrock upon which neoliberal philosophy has been founded and they remain the main thrust of present-day development policy.

6

WEBS OF COMMITMENT AND DEBT

The significance of money and social currencies in commodity networks[1]

This chapter identifies the different types of 'social currency' that shape the webs of social commitment and debt generated within commodity networks. It highlights the strategic interplay and handling of cash and non-cash values as they relate to diverse transactions, organisational practices and cultural meanings associated with the trajectory of a specific Mexican product – maize husks. It argues that commodity configurations should not simply be visualised, as they often are in commodity-chain analysis (e.g., Gereffi and Korzeniewics 1994, Bonnano et al. 1994), as disembodied sets of relations generated by the demand for a product in national and transnational markets. They must also be viewed as the outcome of the series of interlocking encounters and relationships that take place between the various exchange actors who endeavour to defend and reproduce their own enterprises, livelihoods and cultural repertoires.[2]

From this standpoint, the concept of 'exchange value' has to be extended to encompass a wider array of values and institutions than just monetary value and the market.[3] In a strict sense, values do not reside 'in', nor are they incrementally 'added' to products, as implied by the widespread use of the notion of 'added value' in analysing commodity trajectories. Instead, they emerge out of the ongoing struggles and negotiations that take place between diverse social actors located at strategic points in a network of commodity relations, and thus are *jointly* created and transformed by the parties involved. In a recent paper – fittingly entitled 'Unchaining value in a new economic age' – Rafael Ramirez (1999: 129–32) emphasises the same issue. He argues that value-chain models 'are difficult to apply to complex real-world decisions. Today we know that values are contingent and inter-subjectively co-produced. They do not reside in individuals or goods independently of the interactions to which they are subjected' (1999: 130, see also Normann and Ramirez 1993 and 1994).[4]

This analytical position carries with it two further implications. First, we should not assume that exchange value is simply determined by the perceived utility value of buyers and consumers, as in neo-classical economic theory; nor should we link it directly to the appropriation of 'surplus value' under conditions of capitalist production, as in Marxist theory. Second, we must distance ourselves from the hegemonic view that it is the power of so-called 'macro actors', such as multinational corporations and international financial and trading bodies, that determines market prices and commodity flows and transactions.[5] Though international bodies, trade agreements and protectionist policies undoubtedly play an essential role in setting commodity prices and delimiting the types of transactions that can emerge, it is equally important to acknowledge the dynamic of livelihood strategies and how they shape commodity flows and networks. This chapter centres principally on the latter, reserving for a future occasion a detailed account of the workings and 'scaling down' of macro processes.

The focus requires an understanding of the complex interweaving of social relations and discursive practices in which apparently dissimilar and incommensurate values and commitments are mobilised and reconciled by a variety of actors in the organising of commodity networks that supply distant national and transnational markets. It is not enough to assume – as many commodity studies do – that it is the omnipresence of money as a standardised, universal measure of equivalence that constitutes the common thread that binds together and dynamises commodity flows and transactions. Indeed, as many anthropological studies have convincingly demonstrated, commodity production, market transactions and various forms of economic enterprise, including also distribution agencies and supermarkets, are underpinned by non-market values and relations (e.g., Hutchinson 1996, de Haan 1994, Arce and Marsden 1993, and Arce 1997). These vary according to the field of activity (i.e., production, distribution, exchange or consumption) and to the ways in which different social domains (e.g., based on family, community, or socio-political interests) intersect.[6]

Recently the discussion of non-market elements has taken a new direction by being subsumed under a new international development buzzword: 'social capital', a concept vigorously promoted by the World Bank. Within this school of thought, social capital is conceptualised as a set of social resources or assets that yields a certain stream of benefits (e.g., increased income, improved material conditions and social leverage) for specific individuals or groups. These social and cultural assets are described by Uphoff (2000) as consisting of structural factors such as institutional frameworks composed of bundles of social rules, roles and commitments, and of cognitive and normative dimensions that do not depend upon and cannot be reduced to market modes of rationality. Though underlining the importance of non-market factors in the organisation of responses to changing market or other opportunities, this way of conceptualising social capital is deficient since it assumes that, like other resources and assets, it is 'out there' waiting to be mobilised, accumulated or stockpiled for future use; that is, social capital is seen as external to the social actions that invoke, generate and constitute it. In contrast to this way of looking at the issue, we assume instead that the co-existence and interplay of a variety of what we prefer to call 'social currencies' are intrinsic to the production and reproduction of commodity networks. In this manner, non-commodity values and relations are treated as an integral and often central component in the negotiation and creation of exchange value.

While most studies on commodities and markets in the end assume that money functions as the standard measure of exchange value, our approach aims to highlight the coexistence and interpenetration of different currency forms and the diverse meanings and guises that money takes on. An important consideration here is the fact that money is often not materialised at the point of exchange when purchases are made, goods bartered or services provided.[7] Indeed, as the following ethnography shows, various non-materialised versions of money play an important role in the functioning of maize husk commodity networks in California and Mexico.

The maize husk trade forms part of the flow of 'ethnic' food and food-related products that links Mexican migrants in the United States to production sites in their country of origin. Our account begins at the Californian end of the chain, where we map out the trading networks and marketing enterprises involved in the distribution and commercialisation of maize husks, focusing principally on systems of payment and money management. After this we shift to western Mexico, where we explore the webs of commitments and debt within the livelihoods of small-scale maize producers, day labourers and traders in Jalisco – an important zone for the production of the product. These two contrasting scenarios form part of a larger transnational economic landscape that connects various types of commodity production to commercialisation and trading in Mexico and the US.

As in Chapter 5, the case raises issues concerning the dynamics of commoditisation.[8]This chapter concludes, therefore, by identifying a number of topics for further theoretical and empirical exploration. These focus on the significance of multiple currencies and money forms, and the interrelations of market and non-market values.

Cash and non-cash values: maize husk trading and market spaces in California

The Latino[9] population in California – which is rapidly becoming a statistical majority (Rosaldo and Flores 1997) – constitutes only part of the clientele for maize husks in this American state. Maize husks are the dry leaves that protect the ear of maize and are used in the preparation of tamales, a typical Mexican dish.[10] But Mexican food has grown in popularity and is now enjoyed by people from all backgrounds and walks of life. In California it is associated with the idea of a Mexican heritage that stretches back over two centuries to the time when California formed part of Mexico. Tamales are made in small factories by a regular labour force, or freshly prepared by Mexican women migrants seeking to supplement their family income. They are sold mostly in Mexican restaurants and in supermarkets – where they can be bought canned or frozen. Husks for the making of tamales are available at supermarkets and at small corner shops within Spanish-speaking neighbourhoods.

Maize husks are only supplied from Mexico. The modern machinery used to harvest maize in the US, and the amount of labour entailed in separating the husks from the ears of maize, make it uneconomic for American growers. Thus traders in California need to establish close links with Mexican suppliers and/or with distribution agents in California. The latter are usually Mexican immigrants who have family contacts in Mexico. Although they occupy a small place in the world of market enterprises in California, they have been able to take advantage of the spaces that opened up as demand for the product increased among the expanding Mexican migrant population. This coincided with the creation of market niches for 'ethnic' products and with the abandonment of central city sites by the larger-scale chain stores.

The distribution of husks is mostly carried out by small and medium-size, family-run firms specialising in Mexican food products and spices, including bottled drinks, tropical fruit and a variety of chillies. Their survival chances depend on their ability, on the one hand, to procure and deliver the needed merchandise on time, and on the other, to juggle effectively with various assets and liabilities. Assets might include a stall in a particular market, a vehicle, existing supply networks or sources of credit; and liabilities or draw-backs could entail discrimination or harassment from other social and ethnic groups, or a lack of cash for buying merchandise or paying taxes and meeting other government oper-ating requirements. A stall owner in a San Diego market showed us at least nine different receipts proving that he had paid fees to the municipality and the health department, and had taken care of workers' pension contributions, social security, etc. He explained with some annoyance that if he did not cover these payments he would be liable to huge fines. While he had some leeway for manoeuvre in his financial agreements with suppliers and buyers, his options were strictly limited when it came to meeting government requirements.

Various systems of payment and management of money have been developed by traders to handle these problems and in order to compete in Californian markets. Money is frequently earmarked for specific types of payment (i.e., it is assigned to special funds), although this should not imply that such arrangements are always rigorously respected. Indeed, traders often find themselves in difficult situations that necessitate drawing upon money put aside so as to grasp the opportunity of a 'juicy bit of business' or to pay off a pressing debt. Earmarking money for the payment of government fees and taxes is viewed in different ways. The larger traders tend to see it as a necessary part of the costs of their investments, whereas the smaller ones – that is, most of the maize husk distributors in California – regard it as a hindrance and a drain on scarce capital. For the latter, it implies channelling liquid assets into a barren field, where they cannot reproduce or yield returns, while cash-in-hand can be used in many ways to promote business and is therefore fungible or capable of serving several purposes.

As Barros Nock – who also studied Tijuana–Los Angeles market networks[11] – indicates, cash can be used to 'entice' business partners and to enter particular networks. At times of great demand for a scarce product, when stall owners risk losing a client if they do not supply in time, they will resort to buying from fellow wholesalers or they will try to break into the networks of other firms by offering immediate cash for goods. In a similar way, credit is not simply provided on the basis of need, but given to partners whose businesses are viable, or used for the purpose of building a social network that gives access to types of produce that can be bought and readily sold both in Mexico and the US. Barros Nock also found that the use of cash in trading transactions was often an indication that the firm in question was facing difficulties, and had not yet built up a sufficiently solid reputation and network of suppliers and buyers.

Traders, then, often buy and sell without resorting to immediate monetary payment. Indeed, most transactions are carried out through various forms of credit and debt, whether arising from direct credit in cash or kind or from advanced or delayed payment. Although, sooner or later, debt is expected to materialise into some form of money, the social implication of these different economic practices is highly significant. The need for liquidity in economic transactions requires processes of translation wherein the expectation of future income becomes an asset to be drawn upon in the present. Hence, having a reputation as a wealthy producer, successful entrepreneur, honest trader or solid worker can be translated into access to credit, loans and advanced payment (see also Villarreal 2000). It can also make a difference to how tolerant individuals or entrepreneurs are with respect to delayed payment. Here issues of skill, knowledge and reputation may be taken into account, and cultural identities are also likely to come strongly into the picture. But in the end, whether dealers or clients are categorised as Mexican or American, illegal immigrants or Chicanos,[12] it is usually a reputation for reliability and trustworthiness that is critical. Hence issues of language, race and culture enter but do not determine, the negotiations involved in accessing market spaces, jobs, wages, and commercial transactions and networks.

Each stage in the itinerary of maize husks as they make their way towards consumers in the US entails a myriad of negotiations over value and its definition. Prices are not unimportant in the appraisal and valuation of products, but the relation of price to social value cannot be left out.[13] Values entailed in the specification of quality constitute an obvious example of this. Negotiating a precise definition of the quality of a particular commodity within specific markets is an everyday issue for traders, and entails dealing with diverse cultural norms, standards and procedures.

Juggling assets and liabilities in the Californian market: the case of Pedro

Pedro's stall near the centre of San Diego is one of a dozen or so stores that specialise in Mexican products. But although he distributes maize husks, chillies, spices, avocados and Mexican brands of soft drinks, his wares also include potatoes, plastic cups and other non-Mexican products. He explains that he will supply whatever his clients need, whatever brings in cash ('lo que traiga plata'). His clients mostly include supermarkets, restaurants and small shops, but he also supplies other distributors upon demand.

Pedro is from Michoacán, a state in western Mexico. He arrived in the United States twenty-seven years ago as an illegal migrant in search of work. Although he is now an American citizen, Pedro still speaks of 'them' and 'us'. It has not been easy for him to make his way in the United States. He claims he is often discriminated against due to his Mexican background and because he is uneducated. There was no school in the small town where he was born, and what he has learned has been from experience alone. 'Education,' he says, 'does not make you smarter. Take my nephew, for example.' Pedro points to a young man who is loading a small lorry on the street. 'He is a student of law, but Americans think he is ignorant because he is Mexican and doesn't speak English. He came here to work with me for a few months and to learn about the trade. Schools don't give you experience.'

For Pedro, experience has to do with learning, what he calls American 'double-talk'. It is not only to do with English, he says, since he now manages reasonably well in the language; it entails learning how to cope with discrimination, uncertainty and ambiguity, and working out how to make the best of things.

He explains that Mexicans stick together and support each other. Although there can also be problems between them, they learn that loyalty and honesty between them is important for business. Pedro himself first worked for a relative who was also a trader, but later he decided to set up on his own. He describes how, at the time, he possessed only a small vehicle, but that his close links to other Mexican traders helped him, stressing that there is much solidarity among them. Such partners supply products whenever he requires them and he is not expected to pay immediately. They even provide loans when he is in urgent need of cash, and he likewise. Also, because he is on good terms with friends who cross the US–Mexico border every day, it is quite easy for him to get hold of consignments of Mexican products at very short notice, which is often much more difficult for larger, more established traders.

This is especially the case with maize husks. Pedro does not have enough space in his stall to stock a large amount of husks. And it would not be convenient for him to do so, since in order to maximise his investments he needs to be able to shift rapidly, in the face of changing demands, from one product to another. This is facilitated by the fact that he has quick access to a wide network for obtaining maize or other Mexican products. Other traders are well aware of this, which is why they often seek him out. Thus, being Mexican

– which carries with it certain disadvantages in California – becomes an asset for Pedro, because it links him with networks of personal support as well as providing access to specific products. These networks help him span time and transnational space much more rapidly than is usually the case for American-run businesses.

Pedro's case illustrates, then, how Mexicans located in what appear to be marginal markets and social spaces are able to juggle with their various liabilities and commitments so as to convert them into assets. This has less to do with bank balances and financial collateral than with their ability to manage interpersonal relations and the interfaces between different domains of the commodity networks in which they operate. Hence, cash and non-cash values intertwine in the organisational practices and meanings associated with maize husk distribution in California. The kinds of commodity and enterprise relations that result cannot be reduced to the economic law of supply and demand, since they are clearly underpinned or anchored by certain culturally defined normative frames and expectations.

Building cross-border networks

As a general principle, both large- and small-scale enterprises must develop networks in order to secure timely supply of relevant products and to build and sustain their clientele. In the case of maize husks these networks are very versatile and involve a variety of products that fluctuate according to changing demand. Even if a trader has never traded maize husks before, if a client asks him for some, then it is likely that he will try to procure some through contacts who deal in Mexican products such as coriander or chillies. Or he may make enquiries through his existing network of relatives and friends living in Mexico. When we first approached dealers to inquire about maize husks – even among stallholders where the product was not among their wares – we were almost invariably asked: 'How much do you need? We can get it to you by tomorrow!' When we explained what our intentions were, the response was: 'We have whatever the client needs. We might not have it just now, but we will do what it takes to get it quickly!' This implies that maize husks (like many other products in the market) undergo quite a bit of movement from one stall to the other and from one trader to another before they reach the consumer. Buyers become suppliers and suppliers buyers. One of the distributors explained to us that husks can move between as many as six dealers, maybe even more, before finding a buyer. It is often easier to 'borrow' merchandise from another dealer than to wait until one's regular suppliers from Mexico manage to cross the border. In fact some of the larger distribution agencies have set up their own agencies in Mexico; yet even they must resort to smaller distributors when demand is pressing.

Networks are constructed on the basis of shared interests, trust, cultural identification and loyalty, and so forth. However, they also involve elements of exclusion, competition, power and control. It is the kinds of bonds established, the ruptures that emerge, and the multifarious commitments and obligations they entail, which shape the overall patterning of social relations. Hence the structure of networks and the precise elements that comprise them are not as fixed as they are often assumed to be. A word from one 'good contact' can open many doors. A skilled trader can make use of seemingly trivial information to establish common reference points and open a small crack that could be the door to some new opportunity. While intuition and the capacity to take risks are relevant, so is information.

However, access to such information is not easy for many Latinos who are not in tune with American regulations, hardly speak the language and are often stereotyped in the US as ignorant and untrustworthy. For them, American partners and networks are often difficult to enter.

In fact Latinos have managed to carve out space for themselves within Californian marketplaces, although such spaces tend to be small as compared to the large transnational firms operating in California. For example, the Seventh Street Market in Los Angeles was the most important wholesale market until 1986, when a better-equipped Terminal Market was constructed. Mexican immigrants, who had started occupying stalls in the former, were not among those who moved on to the more modern installations. Thus the Seventh Street Market became Mexican and Latino.[14] In a similar way, the San Diego market stalls located near the centre of the city were left to Latin Americans when the big firms moved out to the suburbs. However, the Latinos themselves are now faced with the problem of having to move, since the area they occupy is destined to become a huge parking lot. This seems to be a common pattern in California. Rosaldo and Flores (1997) describe how the centre of San Jose (the state's third largest city) was left to decay when shopping centres sprang up in the suburbs, pulling business from the downtown area. Mexican restaurants and businesses then took over. Rocco (1997) documents the same process for Los Angeles.

Differences in ethnicity, colour and citizenship thus have a heavy impact on the kinds of network that are constructed and the nature of the relationships established. Vulnerable to discrimination, harassment and exclusion, Latinos have created their own specific networks. Distinct Latino spaces, contacts and values are built and redefined to create and sustain their livelihoods and to give room for manoeuvre. Maize husk distribution is one such space. Chicano or Mexican traders run most of the distributors – including larger companies – and their employees tend to be Latinos as well. The distribution agencies are mostly located in downtown areas of Los Angeles and San Diego and in the Mexican market. Discrimination has also had the effect of strengthening loyalty among Latinos and closing ranks against Anglos (white Anglo-Saxon or Caucasian Americans) who attempt to create space within their networks. Indeed, many Mexican traders view Anglo dealers with suspicion and resentment.

However, ongoing relationships must be developed between members of these different social groups. The encounters that take place between them present interesting interface situations in which values (not only based on commodity notions) are contested and negotiated. For example, Chicano, Mexican and American traders negotiate the stereotypical notions of their cultural and ethnic personas and attempt to cross or rework these imagined boundaries and social worlds by building upon different images of trustworthiness, reciprocity, accountability and entrepreneurship. We were introduced to the owners of a Mexican supermarket located in a Mexican neighbourhood in the Los Angeles area – two tall, blond, Anglo-looking brothers who spoke a little Spanish with a heavy Anglo accent – who presented themselves as Mexicans. When we enquired about them, our friends explained that they were of Mexican descent. Their grandfather, who started the enterprise, was Mexican, and they interacted in a very familiar way with Mexican clients. They had *compadres* among their clientele and they attended beer parties and other celebrations in nearby neighbourhoods. Drinking with Mexicans encouraged sentiments of affiliation, which were instrumental in running the business and keeping their clients.

Thus, in addition to the obvious economic interests entailed, such encounters represent cultural interfaces where new social identities are forged and redefined. Furthermore, as Roberts and Spener (1994) suggest, the cross-border area itself becomes an integrated transnational space in which issues of identity are contested on the basis of common historical roots and everyday social interaction.

Maize husks enter the United States through a chain of traders who move the product through several hands to feed into the specialised border intermediaries who are *au fait* with the complicated US frontier import regulations as well as those of Mexico. The Mexican traders we interviewed all agreed that the first requisite for exporting is to have good contacts in the United States. 'Otherwise they will make you wait, and buy at very low prices.' To make a good deal a trader requires detailed information, not only on clients, prices and costs, but also pertaining to the workings of insurance companies in a foreign country (the US) and the criteria for defining quality.

Another example is the wholesale market in Monterrey, an industrial and big business city located within relatively easy distance of the US border and with close links therefore with the US economy. Tomás, a maize husk trader and exporter, owns a stall in this market, a central site for the commercialisation of maize husks in Mexico. Although there are only a few traders specialising in this product, they maintain strategic links to owners of the maize husk packing plants[15] as well as to intermediaries in the United States and Mexico. Tomás owns a small packing plant himself in the neighbouring state of Tamaulipas. Commenting on the difference between the Mexican and US customs posts, he explained:

> In Mexico we have the advantage – or the disadvantage – of having the same group of people in the shifts at the customs office. You know that your contact person will always be there at certain hours of the day, and in all likelihood will remain there for years, sometimes even a lifetime. Then posts get inherited if the person keeps his networks in good shape. Contacts are also inherited. My father passed his contacts on to me, and I often pass them on to friends. In the United States it is not like that. Sometimes you are lucky and you get the same person two or three times, but you never know who will be in the customs office.

Manoeuvring his way through the thicket of Mexican commercial risks and government restrictions is also a trial for Tomás: he will need to access information concerning the ins and outs of tax regulations and identify in advance any other possible hindrances. Here again, values and definitions are negotiated and contested. For example, the category of goods under which husks are to be classified is critical, since this determines the levy imposed on particular transactions. Because the maize husk industry is relatively new in Mexico and is not sizeable enough to be included in formal trade statutes, Tomás claims he is able to register his husks as 'unprocessed rural products' (*productos de campo no procesado*). Although husks do pass through a process of cleaning and classifying, he argues that they are not in fact processed, only packaged. Consequently he should not expect to pay Mexican tax on this. On the other hand, when dealing with the large supermarkets in Mexico, he will register his transactions under the 'fruit and vegetables' category, instead of 'groceries'. The reason for this is that Mexican supermarkets generally settle payments for fruit and vegetables within no more than two weeks, while for non-perishables they can delay up to three months.

Similar considerations are taken into account in transactions crossing the Mexico–US border. Negotiating the definition of the product and the classification under which it is to be regulated and commercialised depends then on the skills of the entrepreneur or broker, who must in the process also maintain good relations with bureaucrats and their secretaries.

Traders become experts at managing complex sets of social relationships, comprising not only face-to-face personalised encounters but also more distant institutional contexts that include a number of technical and administrative components, financial and other resources, and media-generated information and discourses. Throughout the process, organising capacity – whether at the level of decisions taken by small-scale traders or in terms of the coordinated actions carried out by consortia of transnational businesses – is crucial and involves the interlocking of diverse elements.

Debts and payments in the maize husk trajectory

We now turn to consider the other end of the commodity chain. The route followed by maize husks from the site of production to their commercialisation can be summarised in the following way. Maize is produced by farmers, or what are called *parceleros*,[16] it is harvested by *cortadores* (cutters), organised in squads by *cuadrilleros* (squad leaders) but paid for by packing plant owners, who also hire workers – mainly women – to clean and pack the husks. The husks are then sold to traders, of whom most own warehouses in the Guadalajara, Monterrey or Tijuana wholesale market places.

From there, husks can take three directions. Those that remain in Mexico are sold directly to enterprises specialising in the making of tamales, most of which are very small-scale, to artisans who transform them into craft work, and to supermarkets and other retailers. Some warehouse owners will directly export them to the United States. Exactly how much is exported we do not know, since the product crosses the Mexico–US border under different classifications and is not properly registered, but we calculate that more than 50 per cent of the product is exported. However, most of the warehouse owners prefer not to export the product themselves, since this is more costly and entails knowledge of the US markets, as well as the skills to deal with the customs authorities at the border. They thus leave this task to trading companies or specialised brokers, who may also move the product within different Mexican cities before crossing the border. Some of these companies have warehouses in the United States where they concentrate the product – always in combination with other products, which is not always the case in Mexico – and then distribute it to retailers or other distributors – mainly those who also pack and distribute Mexican food and spices. From here it goes to supermarkets and small-scale tamale enterprises and restaurants. Consumers in the United States are mostly Latinos, but also Americans and tourists.

Following the flow of credit/debt in the trajectory of maize husks yields interesting insights into the social relations of the transactions that take place. The following diagram illustrates such flows – albeit in simplified form. We have not included all possible flows since that would complicate the figure unduly. We have also left out consumption and the retail end on the Mexican side. The flows here are quite similar to those in the United States, except that in Mexico some distribution takes place at the packing plant itself, and the rest is deposited in the warehouses located in the wholesale market, from where it goes directly to retailers.

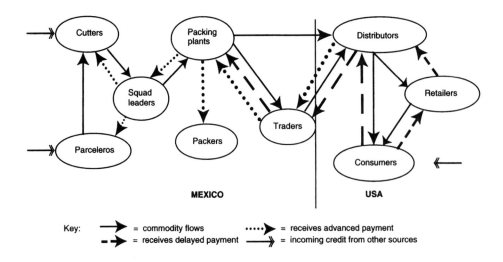

Key: → = commodity flows   ·····▶ = receives advanced payment
      ▪▪▶ = receives delayed payment   ──» = incoming credit from other sources

Figure 6.1 Commodity flows, payments and credit relations

As the diagram shows, a chain of debt can be traced from the *parceleros* and cutters all the way to the consumers. Debt, of course, or – as seen from the other side – credit, does not simply begin with the cutters and *parceleros*, since it is a circular process, outlined in more detail below.

The cutters, indebted to others in their villages, welcome payment in advance from the *cuadrilleros*, who need advanced payment in turn from the packing plant owners in order to cover these payments. The chain or circle continues, since the packing plant owners need advanced payment from the traders to cover such costs. In this section of the chain, what we see is mostly the need to secure links in order to guarantee a sufficient supply of quality products. In the next part of the chain, that of the traders and distributors, the form of credit/debt most resorted to is that of delayed payment. This manifests a different process of negotiation to that of advanced payment. For traders and distributors, there is a tension between the need to secure clients (thus allowing clients a degree of latitude regarding when they pay, and recognising their need for liquidity) and the need to secure better prices (and thus not be tied to a particular buyer through advanced payment). To make this possible, they must possess or be able to access enough liquid capital (often transferring cash from one line of business to another – hence the value of diversification), make use of delayed payment, and acquire debts through sources not related to the particular line of business.

Delayed payment is often a strategy used by retailers and medium-scale consumers, such as restaurants and small-scale tamale factories. Small-scale consumers incur debts through the use of credit cards and other similar means. Direct person-to-person debt is to be avoided whenever possible, and is mostly evident at the tail-ends of the network.

Debt and commitments in the interlocking livelihoods of cutters and cuadrilleros

Cutting husks is a heavy and risky activity and only those most desperate for work are willing to undertake it. They must rise early in the morning and finish picking the ears of corn before the sun is too high, because the husks will dry out and crack. They finish late in the afternoon, sometimes sleeping in the fields when far from their village. The *cuadrillero* knows that no one will last the whole season because of the nature of the work. Thus it is not easy to recruit labour and there is competition between *cuadrilleros* to secure the best cutters for their squads. *Cuadrilleros* earn a percentage of each kilo of husks delivered to the packing plant, and so they are eager to enrol the most experienced men. Although *cuadrilleros* can themselves establish the percentage they will take of each kilo, since they need to keep their men they stick to around 20 per cent of each cutter's production. On top of this, they try to keep their men happy by offering other perks. If the cutter is hard-working, the *cuadrillero* might establish *compadrazgo* – that is, fictive kin ties – with him and his family, to secure his loyalty. In general, *cuadrilleros* try to establish friendship ties with the men. They offer them drinks at work and sometimes at weekends. Drink makes the workload easier to handle, but they must be careful not to overdo it, since the task of cutting the husks off the maize cobs is a risky operation. Cutters must have a steady hand in order not to cut themselves on the metal cutting discs. Friendly gestures include being understanding of the men's problems, offering them rides in their vehicles, collecting a warm lunch from each cutter's home and bringing it to them on time, taking them hunting at night if they sleep in the field (and providing the guns and lamps to do so), and lending them money when the cutters face problems at home. Most *cuadrilleros* will also advance the cutter cash when the harvest is almost ready. Since harvesting takes place at the end of October/beginning of November, immediately after the 'bad months' (*los meses malos*), months when there are few possibilities for employment, day-labourers generally welcome the opportunity to cover their immediate debts. Tensions between cutters and *cuadrilleros* are partly over the possibility of securing the best workers for the longest period of time. The cutters need the advanced payment, but they want to be free to take other jobs when the opportunity arises.

Hence the transaction between *cuadrillero* and cutter is not only a matter of labour for money, but also concerns working conditions. A tentative equation would be something like: labour + loyalty on the side of the cutter = money + perks (including food, favours, alcohol, loans) + friendship + job security on the side of the *cuadrillero*. The value of the equivalences is a constantly negotiated issue. The cutter may complain, for example, that the alcohol provided is of poor quality and be inclined to desert his boss or use this to negotiate favours. The *cuadrillero*, in turn, will not offer the same gestures of friendship to all workers. For example, if conflicts arise, he will tend to favour the best workers, those he wants to keep for future seasons. He will also be more inclined to lend money to such workers, instead of to those he predicts will drop out.

Having said this, it is important to note that value equivalences are not always established in strict rational terms: *cuadrilleros* will often contract and favour a bad worker out of charity, loyalty to his kin or for religious or political reasons. This highlights the untidiness of social relations and the somewhat unpredictable nature of social and moral currencies. However, it is clear that it is in the non-monetary rewards that power relations and forms of resistance are generally established and identities and reputations weighed up, disowned, negotiated and drawn upon when applicable.

The cutters know in advance in which fields they will be working in the days ahead, and although not told, they quickly inform themselves about the quality of the harvest in those fields. Some of the cutters simply do not show up when they know the harvest is poor. It is said that this is why many *parceleros* offer them drinks as an incentive. This ensures that they harvest the maize with 'gusto' and do a proper job. Offering drinks is also linked to the tradition of celebrating the end of the maize harvest by recognising all the hard work put into it. Hence cutters have come to expect drink as part of their reimbursement. They speak of *cuadrilleros* who do not offer drinks as stingy, and may show little willingness to work for them in the next season. On the other hand, cutters have a reputation for being *borrachitos* (drunkards) because they go from one field to another throughout the season where they are offered drink. They start drinking in the fields, continuing at home and in the streets during weekends. In the eyes of local people, this reinforces their marginalised or stigmatised social position within the region and serves to mark cutting as a low-status activity, thus discouraging other day-labourers from engaging in it.

Livelihood issues and circuits of debt: the case of Manuel, a maize husk cutter

In August 1997, Manuel, one of the best maize husk cutters in the Autlán–El Grullo valley,[17] was already heavily indebted. He explained that he had found very few opportunities of work that summer, since the tomato companies that had been working in the valley had moved to other regions or been declared bankrupt. He had carried out a few odd jobs, had at times gone out to fish and, when he was lucky, had managed to earn a few *pesos*. He and his wife and children gleaned the fields for leftovers from the harvest – *repepenar* – and had been living on the maize collected[18] in this way. Manuel was never invited to harvest fresh maize, one of the most lucrative jobs for day labourers in the valley. This work is hard. Fresh corn is heavier than dried out maize, and they have to carry huge baskets of it on their backs – which they later empty directly into lorries to be traded the same day, before it loses its freshness. But the pay is good and only the younger, stronger men are invited, especially in summer, when less fresh corn is ready for harvesting in the region. Manuel recognises that his problem is in part due to his drinking habits. He says he likes to drink now and then, especially at weekends – at which point his wife interrupts angrily, saying that he often drank during the week as well. She pointed to maize on the cob piled in one of the rooms of their makeshift house, and explained that the pile had been growing smaller and smaller. She would sometimes degrain (*desgranar*) a few kilos and take it to the store to exchange it for salt, rice, cheese or milk, but had recently discovered that Manuel did likewise, in exchange for alcohol. Later she softened, and explained that it was difficult for him. He worked so hard that he had to let go and relax a bit. But it was even more difficult when he did not find work.

Manuel agreed with her, and blamed the government for the situation. Had he been granted a piece of land, Manuel insisted, his situation would have been different. Like most of the maize husk cutters, Manuel and his family live in *El Cacalote*, considered to be the poorest settlement in the valley because its inhabitants possess no land. Manuel himself was part of a group of land claimants who struggled for more than ten years in the hope of acquiring land under the Agrarian Reform. They gave up when their leader betrayed them and made deals with the government against the interests of the group. 'They virtually send us out to steal,' he said. 'They leave us no way out.' He immediately added that he was an honest man and did not steal, but that debts were practically driving them from their house. He had accumulated debts in two local stores. In one, his family was already denied credit, since not only had he not paid, but also the shop owner had discovered that his wife was buying in the other store and therefore refused to deal with them further. To the other, he paid off small amounts when he had money. This at least showed a willingness to pay and they continued to be able to get indispensable articles on delayed payment (*fiado*). He was no longer on speaking terms with his brother, who was tired of lending him money and not being repaid.

Thus, at the beginning of September 1997, Manuel received payment in advance from Juan, one of the youngest *cuadrilleros*, thus binding himself to work on the harvest as soon as the crop was ready. Manuel's urgent need for cash led him to overvalue the job, since he accepted a deal that was in some ways detrimental to him; that is, he agreed to work for this *cuadrillero* irrespective of the level of remuneration.[19] Although in theory he had the option to drop out if a better working opportunity came up later, in practice this meant paying off his debt to Juan first. And there was a moral commitment, since Juan had helped him out in time of need and he could not let him down, especially since he knew he would probably require him again the following year.

Manuel's case is illustrative of the various currencies, discontinuities and social commitments entailed in debt circuits. Due to his lack of land, his low status as a husk cutter and his lack of trustworthiness because of his drinking habits, it was difficult to get loans from moneylenders. In other words, he was excluded from this sphere for not possessing the right currencies; that is, the right moral, social and financial collateral. His sources of debt were thus his brother, the local stores and the *cuadrillero*. Kin networks usually do not require high status or land ownership to provide loans, but limits are generally placed on the failure to comply with moral standards; hence the breaking of relations with his brother.

Let us now, in the concluding part of this chapter, discuss a number of general issues that arise from the above ethnographic account.

Diverse meanings and multiple currencies

The significance of money as a medium of exchange differs according to the kinds of transaction involved, but money is never the sole value-determining currency. As we define it, the notion of 'currency' implies attempts to define and frame equivalences in value between specific commodities, goods and services (e.g., labour, information, provision of equipment and social contacts) and how these might be 'remunerated' or 'rewarded'.

Several issues need further exploration. In the first place, various currencies can be identified in money itself, such as cash deployed to lure or attract clients or partners, or used for gifts, advanced as credit, or used to oil relationships and offer perks. This movement of cash highlights the different modalities in which social identifications are constructed. For example, gifts move within particular kinds of relations, but do not operate in the same way as bribes. Also, in certain exchange circuits, cash may be tied up with calculative financial concerns, whereas in others it involves prestige and status issues. Related to this is the earmarking of money for special purposes whose categories are not treated as equivalent and therefore are not easily convertible from one into the other.[20] As Lave (1988) shows, households often process parts of their income into special compartmentalised funds ('stashes') which are set aside for particular types of expenditure, individual and collective.[21] Examples include rent money, school fees and funds for burials, weddings, Christmas and recreation. And the same applies to state and private institutions that decide to earmark some of their capital reserves for particular purposes such as contributions to charities or 'good causes', insurance and mutual-fund shares, and special educational and skill acquisition programmes. Some large firms have devised schemes to divide workers' wages into direct cash and voucher payments that can only be redeemed through making purchases at the company store.[22] These and many other similar examples of earmarking highlight the many ways in which the use of money is hedged around by moral and social concerns.[23] It is important to point out, however, that in emergencies, money put aside may be released to meet critical needs.

Earmarked money often moves in clearly defined circuits. For example, money may be set aside for gifts which move within certain kinds of relationships, implying notions of reciprocity and sometimes entailing inter-group affiliations. Bribes (which may also be earmarked) operate on different social and moral principles. In both cases money either directly changes hands or underpins the transactions, but the principles of reciprocation have different social, moral and often temporal dimensions. Gifts may not incur a direct obligation to reciprocate, although they are framed within some notion of reciprocation: take, for example, the giving of presents to relatives at Christmas or the delivery of company gifts to clients. Christmas gifts may in fact be evaluated by givers and receivers alike in terms of some calculation as to the monetary values involved, thus placing a moral or social pressure on people to reciprocate in equivalent value. Company gifts are somewhat different, in that the reciprocation by the client is not expected in equivalent money or goods, but rather is used to cement client/company relations. Such gifts are rarely described as bribes, though their intention is to facilitate further business. Hence the boundaries between gifts, bribes and perks are not always clear. In certain cultural contexts bribes are openly acknowledged and sometimes clearly earmarked in company and individual money management practices.

In yet another circuit or social sphere, cash accompanies the setting-up of social ties, as in the case of marriage arrangements, where money is gifted, or expected to be gifted, by specific categories of kin to the bride and/or groom or relatives. The main aim of this exchange is to cement the consanguineal and affinal links and obligations between the parties concerned. There is of course a wide variety of marriage systems that involve the gifting or exchange of money, goods and services, including the return of some or all of the assets invested in the marriage in the case of divorce.

Another area to explore is that of depositing money or borrowing from banks, moneylenders, savings associations or other private or public forms of enterprise. These institutions establish ground rules for depositing, accessing and withdrawing cash and for returns on investment. Clearly the criteria for the giving of loans or the making of advanced payments for goods are generally governed by the personal standing of the potential borrower. As we saw in the cases presented, such evaluations centre upon social notions of the 'trustworthy individual' – client or partner. Insurance brokers and their like also feature prominently in the management of commodity networks. The insurance function is particularly important in the case of the production and commercialisation of perishable products. This affects farmers and traders alike, especially those facing high-risk conditions occasioned by the uncertainties of harvest yields and the vicissitudes of competitive and sometimes unpredictable markets. While some farmers and traders may take out insurance policies to protect themselves, the majority take their chances and hope their social networks will bale them out. This latter strategy, of course, requires considerable ongoing investment in a wide range of social ties. These ties carry with them their own currency requirements, which range from providing unpaid labour for family members, to giving support to local political bosses, to making available trucks or other resources, to sponsoring major religious events or fiestas with all their financial and other implications. These various ways in which cash and security are managed involve a complex mixture of values and relationships, which in one way or another work towards the construction of viable market-embedded livelihoods.

A focus on these multi-stranded processes of exchange has three implications:

1 It helps to understand how apparently similar monetary valuations are earmarked and given different social and economic properties.
2 It shows how dissimilar social and monetary rewards can be judged equivalent. This results from the ways in which different currency circuits, clusters of relationships and goods are attributed specific meanings, priorities and weightings.
3 It draws attention to the incommensurabilities that lead to contests over relevant social values and equivalences.

Processes of decontamination

Money, in certain situations and circumstances, is hedged around by cultural values that pressure people into adopting ways of decontaminating or purifying money from market values.[24] The presence of money in relationships may be de-emphasised or 'cleansed' in order to shift the emphasis more towards the demands of existing kinship or friendship bonds and values. The opposite might also be the case, and relations of kinship denied in favour of market rationality. This is illustrated where kin or affinal relations are seen as a drain on the person's capital and resources, which leads him or her to impose conditions on access to these through charging interest on capital and a price for the use of resources. This can rupture, or certainly jeopardise, existing social relations. On the other hand, dealers and traders may firmly refuse to offer credit or loans in cash or kind to relatives or close friends, preferring instead to give it in the form of a gift. In this way, they avoid contaminating kin relations with market values and obligations. Sometimes such gift-giving operates as a calculative strategy to control the market relationship. Such patterns of behaviour stress the contest of values implicit in the functioning of multi-stranded relationships and cross-border confederations of enterprises and households (cf. Smith 1984 for an exploration of rural/urban confederations of households in Peru).

The framing of social currencies

Linked to these issues are the ways in which unequal and hierarchical relationships between commodity buyers and sellers are generated and maintained by existing interpretations of power. It is often assumed that power simply results from control over the market or economic resources. Power in the market is also sometimes seen as emanating from existing political positions and status hierarchies that lie outside the market. Both interpretations fall short, though, because they emphasise how externalities forge power relations. Thus, while recognising the interrelations of these different dimensions of power, we should instead give closer attention to the embedding of social, cultural and political relationships and resources within the social fabric of commodity relations in specific market places and at the sites of production and consumption. Relations of domination and power are inscribed and negotiated within the transactions and commodity networks that tie together the organisation of production, commerce and consumption. As we have argued earlier, the relations that develop entail an intermingling of many elements, not only those associated directly with negotiating the cost/value or price of the products and transactions entailed, nor with how status hierarchies may influence this process. Although these latter considerations must undoubtedly be taken into account, the parties to the negotiations have interests and draw upon meanings that extend beyond strictly economic or socio-political matters. The moneylenders and other local economic brokers, identified in the cases described above, live in a world full of pushes, pulls and balances between conflicting interests and obligations, where they often cannot simply apply the stick or carrot to persuade people to repay their debts. Indeed, it may be in their interests to extend credit to debtors in order to wield a measure of control.[25] A similar situation applies to the larger product distributors and trading companies that offer advanced payments for goods to help with production costs, while others delay payment until produce is delivered or sold. These various deals struck during the commercialisation process are founded upon the previous track records and other considerations of the individuals and companies involved. It is through the framing of these social currencies in relation to specific exchanges that meanings, reputations, partnerships and hierarchies are established or contested.

'Virtual money' or non-materialised cash

Although money is reckoned at the time of the transaction in units of dollars or other hard currencies, money is not always immediately materialised at the time of transaction, although presumably it must be so at some point. This is complicated by the fact that this 'virtual money' is often carried across several parties. At different junctures there is the potential to materialise the money on the books through payments given or received. Another variation of 'virtual money' is the idea people have of what a particular product might realise on the market after harvesting. People are aware that they have capital wrapped up here, but the materialisation is in the future, and is hypothetical. This idea of future money of course pertains not only to international financiers and to electronic digital stocks and 'futures', but also to the small-scale producer and entrepreneur.

However, whether wealth is virtual or real remains an ambiguous issue until, of course, events precipitate the need to define its nature. In markets where produce is bought and sold and continuously moving, and money likewise, one's wealth and credit standing will depend at any one moment on the social networks that one is involved in and the velocity of the bulk of commodities that passes through one's hands. Moreover, if there is a need at some point to assess how much in the way of financial assets one has, then such considerations such as the advance of the agricultural season, the maturity and quantity of produce and the availability of trucks, warehouse space, etc., will become critical. Such wealth, or its evidence, is then virtual in the sense that what actually has value are the contacts, their stability, and the commitments and reciprocities of network members, in local, national or international arenas, and the images by which their perceived wealth, collateral or ability to pay is portrayed. Here, calculations or predictions concerning future opportunities for exploiting or accessing wealth or economic resources must include the relevance of processes of building images and reputations. These processes are at the essence of what Bourdieu (1977: 171–82, 1990: 112–21) calls 'symbolic capital'.

The issue of money fetishism

A fuller appreciation of the role of money in market economies requires some discussion of the notion of 'money fetishism', which signals the reification of money at the expense of understanding how money is interwoven with other value components. Money fetishism leads to an over-concentration on aspects based on market rationality and economic cost/value calculations. This leads to the neglect of other modes of strategising and managing livelihoods and enterprise. Even though commodity networks are geared to the supply of goods and services, and prices and capital assets are represented in denominations of money, the organisation of production, trade and market transactions necessarily entails the combining of skills, knowledge, social relations and discursive practices. These various social factors are of critical significance for creating viable organisational solutions and for shaping economic performance. This remains true even when labourers, farmers, traders, distributors, retailers and consumers frame their activities and decision-making in terms of the maximisation of economic goals and benefits, which they measure or evaluate in monetary or quasi-monetary terms.

Undoubtedly then the 'power of the market' – the central rhetoric of neoliberalism – must find a place in our analysis; not as a self-evident fact of life, but rather as a set of images and ideas that invades the consciousness of actors and predisposes them towards seeking market/economic explanations for their present predicaments and future expectations. At the same time, these very same individuals and groups may also formulate or draw upon pre-existing counter-representations which may eventually or situationally serve to challenge the rationalisations and authority of certain 'dominant' discourses and interests embedded in the economic policies of the state and international agencies. These counter-representations are often grounded in everyday life experiences and draw upon values and social practices which, for various socio-historical reasons, have escaped from being fully 'colonised' by the idea of the market and by the oratorical skills of its protagonists. On the other hand, we must also note the paradoxical ways in which such counter-representations, linked as they are to ongoing everyday lifeworlds and modes of organising, may serve to sustain existing market relations.

Thus, as this chapter has attempted to show, the entanglement of relationships and values intrinsic to various types of exchange and commodity networks generates specific webs and chains of commitments that tie together specific actors, the arenas in which they operate and the framing discourses they draw upon. Adopting this analytical approach, we believe, allows for a better understanding of the nature of the multi-faceted bonds and patterning of currency circuits that constitute commoditisation processes.

7

NETWORKS, SOCIAL CAPITAL AND MULTIPLE FAMILY-ENTERPRISE

Local to global[1]

The reinvention of social capital

As I indicated in Chapter 6, social capital has recently re-emerged as a central concept for exploring the workings of the social fabric of markets, enterprise and civil society. By social capital is meant the 'capacity of individuals to command scarce resources by virtue of their membership in networks or broader social structures...[T]he resources themselves are not social capital, the concept refers instead to the individual's [and group's] ability to mobilise them on demand' (Portes 1995: 120). Hence social capital is embedded in a set of socially situated and culturally defined relations. These connections and commitments acquire particular significance once they are activated by specific actors in cooperation and/or competition with others in seeking to gain access to critical resources, or in attempting to deny or block access to others. Such resources encompass not only material or tangible benefits but also less tangible properties such as knowledge, skills, trust, shared values, organisational principles and representations.

Recent literature has used this notion of social capital to demonstrate the importance of networks in ordering new forms of flexible economic enterprise at the level of firms, business groups and regions (for an overview of these studies, see Powell and Smith-Doerr 1994: 385–91), and in relation to the social underpinning of market transactions and commodity forms by non-commodity values that stress the importance of trust and reciprocity in economic and political life (Granovetter 1985, Putnam 1993, 1995). A special issue of *World Development* (1996, edited by Peter Evans) examines these same issues across the divide between the public and private domains, emphasising the potential benefits of networks that span state and civil society, since 'synergy is produced by the intimate entanglement of public agents and engaged citizens' (Evans 1996a: 1036).

The idea of the social embeddedness of economic and political life and the significance of the mobilisation and deployment of social and organisational resources for the pursuit of economic and political goals is, of course, as old as the disciplines of economics, sociology and anthropology themselves. It boasts a distinguished pedigree that stretches back to the founding fathers (Adam Smith, Marx, Weber and Durkheim) as well as a long list of twentieth-century social theorists who have used the concept – of whom Polanyi (1944), Bourdieu (1980) and Coleman (1988, 1990) are perhaps the best known. As Coleman (1994: 170, 175–7) explains, the term 'social capital' first appeared in response to what were seen as the deficiencies of mainstream neo-classical economics which accorded 'little place for...social organisational elements, treating them merely as empirical disturbances to

132

theoretical predictions'. Social capital, it can be argued, facilitates the workings and repro-duction of the economy and polity, but, unlike economic capital, it cannot be consumed or depleted merely through use; instead, activating it is likely to increase its potency and generate increased possibilities for its continued utilisation.

In spite of these theoretical developments, social capital remains a broad, and at times an illusive or empty concept. In many studies it serves merely as a way to signal those social resources that are considered to be highly significant in the making of viable (or 'productive') economic, political and community attachments and organisation, thus adding social capital to the list of other forms of capital labelled 'economic', 'human' and 'symbolic' (Bourdieu 1980, 1986). Only in a few exceptional studies is there any attempt to dissect in detail how, in particular circumstances, certain institutions or networks are put to use as social capital in order to attain specific goals (see, e.g., Putman 1993, Portes 1995, Waldinger 1996).

Another shortcoming of the literature to date is the uneven treatment of different types and operational levels of social capital. There are a number of micro-level studies that document the advantages and opportunities achieved through membership of certain ethnic groups, churches, families and interpersonal networks (e.g., Long 1977a: 105–43, Bourdieu 1977, Lomnitz 1977, Lomnitz and Perez-Lizuar 1987, Waldinger 1986); Caroline Moser's World Bank Studies on responses to poverty and vulnerability in poor urban neighbourhoods (see Moser 1996, and Moser and Holland 1997); and a few regional- or national-level studies that elucidate the differential benefits of membership of particular civic, regional or national cultures and networks (Putnam 1993, 1995; Fukuyama 1995). But the challenge remains of specifying more precisely the nature and significance of forms of social capital at different levels and in different social arenas, and how these varied forms may interact.

A further serious limitation in many discussions is the almost celebratory conviction that the acquisition of social capital is always positive; in fact, the more the better. Social capital entails 'networking', 'cooperation', 'building trust relations' and the like, while 'competition', 'conflict', 'exclusion' and the historical liabilities of particular forms of social capital are conspicuously put to one side and ignored. Thus there is an almost inherent blindness to the conflictive and unequal nature of social capital (see Portes and Landolt 1996, Putzel 1997, and Harriss and de Renzio 1997: 926, for accounts of its nega-tive aspects). Social capital is also frequently discussed in a gender-neutral way, when it is abundantly clear that asymmetries in gender relations (such as those shaped by class and race difference) affect the capacity for social action, thus giving a particular configuration to networks, forms of knowledge and identity and social position. Thus, as Moser (1996) points out, although norms, trust and reciprocity networks may facilitate certain forms of cooperation in a community, women are often affected differentially depending on the time they can devote to voluntary community activities because of their need to secure income for the family.

Another blind spot is the almost deliberate ignorance of a vast body of previous social research that has already contributed importantly to the understanding of the phenomena and dimensions, now 'revealed' under the rubric of social capital, without ever using the term. Such amnesia is clearly counterproductive and underlines the urgent need to identify more explicitly the types of problems and areas of research where the notion of social capital can fruitfully be used to open up new insights and lines of analysis.

In the present chapter I explore networks and social capital through an analysis of the history of one highland Peruvian family and its multiple enterprise. Although the original case material for this account was collected in the 1970s, well before the recent explosion of literature on social capital, clearly many of the processes identified bear directly on current debates. In a postscript I update the case to include the period up to 1998, which allows us to appreciate the transformations in the enterprise and family relations over a thirty-year trajectory.

Multiple enterprise

One ubiquitous feature of poorer economies and of certain sectors of more affluent societies is the phenomenon of multiple occupations or enterprise; that is, the simultaneous participation of individuals or groups in more than one branch of economic activity. This tendency towards economic diversification has been explained by reference to the structural conditions associated with situations where resources are scarce, fragmented and disproportionately distributed. Early studies suggested that multiple job holding was a feature of 'transitional' societies experiencing incipient industrialisation and a rapidly expanding opportunity structure, or that it reflected the essentially multi-structural character of underdevelopment, where non-capitalist modes of production persisted alongside, and were functionally related to, the dominant capitalist mode. Other interpretations of multiple enterprise have focused more specifically on the particular life situations and interests of the social categories in question. For example, it is contended that members of elite groups develop diversified investment portfolios in order to optimise their control over basic financial, commercial, and industrial resources, whereas poorer people, who also spread their more limited assets over several fields, do so in order to reduce risk and supplement their inadequate incomes.

While such interpretations have the merit of placing the phenomenon of multiple occupations in some macro- or micro-structural context, we often lack the detailed data to show precisely how particular social categories of actors build the necessary networks of relationships for combining or switching between economic activities or occupations. No individual, whether a poor urban worker, a peasant struggling to make ends meet, or an entrepreneur wishing to expand his businesses, has a ready-made matrix of relationships and investments that remains constant over time. Even those who inherit businesses or occupations from their parents or other kin must, during the course of their economic careers, reconstitute and modify the sets of relationships involved.

The aim of this chapter, then, is to develop an analysis of economic careers that combine different fields of activity and investment. A second point of interest is that of examining the usefulness of viewing social networks as repositories of social capital. The argument is elaborated by reference to data (collected in the 1970s) on one family-based multiple enterprise in the central highlands of Peru, focusing on what Ansoff (1965) has called 'strategic decisions' which lead to the emergence of new branches of production or business. The final part of the chapter describes the structural conditions associated with such careers and updates the family history. It shows how, within the space of one generation, education and migration to the United States have facilitated the pursuit of new, more specialised, but still family-based entrepreneurial careers, as well as professional livelihoods.

Social networks and economic careers

A central issue running throughout the case study is the question of how social networks give direction to economic careers and influence decisions to combine or switch between branches of economic activity. I am especially interested in showing how specific social networks, once established, become a constraint as well as a positive influence on future decisions. New economic investments emerge out of a set of social investments in personal relations, which themselves generate new or modified sets. A person's ability to combine different branches of economic activity and to develop certain entrepreneurial careers is thus crucially affected by the content of existing personal networks. Such networks are significant not only because they may provide access to essential resources such as capital or labour, but also for the flow of information and for the support they may offer for various courses of action. Certain aspects of a person's network may be pre-selected by family and community background, but other aspects must be developed from scratch, such as those based on friendship or occupational criteria.

In earlier papers (1972, 1973, 1977: 122–8) I discussed the management of interpersonal relations based on kinship, *compadrazgo*, and other ties in the running of small businesses in the central highlands of Peru. I also explored the operational requirements and types of networks associated with running particular enterprises, showing how these networks were established and sustained. A third theme was the analysis of the mechanisms by which entrepreneurs attempted to increase the predictability of outcomes of specific relationships by injecting into them extra normative and symbolic contents (e.g., associated with membership of specialised clubs and participation in fiesta activities, see Laite and Long 1987). This they hoped would create a higher degree of trust or specificity in the exchanges that took place between the parties concerned. This chapter considers the broader problem of how networks influence both the setting up of new branches of economic activity and the types of economic careers pursued.

The earlier work of Anthony Leeds (1964) on Brazilian social careers provides some valuable points on how to develop such a perspective. The main focus of Leeds's analysis is an identification of the mechanisms by which people advance their political and economic careers, giving particular attention to the higher status levels of Brazilian society. One of his conclusions is that patterns of informal organisation based on personal ties are critical at every promotional level. These ties are loosely established in groups sharing a common interest. Usually, they represent a roster of all key socio-political and economic positions. Such groups, *panelinha*, are operative at every level in the national hierarchy, so that the ambitious and successful leader must pass through a number in succession. He must, in addition, spread his tentacles out into differing fields of activity, thus keeping in touch with the potentialities of various types of social resource. Involvement in several niches or jobs at once is characteristically described in Brazil as *cabida de emprego*, the 'employment hanger'.

Leeds goes on to suggest that for each person there are specific 'springboards' or 'trampolines' that will project him or her into new branches of activity and into new levels of control and influence. These springboards consist of such ties as family, kinship, *compadrazgo*, politico–bureaucratic affiliations, commercial and industrial connections, and recreational and educational bonds. A major task for the ambitious, therefore, is to establish the right network of contacts that will propel them into a more widely spread and influential circle – something they hope to accomplish by cultivating and publicising a positive image of themselves and their capabilities. In the early and middle stages of a career, this normally entails investment in an ever-widening network of ties so that the sources of support can be multiplied to cover a wide spectrum of contingencies. They will also aim to build around themselves a 'tactical corps of supporters or aides ("a little church")' (Leeds 1964: 1336). If successful, they will later join a *panelinha*, composed of a body of individuals sharing roughly equivalent power and status, and hope then to move through a hierarchy of such informal networks at municipal, state and federal levels (cf. Shirley 1971).

Leeds's discussion relates primarily to political careers at the regional and national levels. It describes a system probably far more structured and hierarchical than that of other Latin American situations. None the less, his analysis raises considerations that are highly suggestive for the study of social careers in general. The notion of springboards is particularly useful as it directs attention towards the identification of major sets of relationships that become available to individuals at certain stages in their careers, and which subsequently provide the means by which they are able to initiate new branches of activity. These relationships may be based on a variety of membership criteria (e.g., kinship, friendship, or political and religious affiliations) and be characterised by different types of transactions and social investments. Important foci for analysis, then, concern the conditions under which these relationships emerge; how they are maintained, consolidated and manipulated to achieve desired ends; and how they serve to promote career prospects or send one off in some unexpected direction.

On the other hand, involvement in a specific network of relationships may carry with it some negative consequences for career mobility, since dependence on particular relationships will tend to impose boundaries or limits on certain actions or rule out some decisions. Hence it may be necessary at critical times in a career to seek actively to reduce or repudiate sectors of one's effective network. Also individuals may fail to recognise fully the opportunities available and find themselves immobile and encapsulated within a specific set of relationships. An understanding of the processes by which people spin new webs of relationships, shake off old ones or remain trapped in highly involuted networks remains central to the analysis of careers. As I stressed earlier, my main emphasis here is on viewing changes in economic careers as resulting from prior investment in certain networks of social relationships as opposed to interpreting such changes as the direct outcome of rational or purposive choice.

Multiple enterprise in Matahuasi: the case of the Jiménez family

In developing my argument, I examine the history of one multiple enterprise based in the village of Matahuasi, a settlement of some 4,000 inhabitants located in the Mantaro Valley of the central highlands of Peru. Besides agriculture – its major form of livelihood – Matahuasi has an important commercial and transport sector. It has close connections with Lima, which is a five-hour drive by all-weather road, and with the Cerro de Pasco mining towns, especially La Oroya.

The Mantaro Valley itself is one of the largest highland valleys of Peru and a primary source of foodstuffs for Lima-Callao. It is predominantly a *minifundia* (smallholder) zone specialising in the production of maize, grains, potatoes, vegetables and livestock products. Attempts have been made to develop a high-quality milk industry. In addition, certain villages are well known for both traditional and modern craft products, which are sold either in the Sunday market or *feria* of Huancayo, the main city of the region, or directly to Lima-based export agencies. Huancayo acts as the administrative and service centre of the area, and, situated at the south end of the valley, is the gateway to the highland cities of Huancavelica, Ayacucho, and Cuzco.

Matahuasi is in the middle of the valley on the main road from Huancayo to La Oroya, which continues to Lima and the coast. Partly because of its location, the village boasts a fairly substantial commercial and transport capacity that serves not only its immediate environs but also spreads out to capture some of the business of the mine and coastal towns. Over the last century Matahuasi has become increasingly integrated into the regional and national economy. Its response to the opportunities brought by the development of mines and the growth of Huancayo has always been positive. A great number of Matahuasi residents have migrated to various towns and cities and they constitute one of the two largest populations of valley-born natives in Lima. In the last twenty years this flow of migrants has expanded to cover various locations in the United States and Europe.

Family background and early work history

Eustaquio Jiménez was born in 1909 of humble parentage. His father was reputed to have been a bandit who operated in the southern part of the Mantaro Valley but who in later years devoted himself to small-scale trading of agricultural produce. His mother came from Matahuasi. During the last part of their lives, Eustaquio's parents settled in Matahuasi, and made their living by purchasing small quantities of vegetables and transporting them by horse or donkey to the ferias (weekly markets) in the nearby towns of Jauja and Concepción. His father owned no land and his mother only a very small plot which she had inherited.

Both parents died when Eustaquio was young and so his mother's kin in Matahuasi looked after him and his elder brother and sister, Isabel. The children never knew their kin on their father's side of the family. The small plot of land and the house left by the mother were inherited by the eldest, Isabel. The others were left to fend for themselves. Eustaquio's brother, Eduardo, migrated to Lima to find work, where he remained and eventually opened a small carpenter's workshop. When Eustaquio was ten he went to live with his mother's brother, Maximo, a livestock trader who worked between the valley and the mining towns. The mining company was installing a new copper smelter at La Oroya and had recruited a large labour force, for which regular food supplies were needed. Maximo seized the opportunity and set himself up as a butcher and cattle trader. Later, through a series of crucial investments, he rose to become a prominent commercial and political figure in La Oroya. Eustaquio at first stayed in Matahuasi working as Maximo's herdsboy, but later participated in the transportation and sale of cattle. With his uncle's help, Eustaquio was able to finish his primary education in Matahuasi, after which he spent one year at secondary school in Huancayo.

During these early years Eustaquio learned the livestock and butchery business. Maximo had cornered a large share of the meat market in La Oroya, and had opened a butcher's shop and several stalls in the markets. As Eustaquio gained in experience, he purchased, again with assistance from Maximo, a few head of cattle for himself and thus began his own small-scale transactions. Then in the late 1920s he married Juana Meza, a woman from Matahuasi, with Maximo acting as *padrino* (sponsor) to the marriage. Shortly after the wedding, Eustaquio and Juana moved to Malpaso, a small mining town near La

Oroya, where, through the uncle's business, Eustaquio already had some contacts. His experience with livestock trading helped to establish him as a meat supplier in Malpaso, while his wife opened a small canteen for mineworkers. This was especially opportune, as there were few comparable facilities in Malpaso at the time and a growing mine population. The canteen was initially financed by capital from the livestock business, though Juana's parents, themselves business people who traded in meat and vegetables, also helped out. Together, the parents-in-law and the uncle provided Eustaquio with the main contacts for the formation of a network of relationships with traders who came from different parts of the central highlands. Several of these early friendships and business partnerships became important for him at later stages in his career.

The move to invest in agriculture

A year or two after opening his businesses in Malpaso, Eustaquio rented four hectares of land in Matahuasi and, with the help of his sister Isabel, he planted maize and potatoes, returning with his wife Juana to help out during the harvesting seasons. Whenever necessary, they would also hire labour. His interest in acquiring land was related in part to the deteriorating employment situation in the mines during the years of the Great Depression. Between 1929 and 1932, Cerro de Pasco Copper Corporation was forced to lay off a third of its labour force. Copper production, which had been steadily expanding throughout the First World War and the 1920s, reached its peak in 1929, but in 1930 world copper prices slumped dramatically. This led to a major crisis in the copper industry. Malpaso and other small mines were completely shut down, and this was followed by a severe reduction in the La Oroya labour force and, early in 1931, by the closure of the mines at Casapalca. This situation had severe repercussions for the many traders and small businessmen who had thrived during the beginning phases of mine expansion. Several businesses went bankrupt while the rest had to operate with much-reduced levels of income. Eustaquio's investment in agriculture helped to compensate for the loss of both clientele and income and ensured that, despite fluctuations and uncertainties of urban income, subsistence needs could be met. The farm also gave support to his sister, who, barely making ends meet on her small plot of land, had to work as an agricultural labourer for part of the year.

For the next five years, Eustaquio and his wife combined commerce with small-scale farming and spent time regularly in Matahuasi. In 1937, Eustaquio learned of the Church's intention to sell its land in the valley. The prospect of obtaining freehold rights over land appealed to him, especially since the plot he then rented was in fact Church property which he thought might be put up for sale. He immediately travelled to Huanuco for discussions with Church authorities. It was important for him to act quickly since several others were also interested. The Church finally agreed to sell the property, and Eustaquio had to raise 3,200 soles[2] for approximately four-and-a-half hectares of unirrigated land.

Although he had some cash of his own, he was short of the full amount. His first thought was to ask Maximo, his maternal uncle, for a loan, but relations between them were strained at the time, as the separation of their business interests, which occurred after Eustaquio's marriage, had indirectly affected Maximo's own entrepreneurial plans. So Eustaquio instead went to another maternal uncle, Enrique, with whom he had more distant, yet friendly ties. Enrique, also a trader operating between the valley and the mines, agreed to advance him some of the capital, though it is not known exactly how much. Eustaquio was thus able to conclude the deal with the Church with a downpayment of 900 *soles* and the rest to be settled over the next two years. The contract was signed and sealed on July 17 1937 in nearby Jauja.

Both Eustaquio and his wife worked energetically at their various occupations to clear the debt. Their efforts were aided by the generally improving economic situation in the mine towns in the late 1930s as the international economy began to revive. They built themselves a small house in Matahuasi with the intention of returning later to take up full-time agriculture. By 1940 they had managed to pay off the outstanding debt and were ready to return. Their decision to settle permanently in Matahuasi and devote their time to agriculture rather than trade marked a major shift in economic career. In retrospect, Eustaquio gives as the main reasons for returning his wishes to take charge of managing his own land, to educate his several children (the facilities in the valley being generally superior to those in other places), and to live in a more agreeable climate. The mine towns were located at an inhospitably high altitude. The land he purchased was well sited – close to the main Huancayo–La Oroya–Lima road then under construction, and to the railway line. It was also situated near a tributary of the Mantaro River from which water could easily be tapped to irrigate the fields.

The late 1930s to early 1940s was a unique period in the agrarian history of the Mantaro Valley. It was the first time in a hundred years that sizeable plots of land were available for purchase. Land registry data in Huancayo since 1900 show very little turnover of any land for sale. The Church's decision to dispose of its landholdings in different communities throughout the valley was thus a once-in-a-lifetime opportunity, which Eustaquio and seventeen other Matahuasinos seized. It is significant that all eighteen purchasers had worked outside the valley and had accumulated sufficient savings to make the investment.

During this second phase of Eustaquio's career, it became essential for him to build a network of dependable relationships in his village of origin. This was important for two reasons. In the first place, he needed a reliable set of ties that could be activated whenever he required labour at harvest or other peak periods. Second, he wished to establish a reputation for himself that would bring some community esteem, thus making his task easier.

Investment in agriculture, however, brought with it a number of unintended and possibly unpredictable consequences. Eustaquio's rapid rise to landowner status was interpreted by many as the result of his discovering *tapado* (buried treasure from the colonial period). They were unwilling to attribute his success to virtue or hard work. His was the luck of a bandit's son, they said, and therefore illegitimate. This prejudice was later reinforced by the conflict that developed between Eustaquio and the community over the purchase of Church land. The dispute centred on the complicated legal issue of ownership, since the Church had over a long period of time accumulated its land through bequests from village people. The land became associated with various local saints and was administered by *cofradias* (religious brotherhoods). Thus, although the title of ownership rested with the Church, it was the community itself, through its *cofradias*, that worked the land and used its production to finance religious fiestas and the upkeep of the saints' images. Consequently, it was argued that the selling of these landholdings to private individuals was illegitimate and against the interests and wishes of the community.

A long-standing legal battle ensued between the community and the purchasers, and in the 1970s it gained renewed vitality with the possibility of the community reclaiming the lands under the Agrarian Reform introduced by President Velasco's military government, which gave the community a new legal status, that of *comunidad indígena* (indigenous community). Litigation had cost the community enormous sums of money for legal advice, but with no positive result. Adjudication always favoured the Church since the Church was able to produce the title deeds. Moreover, at the time of the sales, the *comunidad indígena* did not exist formally as a recognised legal entity (for details, see Winder 1974: 81–91; also Long and Winder 1975).

This dispute produced major social divisions within the village, polarising the poorer households and the larger farmers, many of whom had acquired their holdings through purchasing Church land. For Eustaquio the situation was particularly acute because at various times he even found himself in direct confrontation with his two maternal uncles. In the year preceding the commencement of litigation by the community, Eustaquio had been associated with Maximo and Enrique in an abortive attempt to establish in Matahuasi a consumer cooperative modelled on similar ventures undertaken by the nearby village of Muquiyauyo (Adams 1959). Later, however, these two uncles, who were concurrently Mayor of the municipality and President of the newly founded *comunidad indígena*, became deeply involved in initiating the litigation to reclaim Church land, in direct opposition to their nephew and his fellow purchasers. Under these circumstances it was inevitable that Eustaquio's relationship with his uncles would become strained.

Eustaquio's decision to invest in land, then, led to a lengthy struggle with the local politico-administrative authorities, to the souring of relationships with his maternal kin, and to a gradual disaffection with community affairs. Neither he, nor any of the Jiménez family, has ever held office in local government. His only claim to public service was a period as President of the Parents–Teachers association of the local school, when he helped to raise funds for the construction of a new school building. Later in life he also helped to mobilise funds to finish off the rebuilding of the main church which long before had burnt down.

Eustaquio's difficulties with the authorities and the people of the village were further compounded when he took over a small piece of land close to the main road and adjacent to one of his other plots. The municipality claimed the land was its property and so Eustaquio was accused of alienating it for his own purposes. Taking over the small plot was part of his plan to build a petrol station on the main road through the village.

An expanding agricultural enterprise

Eustaquio's career in Matahuasi was marked by a pattern of gradual diversification and shifts in various activities. At first he concentrated on agriculture, growing maize, potatoes, barley, carrots and other vegetables using his own and his wife's labour, with occasional help from his sister and hired hands for sowing and harvesting. When his children were old enough, they also took part. Each year he marketed his surplus to Lima, transporting it in hired lorries. This marketing was greatly assisted by the fact that his parents-in-law had expanded their trading business into an agricultural intermediary enterprise with sales outlets in Lima. Some of Eustaquio's earnings were later invested in the purchase of dairy cattle, and so he began to move into milk production as well.

During this phase he was a bold agricultural innovator. He experimented with alfalfa, trebol and natural grass in the same field to produce a better quality food mix for the cattle and consequently achieved much better milk yields. He also experimented with the intercropping of barley and carrots. These crops were grown exclusively for the Lima market and, with irrigation from the nearby river, he could produce two harvests per year.

Eventually he rented an additional two hectares of farmland from a neighbouring farmer who had also purchased Church land but was not fully utilising it.

In addition to agriculture and livestock husbandry, Eustaquio built an artificial pond with water channelled from the nearby river and stocked it with fish. Within four years he had raised several thousand fish which he sold locally. This and other farming investments were supported by a loan from the Agricultural Development Bank, guaranteed by his four-and-a-half hectares of land at 9 per cent interest. The loan totalled 50,000 *soles* and took him five years to repay.

The Jiménez family spent fifteen years developing the farm and its various branches of production. Despite frequent problems with labour recruitment – always a source of uncertainty – Eustaquio was able to achieve high levels of productivity and a balanced system of production. In 1952 the government of Peru awarded him a gold medal and 20,000 *soles* for his work as the best farmer of the central region of the country. The award was presented by President Odria himself at the Presidential Palace in Lima. Eustaquio used the prize money to establish yet another branch of his enterprise – one that would eventually shift the balance of his interest away from farming and back into commerce.

Restaurateur and garage owner

On the property close to the main road, Eustaquio opened a restaurant and bar. It took four years to construct the building and to make everything ready. His wife, having run a similar but smaller business in Malpaso, managed the restaurant and organised the kitchen, while the elder daughter, Hilda, was made responsible for its general administration. Eustaquio continued to supervise work on the farm, which had become increasingly concentrated on milk production. He was assisted by his three teenage sons, who herded the cattle and cultivated the alfalfa. Requiring less labour than crops, milk production was developed in response to the growing problems of labour supply, since few local peasant families would work for him if they could get employment elsewhere. He was unpopular due to his isolation from the community over the land litigation issue, and had acquired a reputation as an authoritarian employer who underpaid his workers.

While the bulk of the livestock and agricultural produce from the farm was traded in Lima and the valley markets, the farm also provided food items for the restaurant. A regular feature of the menu was trout from their own fish farm. On weekends this attracted large numbers of visitors from Huancayo and Jauja. The restaurant quickly became a popular location for dining out for the middle classes of Huancayo and other valley towns. It was strategically situated midway between Huancayo and Jauja, and in the late 1950s there were few rival establishments. A temporary setback occurred in 1960 when the trout experiment was suddenly and tragically brought to an end. One morning Eustaquio discovered all his fish floating dead on the surface of the pond. Evidence suggested that they had been poisoned in the night by, as he put it, 'his enemies in the pueblo'. He never kept another fish.

Hilda, his eldest daughter, turned out to be an exceptionally able administrator and became well known throughout the valley for the dinner dances and receptions she arranged. The restaurant was so successful that it became necessary to take on additional help. Hilda worked for her father for twelve years, but eventually quit to attend to her young children and to start a small shop of her own. In retrospect, she complains that she had no real share in the restaurant business and was only given pocket money. The profits, she claims, together with the income from the farm, were used primarily to educate Jiménez' sons, her brothers, of whom several completed secondary school.

Hilda's mother tried to take over the restaurant administration and dealings with the customers. She struggled at the task for three years but gradually the quality of service suffered and the clientele diminished. The work and problems involved were more than Eustaquio's ageing wife could handle, and as a solution Eustaquio decided to rent the restaurant for 900 *soles* a month to his son Atilio. Atilio was less educated than the other sons, had no specific occupation, was married, and had a rapidly expanding family. He and his wife took over the restaurant but, faced with growing competition from new restaurants along the road, they failed to attract customers and so instead he set up what later became a successful transport business based in Matahuasi.

It was at this juncture that Eustaquio launched yet another branch of business. He opened a petrol station, which he saw as a natural extension of the restaurant since lorry drivers could be encouraged to stop and have a meal after they filled their tanks. The idea for the petrol station originated in 1957 in conversations with a friend in Huancayo who knew the garage business well. This friend happened to be the Prefect of Huancayo, a man with whom Eustaquio had first become friends during the legal difficulties with the community. However, it was not until 1961 that the new project got off the ground. A large loan was needed to finance the building of the pumps and tanks. The total loan, eventually obtained from the Industrial Bank, amounted to 1.5 million *soles* to cover the costs for the construction of the petrol installations and the purchase of two petrol tankers. A loan application for a sum of this magnitude required the careful preparation of financial estimates and a presentation of the economic viability of the project. In this Eustaquio was ably assisted by the Prefect, who had the necessary professional and political connections in government and banking circles in Huancayo, and by an old school friend in Matahuasi, a trained accountant, who had worked at one time for a garage in the valley and knew first-hand the problems of running a petrol station.

Even with finance secured and installations completed, the opening of the station was delayed because of a conflict between Eustaquio and the local municipality over the siting of the pumps, which they claimed were illegally on land that was owned by the district. The dispute continued for two years, after which Eustaquio was finally taken to court and ordered to pay a fine. During this time he had applied to the provincial government for an operating license. With a change of municipal authorities and the election of a new Mayor – a distant relative of Eustaquio through his mother's family and a member of the same political party (APRA, *Alianza Popular Revolucionaria Americana*) – the problem was quickly resolved.

The large investment necessitated by the construction of the petrol station and the purchase of tankers meant that the Jiménez family was for some seven years weighed down by heavy loan repayments. Eustaquio says that this kept the garage from showing much of a net profit until about 1969. He then began to enjoy a fair degree of financial success, owning by 1972, in addition to the two tankers, a Volkswagen car and pickup truck. His son Atilio was given charge of one of the tankers and made responsible for its operation and maintenance. His daughter Hilda was then running her own small shop and managed jointly with her father the petrol station, the farm, the restaurant and other assets. The main emphasis of the enterprise, however, shifted from the restaurant and farm to the development of the petrol business. Eustaquio now had a set of regular contracts for the transportation of petrol, diesel and paraffin from Lima to various garages and commercial establishments in Huancayo and other valley towns. At his Matahuasi garage he was beginning to put together a spare parts service.

By 1972 the organisation of the Jiménez family enterprise was as shown in Genealogy 1, which also shows key kin and affines and details of the occupations and places of residence of the children. From this it can be seen that Eustaquio's kinship network contains within it several important entrepreneurial families.

The influence of interpersonal networks on investment behaviour

Earlier I stressed the ways in which economic careers and strategic decisions are influenced by the evolution of networks of interpersonal ties – important for the flow of information and mobilisation of resources. The case of Eustaquio illustrates this point well, for at each stage in the development of the enterprise he became enmeshed in a slightly different matrix of social relationships which opened up new sources of information, assistance and capital. Indeed, his whole career profile can be interpreted as the outcome of successive changes in the pattern of interpersonal ties based on kinship, affinity, friendship and locality.

In the initial phase, Eustaquio was closely involved as a dependent worker with maternal kin who were emerging as important traders and businessmen in the nearby mine towns. In transactional terms, Eustaquio's labour was offered in return for his keep and educational expenses. This period of dependence was significant for several reasons. First, he acquired information and expertise, which later proved beneficial when he sought to establish his own business. Second, it brought him into contact with his future wife and in-laws, who were also trading in the same towns of the region. After marriage he was able to consolidate this set of affinal ties and, together with his previous contacts, spin a wider web of commercial ties. It was this network that determined the direction his investments took in the ensuing years.

The next stage was marked by his decision to rent land in the home community. Although his economic activities were located mainly in Malpaso, the buying of cattle and other products necessitated regularly travelling to the Mantaro Valley and to nearby areas to build a clientele. In this way he was able to keep channels of information open at the village level, and so, when land became available for renting, he was quick to hear of it. On one of these trips he learned early of the possibility of purchasing land from the Church. Eustaquio's situation, in this regard, differed somewhat from that of his two uncles, who had concentrated on developing their businesses in La Oroya and the mine towns and were not so closely involved with peasant production in the Mantaro Valley. Most of their contracts, in fact, were with the haciendas of the Cerro de Pasco Corporation, not with the smaller-scale peasant producers. It is also clear that marrying a local girl, whose family both traded and farmed, was crucial for orienting Eustaquio towards land investment and to permanent residence in Matahuasi.

Their return to Matahuasi to take up farming full-time could have resulted in a dense network of local ties with various sectors of the population. But instead, whole areas of social relationships were gradually closed off to them. The land they had bought was originally cofradia property associated with the Catholic saints, which the majority of residents regarded as inalienable community assets. This was an emotionally charged issue, which isolated Eustaquio and the other purchasers from the rest of the village. He also antagonised the municipality over the siting of his petrol station and his takeover of land that was unused but

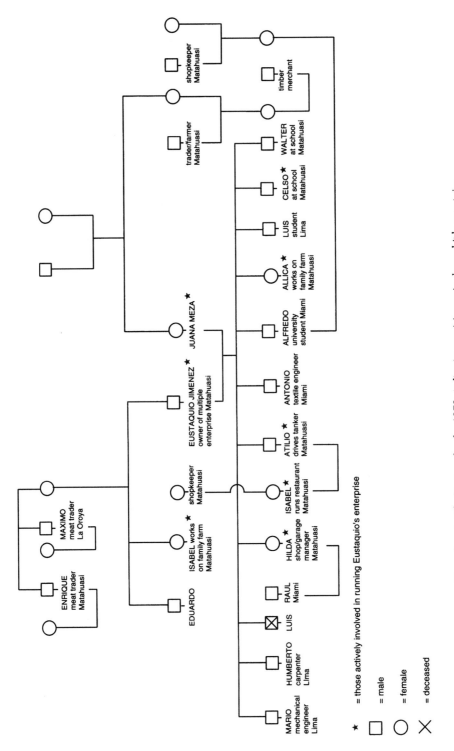

Genealogy 1: The Jiménez family, 1972, indicating participants in the multiple enterprise

officially under its jurisdiction. These problems were symptomatic of his generally poor and deteriorating social relations within the village, which threatened to affect seriously the running of his farm since he faced constant uncertainties over labour recruitment and over whether the community would win its legal case against him and confiscate his land. He had also acquired a reputation as a tough entrepreneur who exploited his employees.

These difficulties affected Eustaquio's participation in community affairs. At no time did he hold office in local government or take a prominent part in organising local fiestas. Even his relations with consanguineal kin were prone to conflict. He experienced major disputes with his two maternal uncles, Maximo and Enrique, who often found themselves supporting the village against the private landowners of the district. Maximo and his brother had always been interested in competing for political status and had held office in local government both in Matahuasi and La Oroya, and when Maximo became too old to participate actively, he devoted time to furthering his son's political ambitions. Eustaquio tried his best to maintain manageable relations with Maximo and publicly manifested this once a year when he assisted him at the fiesta of Candelaria for which Maximo had been responsible for thirty years. Only during fiesta entertainments was there any attempt to reaffirm family solidarity, and this was very short-lived.

Over the years Eustaquio had little contact with his brother in Lima whom he occasionally visited. On the other hand, Eustaquio maintained continued good relations with his sister who helped on the farm. His links with his wife's kin constituted the most secure sector of his network and it was with them that he interacted most frequently in business and recreational contexts. His most successful attempt to build new linkages in Matahuasi was through the marriage of his son Alfredo to the daughter of the largest shopkeeper in the village, Acosta. Acosta was from Arequipa, southern Peru, and married to a Matahuasi woman. He had an extensive set of ties with commercial and professional people both in the valley and elsewhere, and, like Eustaquio, remained somewhat aloof from local affairs.

With the deterioration of his social relations in the village, Eustaquio was pushed into developing new types of external ties. This first arose because of his need for legal advice and administrative support in his disputes with the community. Gradually he established a network of links with lawyers and members of APRA (*Alianza Popular Revolutionaria Americana*) who held important positions at the regional level. During the late 1950s and 1960s, APRA dominated the politics of the Mantaro area and represented a broadly-based rural bourgeoisie composed of farmers, businessmen and middle-class professionals. It was in this context, then, that Eustaquio sought to align himself with persons outside Matahuasi who might recognise his entrepreneurial talents and give him support. Several of these new-found friends became godparents to his children and were thus tied to him through *compadrazgo* (co-parenthood) relationships. As I have argued elsewhere (Long 1973), *compadrazgo* in highland Peru takes two basic forms. It can be used to select relationships of special significance out of an existing kin or affinal network; or it can be used to create a set of strategically important non-kin ties that, for the most part, are located outside one's place of origin. Often the latter type of relationship is with a person of slightly higher social status or with business or political allies. Table 7.1 shows that, of five *compadres* of Eustaquio, only one is a Matahuasino by origin, but even he had spent most of his working life outside the valley and had retired to Lima. Each of these *compadres* gave Eustaquio access to important contacts outside. Two were large-scale middlemen who became important in the marketing of Eustaquio's agricultural and livestock products, one was a senior railway official, and the other two were professionals

Table 7.1 Eustaquio's *compadres* (1972)

Place of Residence	Place of Origin	Occupation	How Contacted and When	Extent of Present Contact
1. Tarma (central highlands)	Tarma (central highlands)	Agricultural Intermediary/ Farmer	Through trading of farm products during 1940s	Occasional visits
2. Miami US	Cajamarca Valley (northern Peru)	Businessman	Was trading partner for livestock during 1930s	By letter only but helped sons in US
3. Huancayo	Huancayo	Lawyer/ Administrator (retired)	When he was Prefect of Huancayo in early 1950s	Regular weekly visits
4. Lima	Matahuasi	Chief Telegrapher on Railways (retired)	From 1930 onwards when he transported livestock and meat products by train	Occasional visits
5. Lima	Huancayo	Lawyer (working in Supreme Court, Lima)	When he practised law in Huancayo during 1940s–50s Was senator for the Dept. of Junin in the early 1960s	Occasional visits but helped with oad accident case

with legal training and an extensive network of friends in regional government. These latter two were crucial in assisting Eustaquio to explore new types of investment. One of them, the Prefect of Huancayo, helped in establishing the garage and put Eustaquio in touch with his relatives who owned petrol stations. The Prefect also helped him to work out the costs and present the loan application to the Industrial Bank. The other played his part by offering legal advice when Eustaquio faced opposition from the municipality over the siting of the petrol pumps.

These stages in the development of Eustaquio's enterprise were accompanied, then, by the evolution of a set of ties with persons of higher social status, who lived and worked in the major urban centres of the region. They were persons with whom he might not in the ordinary course of events have come into direct contact. Paradoxically it was precisely because of the series of complicated legal cases pitching the village against him that the occasion arose for him to develop these relationships. This is also borne out by the list of best friends he named: of the six persons mentioned, two were lawyers who worked for him during the land disputes and whom he used in connection with a road accident case. One lived in Concepción and the other in Jauja, at the northern end of the valley. The remaining four all lived in Matahuasi but had urban experience and contacts (see Table 7.2).

Unlike the petrol business, which was initiated by the development of an external network of friends and *compadres*, the restaurant and shop were primarily a response to the growth of Eustaquio's nuclear family. As Benedict (1968) has observed, it is usual for family firms to begin new branches of production so that their adult children might be

Table 7.2 Eustaquio's friends (1972)

Place of Residence	Place of Origin	Occupation	How Rrelationship Fomed and when	Extent of Contact
1. Matahuasi	Matahuasi	Accountant/ Small farmer	Old school friend	Regular visits, gives advice on accounts
2. Matahuasi	Matahuasi	Bar Owner/ Electrician	Distant maternal kinsman	Regular visits, gives electrical help
3. Matahuasi	Arequipa	Shopkeeper	Commercial relationship developed during 1950s	Regular visits, daughter married to Eustaquio's son
4. Matahuasi	Matahuasi	Carpenter (retired)	Distant maternal kinsman, Mayor of Matahuasi during early 1960s; member of same political party	Infrequent visits
5. Jauja	Jauja	Lawyer	Helped in disputes with Community over Church land during 1940s and 1950s	Regular weekly visits, helped with accident case
6. Concepción	Concepción	Lawyer	Same as above	Regular weekly visits

settled in their own businesses. A similar process occurred with Eustaquio's enterprise, though the question of educational investment must also be considered.

Investment in the education of children often provides an alternative to joining the family firm, for it offers the possibility of entering professions or skilled occupations. Several of Eustaquio's sons were educated to secondary or post-secondary level and practised occupations that seemed unlikely to bring them back to Matahuasi to work with their father. Two of them lived in the United States – one working as an engineer in a textile factory, the other studying fine arts and design – and four lived in Lima – two working in skilled jobs, and the other two finishing secondary schooling in 1972. Of the remaining sons, one was young and still at school in Matahuasi; the other, Atilio, worked with his father in the petrol business. Eustaquio's two daughters both received some education but left school before they had completed their secondary course. The elder, Hilda, played a major part in the management of the enterprise, and her younger sister lent a hand on the farm and in the restaurant.

Eustaquio thus invested a fair percentage of his income in the education of his children, which resulted in several of them leaving home to seek fortunes elsewhere. Two of his sons and a son-in-law, the husband of Hilda, eventually went to the United States, the others to Lima. After one of these sons, Antonio, had unsuccessfully tried to enter the Engineering University in Lima, he was sent to complete his education at a technical college in Miami, Florida, where Eustaquio's *compadre* from Cerro de Pasco had settled. With assistance from the *compadre*, Antonio finished his training and became permanently settled in the United States. In the 1960s he was drafted into US military service and sent to Vietnam for a year. After his return to Miami, he married a Cuban woman and was later joined in Miami by his brother and brother-in-law. In 1972 it seemed likely that they, too, would make their careers in the United States. It was, of course, possible that should their father die then they would return to Peru to secure a share of the family property, but for the time being they remained abroad and uninvolved in the family business. The marriage of the other son, Alfredo, into a prominent commercial family in Matahuasi – a marriage Eustaquio seemed instrumental in arranging – appeared to be designed to encourage closer involvement with the family network in Matahuasi. However, after the wedding the young couple travelled to the United States to live, though the marriage was not to last.

The establishment of the restaurant, following the difficulties Eustaquio faced in expanding his farm, gave his wife and elder daughter, Hilda, an area of special responsibility within the enterprise. Hilda's role in the restaurant business increased and she later shared joint management of the petrol station. She also managed her own shop, operated independently of the family firm. One of Eustaquio's sons, Atilio, also tried his hand at running the restaurant business but he had to rent the facilities from his father at a fixed monthly rate. There was fierce competition at the time and Atilio and his wife had no flair for the task. So Eustaquio eventually offered Atilio financial backing to purchase a petrol tanker to operate himself within the already established petrol business. By handing out financial incentives of this kind, Eustaquio kept these two children closely tied to the family business. This was essential for survival of the family firm because his decision to educate his sons meant, as it often does in such cases, that he was unable readily to utilise their labour and skills in further expansion of the business. At the point when he needed their labour for agricultural production, several of his teenage children, who could have helped, were away at school. This was one of the factors affecting his decision to shift to livestock production and to open a restaurant and make use of the female labour that was available. After this decision, his strategy was to diversify more, moving away from agriculture towards providing services for road transport, and to hire in labour. In 1972 only one of his four permanent employees was from Matahuasi.

This later period in Eustaquio's career, then, was a joint product of increasing external ties, which integrated him more effectively into the system of regional commerce, and the pressures existing within the village and within his own nuclear family due to earlier decisions to promote his children's education. He had become a true cosmopolitan in orientation: his main sets of relationships extended well beyond the village to the towns and cities of the region, to Lima, the metropolitan capital, and to the United States. The only viable set of local relationships he maintained was with the small number of families in the area who had relatively high economic status as traders and farmers and who, for the most part, formed the central links in his network of kin and affines.

Springboards and constraints

Having sketched out the types of transactions and social investments made by Eustaquio in the building of his economic career, I now wish to explore Leeds's (1964) notion of social networks acting as springboards into new forms of economic activity. The notion of springboards, however, deals with only one side of the matter, since continual use of a particular network will eventually impose significant constraints on possible future actions and decisions.

The kinds of springboard associated with Eustaquio's enterprise are a case in point, and illustrate the way in which economic careers evolve in the central highlands of Peru. In the first place, it is the close-knit kin network, which – depending on the skills, contacts and resources of the people concerned – initially determines the direction of a person's early career. This is especially so when entering the urban labour market for the first time.

As we described earlier, the new migrant is likely to gravitate towards fellow kinsmen and persons of the same rural origin who will help him find work, often in the same economic sector as their own (Long 1973, Laite 1975, Smith 1984).

A second springboard is the set of affinal links through marriage that makes it possible to draw upon additional resources, illustrated by the transactions that occur between brothers-in-law in the Andes in respect to exchanges of labour and information (Long 1973). Affinal relationships between members of the same generation do not, it appears, exhibit the same degree of tension and competition or conflict that characterises bonds between siblings. A main reason for this is that the parties involved do not directly vie with one another for control over inheritable wealth.[3]

Other important sets of ties are developed through membership of a political party and regional associations.[4] Ties of this type frequently crosscut rural and urban areas and thus become important in orienting the individual to a wide span of rural and urban contexts. Membership in such organisations seems particularly significant for entrepreneurs specialising in transport or in the marketing of agricultural produce. These fields are highly competitive, and associational affiliations provide protection against competing commercial groups (Long 1972, 1973; Long and Roberts 1984: 181–97).

Another springboard, which in Eustaquio's case was critical, is the set of links with professionals such as lawyers, doctors and administrators. Such a network is valuable for the flow of general information and specialist advice, and for the provision of additional contacts with government personnel and institutions. Like Eustaquio, most aspiring entrepreneurs will attempt to cultivate professional friends who may help them lobby the government or who will introduce them to other persons of political or economic standing. Certain types of entrepreneurial careers require, in addition, a springboard into community relationships at the local level. This is particularly the case if the person is originally an outsider and operates, for example, as an agricultural middleman who requires close connections with farmers in order to know when and where produce is ready for purchase. The maintenance of such a network calls for considerable skill and tenacity on the part of the entrepreneur, who may be expected to participate actively in village fiestas or other voluntary activities.

While emphasising the positive aspects of these springboards, it is equally important to note the kinds of restrictions that they may bring. Continued use of the same set of ties will tend to give rise to a highly dense and involuted network, which can impose considerable constraints (Bott 1957, Long 1973). Sometimes the very restrictions and pressures that develop lead to new ventures and new phases in a career, even if this requires the repudiation of relationships where there is a high degree of affective and normative content. One aspect of this process is illustrated in the case of Eustaquio, when he broke close ties with his maternal kin in order to consolidate an affinal network. The difficulties with his maternal kin were further exacerbated by the conflict with the community over Church land. These same problems, however, led in the longer term to his establishing various external relationships that generated new and different forms of economic investment.

Thus an analysis of economic careers must allow for such changes and shifts in social relations. But rather than interpreting them as the result of clear-cut calculative and instrumental types of decision-making, they should be seen as being contingent upon the person having developed or been drawn into certain webs of relationships and commitments (emotional, material and organisational), whose precise outcomes are likely to be unforeseen and unintended. Moreover, it is characteristic of the kind of situation in which

Eustaquio found himself that careers are discontinuous and not predetermined from the outset by skills, assets and occupational niche. In the Mantaro region, as in other contexts, there are few instances of careers, including bureaucratic ones, where the steps to be taken follow a clear and fixed pattern.

Economic careers and the flow of information

Implicit in the foregoing discussion is the significance of knowledge and information in the development of careers. Several scholars have suggested that, in analysing flows of information, one must distinguish between two zones or sectors in a social network:[5] that composed of tightly organised sets of ties, often focusing upon specific institutional domains or social groupings – for example, family and kinship groups or religious and political associations; and that which comprises a more extended, loosely-knit network of dyadic relationships. The latter, it has been argued, functions as the means by which information is fed from one institutional context or social grouping into another. Hence, the study of entrepreneurial careers requires close attention to the form and structure of social networks and to the ways in which information of various types flows within them, which of course will vary over time. For example, the types of relationships constituting the central core of Eustaquio's career network changed over time, from high involvement with maternal kin, to investment in affinal relations, to a network of friends and *compadres* that extended well beyond the bounds of village.[6] The passage of time also saw certain ties in his nuclear family assume importance.

The two sectors of an entrepreneur's network become especially significant for the flow of information brought to bear on different types of decision. Information pertaining to strategic decisions – that is, concerning changes in the branch of economic activity pursued or relating to new forms of investment – generally flows through a series of relatively weak ties that form part of the extended network, and not through relationships where there is a high degree of interaction and normative consensus. On the other hand, information on the availability of basic resources or inputs necessary for the everyday operation of an enterprise will tend to flow between persons whose ties are strong and consolidated. This latter point is illustrated by the way in which traders and transporters maintain close bonds among themselves and with their business partners in order that information about contracts and available produce can be passed on easily. A similar pattern operates for commercial farmers who regularly organise exchanges for labour and information with their neighbours and kinsmen.

The significance of what are called 'weak' ties in social networks was first emphasised by Granovetter (1973)[7] who suggested that they are important not only for the manipulation of networks but also 'as channels through which ideas, influences, and information socially distant from ego may reach him'. Granovetter develops the idea in relation to information on job mobility and to general literature on the diffusion of innovations. Information, he contends, travels more quickly if it travels through weak ties that link together clusters of relatively dense sets of relationships. Moreover, the more weak ties a person has, the more information he is likely to receive, and conversely the better placed he is to distribute it, directly or indirectly, to a wider range of people. In job seeking, for instance, a loosely-knit network of weak ties will provide access to more varied sources of information from a greater variety of people than a more dense personal network which lacks extensions beyond the common circle. On the other hand, once information is received concerning the availability of a job or the possibility for a new type of economic investment, it is obviously better to activate strong ties based on high levels of trust and support in order to make the fullest use of the information. Weak ties may help with the provision of vital information, but they do not necessarily bring the best results.

The success of an entrepreneur lies in his ability to integrate both these elements into his network. He must spin a wide network of weak ties and keep their channels open while he develops a set of closely-knit, dependable relationships to assist him in utilising his resources effectively. The structure of his network will alter over time; some strong ties will become weak and some weak ties strong. And there will be shifts in the emphasis placed on particular types of relationship and their contents. Depending on the socio-cultural context, the viability of some relationships will thus change considerably. Also there will be differences in the ways relationships within a common frame are activated and consolidated; and the social costs involved in keeping open weak ties will vary according to the type of relationship. Some, such as consanguineal bonds or ties of *compadrazgo*, may require little effort beyond the basic requirement of occasional interaction, since they form part of a generally accepted (though situationally defined) frame of norms and values. Other relationships that are more instrumental or transitory in character, such as buyer–seller relationships or political alliances, will cease to exist once circumstances change and specific exchanges are terminated. The latter will need constant renewal through the joint participation of the parties concerned.

Some weak ties function to link two or more relatively dense sectors in a network or between networks. Granovetter (1973) calls these relationships 'local bridges', while others (Boissevain 1974, Allen and Cohen 1969) suggest the terms 'broker' or 'gate-keeper' for the person occupying such a position. Brokers are important in the flow of information since they command access to socially distant relationships and resources, and hence often play a significant role in opening up new sources of economic activity and investment. Eustaquio's case provides several examples of brokers. Maximo, his uncle, had connections with businessmen and political figures in La Oroya and the mining towns. Eustaquio's *compadre* in Huancayo, at one time the Prefect, provided links with influential people in commerce and politics at the regional level, and another *compadre*, who lived in the United States, offered indirect contacts with various persons and institutions which later proved helpful for Eustaquio's sons. Finally, the Matahuasi businessman whose daughter married Eustaquio's son, Alfredo, was integrated into a network of links with local Matahuasino farmers and shopkeepers which would have been useful had Eustaquio wished to align himself more firmly with the local economic elite. For a while, this last relationship proved useful, because at around the time of the first study, this group had control over the municipal government (Long and Winder 1975).

The structural concomitants of multiple enterprise

I wish now to return briefly to the phenomenon of multiple enterprise posed at the outset. My aim here is to identify the conditions associated with the development of economically diversified careers like that of Eustaquio. I concentrate on depicting the broad features of the regional socio-economic system as it was in the 1970s (cf. Long and Roberts 1984). Later, when updating the Jiménez family history, I will pinpoint some significant changes that have since taken place.

A main feature of the Mantaro region is that it is highly diversified economically. There are important mining centres nearby, and much of the labour force during the 1970s came from the villages of the Mantaro Valley. These same villages also supplied workers for the coastal cotton plantations and were a major contributor to the growth of the urban labour force of Lima. The surrounding highlands were the location of Peru's largest and most modernised livestock haciendas, later organised on a cooperative model following the 1969 Land Reform. In 1972, the principal city of Huancayo had a population of 116,000, and was one of Peru's fastest growing cities (by 2001 Huancayo had expanded to over 400,000 inhabitants). It was, and continues to be, a major commercial and administrative centre, and once possessed a textile industry employing some 3,000 workers.

The rural-agricultural scene exhibits a diversity of interrelated forms of production and land tenure. There exists a system of markets and marketing ranging from traditional barter exchange through rotating village markets and *ferias*, catering for local consumption needs, to large distribution markets that supply Lima-Callao. Alongside these markets, and in many ways more important, have been the individual traders and middlemen of the villages responsible for the movement of a large percentage of Lima's food needs. Some villages engage in small-scale craft production aimed mainly at a tourist market. As a whole, the region comprises a complex mix of agricultural, commercial, craft, industrial and service activities. It also possesses a considerable variety of organisational forms. There exist both household- and firm-based enterprises, production, distribution and service cooperatives, various recreational and welfare associations, and an abundance of government development agencies.

A second major feature of the socio-economic setting has been the relatively low degree of economic integration and centralisation in the region. For example, the bulk of agricultural produce was and still is marketed directly from the villages to the principal centres of the coast; it does not pass through Huancayo or through the hands of Huancayo-based entrepreneurs. Though there are major wholesale markets for agricultural and livestock products in Huancayo, most of this derives from trade with the remoter provinces to the south and east of the area. Moreover, although Huancayo is a distribution centre for dry goods and manufactured items originating from the coast, its function in this regard is diminished by the fact that the major villages make purchases directly from firms in Lima. This practice has been facilitated by the development of excellent road communications with the coast since the 1940s. Even in the field of administrative services, there is a general tendency to negotiate directly with the government in Lima, often using Lima-based associations to represent village and provincial interests in the capital, rather than to work through central or provincial government offices based in Huancayo. The same tendency to use Lima as a focus is reflected in the higher proportion of the area's university and secondary school students in Lima than in Huancayo, which now has two universities and good secondary schools. Labour migration data, likewise, indicate no consistent stage migration reported for some Latin American contexts. That is to say, large villages like Matahuasi, only ten miles from Huancayo, exhibit greater out-migration directly to Lima than to Huancayo or the mines, and nowadays its extra-local village networks stretch as far afield as the USA and Europe.

Another feature of the area is the highly dispersed nature of economic resources. In agriculture it is common for a household to have its land (average landholding in the valley in the 1972 were about one to one-and-a-half hectares) divided into a number of small plots located in different parts of the village or adjoining settlements. Some families also possess land in the distant tropical lowlands or in other places outside the valley. This patchwork of landholdings based on a mixture of private-freehold and community-owned tenure has given rise to various sharecropping and renting practices on plots owned by persons living temporarily or permanently outside the village. On the other hand, villagers may themselves own, and from time to time use, houses in Huancayo, Jauja, La Oroya, Lima and farther afield. This dispersal of property is also often associated with the operation of trading and small industrial enterprise. There is, for example, a group of traders who live in Matahuasi but control property and businesses in La Oroya and Lima, and similarly in the nearby village of Sicaya there is a group which runs a small garment industry with workshops located in Huancayo. The operation of transport, timber exploitation or agricultural trading businesses likewise necessitates networks of relationships in different localities. For example, timber, purchased in small lots from farmers in the valley and the tropical lowlands, is sold in the mining and urban centres of the region.

This dispersal of economic resources is, in part, an outcome of the valley's critical variations in micro-ecology and climate. Another factor is the long history of labour and household mobility that has enabled villagers of the valley not only to colonise labour centres but also to acquire land in the tropical lowlands and the highland pastoral zone. These different places constitute valuable resources for the people of the Mantaro Valley, in the same way that the valley provides for those who reside outside it and wish, for whatever reason, to retain active involvement in village affairs.

Associated with the dispersal of economic resources is the small-scale nature of economic activity. In Huancayo and in the small towns and villages there are few large-scale stable enterprises. This is particularly evident in agriculture, where, due to demographic factors, the tendency has been for holdings to fragment, thus preventing any significant consolidation of land from taking place. The same is true for the organisation of transport, which is mostly made up of independent vehicle operators who maintain close informal ties but have little sense of having a corporate identity. Thus, although in the 1970s there were some several hundred trucks operating in the valley, there was not one trucking company. Transport associations or cooperatives existed, but members owned their trucks individually and profits were based on individual effort. The primary function of each cooperative was the dissemination of information on loads and contracts. Eighty-one bus companies were registered in Huancayo in 1972, but most were made up of individual bus owners who joined forces in order to secure a route, coordinate timetables, and share the expenses of running an office. Similar patterns pertained to trading and industrial ventures. Apart from the Lima-owned and foreign trading companies in Huancayo (now increasingly important), large-scale, formally constituted trading or industrial firms were non-existent in the 1970s. Indeed, the tendency was for the large firm to be replaced by small ones. Huancayo's large-scale textile industry, which at its height employed 3,000 workers in four factories, had been replaced by 400 textile workshops, each with an average of seven employees, and by a newly formed textile cooperative of 250 members. Such textile workshops are still a major feature of Huancayo's extensive informal economy that also includes a host of other small independent workshops, service activities and trading enterprises.[8]

This persistence of small-scale enterprise is largely explained by the diversified, dispersed nature of resources, the generally low-level capitalisation of the economy, which continually suffers a drain of resources to the coastal metropolis, and by the high degree of uncertainty that exists in the regional and national markets. Despite these unfavourable conditions, many cases of successful entrepreneurship by persons of peasant origin can be documented. Such persons have succeeded in expanding their businesses by investing capital in new, often complementary, enterprises. Economic expansion through increasing specialisation of function is still uncommon, since heavy losses can ensue when markets suddenly contract.

Multiple enterprises, like the Jiménez case, are often organised in terms of a division of labour between the members of a household or extended family and operated on a profit-sharing basis. This pattern of organisation reduces labour costs and provides junior members with some leeway in the pursuit of their own economic strategies – though it can at the same time lead to conflicts of authority and status. Much depends on the management skills of the senior partners who, in order to generate profit and maintain a stable set of internal ties, must recognise and negotiate certain 'local' conventions and operating standards. An analysis of these internal organising practices is fundamental for assessing the viability of such enterprises. In addition, one must trace how external networks generate information and other resources relevant to the running of businesses. As I have argued, inputs from external contacts play a major role in the shaping of entrepreneurial careers. Indeed, as Eustaquio's case clearly shows, the setting up of new branches of economic activity is, to a large degree, a consequence of existing interpersonal ties. The opportunities and relationships that emerge, however, are also shaped by transformations in regional socio-economic conditions. Hence, while Eustaquio's career is unique in that it is the product of the evolution of a particular set of interpersonal relationships and strategies, it is also typical of the forms and styles of entrepreneurship that had emerged in the Mantaro Valley in the 1970s.

A further comment on social capital

The foregoing account of the history and vicissitudes of Eustaquio's enterprise brings us back to questions of social capital. As the case demonstrates, trust-based relationships such as those of kinship, affinity, *compadrazgo* or political ties are often beneficial to the building of entrepreneurial careers. So is it useful to conceptualise them as social capital? The case also provides many insights into how particular social networks are built, consolidated and later reworked through the discarding or fading away of previously crucial relationships in favour of forging new ones. In this sense it has many things to say about how social resources are managed and transformed – some particular to the empirical case and others of more general import. But, again, is there much 'added value' in bracketing these processes under the notion of social capital?

To single out certain social components in this way may exaggerate or reify their likely potency. Indeed it can lead, as it does in some policy documents, to the suggestion that a lack of social capital can be rectified through 'engineering' the conditions under which it will emerge and hopefully flourish. A related issue is that, while trust-based relationships may form part of an existing cultural repertoire, there is no guarantee that support and cooperation will be forthcoming when needed. There is always a downside to social networks. Though conceptually based on the mutuality[9] of interests or joint recognition of reciprocal needs and dilemmas (e.g., between the entrepreneur and his workers or partners), this does not exclude the possibility of requests for help, or demands for loyalty, being rejected. In fact without such problems and their resolution networks would become ossified. To stave off the worst effects of not being able readily to mobilise relationships and secure access to critical resources, the entrepreneur and his partners or clients will devote a good deal of attention to the pragmatics of working together. They will test each other's commitments and priorities, and generally learn through experience how best to accommodate to each other's styles, values and presumed interests. Hence bonds of trust and support do not reside in the realm of abstract moralities or cultural dispositions but rather in the strategic management of ongoing relationships, exchange contents and the social meanings that are constructed around them (cf. Kapferer 1976).

As Eustaquio's case highlights, many contingent factors enter into these situations and impact on and shape the effectivity of the relationships. None of these ties and their potential benefits/resources can simply be treated as generating social capital, which can then be tapped and put to work in satisfying the whims of the entrepreneur and the needs of the other actors. Obviously this is too functionalist a view. Furthermore, if entrepreneurs or other social actors adopt too calculative or extractive an approach to partners or subordinates, then the relationships involved will be seen as an encumberance and on the brink of being dissolved completely. That is, the actors involved will repudiate, subvert or ignore the relationships altogether, or, if that is impossible, they will simply 'go through the motions'. Seen from another perspective, the building of a trustworthy set of relationships with one set of kin, friends or business associates, of course, implies denying similar benefits to others. Thus, as Portes, Harriss and others have rightly pointed out, the very idea of the existence of social capital implies negative or marginalising effects for some, often those who are unsuccessful in vying for the same resources or who are generally socially disadvantaged.

Hence it becomes difficult to deduce general principles about the power and utility of specific institutions, cultural frameworks or ideologies for creating social capital. A principal reason why this is so is that social networks are infused with a multiplicity of partial connections, exchange contents, normative repertoires and multiple markers of morality. They are never fully integrated or organised around an unambiguous set of values, rights and obligations. They are entangled and ambivalent. Only detailed case studies can adequately identify and analyse the ways in which differences of value and interest are negotiated in the everyday practices of sustaining or transforming social networks. As amply illustrated in this chapter, such studies must adopt a diachronic approach since the content and effectiveness of the relationships that constitute a social network will shift over time. If ties are not activated regularly, then they may become 'sleeping partners' that are only reawakened in the face of critical events.

If these network configurations and the ways in which they change their form situationally and over time are what is signified by the idea of social capital, then we need to place a great deal more emphasis on its organic and hybrid character. From this point of view, social capital cannot, strictly speaking, be stockpiled, accumulated or invested. Instead it must be considered an integral part of the self-organising processes of network formation and reconfiguration. The foregoing case study offers some suggestions on how we might approach a better understanding of such dimensions.

A postscript: The Jiménez family at the turn of the 21st century[10]

It is now almost three decades since the original data on Eustaquio Jiménez' multiple enterprise were collected. Much has happened in the meantime. The violence brought by the Shining Path movement (*Sendero Luminoso*) and, to a lesser extent, the MRTA (*Movimiento Revolucionario de Tupac Amaru*) reached its height in the valley between 1989 and 1994, even though the *Sendero* leader Abimael Guzman was captured in 1992. The economy had run into serious decline, exacerbated by an increase in the national debt due to large imports of cheaper foodstuffs, and agricultural and livestock production dropped. The younger generation of the Jiménez family had dispersed through transnational and internal migration, and the trucking business had moved its centre of operations with Eustaquio's son Atilio and family to Trujillo on the northern coast.

At the beginning of 1998 when I last saw Eustaquio, he was a frail and sick old man of 93, who struggled to and from the Mass to celebrate the fiesta of San Sebastian, the major annual religious festival in Matahuasi, his daughter Hilda by his side. Although the infrastructure of the garage was still intact, it no longer served petrol. However, the shop at Hilda's house was well stocked with fruit, bread and tinned goods. In the 1980s Hilda had opened a beauty salon in Concepción which functioned well for some years, but by the early nineties, at the height of the violence in Peru, it and the rest of the enterprise went into decline. By 1995 the restaurant, shop, garage and beauty salon were all closed, though the restaurant and the office of the garage were rented out until 1998. The only remaining productive activities of the former family enterprise were the farm, managed by Walter, Allica and Hilda, and one of the trucks; but petrol was expensive and contracts for transporting merchandise few and far between.

Eustaquio and his wife Juana Meza had eleven children: Mario, Humberto, Luis (who died as a baby), Hilda, Atilio, Antonio, Alfredo (Eric Hutton), Alejandrina (Allica), Luis, Celso and Walter. As Genealogy 2 shows, only three remain in Matahuasi. The others live in the southern part of the United States, Europe, and in Peru in Lima and Trujillo. Let me now sketch out what had transpired with each of the children and their families over the intervening years. This way of relating the story enables us to appreciate how educational, occupational and spatial mobility were interwoven to influence the demise of the original, highly successful multiple enterprise, as well as the spawning of new extra-local businesses.

Juana Meza, Eustaquio's wife, died in 1990 and was buried in the nearby cemetery of Concepción. When she died, Eustaquio went to live with his son Celso in Los Angeles, where he stayed until returning to Matahuasi in 1994 to live with Hilda, in the house beside the petrol station. During his stay in Los Angeles he helped Celso and his other two sons, Antonio and Luis, maintain their gardens. He also went to a club for elderly people during the day when his sons were out working, but, after a long and active working life, he found retirement and leisure activities difficult to cope with. Now at 93, he is too frail to move much beyond his house in Matahuasi. During 1999 he lived with his daughter Allica (Alejandrina) who lives down the main road from the petrol station, which was rented to a businessman from Lima. Hilda and Walter had been administering it, but had insufficient capital to invest in it or run it efficiently and the storage tanks were often out of petrol. The family still owns a truck, which Walter operates for transporting goods between Huancavelica, Huancayo and Lima, and which is sometimes hired out. In addition they have a van which is rented to a mining company in Cerro de Pasco. The

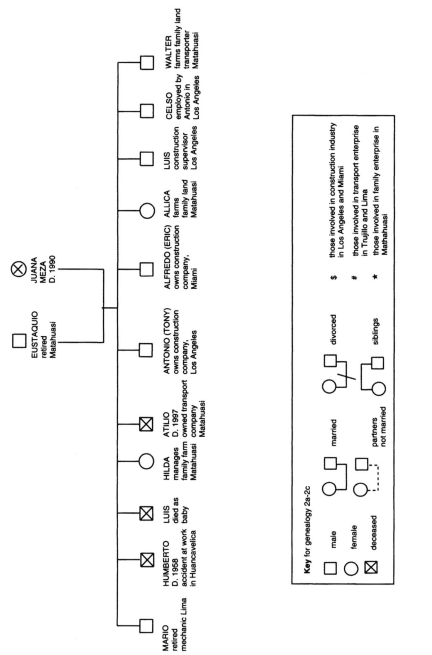

Genealogy 2: The Jiménez family, 1998: Occupations, enterprises and residence (see also Genealogies 2a 2b and 2c)

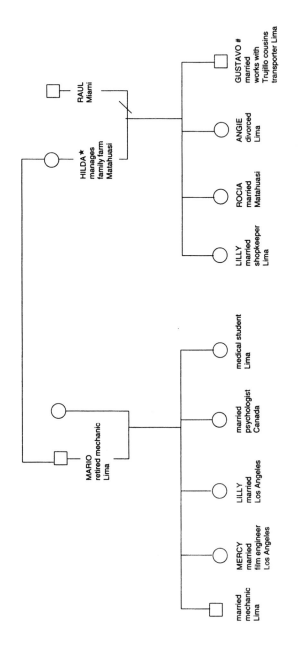

Genealogy 2a: Families of Mario and Hilda (based in Lima and Matahuasi)

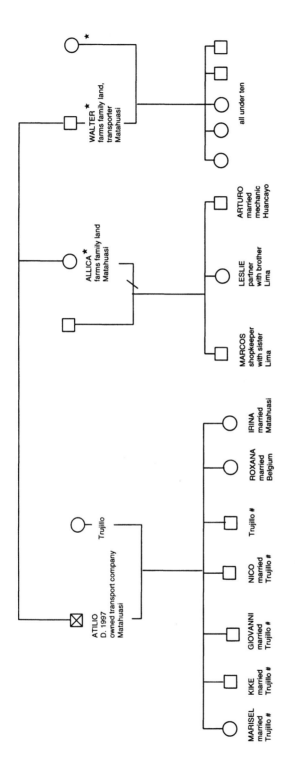

Genealogy 2b: Families of Atilio, Allica and Walter, 1998 (based in Lima, Matahuasi and Trujillo)

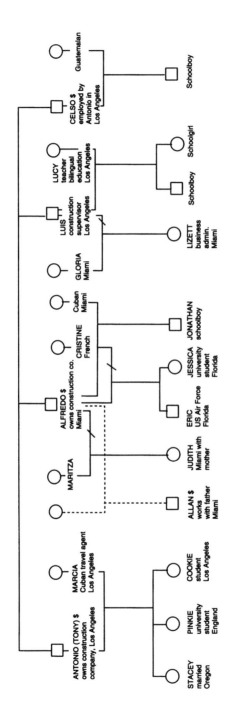

Genealogy 2c: Families of Antonio, Alfredo, Luis and Celso (based in Los Angeles and Miami)

money earned in this way is welcome, but the van is rapidly deteriorating in the harsh and polluted environment of the mining sector. The restaurant had also for a time been rented to a woman from Huancayo, but now stands empty. Hilda had ambitions to open it again as a place to hold receptions and parties, but she had no money to restore it.

Mario, the first born, was 70 years old in 1999. He went to Lima to work when he was 12, and never lived with his family in Matahuasi again. He resides in the district of La Victoria, Lima, with his wife, who is ill, and with his youngest daughter and mother-in-law. Mario was trained and worked as a mechanic at the Endeco factory. He is now retired. He has four daughters and a son. The son lives in Lima with his wife and two children. Two of Mario's daughters live in Los Angeles in California. They are both married to Americans and one of them, Mercy, has two girls. Mercy is an electronics engineer and works in the film industry. The other girl, Lilly, has two boys. Mario's third daughter is a psychologist. She went to Canada in 1993, married a Canadian, and is now living and working there. Mario's youngest daughter is studying medicine at San Marcos University in Lima and lives with her parents. Mario and his wife have travelled several times to both Canada and the US to visit the daughters. Mario has been on five occasions and his wife seven.

Humberto died as the result of an accident in 1958, when in his early twenties. At the time he was working in Huancavelica in the construction industry. He suffered from epilepsy and fell to his death during an attack. He is buried in Concepción at the same spot as his mother.

Hilda, the elder of Eustaquio's daughters, was 60 years old in 1999. She continues to live beside the petrol station not far from where Matahuasi adjoins the municipality of Concepción. Hilda has three daughters and a son – Guilliana (Lilly), Rocio, Angelica (Angie) and Gustavo. Hilda's husband, Raul Quispe, who came originally from Ayacucho, is said to be in Miami. With the help of Hilda's brothers he went to the US and was meant to send for her when he had earned enough money. However, he never fulfilled his promise, and is no longer in contact with Hilda or the children. Since then the daughters have tried to renew contact with him, with a view to moving to the States themselves, but he has never returned their calls and has changed his number to an ex-directory one, which has effectively ended the contact. Hilda is currently living with her father and her daughter Rocio, who decided to move back to Matahuasi from Lima with her two children, because she had problems with her husband – said to be an ill-tempered police officer. As mentioned earlier, Hilda had rented out the restaurant, but in 1999 this came to an end when the tenant terminated the arrangement on the grounds of not being able to make a living from it due to the generally poor state of the economy. The petrol station is rented to a businessman from Lima. The rent money is shared with her youngest brother Walter. They also entered into an *al partir* (sharecropping) arrangement with the daughter-in-law of a land-owning family, who provides labour and seeds, while Hilda's family provides the land. In 1998, they sowed maize and potatoes, the former being divided 1:1, and 1:2 for the potatoes.

Of Hilda's children, Lilly, the eldest, lives in Lima with her husband Tony and their two school-age sons. She has a small grocery store in Ate district, and goes to Matahuasi only twice a year but often helps by sending foodstuffs to her mother and her grandfather Eustaquio. Lilly went to Chile in 1995 through a network of international migrants, where she worked for a year as a cleaner in upper-class homes in Santiago. Rocio, the second daughter, moved to Matahuasi in 1998 with her 10-year-old daughter Joanna and her five-year-old son Pepe. She raises rabbits and guinea pigs, which she sells in the market in Jauja, a town at the northern end of the valley. She also helps her mother on the farm. In June 2000, Rocio took over her cousin Leslie's grocery store in the La Molina district of Lima. However, this arrangement was only until December, when she planned to return to Matahuasi. Angie, the third daughter, lives in Santa Catalina, La Victoria district of Lima. She has one son, Steven, and is divorced from the boy's father, Alex, another police officer. Angie also has a grocery store in Lima. She visits Matahuasi more often than does her sister Lilly.

Hilda's only son, Gustavo, was studying in Lima when his fellow student girlfriend became pregnant, leading to them both dropping out of school to marry. They now live in Lima with their two-year-old son Gustavito. Gustavo works with his cousins in Trujillo (Atilio's sons and daughters) as a truck driver. He mainly drives to the North (Tumbes and Chiclayo) and to the jungle lowlands. Both Angie and Gustavo have aspirations to migrate to the US. However, nothing yet has transpired to make this possible.

Atilio, Eustaquio's fourth son, married Isabel Torres from a well-known and respected Matahausi family. He died in 1997 of a heart attack at the age of 55, after which Isabel moved to live near her children in Trujillo. Atilio owned and ran a transport company and was the owner of three large Volvo trucks. Atilio and Isabel had seven children (three daughters and four boys), all of them now grown up. The oldest daughter, Marisel, married a Matahuasino and has three boys. She lives, like her four brothers, in Trujillo on the northern coast of Peru, from where they run the transport enterprise founded by their father. They now jointly own five Volvo trucks and heavy machinery and plant for construction. Gustavo (Hilda's son) is employed by these Trujillo cousins, but Hilda complains that they do not treat him as real 'family'.

Of Atilio's sons, Kike is married with a daughter, Giovanni is married to a woman from Concepción and they have three children, and Nico is also married with a son. Atilio's fourth son is a bachelor and also lives in Trujillo. Atilio's second daughter, Roxana, is married to a Belgian. They owned a restaurant in Trujillo, but after a break-in robbery they moved with their small son to Belgium some four years ago and established a restaurant there. Isabel, the mother, has been to visit them several times since then. The youngest daughter, Irina, used to live in Trujillo but married Raul Oré from another Matahuasi family and in 1998 returned with their two children to Matahuasi to farm the Oré family land.

Antonio (Tony) reached 56 years of age in 1999. He was the first of Eustaquio's four sons to travel to the US. He went to Miami in 1963 with a friend from Huancayo on a tourist visa. Shortly after arrival he enrolled in the US Marine Corps, and was sent to Vietnam for 13 months. This gave him US citizenship. He now lives in Pico Rivera, a middle-class residential area in Los Angeles. He owns a road construction company and employs his younger brother Celso. In Miami he married a Cuban woman, Marcia, who now works in a travel agency in Los Angeles. They have three daughters. The oldest, Stacey, is married to an American lawyer and lives in Oregon. Stacey is the godchild of Antonio's brother, Luis. The second, Pinkie, went to England when she finished high school in Los Angeles. In 1990 she was studying and working in a clothes shop there. The youngest daughter Cookie is eighteen and lives at home with her parents. Tony went to Matahuasi to visit his father in January 2000, to coincide with the annual village fiesta of San Sebastian, but he only stayed a week.

Alfredo (Eric) Jiménez (54 years old) went to the US in 1967, in the footsteps of his brother who had just returned from the Vietnam War. He also gained US citizenship by fighting in Vietnam, and then changed his name to Eric Hutton. The Peruvian part of the family felt that this was tantamount to denying his Peruvian background, but his argument was that if you have a Latin name, then you are more likely to meet with discrimination in the US, and he wanted to 'progress'. Alfredo does not fraternise with the Peruvian community in Miami, where he lives. In fact he thinks it is bad to mix with 'foreigners'. He has not been back to Peru in 20 years but he frequently sends money to pay for his father's medicines, and occasionally sends photos and writes letters.

Alfredo (Eric) has a large construction company in Miami, engaged in road building. He is the most affluent of the Jiménez brothers. He has not travelled to work in other places of the United States like his brothers, but after Vietnam he stayed put in Miami. Before going to the US, he had an illegitimate son, Allan, by an ex-girlfriend from Matahuasi. But after Allan's birth, Alfredo married another Matahuasino woman, Maritza Acosta, the daughter of a shopkeeper. They went to the States and shortly after their arrival their daughter, Judith, was born. Later Maritza returned to Peru with Judith to organise her papers to apply for US residence, but met with difficulties and so they remained in Matahuasi. She and Alfredo later divorced. When Allan was 9 years old, Alfredo returned to Matahuasi to bring him to the States. When Judith was a bit older Alfredo sent for her also, and when she gained American residence status at the age of 21 she brought her mother to Miami, where they both presently live. Judith is the granddaughter who keeps most in touch with the family in Matahuasi. Allan is also living today in Miami and is married to an American.

After his divorce Alfredo married Cristine, a French woman, and had two children, a boy called Eric after himself, and a girl called Jessica. Alfredo and Cristine have visited Peru once only. Eric is now 21 years old and is in the US airforce, and Jessica is studying at the University of Florida in Gainesville. Alfredo now lives together with his third wife, a Cuban woman, with whom he has a son called Jonathan.

Alejandrina (Allica) lives in Matahuasi on the other side of the petrol station. She also went to the US in the early 1970s but returned after three months because she missed her boyfriend, by whom she was pregnant. She had three children, but was later divorced. She now works on parts of the family land. For a number of years she administered the petrol station, and also ran another in San Jerónimo, a village en route to Huancayo. Presently, she is seeing a retired employee from the Banco Popular in Huancayo. Two of her children, Marcos and Leslie, live in Lima. Up until June 2000 they ran a grocery store together. Leslie had arranged for a cousin to take it over for six months so she could have a maternity break. Her partner Jorge is a textile engineer who operates a small company in Lima. Allica's third child, Arturo, is married to a woman from Huancayo and has a son. He works as a mechanic and runs a small enterprise in Huancayo related to transport activities.

Luis, the seventh Jiménez brother, was 50 years old in 1999. He went to the US in 1971, having finished secondary school in Lima but failing to get a place at the national engineering university. He first lived in Orlando, Florida, where he worked in Disneyland to pay for his studies. He then paid a Cuban American woman 800 US dollars to marry him so that he could get US residence. It was only a formality and he never saw her again. He then worked as an engineer in Miami for three years in different construction companies. Over the years, he has travelled all over the US and Canada, always working in construction, with contracts facilitated through membership of the US Union of Construction Workers. After Miami, he went to Toronto and Montreal, then to Buffalo in New York and finally to California, ending up in 1979 in Los Angeles. Today, he works as a supervisor in the construction industry. His two brothers, Tony and Celso, joined him in Los Angeles. Luis married twice (in addition to the visa marriage). With Gloria, a Lima girl he met in Miami, he had a daughter who now holds a Master's degree in business administration. He has two children with Lucy, his second wife whom he met on a visit to Trujillo in 1982. In 1985 they bought a house in a residential neighbourhood of Los Angeles. They live a solid middle-class American life, Luis earning between 4,000 and 5,000 US dollars a month and Lucy 2,000 US dollars a month. The children are at school and enjoy sports and Lucy works as a teacher in a bilingual education programme, mainly for Mexican women. Luis frequently visits and makes telephone calls to Peru, and it was he who installed a phone in his sister Hilda's house in Matahuasi, so he could communicate with his father.

Celso, the penultimate Jiménez brother, was sent by his father to the US to find work in 1974. He did not want him hanging around the farm in Matahuasi doing nothing. Like several of his brothers, he too lives in Los Angeles, working in his brother's construction firm but also supervising other contract work. Celso is married to a Guatemalan woman and they have a son of about 15 years of age. However, unlike his brothers, Celso often visits Matahuasi, especially during fiesta times when he fulfils *cargos* (duties) as a *padrino*. He participated, for example, in *carnavales* in Barrio Ferrocarril, Matahuasi, in 1997 and 1998. He was also nominated the *padrino de monte* (i.e., the person responsible for the tree-cutting ceremony) during the San Sebastian fiesta of January 1998. But he was unable to attend and so asked his younger brother Walter to stand in for him.

Walter, the youngest of the Jiménez brothers, is 44 years old. On finishing school in Lima, he moved back to Matahuasi and worked with his father. He is married with five children, the oldest of whom is ten. They live in the old family house constructed by Eustaquio. Walter uses the remaining family truck to transport merchandise between Huancavelica and Lima. He owns five dairy cows from which he obtains milk for the family. Walter's wife ran a restaurant in Huancayo until 1998, but when she became pregnant again she decided to leave the business and concentrate on the Matahuasi family affairs.

At present the family based in Matahuasi (i.e., Hilda, Allica and Walter) are disputing access to the family land and the belongings of the family enterprise. Should Eustaquio die intestate, there will certainly be disputes over inheritance.

Concluding remarks

While the decline and imminent disintegration of the original Jiménez family enterprise over the past twenty years can be traced in large part to the internal dynamics and social differentiation of the family, it is also due in no small measure to the more general economic and political forces at work in Peru during that same period.

The enterprise faired reasonably well until the beginning of the 1980s, when it was plainly clear that earlier government policies aimed at redressing the inequalities of land-holding and property ownership, first through land reform and revitalising cooperative modes of organisation, and then through encouraging the privatisation of community lands and market-led enterprise development, had failed to bring any prosperity or stability to the highlands. The first scenario had resulted in an increased presence of the state in the shaping of regional and local development. The second was marked by a decrease in direct state intervention leading to a severe cutback of government services relating to activities such as extension, credit and technical inputs. Hence both policies contributed to a worsening of the economic conditions in the highlands and the country at large, and to a growing national debt exacerbated by financial and other mismanagement. This increased the vulnerability not only of the rural and urban poor but also of the middle sector, including teachers and other government employees, the self-employed, and owners and workers in medium and small industries.

In the face of increasing livelihood difficulties and poverty, which was especially concentrated among the rural highland population and in the poor urban settlements surrounding the large cities throughout Peru, there emerged various forms of social unrest. Eventually this took the shape of direct armed resistance to the state, mounted primarily by *Sendero Luminoso* (Shining Path) and the MRTA. Although in the early days the struggle between *Sendero* and the Peruvian military did not unduly affect the Mantaro region, by the end of the 1980s and until it peaked in 1992, it had massive repercussions for the people of the Mantaro Valley, its surrounding pastoral highlands, and the city of Huancayo. Commerce and transport of goods and people were seriously curtailed. Communications to Lima and the coast became dangerous and on several occasions the main road was blocked and essential foodstuffs prevented from reaching the capital. Agricultural and livestock production was reduced by pillage regularly carried out by *Sendero*, who also exacted tribute in the form of cattle, money and crops to feed its army; pillage also sometimes resulted from retaliatory actions carried out by the Peruvian army. *Sendero* also enforced regulations that reduced the amount of foodstuffs and animal products reaching the market, arguing ideologically for a return to a subsistence-based economy. In addition, they targeted government officials and local representatives of the state such as Mayors, municipal secretaries and provincial governors.

In the case of Matahuasi some ten people were assassinated in the early 1990s by *Sendero*, including the municipal secretary and a resident agricultural engineer who had played a major role in raising funds for and implementing the rebuilding of the municipal offices. It had taken twenty years to raise the capital for this large investment and, on the day after its inauguration, both men were gunned down in their homes and in the presence of family members. They now lie side by side in a memorial grave in the Matahuasi cemetery, a constant reminder to residents of the brutality of that period. It had become dangerous for individual cultivators, householders and entrepreneurs to move about and carry out their normal activities. There are several well-documented local accounts of gunfights between marauding *Sendero* groups and prominent Matahuasi families and businessmen. Not surprisingly these economic and political events had a detrimental effect on enterprise development and seriously disrupted the running of Eustaquio's enterprise. They must also have affected decisions made by members of the family as to whether to return to Peru from the US, or to the village from Lima, or concomitantly to leave Matahuasi for safer havens. At certain times members of the Matahuasino family sought refuge in Lima. It was not practical to move to the nearby city of Huancayo, since this itself had become a centre of violence and was filling up with refugees from the surrounding southern highland regions, where *Sendero* had its garrisons. The Peruvian military, in a bid to dislodge them, evacuated or drove out a large proportion of the population.

Under these conditions petrol was difficult to obtain and many garages were unable to obtain or pay for supplies, including that of the Jiménez family. In addition income from petrol sales had dropped because of the reduced movement in the zone, and this undoubtedly affected the restaurant linked to the garage. There were fewer passers-by, and families or groups were less willing to hire the location for receptions because it had become dangerous to gather in public, especially at night. Support from a wide spectrum of Matahuasino residents was crucial throughout these years, but Eustaquio and his family did not always find this forthcoming because of the ongoing tensions between them and the community and municipal authorities.

It is difficult to say to what extent the out-migration of four of the Jiménez brothers was also a factor, but it obviously reduced the amount of labour available for the various branches of the enterprise. Hilda continued to farm the family land under a sharecropping arrangement, but it is not surprising that Atilio's sons shifted a good part of the transport business to Trujillo and Piura on the northern coast, since *Sendero* was not operative in that part of Peru. By the late 1980s Eustaquio was well into his seventies and no doubt seeking to reduce his commitments and responsibilities. Each of his sons had done well in their own right and he and Juana Meza regularly visited Los Angeles where three of them lived. There was little to attract them back to Matahuasi.

By 1999, only three of Eustaquio's children were living in Matahuasi. Hilda and Walter work together, but neither get along with Allica. Though they live close by, they never see or visit each other. The petrol station is rented out and Hilda keeps the money; she justifies this by saying 'it is not inexpensive to look after my father'. When the absent brothers visit, they do their best to mediate between the three of them.

From a family united around a multiple enterprise in Matahuasi, the Jiménez family is now spread over a good part of Peru and into the US and Belgium. This more global network has resulted in significant social and cultural differentiation within the family, with some members and branches retaining greater contact than others. While a few individual families still retain an interest in their Matahuasino roots, travelling back to play a role in village and patron-saint fiestas, others have detached themselves from these influences and have sought to 're-invent' themselves as Americans, choosing English-American names for their children, putting them through American educational institutions and building household lifestyles around American values. The older generation, that of Eustaquio's sons, except for Eric Hutton, have made some accommodation between Peruvian and Latino culture and American values, performing a kind of balancing act by marrying Latinos based in the States and living a mixed Latino/American way of life. For first-generation migrants, family life is difficult and it is perhaps particularly hard for women to survive without the close support of family, even though they may be able to get work more easily than men (e.g., as low-paid domestic workers). Eustaquio's daughters remained in Matahuasi, and the daughters-in-law who married the sons who migrated to the States each in turn had marital problems, was divorced, and returned to Peru.

The days of the Matahuasi-based multiple family enterprise are now numbered. The interconnections between its various branches of activity have broken apart; it is undercapitalised and will undoubtedly be dissolved on Eustaquio's death when his children attempt to claim their inheritance. It is more than likely that his sons running successful construction businesses in the US will not be interested. But for the rest there are still property issues at stake. The garage with its infrastructure modernised, and the family land and farm better managed, could still offer a viable living for the few resident members in Matahuasi and those strategically located and interrelated, such as the transport branch of the family in Trujillo and Lima. Like all family enterprises, as the generations proliferate so do new branches of activity arise. Hence, while on one level we are apparently witnessing the demise of what was once a successful multiple enterprise centred upon Matahuasi, on another, the enterprise lives on in the skills, experience and entrepreneurial flair of the new generations of family members. From the humble roots of a highland village in Peru, these children and grandchildren of Eustaquio are now carving out important niches for themselves within a world of transnational relations and diversified local/global encounters.

Part III

KNOWLEDGE INTERFACES, POWER AND GLOBALISATION

8

KNOWLEDGE, NETWORKS AND POWER[1]

The sociology of knowledge has a long-established intellectual pedigree, but only relatively recently has the analysis of knowledge processes become a central concern in the fields of development and social change.[2] This chapter explains the significance of this interest in knowledge issues and identifies critical dimensions for further theoretical and empirical exploration.

The significance of knowledge issues

From about the early 1960s onwards, social scientists interested in uneven development, the transfer of technology and the significance of the cultural and institutional factors involved, turned towards modernisation theory and later to political economy for explanations of the dynamics of these processes. Such approaches provided new insights into issues of class struggle, 'traditional' versus 'modern' values, and the roles of the state and international capital in promoting change. In so doing they touched upon questions of power and authority but failed to appreciate the fundamental significance of 'expert' knowledge or science in the social construction of society and social change.[3] Knowledge and science were part of both modernisation and neo-Marxist discourses, but they were perceived instrumentally, either as resources or as part of the toolkit of a 'modernity' project aimed at isolating and promoting the central driving forces and mechanisms of social change.

Later, sociologists concerned with issues of 'popular education' argued that introduced forms of knowledge needed translation in order to become effective in local development. These translation tasks were the mission of so-called 'promoters', 'animators', 'change agents' and the like, whose assignments were linked to the overall goal of using knowledge for transforming society in an effort to achieve greater equity and political participation (e.g., Freire 1970, Galjart 1980, and Fals-Borda 1981). In this way the worlds of research and development practice became interconnected through the discussion of how to organise and use knowledge and science for the pursuit of the 'good society'.[4]

More recently, the sociology of knowledge has embraced a social constructionist perspective that provides fresh insights into how 'expert' and everyday forms of knowledge relate to development processes. For instance, Knorr-Cetina (1981a) has studied 'practical epistemologies' within science and shown how expert scientific knowledge is produced and re-created not simply in the laboratories of research institutions but also in the canteens and corridors of these scientific establishments. Parallel views within the field of development studies have been expressed by Robert Chambers (1983) and Paul Richards

(1985), who argue that the practical everyday knowledge of ordinary people can enrich 'science' and improve development practice.[5] Thus two rather different research strands converge to stress that, rather than exploring the nature and epistemology of knowledge in an abstract and formalist manner, we should open the path to a re-evaluation of 'science-in-the-making'. Such a perspective should take full cognisance of social actors, their values and understandings in the construction of knowledge, and in the scientific design for alternative or competing 'projects of society'. It must also stand against treating science and everyday knowledge as being ontologically different.

Hence the demystification of science through the ethnographic study of scientific practice and everyday knowledge brings into perspective a whole new set of images and representations of how the social world is constructed and organised. From this standpoint, a fresh panorama unfolds in which the interplay and interfaces of local people and scientists become central to the production of more acceptable, 'human' solutions aimed at countering the 'supremacy' and 'excesses' of modern technological and economic development.

These various attempts to study and analyse expert science, scientists' interests and people's knowledge and aspirations opened the way to detailed ethnographic studies on how knowledge is created and used by all sorts of actors in their practical attempts to cope with issues of livelihood and planned intervention by outsiders. The creation and transformation of knowledge, however, can only effectively be studied and analysed through an appreciation of how people – whether peasants, bureaucrats or scientists – build bridges and manage critical knowledge interfaces that constitute the points of intersection between their diverse lifeworlds (Arce and Long 1987, Long 1989, and Long and Villarreal 1993). This requires giving close attention to the practices of everyday social life, involving actor strategies, manoeuvres, discourses and struggles over meanings and identity, since only in this way can one tease out the intricacies of how knowledge is internalised, externalised and reconstructed by different actors (cf. Berger and Luckmann 1967). It is in this way that an actor-oriented perspective on knowledge and knowledge encounters can help to go beyond dichotomised representations of differing forms of knowledge (i.e., in terms of 'modern science' versus 'people's science', 'external' versus 'local' knowledge).[6]

This actor focus concentrates upon exploring how socio-cultural practices are organised and enacted in everyday performances. It does not see these practices simply as the product of some self-contained cultural or institutional orders or systems of social thought. And it refuses to draw sharp distinctions between different kinds of knowledge on the basis of their origin, pedigree and so-called authority. Knowledge is generated and transformed not in abstract but in relation to the everyday contingencies and struggles that constitute social life. It is not given by simple institutional commitments or assumed sources of power and authority, but rather is an outcome of the interactions, negotiations, interfaces and accommodations that take place between different actors and their lifeworlds.

The lack of commonality in the concept of knowledge (i.e., the contradictions, inconsistencies, ambiguities and negotiations that it implies) means that there are many different intersecting knowledge frames – some more diffuse and fragmented than others – that intersect in the construction of social arrangements and discursive practices.[7] These 'multiple realities' may mean many things and entail different rationalities for the actors involved, but somehow they are contained and interact within the same social context or arena. It is these knowledge encounters and interactions that generate locally situated knowledge, whether this takes place within the setting of an irrigation scheme, a rural development project, or in an urban neighbourhood where street children hang out (see Chapter 4). In developing a methodology for studying such processes I distance myself from general epistemological debates on the nature of knowledge and knowledge universals. Instead I aim to understand how knowledge impinges on the 'ordering' and 're-ordering' processes of everyday life (Law 1994). I also build upon previous theoretical work that rejects the simple assumption of a hegemonic Western philosophy of science in favour of a detailed understanding of how the complex practices and beliefs of science (and indeed any other causal theories) are constructed, reaffirmed or reworked through the social encounters, experiences and dilemmas of everyday life.[8]

In order to explore these issues more closely, I have chosen to focus upon one important field of application, namely, that centring on the processes of knowledge acquisition, utilisation and transformation. Such processes are at the core of programmes of planned intervention, and form the critical set of problems that define what is called 'extension science' (Röling 1988).

The systems model in agricultural extension

While extension science was for many years associated with Rogerian models of the adoption and diffusion of innovations (Rogers 1962/83, Rogers and Shoemaker 1971) and with the Land Grant type of applied rural sociology (Lionberger 1960), by the early 1980s this had given way to a more thoroughgoing application of communication and systems theory (Beal et al. 1986). At Wageningen, this was signalled by the mushrooming of research dealing with farmer knowledge and the complex set of links between research establishments, extension services and the farming population. These developments were accompanied by a growing interest in 'farming systems' analysis, which aimed to develop a multi-level, interdisciplinary approach to understanding farming practice placed within the context of wider ecological, technical, economic and social constraints, and in relation to technological change in agriculture (Collinson 1982, Brush 1986, Fresco 1986, Sutherland 1987, Rhoades and Bebbington 1990, Gatter 1993).

Much of this new-style extension, agronomic and rural sociological research was grounded in systems thinking based on four central concepts: emergence, hierarchy, communication and control. It was argued that the interaction of elements within a system gives way to emergent properties that are irreducible, thus producing a whole that is bigger than the sum of its parts. This whole is composed of different sub-systems that nest within each other and are functionally and hierarchically interrelated. For example, Fresco and Westphal (1988) define a system as 'an arrangement of components or parts that interact according to some process and transform inputs into outputs'. They claim that 'agriculture can be described as a hierarchy of systems, ranging from the cell at the lowest level, through the plant or animal organs, the whole plant or animal, the crop or herd, the field or pasture, and the farm, to complex ecosystems such as the village and watershed culminating in the agricultural sector at the highest level' (1988: 401). Another element described as crucial is communication, since it is the flow that holds the system together. In order to maintain a hierarchy, there should be adequate communication of information for purposes of regulation or control (Checkland 1981: 83). This stands at the centre of the analysis, as all systems are said to contain within them factors of control that can be triggered off and manipulated to guide them in the desired direction.[9]

But such systems models are basically inadequate for developing a sound understanding of the complex processes involved in the generation, acquisition, utilisation and transformation of knowledge.[10] I aim to show this through developing a critique of existing attempts to theorise and investigate the nature of knowledge processes and through elucidating the advantages of adopting an actor-oriented approach. This takes up the next part of this chapter. After this, I build upon the argument by showing how one might extend the analysis of knowledge processes to cover the organisational and strategic elements involved in development interfaces. As I outlined in Chapter 3, interfaces are characterised by discontinuities in interests, values and power, and their dynamic entails negotiation, accommodation and struggles over definitions and boundaries. A close-up study of interfaces provides insights into the processes by which policy is transformed, how room for manoeuvre and empowerment are created by both intervenors and 'clients', how persons are enrolled in the 'projects' of others, and how metaphors, images and ideologies shape the contests that take place over competing paradigms and strategies of development.

The legacy of Havelock's communication model

Thirty years ago, Havelock (1969) suggested that the essence of knowledge utilisation is the linkage between two social systems, one of which is faced with a problem and the other with delineating options that facilitate its resolution. Since then this basic idea has been further elaborated and developed by Havelock himself and others, in an attempt to conceptualise in more detail the nature of such linkage processes.

In 1986, Havelock provided a fuller explication of the critical elements involved, arguing that the descriptive term 'link' implies a continuous loop which forms part of 'a chain, a sequence of entities connected to one another in a series and serving a common purpose' and where each link has two sides that interpenetrate other links or elements of the same chain. In other words, one might visualise it as some kind of coupling device, such as that linking the individual carriages of a train. On top of this coupling image, Havelock adds a radio signalling metaphor when he describes knowledge utilisation links as actively engaged in the 'transfer of complex messages' between 'senders' and 'receivers'. He suggests that such dialogue or exchange is based upon the movement of resources from a 'resourcer system' in an attempt to respond to certain needs emanating from a 'user system', although at the same time resource users 'stimulate the problem solving processes of resource systems, at least at some level' (1986: 228). Both images of course stress the discreteness and integrity of the elements or 'systems' that are articulated.

Havelock goes on to maintain that what 'is special about linkage theory is its explanation of how altogether new connections are formed, connections that extend perhaps to far-away resources and far-away users outside the normal environment. What we are looking at is the way in which one system can send messages that penetrate the self-protective layers and become planted in the ongoing routines and problem-solving processes of the other' (1986: 227).

Although some recognition of actor/interpretative processes is smuggled in, Havelock concludes by arguing that linkage is a natural process, but that it is generally slow, inefficient, error-prone and costly. Furthermore, there are many links along potential knowledge-user chains that are either dangerously weak or missing altogether. That is why there is a great need to provide specialists in various linkage processes at strategic points along the knowledge chain (1986: 234).

This leads him to argue that machine and human interventions designed to improve the flow of messages are essential: hence the need for what have been variously called relay stations, transformers and synthesisers, as well as extension agents, animators (i.e., 'user system mobilisers'), and what he characterises as 'linkage catalysts' or 'linkage process facilitators'. In line with these developments – and all the horrible neologisms – was the use of the latest technology such as videotexts and other computerised systems to send massive data sets to farmers in distant regions (Kuiper and Röling 1991, Leeuwis 1993).

Until relatively recently, Havelock's communication model remained a central orienting image for looking at knowledge dissemination and utilisation processes, forming the conceptual bedrock of much work on knowledge systems. For example, the model of agricultural knowledge and information systems originally promoted by Röling (1988: 30) and Engel (1990) in the 1980s, and to some extent still in current use, distinguishes between research, extension and farmer networks and institutions ('sub-systems'). These are interlinked through the flow of information and other resources to form a synergistic whole. Linkage mechanisms, which Röling describes in his earlier work as devices for bridging 'the gap between components of the system', stimulate communication between them, but because of certain resistance to the smooth flow of information, intervention by 'knowledge managers' is also required 'to nudge [them]...into compatible and complementary system roles'. Such intervention focuses upon 'institutional calibration' in which 'institutions can be compared to cogs in a gearbox: each cog transforms knowledge up or down stream' (Röling 1988: 54). In this way, Röling adds a further metaphor to the picture: this time a mechanical engineering one.

Further contributions by Röling (1990) and Engel (1995) have softened up 'hard systems' thinking and imagery characteristic of earlier formulations. In harmony with Checkland (1981, 1985, 1988), they propose a 'soft systems' methodology that takes a more inductive approach to systems modelling. Checkland argues that, whereas clear purposes can be attributed to certain phenomena such as the motor car, making them amenable to hard systems or engineering models, human activity and organisational behaviour are characterised by ambiguous and conflicting goals, interests and procedures, and by hazy and shifting boundaries. The analysis of social phenomena therefore necessitates a softer systems perspective, which views system configurations as the outcome of human endeavour rather than as constituting the conditions or 'prime movers' for social action.

Checkland goes on to formulate – though still retaining key systems principles such as emergence, hierarchy, communication and control – a methodology based on 'the view that social reality is not a "given" but is a process in which an ever-changing social world is continuously recreated by its members' (Checkland 1981: 20). In an attempt to avoid the teleological trap of predefining 'system goals', he suggests that the focus of systems research should be 'problem situations in which there are felt to be unstructured problems, ones in which the designation of objectives is itself problematic' (Checkland 1981: 155). The first step, then, involves a detailed depiction of the social situation and circumstances, leading to the identification of the critical problems facing the actors and to the use of systems concepts to delineate and prioritise them. On the basis of this, one devises a series of procedures whereby the actors and researcher participate in the construction of a systems model and 'make joint decisions in order to enhance the emergent properties of their human activity system' (Röling and Engel 1990: 9). Accordingly, gaps in communication (missing links), latent conflicts, lack of access to critical resources (especially information), problems of coordination and task differentiation, and poor management practice can be exposed and plans laid to correct them. Once such 'pathologies' (Röling 1988: 39–41) are detected, it is simply a question of making the right choices, of identifying the control variables and designing a control strategy to correct them.

Applied to the understanding of agricultural knowledge systems, soft systems methodology, then, entails the search for an understanding of the problems of communication pertaining to agricultural research, extension, knowledge utilisation and technological change. It views (Engel 1990: 29–30) these different activities as interlinked through both formal and informal mechanisms and points to the need to analyse:

1 The multiplicity of actors involved (e.g., farmers and their organisations, specialised research and extension institutions, agro-industrial entities, and more recently environmental and consumer groups);
2 The diversity in the sources and types of knowledge and information available; and
3 Any problems that exist in the integration and coordination of the different sub-systems.[11]

The systems model has been considered a useful tool by policymakers as well as by scientists. Adopting such an approach, a planner is expected to find the appropriate archetype, map out the social situation by taking into consideration the whole and not simply the parts, and look into the information and communication flows that will sustain the vital organisation of the system. He or she will then be in a position to 'target' efficiently the population and establish a good 'package', adequate for each category of user. This is still the basis for much research, especially in the ecological and natural sciences. Differences or failures in the implementation stage may later be attributed to 'the stupidity of the implementer', 'the corruption of government officials', the 'backwardness and false consciousness of the beneficiaries' or 'distortions produced by the capitalist system'. Hence, although the inadequacy of the package may be acknowledged, the categories used and the preconceived representation of the system are hardly ever questioned. On the other hand, it is the frontline worker – who has the mission of presenting the package and making it work – who must figure out the appropriate strategies, possibilities and constraints. It is therefore not surprising that members belonging to what has been labelled and targeted as the 'poorest of the poor' category, and thus subject to the 'benefits' of the 'project', often turn out in practice to be not the poorest but simply those who are willing, able and at hand. And, since it is the implementer who is confronted with the variety of interests, understandings, constraints and abilities of the 'target' population, it is mostly he or she who abandons the preconceived set of categories in favour of a more practical analysis. Here is the critical moment of decision-making, of the actual accomplishment of projects, which is mostly strikingly different from any written plans. Thus any logically-derived set of categories fades away in the face of the exigencies of everyday social life.

Pre-determining hierarchies or the roots of a system likewise overlooks the same ongoing intricate processes, thus rendering a logical but ethereal sketch of the situation. Differences arise in the way constraints influence the conditions of the agent, the space they occupy in his or her immediate world, or the leverage they exert during decision-making moments, but they cannot be depicted in simple hierarchical or systems terms. In fact they frequently cut across diverse structural arrangements or system linkages, and can only be accounted for using more perceptive theoretical tools. This implies new conceptions of knowledge, power and intervention.

Knowledge as an encounter of horizons

By the late 1980s, researchers began to pinpoint certain critical limitations in this linkage approach, or what Dissanayake (1986: 2) has designated 'the transportational paradigm', to understanding knowledge processes. The model assumes that the process of knowledge dissemination/utilisation involves the transfer of a body of knowledge from one individual or social unit to another, rather than adopting a more dynamic view that acknowledges the joint creation of knowledge by both disseminators and users. This latter interpretation depicts knowledge as arising from a fusion of horizons, since the processing and absorption of new items of information and new discursive or cognitive frames can only take place on the basis of already existing modes of knowledge and evaluation, which themselves are reshaped by the communicative experience. Moreover, although knowledge dissemination/creation is in essence an interpretative and cognitive process entailing the bridging of the gap between a familiar world and a less familiar (or even alien) set of meanings, knowledge is built upon the accumulated social experience, commitments and culturally-acquired dispositions of the actors involved. Hence,

> communicative action is not only a [cognitive] process of reaching under-standing; in coming to an understanding about something in the world, actors are at the same time taking part in interactions through which they develop, confirm, and renew their memberships in social groups and their own identities. Communicative actions are not only processes of interpretation in which cultural knowledge is 'tested against the world'; they are at the same time processes of social integration and socialisation...
>
> (Habermas 1987: 139)

Processes of knowledge dissemination/creation simultaneously imply, therefore, several interconnected elements: actor strategies and capacities for drawing upon existing knowledge repertoires and absorbing new information; validation processes whereby newly introduced information and its sources are judged acceptable and useful or contested; and various transactions involving the exchanges of actors involved in the production, dissemination and utilisation of knowledge. However, as several studies of 'experimenting farmers' (e.g., Richards 1985, Box 1987, Rhoades and Bebbington 1988, Millar 1994, Stolzenbach 1994) have convincingly shown, it is unlikely that the critical social divisions will coincide neatly with the distinctions between knowledge 'producers', 'disseminators' and 'users'.

This is illustrated in the following examples. The first concerns research on the use of information technology (i.e., computerised production models) among Dutch farmers (Leeuwis 1993). The study shows that the category of 'users' must be extended beyond farmers-as-clients to cover also government agencies and farmers' organisations wishing to use the technology to improve their competitiveness *vis-à-vis* other producer groups. Information technology should also be extended to include researchers and extension workers who deploy it to promote their own models of farming, as well as to agro-industrial enterprises that seek to tie customers to their business interests. Leeuwis's data suggest that conceptualisations of 'information needs' in terms of information tech-nology are often problematic, since they are viewed as 'static', as if they could be 'predicted in advance and relate[d] to formal decision making models'. Dutch cucumber growers, he claims, choose a specific software programme considering all sorts of 'context' situations, such as solidarity between peripheral groups, personal ties, group composition and the need to avoid isolation (Leeuwis 1993).

The second example relates to the case of Tomatlán, western Mexico, one of the largest irrigation districts in Mexico.[12] It highlights the shortcomings of externally-imposed technical solutions. Drawing upon national and international expertise, major plans entailing the use of the latest high-tech sprinkler systems and massive capital investment were designed to transform a resource-poor, dry farming zone into an area of irrigated agriculture. The scheme was initially intended to promote large-scale rice production, but this proved uneconomic. It was then decided to use part of the land instead for intensive livestock production and the growing of special varieties of grass and sorghum for cattle feed by peasant producers. A slaughterhouse was later to be built and the meat products exported to the United States. But these plans never came to fruition, since the land was unsuitable and the irrigation system too expensive for local farmers to use.

These pressures on local livelihoods led to the search by local cultivators for more viable forms of production based upon their own informal networks and sources of knowledge. One village, composed of a group of immigrant settlers from a neighbouring state, had relatives and friends back home who were experienced in the cultivation of papaya and lemon trees. Some of these immigrant farmers dreamed, then, of starting a similar enterprise in the Tomatlán area, for which they could obtain technical support and contacts for marketing from their relatives. Disobeying strict orders concerning approved crops and water use promulgated by district officials, they began using the small slopes on the edges of their plots to plant fruit trees, later extending these to cover the irrigated plots themselves. Also, rather than relying on official extension workers for information, they carried out their own research, visiting their kin to observe and to ask for advice. In addition, they obtained 'informal' and 'illegal' assistance from certain friendly district officials whom they encountered in various local bars. For instance, a close friendship with the officer in charge of locking and unlocking access to the underground water pipes installed for the high-tech sprinkler systems made it possible for them to borrow his keys at night so that they could irrigate their own plots, despite the prohibition to do so. Somewhat ironically, district extension officers later became the users of this farmer information to promote fruit production among other farmer groups in the Tomatlán district.

Such cases lend support to the argument that, if we conceptualise the issues of knowledge dissemination/utilisation simply in terms of discrete categories and linkage concepts, we will have failed to understand the rudiments of knowledge itself. An understanding of knowledge requires a careful analysis of the transformations of meaning at the interface of actors' lifeworlds. Furthermore, in coming to grips with knowledge processes, we must aim to understand questions of *dissonance* as well as consonance of ideas and beliefs, explore *discontinuity* rather than just the linkage of lifeworlds or social domains, and not so much the transfer of meaning as the *transformation*. Knowledge emerges as a product of the interaction and dialogue between specific actors and actors' lifeworlds. It is also *multi-layered* (there always exists a multiplicity of possible frames of meaning) and *fragmentary* and *diffuse* rather than unitary and systematised. Not only is it unlikely, therefore, that different parties (such as farmers, extensionists and researchers) would share the same priorities and parameters of knowledge, but one would also expect 'epistemic communities' (i.e., those that share roughly the same sources and modes of knowledge) to be internally differentiated in terms of knowledge repertoires and applications. Therefore engineering the creation of the conditions under which a single integrated knowledge system (involving mutually beneficial exchanges and flows of information) could emerge seems unattainable. And if indeed one were to succeed, this would most likely be at the expense of innovativeness and adaptability to change, both of which depend upon the diversity and fluidity of knowledge rather than on integration and systematisation.

Discontinuities and accommodations at knowledge interfaces

In order to explore these issues in more depth it is necessary to develop an analysis of knowledge interface situations. The notion of interface generally conjures up the image of two surfaces coming into contact, or of a computer system whose central processing unit is linked to auxiliary equipment through a mechanism called an interface. It has also been used to characterise the situation where chemical substances interact but fail to combine to form a new composite solution. My usage is different, in that I wish to stress precisely how the multiplicity of actors and perspectives involved in social interfaces merge and combine through processes of accommodation and conflict to generate newly emergent forms of organisation and understanding. This is the case even where the dynamics involved lead to separation, opposition or renewed conflict. Hence, I define social interfaces as critical points of intersection between different social fields, domains or lifeworlds, where social discontinuities based upon differences in values, social interests and power are found (see Chapters 3 and 4 for a fuller explication). A similar idea is conveyed by Röling (1988) when he suggests that interface is not simply a linkage mechanism but rather the 'force field' between two institutions.[13]

Interface studies, then, are essentially concerned with the analysis of *discontinuities* in social life. As I mentioned above, such discontinuities are characterised by discrepancies in values, interests, knowledge and power. Interfaces typically occur therefore at points where different, and often conflicting, lifeworlds or social fields intersect. More concretely, they characterise social situations (or what Giddens calls 'locales') in which the interactions between actors become oriented around the problem of devising ways of bridging, accommodating to, or struggling against each others' different social and cognitive worlds. Interface analysis aims to elucidate the types of social discontinuities present in such situations and to characterise the different kinds of organisational and cultural forms that reproduce or transform them.

Some of the complexities involved in the interaction of outside organisations with local groups are explored in the following two cases. They illustrate how the understanding of different forms of knowledge and technology is central to the analysis of rural development. The first case concerns a Mexican government programme for rural women, which I have referred to in Chapter 4. The second explores the interface networks that emerge between local farmers and private and public technology and market institutions in an English rural county.[14]

Following a new law promulgated by the Mexican government designed to stimulate the formation of new enterprises among peasant women, a group was set up in a village in western Mexico to run a bee-keeping project. Although the women had different expectations and saw their participation in the project differently in terms of the kinds of benefits they might receive individually or collectively, their interests came together at certain points not only in relation to the project itself, but also as their experiences generated a degree of common identity. They shared many of the same difficulties with respect to gender roles and conflicts over them in their households and in the village at large. However, the process of working together and being involved in a common endeavour did not imply a uniform view of matters such as the size of the enterprise (this was crucial as to whether it was a complementary or central activity for the women), the relations they assumed with groups and institutions outside the village, but also their self-definition as beekeepers, as women entrepreneurs or as housewives. The women struggled together against male villagers who labelled them lazy and irresponsible towards household chores, redoubling their efforts to mind their children and husbands. They contested the ideas of ministry officers who pressed them to enlarge their enterprise and to enter into the 'men's world of business'. However, during the process of interaction with each other, with their families and other people from the village, as well as with outside intervenors from the ministry and even with us as researchers, the boundaries of the project and their roles as women were constantly redefined. This redefinition involved not only their aims as beekeepers, but their prospects and projects as women in other fields of their everyday lives.

The second case concerns a study of technological change (Hawkins 1991) which shows how issues of 'knowledge transfer' also necessitate a careful analysis of the interests and strategies pursued by those who produce, sell and/or promote technologies. This case provides suggestions as to how we might integrate such political and economic dimensions into the analysis of agricultural knowledge processes.

Hawkins' study focuses upon dairy and potato production in Cheshire, exploring the following issues: the sources of funding and direction of agricultural research in dairy farming and potatoes, the dissemination of new technologies from manufacturers to individual farmers, and the types of interface networks that emerge within these two contrasting commodity complexes, as well as the ways in which farmers integrate new technologies into farm production. Hawkins argues that new technologies have a dual nature: they are both a product or input into production and an information flow concerned with promoting a particular technological rationale. Technology development and dissemination is managed and shaped by specific public and private interests and influenced by prevailing policy discourse and by market possibilities. As a result, the rate and direction of technological change varies, for example, between dairying (which tends to be production-oriented) and potato growing (which is primarily market-oriented).

However, Hawkins maintains that it is crucial to disaggregate these various sets of interests impinging upon the farm by identifying the particular social actors involved in the process. This leads her to isolate important differences in the commodity complexes and interface networks for milk and potatoes. The provision of technology to the farm and the networks and the channels through which this was achieved showed how the farm itself was enclosed within sets of interlinked agents (providing inputs and advice and organising outputs) that took somewhat different forms depending on the commodity complex. Whereas the potato complex was found to be highly integrated both vertically, with processors and packers also selling seed and providing advice, and horizontally, with agents selling combinations of inputs, the milk complex was more segregated, with little evidence of vertical or horizontal integration for products. The study of interface networks highlighted three other interesting aspects: first, far from being in powerful market positions, agribusiness agents faced uncertain and constrained markets; second, locality was important, since farmers obtained many inputs from the nearby general merchant; and third, the offer of technical advice to farmers was a strategy for intensifying the link, since, as production became more technically complicated, so farmers felt the need for more advice. Hence good technical advice was considered by agribusiness as a way of increasing farmers' loyalty: for example, many dairy farmers favoured ICI fertilisers because they wanted to use ICI's 'Dairymaid' costing service and other facilities.

Technological change was not only important therefore at a product level but also through its advisory, or as Benvenuti (1975) term it, its technico-administrative character, although – as Hawkins shows later in her analysis of how farmers negotiate a degree of autonomy in managing technology, commodity networks and farm production – agribusiness is never able completely to undermine the independent decision-making capacity of farmers nor destroy the heterogeneity of farm enterprise, even within the same commodity complex. Even if farmers' decisions are influenced to a considerable extent by the ideas of their advisors, any such advice is, of course, filtered through the farmers' technological system and their own lifeworlds. In this way there is what one might call 'an internalisation of externalities'. As Hawkins neatly puts it:

> The interface networks are sites for the dynamics of agri-business, extending markets and technical control to farmers and [of] farmers reacting by adapting the offered technologies to suit themselves, shaping the networks and relating their actions perhaps to a slightly different logic to those of agribusiness.
>
> (Hawkins 1991: 279)

Knowledge networks and epistemic communities

Consistent with this emphasis on viewing knowledge as a social process is Louk Box's (1989: 167) argument that agricultural knowledge systems should not be conceptualised as overall structures made up of research, extension and farmer 'subsystems' (as suggested by Röling 1985 and 1988). He proposes instead the notion of a multiplicity of knowledge networks through which certain types of information are communicated and legitimated, and between which there is often a critical lack of communication. Using the case of cassava production in the Dominican Republic, Box shows how the lifeworlds of researchers, extensionists and farmers are partially sealed off from each other. He concludes that '[i]nstead of one knowledge system there are many complex networks, which lack articulation among each other. The lifeworlds of the participants, or their values, norms and interests, differ so greatly that they do not allow for communication and interaction between the parties' (Box 1989: 167).

These differences, often labelled pathological by system thinkers, are intrinsic to the everyday life of the actors, and constitute the social conditions for both change and continuity. A key problem for the analysis and management of so-called knowledge systems is, then, precisely the fragile, changeable or non-existent communication channels between the various parties involved, not the permanence and coherence of existing linkages. Moreover, as Box underlines, the knowledge repertoires of sierra immigrants – who arrive with certain pre-existing social networks but also quickly create new ones – cannot therefore be detached from the social relationships and exchanges in which such knowledge exists.

In another study in the Dominican Republic, Box documents how small-scale traders (not extension officers) involved in the marketing of various types of agricultural produce played a central role in the diffusion of information concerning new varieties of sweet potato. Twenty per cent of farmer respondents indicated they preferred to receive advice from traders, as compared with only five per cent who showed a preference for official agricultural extensionists. In addition, there was widespread distrust among farmers about the quality of the planting materials distributed and the information given out by government agencies. Local producers bitterly recalled the last time government actively promoted a new variety: this tasted so bad that it was impossible to sell it in the fresh food markets (Box 1986: 104–5).

Another example of the way in which agricultural knowledge is embedded within particular social relations and cultural understandings comes from the Tonga of Mola Chiefdom in northern Zimbabwe (Schuthof 1989). Here we find three different and largely separate social networks relating to agricultural knowledge and practice: one centring upon the government agricultural extensionist whose job it is to promote a hybrid maize package, the second upon the religious specialist, 'the spirit medium' or rainmaker who deals primarily with matters pertaining to traditional staples and Tonga farming practice, and the third upon a group of 'innovative' farmers involved principally in market-oriented production. The community is also divided along religious lines between Christians and non-Christians. Schuthof records that, while Christians usually consult the extensionist or knowledgeable local farmers when faced with agricultural problems, most non-Christians go directly to the local rainmaker who gives advice on the scheduling of agricultural tasks, divines the causes and cures of plant diseases, blesses the seeds before planting, and intercedes on behalf of local people with aggrieved spirits for rain or to prevent wild animals from attacking them or from destroying their crops. For the bulk of the population, the rainmaker with his professed 'agricultural' knowledge and network of support and legitimation was more significant for shaping agricultural production decisions than the specialised agricultural knowledge and contacts provided by the extension staff. Indeed, Schuthof's brief study shows that only one per cent of the farmers of the area bothered to visit the extensionist and learn about the maize package he was supposed to promote, even though most farmers did in fact grow some improved maize variety. Understanding agricultural knowledge dissemination/utilisation among the Tonga then required careful appreciation of the differentiated nature of local social networks, beliefs and power.

An early study of differences in the social networks of commercial and non-commercial farmers among the Plateau Tonga of Zambia (Jones 1966) showed how commercial producers developed closer, non-dependent friendship ties with nearby European farmers, from whom they obtained benefits such as advice on maize farming and certain farm inputs. Unlike the non-commercial farmers, however, who also sometimes visited European farmers (mostly ex-employers), usually 'to beg for something...salt, a piglet, and in one case, a pile of old sacks', the commercial farmer avoided placing himself in a subordinate relationship and insisted on paying or reciprocating for any services rendered. One such farmer responded to the cultural information he received by advising his European friend on the purchase of pigs from certain non-commercial farmers. Another case was that of a farmer borrowing money to pay off a debt on a tractor, in return for which he offered to place cattle on the European's land as collateral (Jones 1966: 280, 282).

These examples point to the existence of important differences in the nature and operation of knowledge networks within the same farming population. Hence, network analysis can help to identify the boundaries of epistemic communities and to characterise the structure and contents of particular communicator networks. As previous studies of communicator networks have shown (e.g., Allen and Cohen 1969, Long 1972), certain individuals or groups often become the socio-metric stars of a defined network of social ties, as well as the points of articulation with wider social fields. That is, they operate as 'gatekeepers' or 'brokers' to spatially and structurally more distant networks. Gatekeepers play a strategic role in both facilitating and blocking the flow of certain types of information, and thus they are of crucial importance in understanding the functioning of knowledge networks. Related to this issue is the proposition that effective dissemination of ideas and information within a network of individuals depends upon the existence of what Granovetter (1973) calls 'weak ties' which 'bridge divergent network segments that otherwise would be isolated from one another' (Milardo 1988: 17). Such weak ties have been shown to be particularly significant for obtaining access to diverse fields of information, such as, for example, those associated with seeking employment or housing, or information concerning prices in dispersed market locations. On the other hand, to act on information usually requires that individuals secure some support from others. This entails a minimum of normative consensus and, in some situations, the capacity for making rules and enforcing compliance from members (Moore 1973). The latter presupposes the existence of a relatively dense social network, which can also, paradoxically, hinder the absorption of new information and the quick adaptation to changed circumstances (Long 1984b: 23, fn 14).

These and similar network findings provide a fertile source for ideas on how different types of social networks and exchange contents within networks affect the flow of information and processes of knowledge dissemination/creation. This is a fruitful but still somewhat neglected field of research.[15]

Knowledge heterogeneity and agency in farm practice

As I have repeatedly stressed in previous chapters, farming populations are essentially heterogeneous in terms of the strategies that farmers adopt for solving the production and other problems they face. Varying ecological, demographic, market, politico-economic and sociocultural conditions combine to generate differential patterns of farm enterprise, leading to differences in farm management styles, cropping patterns and levels of production. Implicit in this process, of course, is the differential use and transformation of knowledge; that is, farm knowledge varies and is accorded different social meanings depending upon how it is applied in the running of farms. This is readily seen in the use of different technologies (e.g., tractor, plough, hoe or axe) but is also evident in the specific meanings that a particular instrument or factor of production acquires as it is coordinated with other production and reproduction factors (van der Ploeg 1986). Hence, adopted technology is forever being reworked to fit with the production strategies, resource imperatives and social desires of the farmer or farm family. Knowledge transformation, then, as Engel (1990) suggests, can be defined as the process by which individuals or groups continuously change and adapt their knowledge in response to changing intentions, opportunities and circumstances.

Included in this, however, is not only the process by which 'new' technologies or packages are adopted, appropriated or transformed, but also the ongoing processes by which particular farmers combine different social domains based on, for example, the family, community, market or state institutions. Since each domain (as the word suggests) implies a distinctive normative ordering, the farmer's task becomes that of selecting and coordinating the most appropriate normative and social commitments for organising the process of farm production and reproduction. The decisions the farmer makes, of course, are based upon value preferences and available knowledge, resources and relationships.

Viewed in this manner, the farmer is seen as an active strategiser who problematises situations, processes information and brings together the elements necessary for operating his farm; that is, a farmer is involved in constructing his/her own farming world, even if he/she internalises external modes of rationality (which may include the use of information technologies) and thus, as it were, appears simply to carry out the commands of outside agents. An interesting example of this is provided by Pile (1990), who analyses processes of cultural construction among dairy farmers in England. He shows how their forms of discourse and 'maps of meaning' conceptualise the power relations in which they are involved and how these frames of signification shape everyday social action and farming strategy. In this way, he brings out how dairy farmers perceive the character of the state and reason about the agricultural policies pursued by both the British government and the European Community.

This line of argument leads me once again to emphasise the importance of an actor-oriented approach to the understanding of knowledge processes. As I elaborated in Chapter 1 of this book, central to the notion of social actor is the concept of human agency, which attributes to the actor (individual or social group) the capacity to process social experience and to devise ways of coping with problematic situations. Agency is composed of social relations and can only become effective through them. It requires organising capacities. Effective agency, then, requires the generation/manipulation of a network of social relations and the channelling of specific items (such as claims, orders, information, technologies and goods) through certain 'nodal points' (Clegg 1989: 199). In order to accomplish this, it becomes essential for actors to win the struggles that take place over the attribution of specific social meanings to particular actions and ideas. Looked at from this point of view, particular development intervention models (or ideologies) become strategic weapons in the hands of those charged with promoting them.

This process is illustrated by van der Ploeg's (1989, 1993) analysis of how small-scale producers in the Andes succumb to 'scientific' definitions of agricultural development. He shows that, although peasants have devised perfectly good solutions to their own production problems (here he is concerned with potato cultivation), their local knowledge gradually becomes marginalised by the type of scientific knowledge introduced by extensionists. The farmer, that is, becomes superfluous to the model of 'modern' production methods promoted by 'the experts', and development projects become a kind of commodity monopolised and sold by experts who through the chain of 'commands' exert 'authority' over their 'subjects'. In this way the rules, limits and procedures governing the negotiation between state agents and farmers and the resources made available are derived (in large part) from external interests and institutions. Hence, although it is possible to depict the relations between Andean peasants and outside experts or state officials in terms of an entrenched history of distrust and dependency, it is science and modern ideologies of development that eventually come to have such major influence on the outcomes of dealings with cultivators that they effectively prevent any exchange of knowledge and experience. This creates what van der Ploeg calls 'a sphere of ignorance' in which cultivators are labelled 'invisible men' in contrast to the 'experts' who are visible and authoritative.

Such processes, however, are by no means mechanical impositions from the outside. They necessarily entail negotiation over concepts, meanings and projects, which are internalised to varying degrees by the different parties involved. Thus the ability of extensionists to transform the nature of agricultural practice is premised on two elements: their skills in handling interface encounters with peasants; and the ways in which the wider set of power relations (or 'chain of agents') feeds into the context, giving legitimacy to their actions and conceptions, and defining certain critical 'rules of the game'. Counterbalancing this is the fact that cultivators, too, assimilate information from each other, as well as from external sources, in an attempt to create knowledge that is better in tune with the situations they face.

This process of internalisation is well described by Villarreal (1990) in her study of the bee-keeping enterprise mentioned earlier. From the start, the implementers of the project saw these women as potential entrepreneurs and as *campesinas* (peasant women). But the women's self-images portrayed a different and varied picture. While some of them to some extent went along with the entrepreneurial peasant image, most described themselves as housewives or as lowly and uncultivated people, as *patas rajadas* (having feet like leather) and *rusticas* (rustic types), for whom bee-keeping was only a complementary activity. Nevertheless, the project provided a series of encounters with the 'outside world' involving a confrontation between 'external' categorisations of themselves as women and their own self images. As time passed, these latter conceptions were reflected upon and partly modified, leading after a few years to the point where the notion of 'women entrepreneurs' was not entirely alien to or incompatible with their other conceptions of self.

Power and the social construction of knowledge

A critical issue, given these 'multiple realities', potentially conflicting social and norma-tive interests and diverse and fragmented bodies of knowledge, is whose interpretations or models (e.g., those of agricultural scientists, politicians, farmers or extensionists) prevail over those of other actors, and under what conditions. Knowledge processes are embedded in social processes that imply aspects of power, authority and legitimation; and they are just as likely to reflect and contribute to the conflict between social groups as they are to lead to the establishment of common perceptions and interests. And, if this is the normal state of affairs, then it becomes unreal and foolhardy to imagine that one can gently 'nudge' knowledge systems towards better modes of integration and coordination.

These issues of power and social conflict are poorly dealt with in knowledge systems theory and methodology. At the theoretical level, Röling and Engel (1990: 11) hypothe-sise that 'optimal KIS [Knowledge and Information System] performance requires balance between the intervention power of specialised institutions and the countervailing power of clients'. They also assert that a KIS needs to be endowed with adequate resources, but where these should come from and how they should be distributed among the various parties (e.g., government development agencies, farmers' organisations and research institutes) in order to ensure a sound performance is not made clear. Thus there is little understanding of how power differences affect the interactions between the elements (or 'sub-systems') of the system. Indeed, the matter is avoided by defining 'optimal performance' or 'synergy' in terms of assumed system goals that entail a balance of forces that regulates information flow and promotes the coherence of the system. It is simply assumed that methods such as 'soft systems' methodology and rapid appraisal of agricultural knowledge systems (Salomon and Engel 1997) provide satisfactory answers as to how to choose between the differing goals and interests of the actors in the system. Local participants and researchers, it seems, are able, through a joint process of learning, to arrive at some new 'systematic' interpretation or model of reality that can then be compared to and evaluated against the views originally held by the different actors, in order to design new intervention strategies.[16]

Implicit in all such procedures and theoretical tenets is the assumption that the relations between intervenors (whether researchers or extensionists) and clients takes place in an atmosphere of optimism and willing participation, when experience shows us that the process is far from smooth and unproblematic, since differences of interests, resources and perceptions will always intrude. For systems analysts, there are two practical solutions to this problem. Either one defines the system boundaries in such a way as to maximise the possibility that mutual agreements can be reached – this implies identifying homogeneous 'target groups' or specific institutions concerned with knowledge dissemination and utilisation, and thus excluding other actors or more informal, 'autonomous' social arrangements – or one adopts a view of the situation that is acceptable to the most powerful participants. From an enlightened policy point of view, neither of these solutions is, of course, satisfactory.

The foregoing discussion emphasises that knowledge is not simply something that is possessed, accumulated and unproblematically imposed upon others (Foucault, in Gordon 1980: 78–108). Nor can it be measured precisely in terms of some notion of quantity or quality. It emerges out of processes of social interaction and, as I suggested earlier, it is essentially a joint product of the encounter and fusion of horizons. It must, therefore, like power, be looked at relationally and not treated as if it could be depleted or used up. That someone has power or knowledge does not entail that others are without. A zero-sum model is thus misplaced. Nevertheless both power and knowledge may become reified in social life; that is, we often think of them as being real material things possessed by actors; and we tend to regard them as unquestioned 'givens'. This process of reification is, of course, an essential part of the ongoing struggles over meaning and the control of strategic relationships and resources that we discussed earlier. Knowledge encounters involve the struggle between actors whereby certain of them attempt to enrol others in their 'projects', getting them to accept particular frames of meaning and winning them over to their points of view. If they succeed, then other parties 'delegate' power to them. As I argued before, these struggles focus around the 'fixing of key points that have a controlling influence over the exchanges and attributions of meaning (including the acceptance of reified notions such as "authority")'.

If we now look at knowledge dissemination/creation in this way we are forced to place it fully in its social context, not as a disembodied process made up of 'formal institutions', 'ideal-typical conceptions' or linkage mechanisms, but as involving specific actors and interacting individuals who become interrelated through networks of interest and through the sharing of certain knowledge frames. These networks, of course, are emergent and stretch beyond the immediate interactional context to encompass remoter regions. They also may, as Latour (1987) has remarked, involve more than simply social relationships: embedded in them are various material and extra-somatic resources (such as telephone calls, farm records, genetic materials and machines) that acquire social significance in the process of knowledge dissemination/creation.

The analysis of power processes should not therefore be restricted to an understanding of how social constraints and access to resources shape social action. Nor should it lead to the description of rigid hierarchical categories and hegemonic ideologies that 'oppress passive victims'. Standing back from the tendency to empathise ideologically with these hapless victims, one should, instead, explore the extent to which specific actors perceive themselves capable of manoeuvring within given contexts or networks and develop strategies for doing so. This is not to fail to recognise the often much restricted space for individual initiative but rather to examine, within the constraints encountered, how actors identify and create space for their own interests and for change (see Long 1984b for a discussion of this notion of 'space for change').

For example, in a study of women day-labourers in Mexico, one particular worker had a clear perception of the fact that there was a shortage (or at least no overabundance) of labour and that the company needed skilled and fast workers. Since she herself possessed the requisite qualities, this gave her a certain leverage over the company: she could pace her own work and banter with the foreman and farm manager, thus revealing what she called their 'softer sides'. Yet at the same time she was not prepared to give the company more physical labour than was absolutely necessary and was able, to a significant degree, to 'mould authority', thus enrolling the 'bosses' in her own 'circumstantial projects' (Torres 1994) – such as selecting the job she wished to do, allowing her more time to rest, or obtaining leave on grounds of health or seeking a higher work position. It goes without saying that she did not of course achieve complete control over the organisation of her work, since the management staff were also intent upon enrolling her and the other workers in their projects, otherwise the company would have no *raison d'être*.

As Villarreal (1994) has persuasively argued, making room for manoeuvre implies a degree of consent, a degree of negotiation and a degree of power – not necessarily power stored in some economic or political position, but the possibility of control, of prerogative, of some degree of authority and capacity for action, be it front- or backstage, for flickering moments or for long periods. Power, then, is fluid and difficult or unnecessary to measure, but imperative to describe more precisely. It is not only the amount of power that makes a difference, but the possibility of gaining edge over others and pressing it home situationally. Different people have different ways of enrolling others in their projects, of selling their own self-images and of trying to impose self-images on them,[17] all of which form part of a process of negotiation by which actors attempt to change certain components or conditions, while striving to maintain others. Hence power always implies struggle, negotiation and compromise. Even those categorised as 'oppressed' are not utterly passive victims and may become involved in active resistance. Likewise, the 'powerful' are not in complete control of the stage, and the extent to which their power is forged by the so-called powerless should not be underestimated.[18] Rather, as Scott points out, one must speak of resistance, accommodation and strategic compliance. Although resistance is rarely an overt, collective undertaking, individual acts of subtle defiance and the muffled voices of opposition and mobilisation nevertheless act to divert the possibly coercive or oppressive strategies of others. In this manner, accommodation and strategic compliance – sometimes shielding acts of defiance – become regular features of everyday social life (Scott 1985).

All this suggests that power differentials and struggles over social meaning are central to an understanding of knowledge processes. Knowledge is essentially a social construction that results from and is constantly being reshaped by the encounters and discontinuities that emerge at the points of intersection between actors' lifeworlds. A systems perspective, I contend, fails to grasp the theoretical significance of these processes for analysing knowledge issues. It also evades making explicit the critical value decisions made by researchers or intervenors when applying systems models.

The discourse and dilemma of 'empowerment'

This view sheds light on the concept of 'empowerment', which is strongly encouraged as a goal to be attained in development practice (Huizer 1979, Chambers 1983, Kronenburg 1986). Although the word forms part of a neo-populist discourse supporting 'participatory' approaches that emphasise 'listening to the people', understanding the 'reasoning behind local knowledge', 'strengthening local organisational capacity' and developing 'alternative development strategies from below', it nevertheless seems to carry with it the connotation of power injected from outside aimed at shifting the balance of forces towards local interests. Hence it implies the idea of empowering people through strategic intervention by 'enlightened experts' who make use of 'people's science' (Richards 1985) and 'local intermediate organisations' (Esman and Uphoff 1984, Korten 1987) to promote development 'from below'. While acknowledging the need to take serious account of local people's solutions to the problems they face, the issues are often presented as involving the substitution of 'blueprint' by 'learning approaches to the planning and management of projects' (Korten 1987) or in terms of 'new' for 'old' style professionalism aimed at promoting participatory management and participatory research and evaluation methods (Chambers et al. 1989).[19]

Such formulations still do not escape the managerialist and interventionist undertones inherent in participatory methods; that is, they tend to evoke the image of 'more knowledgeable and powerful outsiders' helping 'the powerless and less discerning local folk'. Of course, many field practitioners, who face the everyday problems of project implementation, show an acute awareness of this paradox of participatory strategies. As Villarreal (1990) describes in her own experience as an external 'change agent', efforts to encourage development in rural communities must necessarily face local patterns of organisation and networking. After receiving many complaints from sesame producers concerning the low price offered for their product, Villarreal and her colleagues brought the issue to a village assembly, where everyone agreed there was an urgent need to look for better markets. Yet, when a good outlet and price was eventually found through peer-group marketing, the initiative met with resistance and apathy. One producer explained his reluctance as being due to the fact that he had already made deals with his *compadre* (fictive kinsman) the middleman, who had good relations with the town mayor. He saw his future lying not in the few extra cents he would gain through selling his sesame along with his peers, but in the help he would receive later from his *compadre* and his contacts. Thus, rather than empathising with other poor producers belonging to what was preconceived as a 'horizontal' category, he identified himself as belonging to a more vertical network which in his eyes placed him in a more advantageous position than the rest of the farmers.

Kronenburg (1986) – also a practitioner – provides an insightful description of some of the dilemmas of 'empowerment' experienced by implementers of a non-formal education programme in Kenya which was strongly committed to participatory and conscientising goals. Discussing the interplay between emancipatory and manipulative processes, he explains:

> There was contradiction looming in the thin line between the use of DEP [Development Education Programme] skills to enhance the capacity of communities and their members to decide on their own development priorities or to attain goals the facilitators themselves had set. Often, discussions on the topic of manipulation emerged at national...workshops usually at a stage that trust between participants and facilitators had not fully developed. Yet, the possibility was always there that unwittingly participants would be following the path laid out by the facilitators.

Closely related to the issue of emancipation versus manipulation is the power of the facilitator to either allow group dialogue to follow its course or to control the discussions by imposing various forms of discipline. By applying time limits on topics judged irrelevant or by emphasising topics familiar or foreseen for discussion, the facilitator could influence the direction of the discussion. This is a dilemma facilitators, applying a non-directive methodology…are faced with continuously…To forestall manipulation DEP workers attempted consciously to develop sensitivity to group needs and feelings. To do this optimally facilitators always operated in teams to provide counterweight to the undesired tendencies inherent to their work.

(Kronenburg 1986: 163)

He goes on to describe what he labels as issues of credibility and integrity versus loyalty:

[M]ost DEP workers were church employed and as it turned out…so were a number of DEP group leaders such as catechists. Other group leaders were civil servants. They included public health workers, social workers, schoolteachers and extension officers. As it happened the high level of credibility DEP had built up towards donor agencies as well as the grass-roots groups carried the very seeds of conflict with their employers: the church and government authorities.

Diocesan development co-ordinators were under pressure from their employers to include request[s] for non-DEP related funds in their applications to funding partners. Others would use DEP's name and claim using its methodology in order to obtain funds for [their] own projects. This threatened to undermine the credibility the DEP had nurtured carefully over the years…[and shook] the mutual confidence among DEP members themselves, thus, risking damage to…DEP's coherence as a movement.

Also…some group action plans, containing social justice components, entered into controversy with government and church authorities. If branded 'political', these actions were likely to fizzle out. A factor in this process was that salaried group leaders risked losing their employment due to disloyalty perceived by their employers…[I]t could well be that due to these 'conflicting loyalties' DEP generated less actions for social justice than were expected

(Kronenburg 1986: 164)

Kronenburg's account exposes the multi-faceted nature of power inherent in the relations and knowledge accounts between development practitioners and their local 'partners' in participatory projects. It also shows how external social commitments intrude into this arena and shape the outcomes of participatory activities. Hence his study adds weight to my earlier argument that social processes (and especially so-called 'planned' interventions) are highly complex and cannot easily be manipulated through the injection of external sources of power and authority. The issue he mentions of conflicting loyalties and ideologies, likewise brings us back to the earlier discussion of negotiations over 'truth' claims, battles over images and contesting interests which are implicit in the interlocking of lifeworlds and actors' projects.

The Kenyan project in fact illustrates the central importance of strategic agency[20] in the ways in which people (i.e. development practitioners as well as local participants) deal with and manipulate certain constraining and enabling elements in their endeavours to enrol each other in their individual or group 'projects'. The case also suggests the significance of social networks for gathering information, forming opinions, legitimising one's standpoint, and thus for generating differential power relations. The idea that designing participatory strategies based upon the effective use of local knowledge and organisation would enable one to avoid what Marglin and Marglin (1990) call 'the dominating knowledge of science and western "scientific" management' is clearly untenable.[21] The question of empowerment, then, brings us back to the central issue of the encounter between actors and their knowledge repertoires.

Conclusion

The foregoing discussion provides a profile of current empirical and theoretical interests essential for developing new theoretical challenges to the analysis of knowledge processes and development. The agenda is extensive and the theoretical issues daunting. It is my view, however, that we have already made important headway towards developing such a revitalised sociological perspective that challenges interventionist thinking and feeds into mainstream sociological and anthropological theory and debates. It enables us, I believe, to build a better bridge between theoretical understanding and social practice. It does this through providing a set of sensitising analytical concepts based on an actor and interface perspective and a field methodology geared to developing theory 'from below'.

9

THE DYNAMICS OF KNOWLEDGE INTERFACES BETWEEN BUREAUCRATS AND PEASANTS[1]

The nature of knowledge

Knowledge is constituted by the ways in which people categorise, code, process and impute meaning to their experiences. This is as true of 'scientific' as it is of 'non-scientific', everyday forms of knowledge. We should not therefore equate knowledge with some professional, specialised or esoteric set of data or ideas. It is something that everybody possesses, even though the grounds for belief and the procedures for validation of knowledge-claims will vary. Nor should the concept of knowledge carry with it the implication of 'discovering the real facts', as if they lay 'out there' ready for uncovering. Such a view is based upon an 'objectivism' which assumes that 'the world is composed of facts and that the goal of knowledge is to provide a literal account of what the world is like' (Knorr-Cetina 1981a: 1–3).

Knowledge emerges out of a complex process involving social, situational, cultural and institutional factors. The process takes place on the basis of existing conceptual frameworks and procedures and is affected by various social contingencies, such as the skills, orientations, experiences, interests, resources and patterns of social interaction characteristic of the particular group or interacting set of individuals, as well as of those of the wider audience. Moreover, knowledge is constructive in the sense that it is the result of a great number of decisions and selective incorporations of previous ideas, beliefs and images, but at the same time destructive of other possible frames of conceptualisation and understanding. Thus it is not an accumulation of facts but involves ways of construing the world. Nor is knowledge ever fully unified or integrated in terms of an underlying cultural logic or system of classification. Rather, it is fragmentary, partial and provisional in nature, and people work with a multiplicity of understandings, beliefs and commitments.

The connection between lifeworlds and knowledge processes

The understanding of the production, reproduction and transformation of knowledge must therefore be situated in terms of the 'lifeworlds' of those individuals and groups involved. A lifeworld is a lived-in and largely taken-for-granted world (Schutz and Luckmann 1973). It is *actor* rather than observer defined.

Everyday life is to a degree experienced as an ordered reality, shared with others (i.e., it is intersubjective). This 'order' appears both in the ways in which individuals manage their social relationships and in how they problematise their situations. According to Schutz (1962), knowledge of everyday life is organised in zones around a person's 'here and now'. The centre of his or her world is him/herself. Around this centre, knowledge is arranged in zones, both spatial and temporal, of different degrees of relevance: first, face-to-face situations, and then more distant zones where encounters are more typified and anonymous.

Everyday life is dominated by the pragmatic motive; that is, it is essentially oriented to solving practical problems. One sort of practical knowledge is that called recipe or 'cookery book' knowledge, which is limited to pragmatic competence in routine performances. This occupies a prominent place in a person's knowledge. Its validity is taken for granted until one encounters a problem that cannot be solved. Then there are other, more explorative types of knowledge: we often have to make decisions involving choice between alternatives, and to do this we intuitively draw upon existing stocks of knowledge, on prefabricated strategic models, or allow ourselves to be guided by certain normative views or social commitments. While certain ideologies discourage innovation, others encourage it. But of course the incorporation of new ideas or modes of behaving simultaneously entails a process of transformation. For example, when a new technology is introduced into an existing farming system, the technology acquires new meanings and uses, often other than those intended by the planners or implementers.

One approach to analysing lifeworlds and the processes by which individuals process the information reaching them is the identification of their cognitive maps. These cognitive maps categorise the world of experience into classes of phenomena, which eliminates the necessity of responding to every unique event in the environment. Bruner et al. (1956) maintain that the learning and utilisation of categories represents the most elementary and general form of cognition by which man adjusts to his environment. Hence it is argued that, in order to discover different strategies of adaptation, we must identify the different category systems that individuals use to reduce the complexity of the environment and to organise their behaviour. Category systems enable the individual to identify those aspects of the environment which are significant for adaptation, give direction to instrumental activity, and permit the anticipation of future events. An ethnographic description of a group and its lifeworld must then tap the cognitive world of the individuals concerned. It must discover those features of objects and events that are regarded as significant for defining concepts, formulating propositions and making decisions.

This approach has been used interestingly by Spradley (1972) in a study of tramps in the United States. He shows that tramps have cognitive maps that differ in essence from the views of them expressed by outsiders such as social workers and medical or legal practitioners. Their knowledge of the world is ordered differently. Any external solutions to their problems are likely therefore to be conceived of in terms that do not conform to their own social construction of reality. Spradley develops a semantic and social classificatory analysis for comprehending their lifeworld. He also brings out the clever way in which they manipulate the welfare and social services in order to extract what they want out of them, a bit like the strategies described for the gypsies.[2] They do this by playing up to the expectations of those who hold different models of tramps' problems.

Spradley does not, however, examine the social interactional basis for tramps' worldviews, or how their cognitive maps are constructed and revised on the basis of day-to-day experience. This points to a general limitation of ethno-scientific models. They assume that cognitive maps or cultural understandings provide the ground rules for social life that remain the same for members of the same 'epistemic community' (i.e., composed of persons who share roughly the same sources and modes of knowledge, cf. Knorr-Cetina 1981b). Clearly this is not the case, and we therefore need a more discriminating methodology. The flows of communication and exchange between different actors – for example, among the tramps themselves and between them and the various types of welfare officers, policemen, etc., with whom they interact – are critically important for defining the knowledge and beliefs of tramps (as individuals and as a group) as against the perceptions and views expressed by the other participants. In analysing this situation it is inadequate to concentrate simply upon 'discovering' through semantic analysis a generalised tramps' map or body of knowledge of their social world. The production and transformation of knowledge resides not in category systems or classificatory schemata *per se* but in the processes by which social actors interact, negotiate and accommodate to each other's life-worlds, leading to the reinforcement or transformation of existing types of knowledge or to the emergence of new forms. These processes and outcomes are shaped by sources of power, authority and legitimation available to the different actors involved.

The importance of studying knowledge interfaces

The concept of 'interface' can contribute to an analysis of these processes. Interface conveys the idea of some kind of face-to-face encounter between individuals with differing interests, resources and power. Studies of interface encounters aim to bring out the types of discontinuities that exist and the dynamic and emergent character of the struggles and interactions that take place, showing how actors' goals, perceptions, values, interests and relationships are reinforced or reshaped by this process. For instance, in rural development interface situations, a central issue is the way in which policy is implemented and, often at the same time, transformed.

However, interfaces contain within them many levels and forms of social linkage and discontinuity. Studies of interface should not therefore be restricted to observing what goes on during face-to-face encounters, since these interactions are in part affected by actors, institutional and cultural frameworks, and resources that may not actually be physically or directly present. Hence, although the methodology of interface studies focuses upon specific social interactional processes, the analysis should situate these within broader institutional and power fields (Long 1989).

The concern for interface entails an acute awareness of the ways in which different, possibly conflicting, forms of knowledge intersect and interact. However, in contrast to more conventional approaches in the sociology of knowledge (e.g., Mannheimian or Marxist analysis), it takes an actor-oriented approach which focuses upon the interplay of different social constructions of 'reality' developed by the various parties to the interface (e.g., government bureaucrats, peasant farmers and traders), and traces out their social implications. Such an approach, we believe, is of value for analysing the production, dissemination/utilisation and transformation of knowledge. But we make no ontological distinction between types of knowledge; for example, between so-called 'scientific' as opposed to 'everyday' knowledge, or between 'bureaucratic' and 'local' knowledge.[3]

The rest of this chapter sets out to explore the encounters between the different actors involved in an agricultural development programme in Mexico from the perspective of knowledge interface issues. The extended case material we use[4] takes as its central figure a *técnico* (technician) working for the Ministry of Agriculture and Hydraulic Resources (SARH) who is assigned to a fairly remote area of the Rainfed District of Zapopan, Jalisco.

Setting the scene for bureaucrat–peasant interactions in rural Jalisco

Before moving to the actual incidents to be analysed, we need to give an overview of the type of agricultural development programme we are concerned with and to describe briefly its administrative structure and implementation.

The focus of the discussion is the impact of SAM (*Sistema Alimentario Mexicano*, the Mexican Food System) which was one of the most comprehensive attempts in the history of Mexico to develop a rural development programme oriented to the needs of rainfed agriculture rather than irrigated, export-oriented production. It was also conceived of as an assault on rural poverty aimed at increasing the production of basic staple foods such as maize and beans grown by small-scale peasant producers. As Carlos (1981: 11) has commented, 'SAM is Mexico's version of a rural War on Poverty.' It set out to recover Mexico's self-sufficiency in grain (mainly maize), reduce the risks of rainfed production through technological innovation, improve peasant income and diet, and organise peasants in what were called 'superior forms of organisation' designed to increase producer participation and negotiation *vis-à-vis* outside interests (see SAM 1980).

The programme was launched in March 1980 during the presidential period of Lopez Portillo. A central tenet of the policy was that of linking the peasant producer to a new government-promoted structure concerned with the development and management of a basic food chain (*cadena alimentaria*), concentrating primarily on maize. This notion of a food chain emphasised the necessity of a closer interaction between peasant production, marketing, food processing and consumption.

In order to carry out the new strategy,[5] it was necessary to transform the existing administrative system and to establish a more technocratic approach to rainfed agricultural development. A core element in this was the establishment of a new type of administrative unit called the 'Rainfed District'. These rainfed districts were to be organised and coordinated under the Ministry of Agriculture (SARH, *Secretaria de Agricultura y Recursos Hidraulicos*). Each region of the country was divided into districts, coinciding with existing politico-administrative divisions of the individual states. At state level a body (*La Representación Regional*) was set up to oversee and control the personnel and operations of the districts. It also organised the planning and allocation of funds for the different agricultural, livestock, forestry and irrigation activities, which were to be implemented by the lower-level district staff. The latter consisted of a Head of District, his deputy, the heads of specific sub-programmes dealing, for example, with mechanisation, fertilisation or the organisation of producers, and various supporting administrative and secretarial staff. Below this level were the operational units (*Unidades de Temporal*) that dealt directly with the farming population. Each unit was made up of a Head of Unit, his deputy, a secretary and several *técnicos* (technicians trained in agronomy, animal husbandry, irrigation, etc.) who were themselves heads of operational zones (*Zonas de Operación*) that normally consisted of about 2,000 hectares. The original idea was to provide the head of the zone with a team made up of several *promotores* (organisational promoters and extensionists), but this never materialised. The *técnico* was, then, the 'frontline' implementer of SAM in direct and regular interaction with his client population. He was accountable to his superiors in the Unit and District and was expected to follow certain administrative procedures in the implementation of the programme. At the same time, however, he accumulated experience in dealing both with the demands of the administrative system and its routines, and with those of his peasant clients.

A *técnico's* involvement with these two contrasting, and often conflicting, social worlds produces a body of knowledge based upon individual experience which leads him to devise his own strategies of intervention in both the village and official administrative arenas. Although it might seem that such strategies are highly idiosyncratic, being based upon the chronologies of experience of particular individuals, in fact they are shaped by the possibilities for manoeuvre and discourse that already exist within the two arenas and by the dynamics of the structural contexts within which the different parties interact. The different social actors (e.g., government officials of various kinds, rich and poor peasants, and others such as traders or even researchers) develop their own everyday shared understandings or models for action that originate from and acquire their potency and legitimation through social interaction and confrontation with opposing views and forms of organisation. As we shall show in the case that follows, a *técnico* cannot simply escape these influences and constraints by attempting to ignore their existence; and if he does do so, he is then likely to lose legitimacy as a *técnico* in the eyes of both peasants and bureaucrats.

This is a complex process which we intend to elucidate through the analysis of an extended case-study which focuses upon the dilemmas of Roberto, a *técnico* who tries to bridge the gap between the interests of peasant producers and the programme administration and its priorities. He launches a criticism of the shortcomings of the SAM programme and gives recognition to administrative malpractice. On the basis of this he tries to introduce new initiatives to assist producers, which he sees as both enhancing his prestige and social position as a *técnico* and also facilitating a more positive involvement by the producers themselves. However, the end result is that he is labelled a 'troublemaker' (*un grilloso*)[6] and sent to a special 'troublemakers unit' for remedial treatment. His lack of success in persuading his administrative boss to accept his solution for bridging the gap between peasant and government interests has the further repercussion that the peasants can use his case to confirm and reinforce their existing model of government practice and personnel. Their experience with this particular *técnico* refurbishes their beliefs in how the dominant system works, although this same set of events may later also be used to justify further attempts to restructure the interface between them and the intervening agencies and interests. The situation also becomes an important factor in the reproduction of their particular livelihood strategies, which they effectively conceal from government, and in the reproduction of their own local forms of knowledge. The combined effect of these various processes is to keep the social worlds of peasants and bureaucrats in opposition through the linking of contrasting types of everyday knowledge and through the mutual generation of socially constructed systems of ignorance.

The first encounter with the lifeworld of the *técnico*

We first met engineer Roberto, the *técnico* of the *ejido* of La Lobera, which falls within the Municipality of San Cristobal de la Barranca, at a Sunday lunch at the municipal centre. San Cristobal is located about 100 kilometres to the northwest of Guadalajara city, close to the border with the State of Zacatecas. San Cristobal is one of the least developed areas of Rainfed District No. 1 of Zapopan, which, until the beginning of the 1980s, was cut off from the main communication routes. Access was partially solved with the construction of the Guadalajara–Balafios highway, which has made it possible to travel from San Cristobal to Guadalajara in one hour.

This area of the Guadalajara region is mainly devoted to livestock production, supplemented by agriculture and independent, small-scale opal mining carried out by local exploiters. The municipality, made up of a population of about 3,700 inhabitants, has a romantic tradition of *gavillas* (bandits) who robbed gold from the Zacatecas mines and who hid it in the deep gullies of the municipality. Today the municipality still retains an image of being associated with illegal activities, such as the production of *agave* (a cactus plant from which tequila and other products are manufactured) and marijuana.

Our meeting with Roberto was by chance. The Municipal President had invited the Head of Zapopan Rainfed District, the Head of the Unit, the agricultural *técnicos* from San Cristobal and Lobera, several 'sons of the municipality' working in Guadalajara, such as a lecturer from Guadalajara University and *compadre* ('co-parent') of the Municipal President, and other local dignitaries resident in the area. The ostensible purpose of the occasion was to press them to provide more government development assistance for the Municipality.

During the lunch the Head of the District said that, in his opinion, the only future for San Cristobal was to develop tourism. This is, he explained, 'the first restaurant I have seen in this area and this can be the beginning of the "take-off" of the municipality'. He went on to say that 'as you can see, this is a place of hot springs' and therefore good for this type of trade. He also added that San Cristobal, like Cuquio to the northeast, is one of two extreme cases of low maize productivity in his district. Then, referring to the theme of out-migration, he said: 'this is a historical tendency of several municipalities around Guadalajara, which cannot be stopped with agricultural development because it is in the blood of the producers. It is natural for them to go to the USA instead of going to Zapopan or Guadalajara.' At this point, several local residents objected strongly to this view; so he rephrased it more sharply by underlining 'the laziness of the Mexican people', and by re-emphasising his point about the problem of poor communications. He went on to say that 'if I just had enough steamrollers and excavators then I would send them here to build roads, but I don't have them'.

After lunch we talked with the *técnico*, engineer Roberto, from La Lobera. At this time of the year, during the rainy season, the *ejido* of La Lobera is cut off and the only way to get there is on foot, a journey that takes about six hours. Roberto described the place as being populated by about 70 producers who, due to their isolation, were not receiving fertilisers regularly. A government programme of credit had been officially operating in the *ejido* for some years but, according to him, these producers had still not received last year's subsidies for agricultural inputs. He also said that people were friendly but suspicious of outsiders. They feared that outsiders came to steal the few possessions they had. He added:

> These feelings of mistrust were the reasons why they did not wish to obtain credit from Banrural [the state agricultural bank], because they run away from situations where they have to sign or put their names to paper. I have been working for a year with them. La Lobera is a rough place, but I like it because I am not one of those *técnicos* who likes to be a *chupa barba* [a 'yes man' or someone who sucks up to his boss][7] and these are the qualities needed to work in Zapopan. In La Lobera I am direct and honest with the producer and as a result have persuaded about 50 producers to join the fertiliser programme.

He went on further to explain:

194

The *ejido* is poor in terms of cash, maize is grown principally for self-consumption; they keep cattle but do not eat meat unless one of the animals falls [in the ravine], and the main diet is beans, tortillas, milk and eggs....The *ejido* has no electricity but they have some televisions operated by car batteries....Concerning customs, the people are very traditional. We young lads [*muchachos*] had to peer through small holes in the billiard hall at the girls [*chavas*] passing by. To wander around with them, chatting and so on, implies that the man is a *cabrón* [a bastard]....Before I went to work in La Lobera, no *técnicos* had been there for a long time. They do not like working there. I managed to survey the *ejido* but I believe that much of the information given was untrue. The producers tend to exaggerate the inputs that they invest in production and underestimate the number of cattle they possess. I am supervising 750 hectares when a *técnico* is required to be in charge of 2,000. It is impossible to know the profits made from cattle because producers market them [illegally] in Zacatecas [rather than in Guadalajara]. My first contacts in the *ejido* were with the young men [*chavos*], after that the older women, and only much later the *productores* [producers, here implying 'heads of household' who are usually male]. Some young producers were very suspicious because they cultivate marijuana: they thought that since I worked for *el gobierno* [the government] I was going to report them.

After this, Roberto shifted the subject of the conversation to ask us whether we thought SAM was a failure. Our reply was 'Yes, but we have to study why it failed.' He answered us directly:

I know why it failed: many of us pocketed the money that was meant for the producer. And we acted irresponsibly. During this period they gave us 2,000 *pesos* (about 40 US dollars) weekly for petrol, even when they knew that it was impossible to spend that amount of money. When I had to handle the tin containers of insecticide [for the *ejido*], sometimes they overturned in the truck. I just used to dump it, and I did the same when it went bad, and reported to the office that it was lost. No questions were asked, and things that were not accidents, but due to one's own negligence, were simply written off as lost, and no more. A colleague from my unit was actively involved in collecting the bills for buying fertilisers, insecticides and seeds from the producers. He took charge of handling producers' claims for subsidies. This person took more than 20 per cent of each subsidy, which was paid directly to him in cash. For the producer, who never knew the details of the programme or the amount he should receive, this was a gift [*una ganancia extra*]. Therefore here comes the contradiction: these same people who received 20 per cent less than they should, organised in his honour fiestas, barbecues, and invited him to eat gratis in their homes, because they saw this *técnico* as the person who got them money they never expected to receive. In this respect, *un funcionario corrupto* [a corrupt civil servant] from the point of view of the government institution is seen as *un funcionario excelente* from the side of the producer. When you are a *técnico* it is often difficult to understand exactly when you are acting in a good or bad manner. It is strictly prohibited to take money from the producer, but last year on visiting this particular plot [here he pointed to a field owned by one of the leaders of the *ejido*], which we do so regularly because it is close to the road, we were always offered watermelons, courgettes and tomatoes to take away with us.

At this point, we intervened to suggest that surely it was quite different to receive products other than cash, to which Roberto answered:

No that is not relevant [*no le hace*]. It's the same thing. What was I going to do with four or five boxes of watermelons and courgettes? After I gave some kilos to my family and friends, I still had some boxes left – which I could not just give away as gifts in the neighbourhood – so I took them to sell in a *puesto* [stall] in the Guadalajara market. Whatever I get for them is simply profit for me. In the end then [to receive cash or products] it is the same thing. The producer sees technical assistance from a totally different point of view...Nowadays it is prohibited to receive any kind of thing from the producer but things continue as always. Take for example that the producer needs to process certain administrative papers. If there is no incentive then we do not move [*tramitar*] the papers. I can give a thousand and one reasons for not doing so. So the producer, despite the regulations, will bring gifts for the *técnico* to speed up [*se mueva*] the process. In these things regulations do not serve. The failure of SAM was due to the fact that they wasted resources madly, *a manos llenas* [throwing away armfuls of resources]; and we were guilty. This is the cause of the present-day economic crisis: a crisis which means that they cannot even finance the travel expenses of *técnicos* to go to communities like La Lobera.

The *técnico's* vision of the lifeworlds of peasants and bureaucrats

A spatial image underlies Roberto's view of the peasants of La Lobera, namely that the community is isolated geographically. Geographical isolation is associated with being a 'rough place', poor in services and resources, and being culturally 'traditional' and therefore outside the mainstream of 'modern' life. A further implication is that they are outside the area of major influence or priority as far as government development schemes are concerned.

Being isolated, the people are suspicious and do not trust outsiders, whom they suspect of threatening or stealing their few possessions: their material resources as well as their girls. This reference to the need to protect daughters must be interpreted in the context of the local custom of 'wife abduction' whereby the man 'steals' the bride-to-be before negotiating with the father of the girl. The *técnico* was ignorant of the full significance of this attitude towards the protection of daughters. In later discussions with peasants from La Lobera it emerged that heads of households do in fact allow marriage to take place with outside men from San Cristobal de Barrancas, providing these marriages give them benefits in the form of political leverage or contacts. This is balanced by trying to press the young men to find women from the community of Cuyutlán where they could obtain, through marriage, easy access to credit, since this community specialises in the production of marijuana. Thus, far from being simply 'backward' or 'traditional', this prescription and control of women was central to La Lobera's political and economic survival and relative autonomy from the wider system.

A second image that relates to the first is Roberto's view that the peasants consider the *técnico* as part of a system of intervention based upon trickery,[8] since some peasants engage in illegal activities, such as marijuana and poppy cultivation, and the marketing of live-stock in Zacatecas in clandestine slaughterhouses, which it is the business of *técnicos* and others representing central government to report. *Técnicos* therefore represent a threat, which it is best to avoid by engaging in counter-trickery. Roberto emphasised this by describing how he surveyed the community but got inaccurate information. His comments thus reveal a degree of awareness of the lack of fit between the reality of peasant life and the assumptions made by government development programmes.

This element of counter-trickery based upon a lack of trust was later illustrated for us by an account given by elders (*viejos*) of the community who told of an incident when a bank official arrived in the community to check on the results of the harvest with an interest in determining how many producers could repay the credit. The official credit system of SAM operated to protect those who suffered a complete loss by exempting them from the need to repay their debts. This meant they could reapply the following season. In these circumstances, the peasants of La Lobera, many of whom had suffered some but not a complete loss, declared to the official that more than half of the *ejido* had suffered a complete loss, and when he doubted this statement, they said: 'Are you questioning our word! Shall we go to the fields?' At which point they stood up and hoisted their trousers, adjusting their belts. This, it appeared, was interpreted by the official as a sign that they were moving their hands towards their revolvers. So, at that moment, the official said he did not wish to see the gardens, and simply signed the claim application. From that day on they have not seen another bank official!

This incident shows not only that the official failed to read or respond to the peasant cue to negotiate a settlement, but that, in the eyes of the peasants, his reactions merely confirmed their general suspicions of government personnel. The combined effect of these types of encounter is that government services to the area remain inadequate and ineffec-tive, thus underlining the 'isolation' and 'marginality' of La Lobera.

This type of mutual mistrust is part of the everyday reality of the people of La Lobera when they have to deal with outside intervening parties. Although officials such as the bank representative or the *técnico* command control over resources and have the support of outside authorities, according to the *técnico* they are clearly vulnerable when they operate outside their own social space. In the same way, the peasants of La Lobera were 'ignorant' of the newly enforced laws of *depistolización* (i.e., the disarming policy enforced in the 1980s) when, one day, they set off for Guadalajara, only to be disarmed by the municipal police in San Cristobal. In order to recover their arms they had to bribe the authorities, since the law said arms should be confiscated.

Roberto's comments on the nature of the peasants of La Lobera coincided partly with those of his superior, the Head of the Unit. The latter stressed that the area was exotic and could therefore be a centre of tourism (on another occasion he suggested that a funicular railway could be constructed from Guadalajara to La Lobera to promote tourism). This implied that the area was not considered to be within the main area designated for the implementation of agricultural development programmes, even though the *técnicos* were expected to promote the production of basic staples.[9] The mention of migration and the 'laziness of the Mexican' simply confirms this view and draws upon a well-established stereotype, current in popular and sometimes also in academic circles, that peasants lack commitment to local development and therefore migrate away. There is in this model no understanding of the cyclical nature of labour migration, nor of other alternatives to agriculturally-based development.

Another dominant theme that emerges from the first encounter is the notion that, for a government official, self-criticism is fine, although at the same time the administrative system tends to neutralise this by providing these same people with flexible and ambiguous concepts, such as notions of 'corruption' and 'negotiation' that justify a degree of criticism of the system, as well as some space in which to develop their own strategies. In this way 'deviations' can be legitimised by the fact that peasants may gain better returns: that is, they may give gifts to the *técnico* in order to obtain support for credit or other services. The element of deception reappears, however, in the fact that the peasants may not be told precisely what their rights are. Hence the *modus operandi*, which may bring mutual benefits to the *técnico* and peasant farmer, works to create areas of ambiguity and ignorance in both bodies of knowledge. In this way, both sets of beliefs are kept basically intact.

A view from below: a sketch of La Lobera and its agricultural problems

This first encounter with Roberto and with the other agricultural staff present at the lunch in San Cristobal motivated us to learn more about the *ejido* of La Lobera. We decided to collect basic background information, drawn mainly from the Agrarian Archives in Guadalajara, and to plan a trip to the community.

According to the Agrarian Archives, La Lobera was originally part of a hacienda of that name. However, in 1970, under the agrarian reform law, it was granted land, although it was not legally recognised as an *ejido* until 1976. The reform affected 150 hectares of rainfed and 1,100 hectares of pasture land, benefiting some 47 households. This area was extended in 1981 to benefit a further 25 households, although at the time of the research this land had not yet been allocated.

As we indicated earlier, La Lobera is located on the *cordillera* of the Zacatecas Sierra, approximately 25 to 30 kilometres to the northeast of San Cristobal de la Barranca. The track to La Lobera starts on the western side of San Cristobal de la Barranca and the journey can take up to five hours by jeep. The track crosses the river Cuixtla which, during the dry season, does not carry much water. During the rainy season, however, the river increases its height to five or six metres, leaving the *ejido* isolated. The track is very narrow with many slopes and precipices.

On the way to La Lobera there is a remarkable change in vegetation. There is an abundance of papaya, mango and banana trees in San Cristobal, due to the humidity and hot climate; but as you journey towards La Lobera, this tropical vegetation is replaced by *nopales* and *pitayos* (prickly pears and their fruit) and is populated by *huizaches* (lizards) better adapted to the dry and hot climate of the Sierra. At an altitude of 2,000 metres, the landscape around the *ejido* is composed of a forest of dwarf oaks and pines.

The *ejido* has a public school, which at the time of the study had operated for eight years, though the building was only finished in 1982. There are two small shops and also a billiard hall where producers meet to talk in the evenings. The community has no electricity, adequate drainage system or telephone. The *ejidatarios* have built a small water tank, supplied by spring water from the Sierra. The tank serves as the most important meeting place for the women of the community, who come together during the mornings and in the evenings. La Lobera's only rapid communication from the outside is through messages that are transmitted over a commercial radio based in Guadalajara. There are three tractors in the *ejido*, two of which had just been bought at the time of the research. The oldest arrived during the SAM project and was owned collectively by the *ejido*, but due to mechanical breakdown it had lain idle for a year. There is one lorry in the community and a few pick-up trucks. The present-day structure of production consists of *ejido* agricultural land, which is allocated to households each year in small plots, *ejido* pasture land which is used collectively by those who own livestock, and some individually-owned plots. Our sample of 23 households showed that 87 per cent possessed between one and five hectares, one household possessed 10 hectares, and two owned more than 11 hectares.

According to *técnicos* at the SARH District office, agricultural production in La Lobera is classified as falling under a model of production for self-consumption (*producción para el autoconsumo*). Yet, according to our research, the situation is more complex. Producers declared that approximately 70 per cent of their maize production was for self-consumption, while 30 per cent was for the market. The latter was marketed outside official state-controlled channels in small quantities in response to the immediate demands for cash to meet household needs. Also producers preferred to feed their cattle on maize and to sell the livestock later. According to producers, this was the only way for them to make a profit from agriculture. In other words, La Lobera is a commercially oriented agricultural community where, in spite of its isolation, money is highly valued. This commercial character has encouraged some producers to develop their means of production, although the majority still operate with relatively low levels of technological input. Thus they use tractors only for opening up land, while the rest of the agricultural tasks are organised using animal traction and with the help of family and seasonal wage labour. The majority of households, however, use fertilisers and insecticides, which were introduced in 1980. Family labour remains the main factor in this system of production, although during peak agricultural periods some 44 per cent of households hire temporary labour. Farmers must rent tractors from one of the three persons owning them. The use of a tractor reduces the risk of not having the land prepared in time for the first rains.

There is constant pressure to produce maize, and a high commitment to agricultural work. With an average crop of two tonnes of maize per hectare, La Lobera in fact manifests the highest productivity level in the Municipality of San Cristobal. Producers use a fallow system called *año y vez*, which consists of dividing the *ejido* land into two areas, one of which is cultivated, while the other is left for livestock. Every year producers rotate the area of cultivation. They explained that this system had proved itself to be the best way of avoiding soil disease; as they put it: 'the soil knows the seed' and therefore will reject seeds used in the previous year.[10] This view contrasted sharply with that of Roberto, the *técnico*, who regarded this form of cultivation as 'traditional and uneconomic'. In his opinion all land should be ploughed, and the amount of insecticides and pesticides increased to promote a more intensive system of production. Producers argue against this, emphasising that crop disease has increased since insecticides and pesticides have been introduced.

These two different perceptions of agriculture and agricultural development reveal a conflict of interests, objectives and beliefs between development agency personnel and producers. This is also seen in attitudes towards the use of the tractor. While some producers regarded the tractor as necessary to save time, many argued against its use, because the soil did not receive proper preparation, making it necessary to plough with animals afterwards. The use of animal traction, it was maintained, achieved a better soil consistency for sowing. And another factor shaping attitudes towards the tractor was that the tractor owned by the *ejido* and introduced under the SAM credit programme had broken down quickly, and this created conflict among producers over what to do with it. It took a year and a half for the community to resolve this. Finally, they sold the tractor to two *ejidatarios*, one of whom was a shopkeeper. The latter each paid *ejidatario* 5,000 *pesos* (50 US dollars) and invested 200,000 *pesos* (2,000 US dollars) in repairs. The tractor was sold complete with all its agricultural implements. *Ejidatarios* recognised that it was sold cheaply, but they pointed out that the important thing was to repair it and solve the community's problems. It was this experience that made some producers oppose the use of the tractor and blame the government for giving them something that was unprofitable and which finally ended up favouring only two producers in the community.

As we pointed out earlier, the increase of maize production was the central aim of the SAM programme offered to communities such as La Lobera. The apparent resistance to such modernisation, seen for instance in their unwillingness to adopt what was regarded as a more intensive system of maize production, presented major obstacles to the 'mission' of *técnicos* in the community. This is, in effect, a 'Catch-22' situation, since *técnicos* cannot ask for more government assistance if they are unable to improve maize production in their areas of responsibility.

An additional problem with the SAM model was its failure to recognise the fundamentally diversified nature of local rural economies. In a public meeting with ejidatarios in La Lobera, one of them exclaimed forcefully:

> The potential of the *ejido* is in livestock and in opal mining. If you ask us, you will find that we have more experience as miners than as agricultural producers. In the dry season, the people who don't go to the USA, go to work in the mines as labourers or as *pepenadores* [i.e., those who scavenge among the discarded deposits around the mines]. We cultivate maize and the introduction of improved seeds is good for us, because we can feed it to the livestock. Simply to produce maize is not good business for us, because our costs are greater than those producers in Zapopan. We have to pay for the transport of the agricultural inputs and after that the cost of moving the harvest down again. So we try to sell the least possible maize because our profit lies in feeding our cattle and selling three or four cows during the year.

This economic rationale was further explored in interviews with one of the most prosperous, and one of the poorest, producers in the *ejido*.

The views of Don Pedro, a rich peasant

Don Pedro was born in 1933 in the locality of El Salvador, in the neighbouring Municipality of Tequila, and has lived for 20 years in La Lobera. He was invited to join the *ejido* by the producers who founded it. His wife is also from El Salvador, and they have eleven sons and one daughter, a fact that allows him to say:

> I am a real Mexican. I don't believe in family planning, because for me, my sons have never been an obstacle. On the contrary, they have helped me to overcome difficulties. The first years of my marriage were hell, because I had to rent land and production was just enough for the family to survive. During that period my parents gave me economic help.
> My situation changed in La Lobera. The *ejido* gave me land and my lads [*muchachos*] began to help me with the work. They helped me from the time they were

200

seven years old, but the assistance of my parents and friends in La Lobera were important too.

The first five or six years I adapted myself to the *ejido* and, as my sons were still growing up, my situation didn't change too much. But, after the seventh year, I was able to buy my first cow. The year after that, I bought another two, until finally I had nine or ten cattle. As the cows started to have calves, I began to sell them in Guadalajara's slaughterhouse. This is when my economic situation improved.

Then my sons started to go to USA and, as they were constantly sending back money, they eased my financial situation. The eldest left at the age of twenty and came back three years later with some money; enough to get married and establish his household. He is building his house now in the pueblo. My second son is still there; he has only been back once. His situation is difficult, because he has no papers; so he works illegally. My third son went to the North (USA), but he has already come back.

Our future as a family is in agriculture, but I want education for my sons too, so the youngest are still at school finishing their primary education. In 1981 my son and I decided to buy a tractor, and I realised one of my dreams. With the machine maize production increased three times. Before buying the tractor, my eldest son and I talked about our needs and we decided that, if we were to work together, we could share the tractor among us and get some money from *maquila* [renting out the tractor to other producers]. Our family works together and all main decisions are taken by my three older sons and me.

In recent years, the land has been producing more than just for *el gasto de la familia* [household consumption] and we can now begin to do business. We have been able to improve the quality of the livestock, but our problem is that we are too far away from markets, so we have not received much attention from the government. Now we are starting to fight for electricity in *el rancho* [i.e., the community]; but we don't know how long that will take.

Progress in the community has been by our own effort. We don't like the agencies very much, because when they come here their objective is to *chingar* [to harm] the producers. We have had several conflicts with Banrural and some of us are thinking of stopping working with its credit. When they came here, they disliked our system of production and wanted to force us to sell our maize in Zapopan to CONASUPO. Because they know we depend on our livestock, the bank won't increase our credit.

And the insurance is always against us. So, producers are not interested in increasing maize production. Credit is given by government to control us: they don't like it when we use our money for livestock.

The views of Don Jorge, a poor peasant

Don Jorge is 35 years old, married, with three small children. He cultivates two hectares of land and he claims that it is the need for cash among poor producers that compels them to sell maize in Zapopan.

We usually sell between ten and twenty *cargas* of maize in Zapopan every year [each *carga* is nine tonnes]. To sell the maize two or three producers contract a truck; the driver takes charge of selling the cargo. He deducts the cost of the transport and gives us the rest.

There are between eight and ten poor producers in the *ejido*, and we have to work in *lo ajeno* [the land of others] to get money. In the *ejido* producers need our labour for agricultural tasks, because it is not always possible to use weedkillers. So we have to be the first to finish our agricultural tasks, in order to have time to work for others. They pay us 1,000 *pesos* (1 US dollar) per day, for eight hours work.

It is better for us to sell maize, because we don't have livestock, but for the rest of the producers who have four or five animals, or the richest ones, who have over 90 animals, it is better to keep the maize and feed it to their animals. On *ejido* land we sow hybrid maize, only for the market. It is much heavier than the *maize criollo* [local maize], which we use mainly for household consumption. Sometimes because we have sold too much of our maize, we have to buy maize from Zapopan later in order to have enough food to see the year out. The hybrid maize is a seed that the bank gave us three or four years ago and we sell it as animal fodder. For household consumption, I also cultivate maize in the *coamil*.[11] For that I cooperate with a friend to burn the bush, which we do during May. In the clearance of the *coamil* we capture rattlesnakes, which we sell later in the Guadalajara market for a good price. The meat of the rattlesnake is a good medicine and is difficult to get, because the capture of snakes is banned by the government.

We sow *maize criollo* because it resists well the conditions of the bush [*el monte*]. We don't have disease in the *coamiles* and we have discovered that if you use insecticides there, it is easy to control the weeds. To work in the *coamil* we form a task group and our wives and children help us in the whole process of cultivation. The harvest of this maize is only for household consumption.

We have to sow *coamiles* because this is the only way for us to save money to buy an animal. Usually you buy the first with a friend, and, after that, it's just a matter of time before you improve your economic situation.

We would like more help, particularly credit from the government, but they won't give us more, because they say we cultivate too few hectares of maize. When we sell our maize we don't sell it to CONASUPO but to the middleman in Zapopan (Cristobal), because, even though he pays 500 *pesos* per tonne less than government, he accepts maize on the cob and CONASUPO will only take it in grains. As we don't have access to a combine harvester, we have no alternative.

Peasants' visions of their lifeworld and that of el gobierno

The foregoing account shows that the peasants of La Lobera do not regard themselves as being outside the market, as assumed in the bureaucratic model which classifies their agriculture as directed primarily towards self-consumption. In fact, their everyday experiences are geared to maximising, where possible, economic return through the market. This was the reason why they did not market much maize and found it more profitable to feed it to their cattle, which they later sold in other markets. Moreover, much of the maize marketed was traded through unofficial channels and therefore not included in government figures.

These two elements – their commitment to the market and the use of alternative channels for marketing – are crucial for understanding the peasant economy of La Lobera. The model perpetuated by the administration fails to grasp these critical dimensions, providing the *técnico* with a frame of reference which systematically ignores the actual situation of the *ejido* and the need to understand its problems. This serves the administration well because it allows them to classify the *ejido* as not worthy of much attention, or of programmes of major investment. This aspect is further highlighted in the section that follows, when engineer Roberto suggests that La Lobera is institutionally classified 'as a punishment area for troublesome *técnicos*'.

However, the peasants' situation is more complex than simply recognising their relation with the market. It involves, in addition, relations within the community between the richer and poorer households, as expressed in the hiring of temporary wage labour for agricultural production. It also covers the ways in which ideas about technological 'improvements' have been processed through a body of local knowledge, thereby creating certain incompatibilities with the model of development promoted by the *técnicos*. This is illustrated by peasant views about tractors. The majority of peasants agreed that tractors save time by making it possible for them to delay ploughing until the last moment before the rains come. But they also know that this does not allow enough time for the night frost and the sun to kill the bacteria (*plagas*) that attack the plants. Most people therefore maintained that tractors do not provide proper care for the soil. This is linked to the belief that the land is a living entity that requires careful nurturing. A further point is that people stressed that tractors generate conflicts between households within the *ejido* over their use (note the difficulties that arose with the collectively owned tractor).

These views should not be interpreted to imply that there is a reluctance to use more advanced technology for increasing production or productivity; rather, they point to a different conception of soil conservation and the management of agricultural production. Newly-introduced inputs must find a place and be given social meaning within local bodies of agricultural knowledge and practice, although at the same time it must be recognised that this is a dynamic process which transforms these new elements as they are incorporated. New instruments and methods acquire meanings and uses not anticipated or intended by the agricultural planners. This process is clearly shown in the example of Don Jorge, the poor peasant, who breaks up the technological maize package in order to use the insecticides to reduce weeding within the *coamil* system of production.[12]

The successful reworking of both new and existing elements of knowledge in order to devise viable household strategies leading to 'a better life' (*una mejor vida*) is further illustrated by the case of Don Pedro, the rich peasant. Don Pedro's view of how to achieve a better life includes three crucial elements: sound enterprise, education and technological innovation. These elements, however, cannot be realised without some strategy for obtaining them. This entails organisation and resources so that he can implement his 'project'. This he does by drawing upon the labour resources of the household and consolidating his ties with his sons. For him, family planning makes no sense since, as he puts it, 'my sons have never been an obstacle. On the contrary, they have helped me to overcome difficulties' – one example of this being the way they jointly coordinated trips to the USA to obtain money for a tractor, which they later rented out to their neighbours at a profit.

Don Pedro is acknowledged in La Lobera as someone who has made it, as a kind of reference model for others wishing to achieve a better life. In fact one can trace similar elements in the strategies of Don Jorge, who is still struggling to accumulate enough cash to buy his first cow. Don Jorge points out that, once one has acquired the first animal, then it is just a matter of time before one improves one's economic situation. Although he lacks sufficient resources to make the trip to the USA, he participates together with a group of poor producers in the organisation of the trading of maize to Zapopan. Being much younger than Don Pedro, he lacks family labour and other resources. This leads him to set up a network of close bonds with three good friends who collaborate in agriculture and small-scale trade. Thus both Don Pedro and Don Jorge – though placed at opposite ends of the status spectrum – manifest a strong commitment to organising their own affairs, outside government control. They also place premiums on cooperating with family or long-standing friends who are status equals.

Despite evidence of increasing social differentiation in La Lobera, these two contrasting cases share, more or less, the same perceptions and opposition towards the 'world outside', and especially towards the government agencies. Don Pedro declared: 'They dislike our system of production'; and Don Jorge said: 'They won't give us more money because they say we cultivate too few hectares of maize.' These expressions capture in a nutshell the common assumption made by peasants, whether rich or poor, that government works against them and has little interest in understanding their own systems of production and their problems. And this functions as an ideological barrier to developing relationships of *confianza* (trust) with government personnel. This view of course is legitimised by the 'bad' experiences they have had, either individually or as a community, with visiting government officials, and which now constitute a kind of collective memory. We shall return to this point later when we discuss the confrontation of peasant and bureaucratic models in the final section of the chapter.

This discussion of peasant views and ideology leads to the conclusion that producers are basically oriented towards keeping control over the organisation of their households and local enterprises, whilst at the same time attempting, where possible, to profit from whatever outside resources may come their way. In this way they operate within what Moore (1973) has called 'semi-autonomous social fields' wherein, in the face of both internal and external pressure, individuals or groups possess the capacity for preserving some normative consensus and control over their own social arrangements. Thus, despite their geographical and institutional 'marginality' and their poverty *vis-à-vis* other social strata or sectors, they nevertheless know how to live with their 'isolation' and extract some benefits from it.

Bridging the gap between different lifeworlds

Engineer Roberto had been working in La Lobera for a year and a half at the time of our research. He was 23 years old, and his father worked in the central offices of the Ministry of Agriculture and Hydraulic Resources (SARH) in Mexico. He recognised that it was due to his father's influence that he had obtained his post as *técnico*. According to Roberto, he did not know much about agriculture, since he had studied electrical and mechanical engineering, but, he said, 'I have learned by experience'. He was working in La Lobera as a result of an institutional sanction: according to him, 'In the District, La Lobera is considered *un area de castigo* (a punishment-area) for troublesome *técnicos*, who are sent there as a way of making them resign from the Ministry'. Roberto went on to tell the circumstances of his placement in La Lobera:

I was working in Cuquio and, as in this Unit, I didn't appear very often at the office; but that didn't mean I was not working. One day after I came back from a field visit and reported my findings to the Unit, I had a shock. There were three memos accusing me of having been absent from work for a month, so the District had decided to deduct those days from my salary. I got furious and went to sort out the problem at the District [office].

When I found the senior staff member who had sent me the memos, I said to him: *'Oye cumpa...porque me has puesto los memorandums?'* [Hey, mate, why have you sent me memos?] He then became aggressive, saying, 'Hey what?' That was enough, and I said: *'Oye hijo de la chingada, porque me pusistes estos memorandums que no son ciertos?'* [Hey, son of a bitch, why did you send me these memos which are not true?] Then things exploded and he said that my attitude was going to cost me the post. I laughed at him and, in front of the staff, I challenged him saying: 'I bet you won't be able to throw me out.' He replied, quite sure of himself: 'OK, be ready then, because tomorrow we are going to carry out an inspection of your area.'

The next day I picked them up from the office. They were dressed as if they were going on a safari. I laughed and said that Cuquio was not the other end of the world. When they arrived and asked the producers they didn't find anything wrong with my work, but they still recommended a change of Unit. So, I was sent to Unit No. 3 because the Head of the Unit had a reputation for being an organiser and a *chambeador* [hard worker]. The Head of the Unit received instructions to make me work hard and that was how I finally ended up in La Lobera.

The *técnico* was proud of his attitude and considered himself different from the rest of the *técnicos*. He disliked their behaviour as a group, because they were obedient to the Head of the Unit, spent their money in *convivencias* (office fiestas)[13] with him and did not give a damn about the producers' situation. Roberto said he was hated by other *técnicos* in the Unit, to the extent that several times they had stolen his field notebook and stopped him from doing his reports. Roberto claimed he did not conform to the expected norms of behaviour in the Ministry and the reason he could get away with it was that his father protected him.

Roberto did not value organisation or professional training as important qualities for a *técnico*. Thus, part of this hostility was directed against the professional agronomists because, according to him, 'all that was needed was *cojones* ['balls', testicles] to gain the *confianza* [trust] of producers, and the rest depended upon how influential your contacts were at the agency'. Roberto constantly emphasised that, while he had to walk six or seven hours to get to La Lobera, the 'others' had their *ejidos* near the Unit.

The técnico and the producers of La Lobera

On our first visit to La Lobera we went with *técnico* Roberto, because he offered to be our guide and to introduce us to some producers in the community. This first stay in La Lobera gave us the opportunity to observe him at work for a period of a week.

The first problem Roberto was confronted with was the death of several cattle. Producers said that they had sent for the veterinarian, but that the medicines he had prescribed had not solved the problem and that the animals were still dying. So Roberto went to see one of the more severe cases. He asked the producer about the symptoms of the disease, and the producer explained: 'Before dying the cows became mad and rejected food and water'. Roberto replied:

> This looks like rabies, but to be sure you have to take the head of a dead cow to Zapopan, because the laboratory has to confirm the diagnosis. Rabies is carried by the vampire bat that lives in the caves of the Sierra, and I am afraid the only solution for this disease is to bring the fumigation brigade here. For that to happen we have to persuade the Head of the District that this is a serious problem. To get his interest I need to show him that producers are interested in participating in the Ministry programmes.

Roberto had the idea that a baling machine was necessary in this area. He was sure that, with a petition signed by the majority of the producers, the District Head would accept the petition. So he asked the producer if he was interested in the use of this type of machine and asked him to sign the petition. Given the producer's concern for his livestock, he signed the petition. He then tried to get something concrete from the *técnico*, saying: 'So what about the cattle then?' Roberto, having obtained the signature of the producer, had lost interest in the producer's problem. It appeared that if he showed too much sympathy he could end up with extra problems to solve. So he suggested: 'What I would like to do is take you to talk with the *mero jefe* [the real boss] in the District, so you can explain the problem directly to him.'

The producer, realising that the *técnico* was not considering his case important enough, demanded: 'Why do I have to go to the District? Is it because you don't report what is going on here?' Roberto replied:

> Of course I do, but it's the staff. They always take time to decide what to do. So, in my experience, the best thing is to go directly to the persons who can solve the problem. Let's go together next Monday, and I will introduce you to the boss.

The producer was doubting: 'Well, I have to go to Guadalajara this Friday, so I will try to stay there until Monday, but if I can't go to the District would you please report the disease to your superior?'

All that evening the *técnico* worked hard convincing producers of the importance of the baling machine, and he collected some signatures for his petition. Producers listened to him, but without much enthusiasm.

During our second night in the community, after we had lit the firewood and warmed ourselves with *tequila de la Sierra*, producers started to come to have a drink and to chat with us. Don Martin, an influential person in the community, told us about his life; the hard experiences of raising a family and of how his sons had migrated to the USA in search of a better situation. Roberto sympathised, saying that those who suffered should be compensated. Then he changed the topic of conversation to much more practical matters, telling Don Martin that the community did not yet know him (i.e., Roberto himself), because they showed no *confianza* in him.

'If you had *confianza*', he said, 'I could bring things to the community, projects from the Ministry to benefit all of you, but I can't do it alone. I need the producers' support. You have to sign the petition. We have to put pressure on the Ministry so that resources are allocated to La Lobera.'

To this, Don Martin replied: 'Look, *técnico*, the government has promised a lot of things and nothing has happened yet. This is the reason why the producers listen to you politely, and why they don't believe in your promises too much'.

At this point, Roberto became annoyed and said:

> I recognise that *el pinche* [the bloody] government is only concerned with one thing – *chingar al productor* (cheating the producer) – and that is why the producers don't support our work. But if you organised yourselves I could get things done. I have good contacts in the Ministry. My father is *el mero jefe* [the boss] in Mexico, and if I ask him to do something I know he will support it. Even my boss in the Unit can't touch me. He wants me to live here, but I don't take any notice of his orders. I come every one or two months.

Roberto was beside himself. So we explained that things could not change overnight, but nevertheless he began to cry, saying to Martin: 'I have discovered that after a year producers don't even know my name and that means no *confianza* in me and, without *confianza*, I can't work. I need your support to put pressure on the Unit. I am not interested if the producer is an *ejidatario* or a small private producer. I want to help, through my actions, to increase production.'

Then he turned to one of us and said, 'Listen *licenciado*, don't tell me things can't change overnight. I am 23 years old and want my idealism to be realised.' He then went into the school and shouted: 'I am fed up with people telling me that things can't change. Sometimes I feel like taking a weapon. The first *cabrón* [bastard] I would shoot is the President, because he is at the centre of the web and I am caught in it. I can't take it any longer.'

With this comment, general criticism against government policies started. The *técnico*, in an excellent performance, separated his position from that of the institution and presented his sentiments as proof of his honesty and idealism. It was late, and Don Martin had been impressed by the *técnico's* performance. He said: '*Técnico*, tomorrow you will get all the signatures you need for your petition', and added, 'Our problem is how to use the resources of the *ejido* more profitably. My opinion is that what we need to do is to plant fruit trees. I got the idea after a visit to the USA. A cherry orchard could be very profitable.'

At this, Roberto realised what Martin's support would cost, and began to make promises again: 'OK, if that is what you want, I can get the trees for you. As a matter of fact, I just bought some for San Cristobal. We have to do this through petitions, and people have to give me the money immediately after the trees arrive here.'

Martin replied, 'If it is just a matter of money, tomorrow I can collect it for the trees'; to which Roberto responded: 'Well then, I think we can work together, because I have contacts in...'

The group was now small, most producers having withdrawn to rest. Only Roberto and Martin remained talking, reassuring themselves of the importance of their deal and how profitable cherry trees could be in the Sierra.

After the promises, the aftermath

Next day Roberto radiated optimism. And, as Martin had promised, producers signed Roberto's petition. At last he had aroused interest about the baling machine, and producers came to us in a much more relaxed state than in the previous days. They told us about the needs of the *ejido*. We were able to work with them, and we were invited to play billiards and to visit their homes. The producers showed us what *confianza* was – that variable which it was difficult for the fieldworkers of the Ministry to manufacture. We left the community with our survey completed, the petition for the machine signed and a briefcase full of promises that the *técnico* was expected to fulfil.

Roberto reported his work to the Head of his Unit and suggested that producers were interested in obtaining access to a baling machine, and that he had collected signatures. The Head of the Unit pointed out, however, that the policy of the Ministry was not to support livestock activities, but the production of maize. So he suggested that Roberto should explain to them the Ministry's policies and make clear that the Unit could not provide them with such a machine.

Roberto said that he could not do that because this petition was the first he had managed to get from them. It was the first sign that producers wanted Ministry assistance. Therefore, like it or not, he could not fail the producers. He would take the case to the District. According to Roberto, the Head of the Unit tried to get hold of Roberto's petitions. 'He was too late; the petitions were already in the District. These were signatures for the trees.' The Head then became angry because he had been challenged in his authority by a subordinate. He said that Roberto had taken on responsibilities that were not approved of by him, and that this was insubordination which would cost Roberto dearly.

Roberto bitterly remembers that the Head of the Unit then went to the District, withdrew the petition, and made the papers 'disappear'. According to Roberto: 'The Head of the Unit knew that he was creating a problem for me by this action, because I then had to explain to the producers why the petition did not receive attention.' Roberto's interpretation was that the Head had acted in this way so as to assert his authority and show the Unit who was in control. He had failed to see the importance of the machine in terms of the work of the *técnico* in the field. Roberto explained that this was the traditional way in which bureaucrats in the Ministry killed off the initiatives of the *técnicos*.

Some weeks later, Roberto was once again transferred to another Unit. The promises of the *técnico* had clashed with the interests of the administrative hierarchy.

Epilogue

We returned to La Lobera during the rainy season to stay another week with the producers. After we had exchanged greetings and were brought up to date with the latest community events – a new *ejidal* President, the arrival of a new tractor, how the old one was repaired, etc. – producers started to enquire of Roberto.

One peasant said: 'What has happened to Roberto? He hasn't appeared again since the last time he came with you.' We informed them that he had been moved to another *ejido*. A producer, with a resigned attitude, shrugged and said: 'You see, the government doesn't help us. We pay taxes, but for what, do we ever receive any service?' Another producer said: 'That's the problem: just when we were starting to get to know the *técnico* and *tenerle la confianza* [have trust in him], the government withdraws him and now we have to start all over again.'

Producers recalled that they had had three *técnicos*. The first one only came to introduce himself to the community but never returned. The next was the best, because he came often and was always present for the meetings. The last one (Roberto) they did not know well. He had promised a baling machine and trees, but he had never come back to tell them what had happened. Producers were convinced that the government had deceived them once again. Their irritation led them to tell us of a recent incident involving the Agrarian Reform Agency, with whom they were trying to legalise the *ejido*'s land area:

Last week we were called by radio to San Cristobal, because personnel of the Agrarian Reform wanted to have a meeting with us. We went there, but we arrived in the *pueblo* one hour late. Well, the official had already gone, leaving the message that he was not there to accept the irresponsibilities of the producers. This is *el gobierno* [the government]. Why doesn't the official come here if he wants punctuality? They know where we live, but they don't like to get their shoes dirty. These are all tricks because we are not important to the government. They don't give a damn about us.

Don Jesus added:

Yes, the government only comes here when they are suspicious about us because we plant *mota* [marijuana]. The last time the army was here in January, they broke into our homes [*allanaron*] and ransacked our possessions. The officer assembled us and said that in Cuyutlan he had found 70 plants of *mota* and that he knew that it was planted in La Lobera too. He asked us to name the people who were cultivating *mota*, otherwise he could use other methods to make us talk. The government likes to humiliate us, but not to help us.

Don Tomas recognised that the producers had only two ways to make cash quickly:

One is to migrate to the United States to work there, and with some luck, to come back after three or four years with some money. The other way is to cultivate *mota*. Its cultivation is easy, the only thing necessary is fertiliser. It is worth the risks because a kilo of *mota* is bought for 60 or 70 thousand *pesos* in Guadalajara. With maize you can't make money, but with *mota* it is different.

Last year, the family of Donoso bought a new tractor, complete with all its implements. They could do that because they cultivated *mota*. From where else do you think they got 3 million *pesos* (3,000 US dollars) overnight?

The producers did not expect to receive help from the government. Migration and the cultivation of marijuana provided cash, which could then be invested in livestock. Livestock were perceived by them as their only way of improving local production. A recent economic assessment of the *ejido* shows that they possess more than 700 head, valued at over 25 million *pesos* (25,000 US dollars). Maize is a less important factor in their economy and the *ejido* falls largely outside the area of agency control.

As we emphasised earlier, the producers' lack of interest in cultivating maize for marketing through CONASUPO is not because they lack market orientation, or because they are not eager to receive the benefits of the programmes in the form of credit, fertiliser and insecticides. Indeed, where possible they use these inputs to further their own economic interests and not the targets set by SARH. This is why implementers, such as the Head of the Unit, are opposed to distributing extra agency resources to an area that is outside their control. The isolation of La Lobera, then, is perceived institutionally as acting in favour of the producers, since they can easily divert programme resources to finance their own economic ventures.

On the other hand, technical assistance in the production of maize is perceived by producers as marginal to the way households organise their production and livelihood strategies. Hence the influence of a strategy such as SAM was resisted by a production system much more complex than that portrayed in the rainfed policy plans. The assumed isolation of the community is relative, since 57 per cent of the producers claimed to have heard about SAM, even if only 31 per cent of them knew its aims, and only one person had received information about it from the Ministry. In other words, resistance to SAM must be understood in terms of the programme's emphasis on the specialisation of maize cultivation; and, on the other hand, in terms of the low agency diffusion of its aims among producers. The area, in spite of its potential and its need for agricultural development, was not considered a priority region for the implementation of Ministry programmes.

Roberto's double dilemma: administration and the peasants

Our central actor in the final phase of the case study is engineer Roberto, who apparently obtained his position in SARH through the influence of his father. Surprisingly, he had no proper agricultural training. He was also special in the way he perceived the careers and motivation of his colleagues (he called them 'chupas barbas'), and in terms of his negative assessment of the administrative system which did not, in his view, deliver the promised services to the farmers. Finally, he was very disparaging of the value of an agricultural training for working in the countryside, maintaining that all one needed was drive and commonsense. These characteristics and attitudes meant that people perceived him as an odd-man-out, the target of ridicule and of pranks within his field unit, and he was institutionally seen as a 'troublemaker'. In his account of how he came to La Lobera one can identify some of the reasons why he was continually in conflict with administrative authority. He showed arrogance and a lack of respect towards his superiors. He did not conform to the expected patterns of administrative behaviour, and he hid behind the presumed support of his father. However, he did show some commitment to bridging the gap between peasant and bureaucrat or técnico. This he saw largely as a matter of establishing the right personal style, understanding and confianza, rather than as a structural problem involving the differential power positions of public authorities and their clients. In practice, of course, as we see from the case, he did not hesitate to present himself – whenever he considered it strategic to do so – as an authority with access to centres of power, as a well-doer actively trying to improve the lot of the peasantry, or as a government official fulfilling his administrative tasks.

In all these respects he was a bit of a madcap. Even so, in several of the social situations described, he managed to manipulate the negotiations to his advantage and to create a further basis for communication. When he first arrived in La Lobera he quickly established his authority through diagnosing the illness suffered by the cattle as rabies. This diagnosis confirmed his status as an 'expert' and placed the other parties (both the farmer and the researchers) in an inferior position. After this he went on to provide a solution, namely the fumigation of the cave of bats.

This opened the way to establishing a defined context for the interface between the peasant and the técnico, both carrying with them, or somehow 'representing', their own social worlds. This relationship was unequal not only in terms of their perceived levels of knowledge or expertise but also in terms of their assumed ability to command resources. Roberto suggested that outside authorities (i.e., the Head of District) should be involved and that the farmer should take the head of a dead cow to Zapopan for analysis. He offered to assist by making the necessary contacts, providing the farmer signed the petition for the baling machine. This baling machine had become his latest obsession (not surprising, really, given the fact that Roberto was trained in mechanical engineering and that livestock was the crucial element in the economy of La Lobera which was something he at least, if not the Ministry, had come to realise).

Once the farmer had signed the petition, Roberto's next move was to invite the farmer to accompany him to Zapopan to present the issue to the boss, knowing full well that this was likely to present a problem since peasants did not like to leave their sick livestock and the distance was large and transport difficult. There was also no surety that the meeting with the boss would solve the problem. The farmer procrastinated, saying that he might be able to be in Guadalajara on the Monday morning when they would meet the boss. The outcome was that Roberto had managed to shift the centre of attention away from the immediate problem of the cows dying to fulfil his own obsession for getting signatures for his petition for the baling machine. This incident shows the facility with which he could defuse the situation, having securely established his position as the *técnico*. This demonstrates the extent to which power enters the scene in favour of the knowledge of the *técnico*, irrespective of the scientific validity of his advice – the power of the 'guru' in situations of emergency! Roberto wove his way through all this with considerable skill, displaying good understanding of different types of knowledge, but in the end achieving nothing effective for the peasant in question. In this respect Roberto is probably not exceptional, since Mexican government fieldworkers have to acquire the techniques of managing these different, and potentially conflicting, bodies of knowledge and cultural frameworks if they are to survive in the field.

The second incident illustrates a different interface situation. As a background to the events, it is necessary to fill in some of the context. The researchers had originally accompanied the *técnico* in order to carry out a social survey of the *ejido*. During the evening we were drinking tequila with one of the more important leaders of the community. The *técnico* was enjoying himself reading the results of the survey, when he suddenly erupted and burst into the group to confront the peasant leader with his observation that the survey had revealed that, after a year or so of sacrifice, walking many kilometres to visit the *ejido* and so forth, the producers still apparently had no *confianza* in him. The peasant leader intervened to stop him, exclaiming that it was not so much due to his person but to the fact that the government made many promises that it did not keep.

This occasioned a redefinition of the terms of interaction whereby the notion of *no confianza* [lack of trust] came to characterise the link between the peasant and bureaucratic worlds. Having established this, Roberto then proceeded to try to win the *confianza* of Martin, the peasant leader. This he achieved through his heart-rending drama, which included tears and an outright verbal attack on the principal researchers and the President of the nation. He viciously accused the government of 'shafting' or 'cheating' the producer, and the researcher of destroying his idealism. Although somewhat inebriated, he managed to seize the initiative to argue that, despite the shortcomings of the bureaucracy, some *técnicos* were able to do something for the peasantry, a remark countered by Martin who used it to put forward his own slightly crazy cherry tree 'project', which he justified in terms of his own experience in the USA. In return, he promised the *técnico* that people would sign his petition. This was accomplished in the morning very smoothly, after which Roberto and the research team left.

Roberto was, however, much less successful in manipulating cultural attitudes and administrative priorities within his own administrative domain. Hence Roberto's plans for 'helping' the peasants and for bridging the gap between the two worlds were shattered. His boss's opinion was that he had stepped beyond the competence of a *técnico* responsible for implementing the rainfed policy, and had not strictly followed administrative rules and priorities. So his fate was sealed: he would be resocialised in a new field unit made up of 'troublemakers' or 'hard cases'.

In the end, therefore, the critical factor affecting Roberto's attempts to link the two worlds was not so much the resistance of the peasantry, but more the constraints, development priorities and ideology of the administrative system under which he had to perform and was evaluated. At the time, he was one of the few *técnicos* who tried to bend the rules a little in the direction of certain perceived mutual interests between him and the peasants. If he had succeeded, he might have helped to create an organised interface between the two parties and to integrate them into a long-term and mutually beneficial set of working relationships. As it was, however, Roberto's case simply revealed for the researchers the enormous gaps in communication and in power differentials in Mexico between peasants and state development agencies. On the other hand, from the peasant point of view, his case showed the possibilities for establishing *confianza* with individual *técnicos* who could bring some benefits, but the impossibility of having close and trusting ties with central government agencies, which peasants continued to see as merely coming to La Lobera to enforce 'the law' and to destroy the basis of their economic survival and autonomy. This view was shared by both rich and poor peasants from La Lobera.

There is, of course, always some room for manoeuvre and some space for *técnicos* to devise ways of accommodating the different and often conflicting sets of interests; but they may be rewarded or penalised both by the administration and the peasantry, or by one or the other. But the struggle goes on. The set of relations is never in equilibrium. The struggle is, as we have tried to show, as much a struggle over types of knowledge and devices for creating ignorance, as it is a struggle over material resources or political power.

Conclusions

This chapter has presented a detailed account of the complex set of relationships existing between peasants of one *ejido* and members of the Mexican agricultural bureaucracy. We focused upon the problem of the interplay of different lifeworlds and bodies of knowledge, exploring this from the point of view of the dilemmas faced by one *técnico* who had to deal with the demands of his peasant clients and those of his administrative superiors.

On the basis of this actor-oriented analysis, we were able to identify the opposition between peasant and bureaucratic views of development. We also showed how bridging actions initiated by the *técnico*, aimed at resolving or ameliorating the difficulties and incompatibilities, simply exacerbated the situation, leading to the further separation of the two worlds and to the reinforcement and legitimation of each body of knowledge. The interfaces that developed between the *técnico* and his peasant clients created a basis for communication and negotiation, and a potential for cooperative endeavour and the sharing of agricultural knowledge and experience; but, in the end, this emergent process provided no more than a springboard to action entailing further confrontation and separation of interests between the parties concerned.

Underlying our analysis is the conviction that a sociology of the everyday life of actors involved in shaping the processes and outcomes of rural development programmes is needed if we are to develop a more adequate understanding of the significance of human agency in such situations. This raises a number of complex issues for research, including the question of how different bodies of knowledge, as well as systematic forms of ignorance, influence the strategies adopted by the participants.

Although we have contrasted the general nature of the lifeworlds of bureaucrat and peasant in order to highlight how their different corpuses of knowledge are manufactured and interact, we wish to emphasise that each is highly differentiated internally (a bureaucrat, for example, might come from peasant stock). This differentiation arises from the specificities of the lifeworld experiences and careers of particular individuals, as illustrated by Roberto's behaviour and perceptions. At the same time, of course, Roberto and his administrative colleagues share a number of representations and prejudices about the nature of the 'peasantry' and the prerequisites for 'agricultural development', as do the peasants of La Lobera about el gobierno and its intentions. These images and attitudes have developed out of the history of peasant–bureaucrat encounters in this and other areas of Mexico, and constitute a kind of recall of the 'imagined' past which individual actors may draw upon and reinterpret in organising their own responses to new intervention scenarios. Shared understandings and taken-for-granted ways of doing things are in this way re-evaluated and modified in the face of new experiences. The analysis of Roberto's interactions with peasant clients and bureaucratic colleagues is, then, far more than the story of a somewhat eccentric técnico confronting an assortment of peasant pragmatists and his tough boss. It offers us a window on the more general issue of the significance of knowledge interfaces in the context of state intervention in rural Mexico, and possibly more widely.

Finally, we wish to conclude by mentioning several other important issues relating to the sociology of everyday knowledge and to knowledge interface situations that are suggested by this case-study that require further investigation.

First, we need to understand how ideologies are represented in 'untheoretical', 'practical ways of life', and how these influence social behaviour in interface situations. Second, we should explore more systematically the significance of different patterns of local social organisation for containing, absorbing and generating particular bodies of knowledge. Third, more work is required on identifying the boundaries of 'epistemic communities' (i.e., those composed of persons sharing the same sources and types of knowledge) through the characterisation of the structure and contents of particular communicator networks. A fourth priority for research is the need to analyse how the systematic exclusion or neutralisation of new items of information or new cognitive frames prevents the merging or transformation of existing bodies of knowledge, thus perpetuating structural contradictions, power differentials and uneven development. Finally, we need to develop a methodology for handling the complex set of relations that evolves in interface situations that would allow for a more thorough appreciation of how bodies of knowledge shape the struggles and negotiations between local groups and intervening parties.

10

GLOBALISATION AND LOCALISATION

Recontextualising social change[1]

Introduction: a turning point in history?

It is now commonplace to stress that we are living in an era of significant change: a turning point in history, a time of transition and radical social change; the end of industrial society and the promises of the Enlightenment (Touraine 1984, 1989), the beginnings of a digital age; and perhaps the 'end of history' as the West has envisioned it (Fukuyama 1989). Important dimensions of this change involve the rapid production and dissemination of scientific knowledge and technology, cultural styles and modes of communication, the restructuring of work, industry, markets and economic life, and the fragmentation and reorganisation of power domains leading to the emergence of new social and political identities.

Such change-processes – whether interpreted as the latest manifestations of some 'modernist' conception of history and 'progress' or as the beginnings of a 'postmodernist' era – not only affect the most affluent but also the poorer nations of the world. Indeed much of what we now witness is essentially 'global' in scope, entailing the accelerated flows of various commodities, people, capital, technologies, information and images across many national frontiers – what Albrow (1996) calls the 'Global Age'.

But we should not be seduced into believing that globalisation is a totally new phenomenon. Indeed some commentators have argued that 'in spite of increases in global flows of trade and money around the world, these are not substantially different to the economic and social interactions that have occurred between nations in previous historical times' (Cochrane and Pain 2000: 2).[2] In a similar way, Standage (1998) documents the enormous impact of the invention of electric telegraphy on communications and social relations during the Victorian era – something on a par with the present-day Internet revolution (see Mackay 2000: 69–71).[3] It would likewise be misguided to expect globalisation to have a uniform impact everywhere. To do so would be to fall into the same trap as previous attempts at formulating general (or universal) theories of social change, namely that of reifying certain 'driving forces', 'prime movers' or 'cultural facilitators'. Globalisation should not be visualised as some kind of overarching hegemonic process that structures outcomes at the level of nations, cultures, economies and people's livelihoods, but rather as a convenient shorthand for depicting the ongoing complexities, ambiguities and diversities of contemporary patterns of global/local relations.

Discerning and interpreting these complex and often contested global/local scenarios is, of course, an enormous task that goes well beyond what is possible in this chapter. My task here is more modest. I aim to outline the main features of global change at the turn of

214

the twenty-first century and to identify certain key theoretical issues entailed in developing a new agenda for research on globalisation and localisation.

Three interwoven fields of change

As I briefly sketched above, we can distinguish three fields in which significant restructuring is taking place.[4] The first concerns changes in production, work and economic life more generally. This entails the following critical dimensions:

1   Changes in the patterns of commoditisation consequent upon the rise of new, and the 'reinvention' of old, modes of value, as consumer markets and interests become more diversified in the types and qualities of goods required;

2   An uneven transition from 'Fordism' and the vertical integration of firms towards a more flexible and global pattern of production and accumulation marked by the growing importance of more loosely structured horizontal linkages covering subcontracting, industrial and artisan homework, and a multiplicity of linked service and consumption-based activities;

3   Changing notions of 'work' and 'occupational status' resulting principally from increases in unemployment and part-time work and a reorganised gender division of labour;

4   A move towards greater 'informalisation' and fragmentation of economic life within the family/household, small-scale enterprise and local community, in some cases resulting in the demise of local systems of care and social support.[5]

The second field of change concerns the changing nature of the state, changing power domains, and the appearance of new social movements and socio-political identities. Central dimensions here include:

1   The decline of corporativist modes of regulation and organisation, and the 'hollowing out' of the state as it relinquishes more of its functions to non-state bodies;

2   The emergence of new forms of coalition at local and regional levels as the politics, policies and organisation of nation-states are transformed under the impact of more global interests, and as central government authority and control becomes weaker and increasingly delegitimised;[6]

3   Shifts in the relations and meanings of the 'public' versus the 'private' domain, bolstered by neo-liberal 'free enterprise' and 'back-to-the-market' discourse;

4   The development of new social and political identities and movements based on diverse social commitments, where class constitutes only one among many forms of association and social difference (such as gender, ethnicity, locality, religion, membership of environmentalist or human rights groups, or a commitment to 'transnational' or 'cosmopolitan' notions of 'citizenship').[7]

The third field relates to issues of knowledge, science and technology. Here the focus is on debates about the nature and impact of 'information society', where sophisticated information, communication and media systems, production technologies and computerised modes of reasoning shape the social relations and cultural orientations of contemporary societies.[8] This field also encompasses issues concerning knowledge generation, dissemination, utilisation and transformation; the encounter between so-called 'expert' and 'lay' modes of knowledge; the clashes and accommodations that take place between contrasting cultural and epistemological frameworks; the affirmation of the 'power of science' to transform social life and steer change; and the transformation of knowledge and technology at the interface between intervening 'development' institutions and 'recipient' groups (see Chapters 8 and 9 for exploration of these themes). In addition, it raises questions about the time–space compression[9] of contemporary social life hastened by information technologies, as well as the central role that information-processing plays in the development of 'institutional reflexivity' (Giddens 1991) which, it is alleged, facilitates the quick response of modern organisations to rapidly changing scenarios.

Globalisation: diversity and policy dilemmas in a global scenario

At this juncture, having dwelt so far on delineating broad trends and identifying critical dimensions, it becomes important to acknowledge the diversities and contradictions that are generated within and between these different fields of change. This is imperative if we are to distance ourselves from essentialist and reified interpretations of globalisation that assume rather than demonstrate the force and uniformity of such change. It is also necessary to make a case against centrist and simple hegemonic modes of analysis.

As a first step, I wish to reassert the significance of social heterogeneity – a central leit-motif of this book. The revolution in information and communication technologies has made the world look more uniform and interconnected. But in fact we live in an increasingly diversified world with only the trappings of homogeneity. Even the most sophisticated communication and media systems and the most integrated international commodity markets have far from eliminated cultural, ethnic, economic and political diversity. On the contrary, globalisation represents a whole new set of diversified and constantly changing patterns of response at national, regional and local levels.

Awareness of such heterogeneity is reflected in the questioning, in certain policy circles, of standardised solutions to problems of economic development, employment and welfare, in favour of what are described as more flexible, localised and 'sustainable' strategies. This shift implies, at least in public rhetoric, a greater recognition of the strategic contribution that local knowledge, organisation and participation can make to development intervention. Concomitant with this is the apparent decline of hierarchical and corporativist forms of organisation and the emergence of new groupings and coalitions that delegitimise centralised political control and authority, thus reshaping power relations. But we must also remember that decentralisation policies often mask 'top-down' measures aimed at reducing the administrative and financial burdens of central government.

Alongside these trends is the swing back to 'market-led' development where the language of 'free enterprise', 'competition' and 'deregulation' prevails. But, again, we should not assume that liberalising and privatising strategies, spearheaded by international bodies such as the World Bank and the IMF, mark the end of interventionist measures undertaken by the state. Indeed, the very implementation of liberalisation policies requires a framework of state regulation, resources and legitimacy, and the use of a persuasive political rhetoric aimed at mobilising people and enrolling them in this new type of strategic thinking. Moreover, policy measures that address themselves to the 'solution' of pressing economic problems often fall short precisely because they fail to come to grips with the everyday practicalities and diverse modes of making and defending a living. Thus strategic planning by government is always difficult to realise successfully when faced by a myriad of local and regional adaptations, but especially so when the political conditions militate against the state being able to govern effectively and steer change. Many domains of state activity in fact increasingly require international backing to function at all.

These processes have exacerbated the fragility of many contemporary post-colonial states, generating high levels of political and ethnic conflict. At the same time there is mounting frustration at the impotence of UN agencies, other international bodies and development aid institutions to prevent conflicts from erupting or to find viable solutions to these daunting problems. Likewise there is a growing concern for issues of environmental damage, food quality and health risks due to the pollution or depletion of natural resources and to the application of inappropriate or over-elaborate management and high-technology solutions.

Given these persisting conditions, it becomes increasingly difficult to design models to promote clearly delineated development trajectories, identify alternative scenarios, or to predict the side effects of development policies. Indeed the side effects of planned interventions have become a central predicament for international development organisations since they have often exacerbated rather than ameliorated existing socio-political and ethnic conflict or deteriorating ecological imbalances and disasters. An additional reason for their poor performance, especially in humanitarian aid situations, is the lack of coordination between the multiplicity of agencies (government and non-government) involved. Even in more stable situations of intervention, livelihood options are frequently affected by global processes, which fall outside the scope of the implementing bodies. For example, diversified local economies exhibiting high levels of informalisation and casualisation of work and incomes (sometimes resulting from the contracting strategies pursued by foreign companies), depending heavily on remittances from international labour migrants, or on producing crops or animals for sale in illegal external markets (the drug trade being the most striking example) present major problems for policy-makers and implementers since critical domains of economic activity lie outside their influence and control. This situation is further compounded by the fact that the outcomes of policy intervention are made up of a complicated mix of intended, unintended and unanticipated results, which are impossible to unravel.

Global domains and 'new' social movements

The problem of governability arises, then, from the complex nature of the relationships affecting different domains of human practice. Geo-political transformations, such as the break-up of the Soviet Union and the socialist bloc countries and the establishment of new regions of cooperation such as the European Union (EU) and the Northern American Free Trade Agreement (NAFTA), as well as the new agreements or 'conditionalities' concerning development aid, debt and trade enforced by the World Bank/IMF and the World Trade Organisation (WTO), throw into question the sovereignty of nation-states, since their rights and obligations, their powers and autonomy, are clearly challenged and redefined. The immense flows of capital, goods, services, people, information, technologies, policies, ideas, images and regulations that these changes imply are not organised from a few centres or blocs of power, as World Systems theory might suggest (see

Sklair 1991: 33–4). Global organisations of this type, as well as transnational businesses, may well have localised sites of operation (for example, in London, New York or Tokyo) but they are not able to dominate completely their global spheres of influence and investment. Instead, they are constantly thrown into contests with competitors and clients, and increasingly have to deal with the criticisms and counter-actions of organised transnational protest groups, brought together through information and contacts supplied by specific websites on the Internet.[10]

It is difficult therefore to conceptualise nation-states or transnational corporations as the principal power-containers of important economic and social relationships in the new global political economy. We must replace this model with one of global *orders* whose constituent parts extend beyond states and transnational corporations to include a variety of civic groups and associations operating within multiple and overlapping networks of power. These various networks are constantly reordering themselves in the face of changing global conditions, and in so doing they draw upon a diverse range of resources and values that appeal to and propagate images of the new 'global' scenario.

Globally-oriented groups and associations include not only recognised multilateral organisations, financial and trade bodies and newly-emerging inter-state political alliances, but also social movements where people group around what they perceive as pressing problems of a global nature. As Castells (1997: 68–109) shows in his analysis of three such movements pitched against the 'new global order', these movements can differ markedly in the way they define themselves, their goals, means and strategies, their ideologies or beliefs, and their social location. He takes the case of the 1994 Zapatista uprising in Chiapas, Mexico, that opposed Mexico's signing of the North American Free Trade Agreement (NAFTA) and the implementation of neoliberal policies (see p. 60); the American 'Patriot' movement of the 1990s, a large network of extreme right-wing groups – including militias – committed to destroying (by violent means if necessary) the 'conspiracy of global financial interests and global bureaucrats that have captured the US federal government'; and the Japanese *Aum Shinrikyo* millenarian cult bent on saving the world from the coming apocalypse caused by the increasing competition between Japanese corporations and American imperialism.[11]

These movements represent a growing commitment to new 'causes' that bring people together across the world – sometimes on a local or national basis, and sometimes on the basis of uniting people and groups across different nation-states and cultures. A good example of the latter is the 'green' movement that addresses issues of worldwide pollution, degradation of the environment, depletion of natural resources and the loss of genetic diversity among animal and plant populations (Yearley 1994, Jamison 1996, Castells 1997: 110–33).[12] Other examples are the movements that have sprung up around health threats affecting the world population at large (and especially vulnerable groups), such as the HIV/AIDS associations and pressure groups; and 'alternative development' associations and groups that have launched campaigns against transnational corporations introducing to the poorer nations what are considered to be nutritionally 'inappropriate' products such as baby bottle-feed formulas and Coca Cola, or 'inappropriate' technologies promoting non-sustainable production methods and oppressive systems of labour control.

From the standpoint of consumer interests, there are associations (mostly based in the richer countries) that lobby for better quality or more organically-grown produce and more favourable prices; and farmers' organisations that seek to advance their own particular interests – sometimes at loggerheads with each other. The French and British producers, for example, have for a number of years been locked in battle over European Union agricultural export quotas, which on one occasion led to the slaughtering of imported British sheep in France. In addition to the evidently divergent livelihood interests of the French and British farmers, the critical issue here has centred on the legitimacy and interpretation of EU regulations. Similar food chain problems have increasingly motivated the transnationals and supermarkets to negotiate direct deals with producer groups, especially in Third World production zones, so as to avoid as many state and international environmental, trade and quality controls as possible (Marsden and Arce 1993).

An example of how certain issues can galvanise mass support spanning national frontiers is the recent campaign (September/October 2000) mounted by farmers, haulage companies and self-employed truck operators in Europe against the high price of fuel, especially diesel fuel. Over the years fuel prices had soared, due partly to OPEC's decision to maintain high oil prices by reducing levels of production, but mostly to the high level of fuel tax imposed by European governments. Demonstrations spread from blockades of the ports in France, to petrol storage depots throughout the UK bringing garages, food suppliers and retail businesses practically to a halt, and led to similar protests in the Netherlands, Belgium and Germany. Although at the time of writing this chapter (late October 2000) the protests are in abeyance pending further negotiations with government in the UK, the farmers and hauliers continue to receive considerable sympathy and support from the public at large. The organisation of a massive protest like this would not have been possible without the full use of global communication media. Indeed, it is said that the most visible and effective weapon that protesters wielded was the mobile phone.

Other cases highlight certain shifts in the character of agrarian movements. Latin America in particular has a long history of struggles by small producers and agricultural labourers against landlords and local political bosses monopolising access to the most productive land and to crucial marketing and servicing channels (de la Peña 1994). But now we witness massive mobilisations of indigenous peoples. Around the Amazonian rim several different groups are actively engaged in fighting not just for rights to land (i.e., plots for cultivation or livestock rearing) but for habitat rights (i.e., the right to be left undisturbed by transnationals or ravaged by land speculators, and the right to determine how natural resources should be utilised and by whom). This struggle, of course, has strong ethnic and human rights dimensions to it, which have prompted the International Labour Organisation to become involved in providing logistical support for the coordination of these Amazonian groups.[13] It has also sparked off protest marches directed at the national governments of Bolivia and Ecuador by indigenous peoples, who walked from the eastern tropical lowlands to the capital cities of La Paz and Quito in order to present their cases. The rebellion in Chiapas, which focused on resistance to the Mexican State and its free trade policies, and began on the day NAFTA was inaugurated, presents a similar mix of issues embracing land, ethnicity, political repression and human rights (see Harvey 1998 for a historical analysis). This case is also notable for the rapidity with which the leaders of the uprising were able to disseminate their manifesto and detail their complaints and demands. Almost as soon as they had taken their first offensive, a statement from them appeared in e-mail inboxes throughout the global electronic network. As Castells (1997: 80) reports, the Zapatistas' use of the Internet was linked in the early 1990s to the creation of *La Neta*, a public computer communication network, and its use by women's groups to link NGOs in Chiapas with women's groups elsewhere in Mexico and the US. This initiative was supported by the Catholic Church and the Institute for Global Communication in San Francisco, whose experts gave their time without payment. The network was also supported by a grant from the Ford Foundation. This highlights another interesting dimension, namely, the global expansion of women's and feminist associations (see Basu and McGrory 1995 and Stephen 1997), which has drawn together women from diverse cultural and socio-political backgrounds, leading to a series of World Summits at which they have been able to share experiences and identify areas for future strategic debate and action.

At the same time as these new social movements have been evolving and flexing their muscles, there has been a concomitant re-ordering of power relations consequent upon a decline in hierarchical and corporativist modes of control. The interplay of these two processes has generated a variety of dynamic and contingent situations, which contain both the organisational potential for the creation of new globally-oriented coalitions of interest and the possibility of the fragmentation of existing power domains. While the latter may lead to the opening up of new political spaces, at least for some social groups, it may also heighten cultural and political confrontation, resulting in the worst of scenarios (such as those seen in the Balkans and Rwanda–Zaire) involving ethnic strife, civil war and societal breakdown.

Clearly, then, globalisation processes generate a whole new range of conditions and socio-political responses at national, regional and local levels. These changes, however, are not dictated by some supranational hegemonic power or simply driven by international capitalist interests. Changing global conditions – whether economic, political, cultural or environmental – are, as it were, 'relocalised' within national, regional or local frameworks of knowledge and organisation which, in turn, are constantly reworked in interaction with the wider context. It is for this reason that we need to study in detail the disembedding of localised ideas and relations as they acquire global significance, and their subsequent re-embedding in yet other locales (see Giddens 1991: 17–20; cf. van der Ploeg 1992, which uses the notions of 'internalisation' and 'relocalisation' to describe these processes). Such processes entail the emergence of new identities, alliances and struggles for space and power within specific local/global scenarios.

Although people in remote areas with poor road communications – and perhaps especially these people – can now avail themselves of modern satellite communication systems, it remains the case that, like other social groups, they must still develop their own strategies to solve the problems they face. Even if global technologies mediate, mobilising resources and social support still requires the deployment of interpersonal networks of various sorts, based on family, community or neighbourhood ties, or church and other associational or professional commitments. Moreover, as argued throughout this book, people do not merely respond to programmes or services provided by 'outside' bodies, public or private; nor do they simply react to market conditions, global or otherwise. Rather, they attempt to come to grips emotionally, cognitively and institutionally with the various 'externalities' they confront. And it is in this way that 'states', 'transnationals', 'markets', 'technologies' and 'global images' themselves become endowed with highly diverse sets of localised meanings and practices.

Globalscapes: cultural flows, 'imagined worlds' and changing socio-political identities

Global relations and cultures are products of networks of communication and information (Appadurai 1990, Featherstone 1990a). That is, the symbolic forms transmitted by communication media have become central to contemporary cultural and social repertoires. Technology enables messages, images and symbols to be transmitted rapidly to audiences widely dispersed in time and space, thus creating and reinforcing new types of technically 'mediated' social relations that link individuals to various 'imagined communities' throughout the world (Anderson 1989, Thompson 1990). These 'imagined worlds' (as Appadurai renames them) are made up of 'historically situated imaginations of persons and groups spread across the globe...[and] are fluid and irregularly shaped' (Lash and Urry 1994: 307). Hence spatial contiguity and direct interpersonal interaction are not necessary features of such worlds. Imagined worlds are, as it were, inhabited by 'non-existent' persons, in the sense that there are probably no persons who exactly match the qualities or profiles of those considered members. Individual and collective identities (based, for example, on ethnic or gender stereotypes, or simply on the idea of what it means to be a 'train-spotter' or a 'Man United' football fan) are constructed around these imagined worlds of peoples and places. They are especially salient when people are somehow forced to compare and contrast their own worlds with those of others. This reflexive process may be facilitated by the rapid and widespread diffusion of media-transmitted images and symbols, but since media messages contain a multiplicity of meanings the outcomes are never very predictable.

The many diverse and often conflicting messages and images projected are reworked by specific audiences in very different ways. For example, in rural Zambia in the 1970s, Jehovah's Witnesses watching an American-made video about the coming of the 'New World' assumed that this paradise would offer them modern bungalows set within a beautiful country estate, where they would dress European-style, have handsome wristwatches, splendid limousines, and enjoy endless family picnics on the well-kept lawns. In short, they expected to receive all the material benefits mostly monopolised by the whites. Their reading of the video thus seized upon the materialist setting chosen to represent the paradise rather than upon what the video makers would have deemed to be its 'spiritual' message. And no doubt numerous other interpretations of the same video film would arise among other audiences.

Thus, rather than generating an increasingly uniform cultural pattern, modern media technology helps to expand the cultural universe in many varied and unexpected ways. Some images, for example, are appropriated by 'opposition' movements to champion their own campaigns, as frequently happens with environmentalists or 'Friends of the Earth' lobbyists. In this way images may be deployed to challenge established views; or, alternatively, they may be used in extreme ways to communicate negative attitudes and 'falsehoods' concerning particular cultures. The latter is powerfully demonstrated by Said (1978) in his exposure and critique of 'orientalist' views of Islamic society, which gained added saliency and legitimacy for the West through the media reporting of the Gulf War.

It is essential, therefore, to acknowledge what Appadurai calls the 'non-isomorphic' nature of global cultural flows: that is to say, the many divergent movements of people, things and ideas that do not neatly coincide or accumulate to produce a single overall pattern. In similar fashion, cultural styles and artistic creations do not merely flow from 'global centres' to subordinate 'peripheries'. Indeed, in many cases it is the so-called 'periphery' that brings cultural innovation to the 'centre': see, for example, the constant reverberations of Caribbean, African and Latin American musical and artistic forms that shape the pop scenes of London and Paris.

A further tantalising but complex aspect of global culture and identity concerns how the notion of citizenship, normally linked to the idea that a person's political identity and rights are defined and guaranteed by the nation-state, has become more elastic and unsure. Nowadays, many groups feel themselves less part of a nation-state, especially when the state is divided along sharp class, ethnic, or language lines, and more in tune with the idea of belonging to a nation, such as the 'Scottish nation' to which many Scots claim allegiance, even if this is 'an aspiration rather than a historical fact'. In fact McCrone (1992) argues that Scottish nationhood is partly built upon the *invention* of ancient Scottish kings and queens whose portraits now hang in Holyrood House in Edinburgh.

Others claim to be part of an ethnic population with its own distinctive culture and language or dialect that crosscuts nation-state boundaries. This often involves the creation of 'new' ethnicities, as people from particular 'homelands' seeking work, education or political asylum build ties that span rural and urban locations and national frontiers. These ties and networks constitute specific responses to changes in economic circumstances, such as shifts in the international demand for labour (e.g., Mexican labour migration to the US), or to convulsions associated with the restructuring or breaking-up of nation-states (e.g., the Sudanese and Ethiopian refugees in Kenya escaping from war and famine).

As cross-border ties stabilise around regular flows back and forth, so migrants gradually develop a sense of self that is genuinely transnational. They also tend to form associations to further their own specific cross-border interests. This encourages the crystallisation of a new kind of socio-political identity built upon ethnic bonds but cutting across national frontiers. Hence, for example, we find a growing propensity among migrant groups from Oaxaca, Mexico, in the US to articulate and defend their social rights as tomato workers *vis-à-vis* their Californian employers and the US government. Yet they do this not only as agricultural workers but also on the basis of a rejuvenated Mixtec identity linking them to their villages of origin in Mexico, which they skilfully deploy in arguing their case against unfair treatment and inadequate housing. According to Kearney (1988), this militancy has spread to incorporate Mixtecs in the border cities of Tijuana, Mexicali, etc. in northwestern Mexico, where Mixtec residents' associations have successfully fought cases involving, for instance, police harassment of Mixtec women street traders. Over time, these experiences have contributed to the emergence of a new conception of self which is essentially pan-Mixteca and which therefore goes beyond the normal criteria of citizenship.[14]

This is a common characteristic among international migrant communities; even among those, as Hannerz (1990) suggests, who make up the brigades of international migrant professionals (and, I would add, their children), who travel around the world working for the UN, development aid agencies and transnationals. These professional families quickly develop a cosmopolitanness that transcends national styles and identities, although at the same time their global networks remain relatively closed to outsiders. They are more interested in pursuing lifestyles that are largely unencumbered by the civic rights and duties of national citizenship, and of course they often receive tax-free salaries.

This, in turn, raises the thorny political and moral issue, discussed by Lash and Urry

(1994: 309–10), of redefining citizenship in terms of fundamental consumption rights. That is, 'people in different societies should have similar rights of access to a wide diversity of consumer goods, services and cultural products', including the right to engage in international tourism – to '*consume* other cultures and places throughout the world' – just as do members of the richer nations.

Globalisation, localisation and re-localisation

In developing these lines of argument we must further clarify what is implied by notions of globalisation and localisation, and why it is sometimes useful to speak of 're-localisation'.

In the first place, I choose to use 'globalisation' instead of 'internationalisation' because the latter conjures up the idea of 'inter nation-state' relations, thereby suggesting that the constituent parts are composed of nation-states. Such a view is clearly too restrictive, especially given the present world situation where we are confronted with a complex, changing multiplicity of interconnections based on financial commitments, commodity flows, producer and consumer associations, technology and knowledge dissemination, and political negotiations and struggles that are primarily transnational in character in that they are framed by types of authority and regulatory practice that transcend those of the state.

Second, as I indicated earlier, we must distance ourselves from the 1960s and 1970s idea of globalisation that pictures an emerging 'world order' in terms of 'centre–periphery', or 'metropolis–satellite' relations, thus implying simple asymmetries in economic, political and cultural terms. Instead we should view global ordering in terms of a complex and changing pattern of homogenisation and diversity. Moreover, the autonomy and boundedness of social and cultural units are better conceptualised as a matter of degree rather than as a set of sharply delineated forms. What is needed, then, is a model that concentrates upon global flows, involving movements of people (e.g., migrant workers, refugees, investors, traders and transnational employees), technology and information, money through financial operations, products through commodity markets, images and symbolic representations through various media (e.g., addressing notions of 'modernisation', 'entrepreneurship', 'citizenship'), and institutional designs (e.g., the roles assigned to business organisations, cooperatives and public/private partnerships) promoted by international development agencies. On the basis of this, we should aim to identify the interest groups, organisations and stakeholders involved in stimulating, manipulating, steering or blocking these flows, and to analyse the types and sources of power relations generated.

On the other hand, globalisation must be coupled with the idea of 'localisation', with a view to establishing the *local embeddedness* of global phenomena; that is, we must examine the complex ways in which local forms of knowledge and organisation are constantly being reworked in interaction with changing external conditions. We may also find it useful to reflect upon issues of 're-localisation' rather than simply 'localisation', since these raise questions concerning the resurgence of local commitments and the 'reinvention' or creation of new local social forms that emerge as an integral part of the process of globalisation. In fact globalisation itself can only be socially meaningful to actors if the new experiences it engenders simultaneously gel, intersect or clash with existing experiences and cultural understandings. It is in this manner that new social meanings and organising practices are generated. To argue for the reassertion of local organisational and cultural patterns, the reinvention of tradition, and the creation of new types of local attachment, is therefore not the same as arguing for a *persisting* set of local traditions. Rather, these 'reinvented' patterns are generated through the ongoing encounter between different frames of meaning and action. In this way, re-localisation opens up new theoretical insights into processes of social transformation.

Globalising and localising processes: the rise of new ruralities

The foregoing discussion of global social change serves as a useful benchmark for assessing current rural transformations and for defining the 'new' ruralities.

The globalisation of agriculture and the food chain has led to changes in farm technology and the division of labour, with an increasing diversification of types of rural work, including agriculture, on a part-time basis, as well as new food processing industries. In some areas we see the growth of new consumption and service activities linked to the tourist industry and recreational pursuits, or the consolidation of small-scale workshops that produce or assemble manufactured goods for transnational enterprises. These openings have tended disproportionately to recruit women into new and often poorly paid jobs.

Many such changes have exacerbated existing conflicts over land and natural resources, and reshaped forms of economic and political support. Some have implied changes in the legal frameworks affecting land use and management, in the use of technology, and in the networks of technical and administrative institutions serving the farm. These various changes have in different ways affected status and gender relations in the household and on the farm, with women generally taking a more active role in income-generation and economic decision-making. But none of these transformations can be said to have been simply imposed or dictated by outside authorities or powerful groups. The different actors involved – peasant smallholders, commercial farmers, transnational companies, agricultural bureaucrats, credit banks, various agrarian organisations, property developers, and city folk moving into the countryside to enjoy a more rural lifestyle – all struggle to advance their own particular interests and have a say in what happens to rural resources in both the short and the longer term.

As emphasised in earlier chapters, farming populations are strikingly heterogeneous in terms of the strategies they adopt for solving their production and other problems. Although ecological, demographic, market, politico-economic and socio-cultural conditions differ and shape the choices available to farmers, in the end it is the farmers – or more precisely the decision-makers of the farm/household – who actively problematise situations, process information and bring together the elements necessary for running a viable enterprise or for terminating it in favour of other livelihood options. Clearly they do this in the context of pressures from outside, from government, transnational companies or research stations. But ultimately decision-making rests in the hands of the farm enterprise managers or the farm families (which cater for the concerns of all their members, men and women, old and young). The decisions they make shape their immediate farming worlds, and involve the internalisation and often the reworking of external rationalities relating to the market, technologies and management, in line with their own interests and circumstances.

An actor-oriented perspective alerts us to the dangers of assuming the potency and driving force of external institutions and interests, when the latter represent only one set among a large array of actors who shape outcomes. The organisational forms that result are complex and varied, since each 'solution' represents a specific configuration of inter-locking actors' 'projects' generated by the encounters, negotiations and accommodations that take place between them, even though some may never in fact meet face-to-face (Long and van der Ploeg 1994). The influence of actors who are remote from the action-situation is especially pertinent in an age where information technology penetrates more and more into everyday life. Many commercial farmers in poor countries now communi-cate through walkie-talkies with their farm overseers or foremen in the fields, and possess mobile phones and computers that can directly access foreign commodity markets for up-to-date information on prices and product turnover. And wage-earning migrants living abroad constitute an important source of information, and their remittances subsidise incomes and livelihood activities in their places of origin. An interesting example of the latter is the regular flow of highly skilled shepherds from the remoter areas of highland Peru to work on the sheep ranches of the mid-western USA. They speak no English and often little Spanish, yet their expertise is highly valued since it helps to maintain high levels of reproduction and offspring survival among the sheep. Unlike many international agricultural migrant workers, these workers are legal, have three-year contracts and earn a regular dollar wage, part of which they remit or save to invest in small-scale business and farming ventures on returning home (Altamirano 1991).

Patterns of agricultural development are therefore subject to the combined effects of globalisation and localisation; that is, local situations are transformed by becoming part of wider global arenas and processes, whilst global dimensions are made meaningful in rela-tion to specific local conditions and through the understandings and strategies of local actors. This produces a variegated pattern of responses, with some farms or production sectors orienting themselves towards producing for international markets, while others increase their commitment to local consumption and distribution markets. Likewise, some farmers specialise their production, whilst others hedge their bets through crop diversifica-tion or by combining agricultural and non-agricultural forms of enterprise. Nowadays, of course, such choices are complicated by the fact that technological developments are racing ahead of mechanisation and chemical inputs to embrace biotechnological research, genetic engineering and automation. This throws up new choices and dilemmas, as well as the vulnerabilities and risks associated with the use of modern science and technology, vis-à-vis local farmer knowledge and practice. But, even in this situation, it does not entail a complete surrender to the 'imperatives' of advanced technology and science. As Hawkins (1991) has shown for British dairy farmers using embryo transplant methods of reproduc-tion supplied by agribusiness, farmers still retain control of how they integrate this technology and its organisational implications into their farming activities and commer-cialisation strategies.

The relationship between global and local dynamics is especially important for under-standing the management of agro-ecological resources. Problems can be identified as global in nature when they have widespread ramifications and consequences, but their solution requires 'localisation'; that is, the localised management of available resources in accordance with existing local and regional knowledge, skills, potentialities and restric-tions. They entail a variety of solutions to similar problems, with consequent differences in farm management styles, cropping patterns, levels of production, levels of resource depletion or conservation, and knowledge utilisation. Farm and environmental knowledge varies and is accorded different social meanings. Take for example the difference in knowl-edge and cultural values attached to harvesting farmed as against wild salmon, or growing hybrid as against local indigenous varieties of maize.[15] These contrasts in farm crops and styles of farming often entail different relations with commodity markets of various types – niche, local and mass consumer markets. They also entail a commitment to and use of different technologies (e.g., tractor, plough, hoe or axe, chemical, organic, biological or genetic inputs, etc.). The meaning a particular instrument or factor of production acquires relates to how it is coordinated with other production and reproduction factors (van der Ploeg 1986, 1990). Adopted technology is forever reworked to fit the production strategies, resource availability and desires and cultural values of farm households. Included in this process is not only the manner in which technologies or packages are adopted, appropriated or transformed, but also the ongoing processes by which particular farmers combine different social domains based on family, community, market, or state institutions, as well as the struggles they pursue in order to retain or create space for manoeuvre.[16]

We can no longer take for granted, therefore, that rural space equals agricultural space or that the central problems for analysis can be reduced to the 'agrarian question', the debate concerning the significance of proletarianisation versus peasantisation of the countryside that was a major preoccupation of agrarian social science during the 1970s and 1980s (see Kautsky 1899, de Janvry 1981, Harriss 1982, Goodman and Redclift 1981 and many articles in the *Journal of Peasant Studies*). We should not privilege agricultural production over other income-earning/livelihood activities, and we should go beyond agricultural production and resource issues to look more generally at the utilisation of countryside resources. This means a concern for landscape and environmental dimensions, for recreation and leisure time pursuits, and for the management of forest and water resources and similar amenities.

These issues raise the question of how to accord value to 'nature'. Local actors (e.g., peasants and traders) and outsiders (e.g., agricultural extensionists, pollution officers, conservationists and research scientists) usually differ in their assessments and priorities, and in the way they represent 'nature–man' relations and the 'environment' (see Ingold 1986, Croll and Parkin 1992, Ellen and Fukui 1996; and Braun and Castree 1998 which calls for the abandonment of the simple nature/man or nature/culture divide in favour of the composite notion of 'social nature').[17] There is also the more pragmatic question of what measures to use in the management of so-called natural resources. The focus here is on how the state attempts to control people and territory as against how people *in situ* go about utilising and conserving resources and biodiversity. (For an interesting case of state imposition and its implications for conservation practices, see Peluso 1993.) Governments are frequently faced with the choice of implementing what are called 'centralised' or 'decentralised' modes of control – the latter usually implying some community involvement in natural resource management.[18] One must also take note of frameworks and mechanisms promoted by the European Union and various international bodies geared to regulating sound environmental practice in regard to agricultural production, pollution and the preservation of wildlife and plant populations.[19] Nowadays environmental policies are hedged round with a host of regulatory prescriptions of a global kind and subject to pressures from powerful conservationist lobbies. As many studies have shown, the protection and conservation of wildlife through the setting up of national parks or protected areas does not necessarily ensure the continued preservation of natural resources and endangered species. Furthermore, as cases from Zambia and Zimbabwe have graphically demonstrated, so-called decentralised community conservation programmes seldom adequately address or understand the livelihood problems of people traditionally dependent on hunting, gathering and crop cultivation in close proximity to wild animal populations. The global implications of this are immense, since many wildlife conservation programmes receive the strong financial and political backing from influential conservationist groups. These wildlife and environmental conservation issues – coupled as they are with a booming safari tourist industry – are critically important for the future livelihoods of many rural producers (see the now fairly well documented case of CAMP-FIRE in Zimbabwe, Hasler 1996; and for the Luangwa Valley of Zambia, see A. Long 1998).

A further way in which rural space is being reconfigured concerns the mass exodus of rural producers and their families from comparatively disadvantaged localities or regions to urban or other rural areas. While this may be due to economic circumstances and the pressures of structural adjustment in a global world, many rural areas of poorer nations have been particularly affected by displacement due to civil strife, natural disasters or developments such as dam constructions. Indeed it is striking that in the last few years a new department of the World Bank has been set up to deal specifically with the effects of large-scale resettlement programmes. Resettlement in new habitats (whether voluntary or forced, planned or not) and the sometimes later return of populations to their homes of origin is associated with processes of social dislocation, the rebuilding of livelihoods, and the social reconstruction of communities and groups. This is a field of change which over recent decades has had a high profile in the media and all sorts of global solutions have been offered with the involvement of a plethora of humanitarian aid agencies and NGOs concerned with refugees and displaced persons. Along with this has come a set of policy discourses aimed at solving some of the more critical problems. There still remains, however, a mismatch of ideas on how to solve these problems while taking into account people's own adaptive capacities and wishes. As I will briefly indicate when examining patterns of international migration, these processes of social reconstruction entail rebuilding or reinventing social identities in an increasingly globalised world.

In the next section, I provide short profiles of recent and ongoing research at Wageningen University that focuses on some of these local/global issues. The themes taken up, namely global commodity networks and transnational migration, are highly pertinent to the changing nature of the countryside. An actor-oriented perspective is eminently suitable for researching these processes since it stresses actor-defined problems, looks closely at organising processes and networks of social relations, explores the social meanings invested in new and old experiences, and throws theoretical light on the interrelations of meanings, practices and outcomes.

The construction and transformation of values in new global commodity networks[20]

New, highly differentiated forms of consumption associated with commodities, such as fruit and vegetables, coffee, cocoa, cooking oils, wines, honey and flowers, are nowadays central to the choices and tastes of the consumer. Access to these and their delivery entail sets of linkages between producers, distributors, retailers and consumers. The 'value' of such commodities is, of course, not determined simply at the farm gate. In what is commonly known as 'adding value', commodities go through a complex and diverse set of reconstituting processes organised in various geographically localised sites. Land-based production, while crucial, is only the start of a long and differentially managed transformation process. Proportionally, agricultural production represents only a minor part of the total value of the product in economic terms, while in social terms a large proportion of symbolic and socially constructed value is added at the processing, distribution and retail stages. Recent and ongoing research at Wageningen has focused on developing an understanding of value construction, contestation and transformation in respect to specific global commodities (see Chapters 5 and 6).

New food and other products demanded by consumers often entail new environmental pressures, the reorganisation of labour conditions, the introduction of new technologies *vis-à-vis* both production, processing and transportation, new standards of quality assurance and new notions of what is considered 'natural' and what 'artificial'. Such changes have contributed to the segmentation of the market and to the creation of diverse styles of consumption. By means of this process, different linkages and interactions have emerged between commodities, consumers, producers, marketing organisations, the state and regional economic trade blocks (such as the European Union and NAFTA). These linkages generate different networks of commodity circulation and create uneven socio-economic spaces at the global, national, regional and local levels.

Recent studies conducted across Europe, Latin America and Africa point to the changing pressures exerted on rural producers by European and American supermarket conglomerates, retailers and distributors searching for 'quality' products. Consumer demands for these products place considerable burdens on the capacity of the 'sourcing' areas to deliver goods at the volumes required and to certify their quality. In addition, producers are confronted by complex investment strategies, marketing arrangements and regulation policies. This conjuncture of factors may have the effect of displacing or reinforcing specific local institutional forms and configurations of interest (as illustrated, for example, by changes in production units, household livelihoods and family networks). A related issue concerns how far market relations and institutional regulations (implemented by the state or international bodies) dictate the patterns of production and investment at local level. It cannot be assumed that such 'external' pressures will always succeed in enrolling local producers and other actors in producing for global markets. Several case studies, for example, demonstrate how local actors reject or transform these global demands.

Producers and agricultural workers sometimes fear that, if they become too heavily committed to outside markets and institutions, then critical interests can be threatened or marginalised. People may also show strong allegiance to existing lifestyles, and to the defence of local forms of knowledge. On the other hand, if intervening parties, such as multinational firms, the state or retail organisations, fail to take seriously the ways in which people mobilise and use resources through existing social networks and cultural commitments, then they run the risk of being rejected by, or distantiated from, the life experiences and priorities of local producers. Hence it is important to study how local organising practices and networks facilitate or constrain the production of high-quality commodities and how external market demands are internalised or modified by local populations.

Although our research aims to focus especially on the dynamics of value creation and transformation at the level of local producer populations, the analysis of commodity flows and linkages necessitates following the passage of commodities into the arenas of processing, marketing, retailing and consumption. For example, the organisation of marketing and retailing is, as mentioned above, not simply a process of adding value to the commodity. Rather, it constitutes a series of interlocking arenas of struggle in which various parties may contest notions of 'quality', 'convenience' and 'price'. These contestations and negotiations usually entail the mobilisation of arguments about what constitutes consumer preference, the availability and advantages of particular technologies, and issues relating to the material presentation of the commodity to its relevant audiences (i.e., the supermarkets, small retailers, 'alternative' food shop owners, and an array of different consumer interests). It is in this way that commodities emerge as 'mobilisers' of resources, thus contributing to the construction and reconstruction of markets and particular consumer lifestyles in contemporary society. One aim of such a commodity approach is therefore to identify how new bridges are built between producers, distributors, retailers and consumers.

Following commodities in this way also permits us to analyse how social resources and cultural repertoires are mobilised and how 'old' and 'new' forms of social value are distributed among the different actors. This has implications for defining the types and degrees of authority and power exercised by the different parties at the different stages in the circulation of commodities – a matter for critical re-evaluation, given the rather simple notions of value creation and appropriation found in much of the current literature (see Chapters 5 and 6 of this volume, Long and Villarreal 1998, and Ramirez 1999).

Undertaking a commodity flow analysis, which gives attention to the organising properties of commodities and people (what Appadurai (1986) calls 'the social life of commodities'), opens up a related line of enquiry which has so far been somewhat neglected, namely an exploration of the processes by which people and their 'objects of desire' generate certain cultural identifications that segment markets and reorganise physical and social space around meanings and practice. Linked to this are the processes by which retailing companies and supermarkets develop advertising and promotional strategies designed to introduce new products into 'consumers' "maps of meaning"...through associating them with popular notions of class, healthy living and sensual experience' (Cook 1994: 236). Methodologically this means examining the contestation of value in different domains and arenas of social action: for example, at the level of producers' associations in which they debate production strategies and deal with external interventions; at the points of purchasing, transporting and packaging a commodity during which conflicts often arise between the producers, lorry drivers, entrepreneurs, trading companies and workers at the packing plants or docks; and at the receiving end when disagreements may arise between importers, retailers and consumer associations over issues of quality, shape, taste and price. An additional important element that shapes the nature and possible outcomes of these contestations concerns the deployment of specific language strategies and discourses that represent the 'political' positioning of the different actors in the networks and arenas concerned (Arce and Long 2000). Such language practices help to identify the nature of different actors' expectations and how they justify their choices and actions. Clashes of language and representations in respect to consumption priorities can be illustrated by the present, often-heated debates around food and notions of a 'healthy' diet, nutritional 'needs' and 'environmental pollution'.

Migration, globalisation, and transnational networks[21]

This next theme centres on the construction and transformation of values, livelihoods and identities in the context of transnational migration – an increasingly prominent and disquieting phenomenon in the global political and economic scene.

Previous studies of migration have tended to represent the flows of people to new locations in terms of the adaptation or adjustment of new migrants to their 'host' societies, or they have offered a dualistic analysis of the interrelations of peripheral places of origin and central places of destination. More recently, migration flows have been reinterpreted as an integral feature of the global economy, giving rise to new types of 'nomadic' peoples and transnational communities. Hence an essential aspect of the social life of 'global nomads' or international migrants is the fact that their networks ('real' and 'imagined') reach out into the wider realm of transnational space, linking them not only to their places of origin but also to compatriots living in widely dispersed locations.[22] These networks of persons and places are bound together through 'collective' memories and images of a common place of origin and possibly of places of migration, and the sense of having yet another, 'third culture' identity, that of being a nomad having empathy with all other similar nomads. (For an explication of the notion of third culture in relation to the socialisation implied in cultural mobility, see Pollock and van Reken 1999.)

Though it has been commonplace in much of the literature to depict these migrant flows in terms of the emergence of new international divisions of labour, a more interesting facet concerns the nature and development of particular transnational networks of people and places. This demands an understanding of the interlocking of 'localised', 'transnational', 'nomadic' and 'hybrid' experiences and also of how these constituent elements transmute into new 'globalised' cultural identifications associated with 'migrants on the move'. So far, research has accorded only minor attention to the dynamics of these intercultural processes and their consequences.

This problematic is related to the broader issue of the emergence of globalised cultures characterised by a continuous flow of ideas, information, values and tastes mediated through mobile individuals, symbolic tokens and often electronic simulations (Waters 1995). Such flows take place in culturally constructed social fields and spaces that make possible new 'imagined communities' that are detached from fixed locations or territories. This phenomenon indeed constitutes a major analytical challenge, since it throws into question the implicit assumptions of some formulations that domains and social arenas coincide with delimited spatial and territorialised settings.

In the case of global migrants and refugees, their social lives are still tied to particular notions of 'place' and 'home community', but these are reworked to include a wide network of individuals and institutions physically located in very different places (e.g., localities in Europe and the USA, in city neighbourhoods and villages, as well as in the community of origin). The precise constituency and salience of the particular 'imagined communities' to which people belong will, of course, vary according to the geographical locations of the groups and individuals involved, the relevant issues at hand, members' accessibility in terms of communications media, their visions of the future, etc. Also family members back in the home setting may themselves participate in these practices of constructing 'imagined communities'.

Clearly these elements are central to understanding the lifeworlds and orientations of international migrants and refugees, but equally they are relevant for returnees and for those who choose not to migrate, since the latter, too, are exposed via interpersonal ties and media to such global forms. The flows of 'home-destined' goods (such as taped music, garments, furniture styles, house decorations, 'exotic' posters, foreign mementoes, family photographs, etc.) carry with them specific meanings and values associated with the migrants' 'global' lifeworlds. And in reverse the flow of 'migrant-destined' goods and messages helps keep migrants in touch, and for some provides a strong anchor. This differentiated global space provides a critical field for defining or crystallising new notions of 'community' and 'belongingness' that are now emerging within localities in many parts of the world.

Another way in which migration is linked to globalisation is the diminished capacity of nation-states to control the flow of people and goods across their borders. Here it is important to take account of the fact that migrant lifeworlds include encounters and avoidance of contact with various agencies of migration control that seek to define eligibility of national citizenship and to regulate the movement of 'aliens' in and out of national territories. Hence, research on this topic should include a study of those agencies involved in managing (controlling) the inflow of migrants and refugees seen from organisational, legal-normative, brokerage and cultural points of view. Linked to this is the exploration of precisely how migrants enter national spaces illegally, how they find work and a place to live, and establish themselves within an acceptable social environment with which they can to some extent identify.

This has led to an interest in analysing the emergence of so-called transnational migrant communities, and the associated practices of transnationalism (Appadurai and Breckenridge 1988, Basch *et al* 1994, Gupta 1992, Kearney 1991, Rouse 1991). Transnationalism, however, should not imply that the nation-state has ceased to be an important referent in the imagination of space or in the situated practices of migrants, returnees and villagers. Instead, as Gupta (1992: 63) argues, the inscription of space in representations of the nation-state now occurs in a de-territorialised way. Hence notions of belonging and 'citizenship' become harnessed less to the idea of a particular national political system than to ethnic identities that transcend borders, and to imagined notions of place and home (such as a specific village or mountain valley); and they often take shape under the influence of global debates (launched by new social and ethnic movements).

The other face of contemporary population movements is the displacement of people due to socio-political violence and the consequent dislocation of economic life and livelihood patterns. In the aftermath of violent conflict, many elements are reconfigured: relations of power, techniques of government, modes of organisation, livelihoods, identities and collective memories, and the relations between people and places (see Malkki 1995 and Wilson 1999). Displaced groups are often reluctant to return to their villages and regions of origin after the cessation of hostilities, and if they do they often reconstruct their lives on the basis of new values, desires and organisational assets or deficits. Frequently they continue to depend on support networks and patterns of aid and resources assembled during their period of exile; and some returnees never in fact fully return. Instead they live within 'multiple realities' where, if they have the necessary strategic skills and knowledge, they can access a wide range of livelihood options, which continue to tie them to their places both of origin and of exile. Other less fortunate individuals or households, of course, may become trapped cognitively and emotionally in the traumas of violence and displacement and be unable effectively to rebuild their social lives.

Seen from another point of view, such former conflict-ridden areas become frontiers where new battles are fought out between the engaging parties involved in the reconstruction process, represented by the state, international development agencies, political groupings and various local actors and families (see, e.g., Stepputat 2000). A characteristic of these situations is the emergence of unstable tactical alliances and the continuous clash and transformation of interests, priorities and worldviews. If solutions are to be negotiated between the opposing parties, then careful analysis is required to reveal the rhythm and dynamics of the various social, cultural and political reconfigurations that take place.

Given this growing vulnerability of many populations in the face of global economic change and political violence, the analysis of differing scenarios and outcomes of global networks, transnational migration and the movement of displaced persons will continue for the foreseeable future to be major topics for research. These processes raise critical issues concerning the viability of certain types of livelihoods and modes of organisation, and address fundamental questions about people changing their cultural identifications and social relations in what looks like being an increasingly diverse and complex world.

Refocusing one's analytical agenda

The foregoing reflections on change at the turn of the twenty-first century underline the need for a new analytical agenda on local/global relations. The present situation throws up a number of important theoretical and methodological challenges, some new and others a continuation of previous lines of enquiry. A central concern running throughout such a new agenda is how to analyse the complex sets of relations that develop between policy discourses, modes of intervention, and the responses of various local and extra-local actors. At the present historical juncture, governments, people and organisations have to grapple with the exigencies, dilemmas, vulnerabilities and contradictions of neo-liberal, market-led development, ecological modernisation and sustainability, and the accelerating impact of science and technology on a global scale.

This requires a rethinking of certain critical dimensions and concepts such as planned intervention, state and market relations, agrarian development, commoditisation and commodity chains, changing livelihoods and identities in the context of new patterns of land use, migration and social reconstruction, and questions relating to science and technology. A consideration of these issues would, of course, necessitate a much fuller discussion than can be achieved here. My aim is simply to offer a sketch of some of the more interesting analytical problems we encounter.

An approach to issues of intervention

In previous research at Wageningen University we have explored the importance of treating state intervention and agrarian development as socially-constructed and continuously-renegotiated processes (see Long 1988; Long 1989; Long and van der Ploeg 1989; de Vries 1992; Arce 1993). We have also used this constructionist approach for researching the differentiated nature of agrarian enterprise and styles of farming (van der Ploeg 1990) and the role of knowledge and power in the transformation of small-scale development projects (Villarreal 1994).

We are now building upon these insights by examining further the interrelations between market processes, government and other forms of planned intervention, and the organisation of civil society; that is, the new configurations of market, state and community. As one proceeds, it is important to counterpoise theoretical and policy forms of discourse with the actual ways in which different social actors – including here not only male and female householders, producers, labourers and small-scale entrepreneurs, but also bureaucrats, migrants, politicians and planners – conceptualise, deal with and become agents in the creation and reproduction of these dynamic and often volatile market, state and community relations.

Crucial to understanding processes of intervention is the need to identify and come to grips with the strategies that local actors devise for dealing with their new intervenors so that they might appropriate, manipulate, subvert or dismember particular interventions. Similarly, the question of how far people make use of formal state or market frameworks and resources necessarily entails the consideration of how local knowledge, organisation and values reshape these 'external' structures. In other words, to what extent do the state and the market become endowed with diverse and localised sets of meanings and practices? This can offer new insights into the interpretation and analysis of neo-liberal policies, theories and practices that go beyond the common tendency to explore them solely from a macro-economic or macro-political angle.

The differentiated nature of agrarian structures and interface actor networks

In order to apply this to rural contexts we need to reconsider the concept of agrarian structure. This has most frequently been used heuristically to identify the set of technical, natural resource and production factors involved in a particular farming system and to depict how wider legal, political, economic and spatial relations fashion its reproduction. Until the 1990s onwards, when the innovative work of Jan Douwe van der Ploeg and his research team (see van der Ploeg 1990, 1994, 1999, and Hebinck and van der Ploeg 1997) became widely known, rather less attention was given to the diversity of farming styles and enterprise types that are contained within such a system. This focus has continued at Wageningen through the initiation of new comparative research that analyses the different ways in which local producers and other actors are now tied into global niche and mass consumption markets (see, e.g., de Roest 2000, Laguna 2000, Miele 2001 and Willems 2001).

These networks form part of complex food chains that link producers to traders, state agencies, transnationals, supermarket businesses, agricultural input suppliers, research enterprises, and eventually to the consumers of the products. Each producer or group of producers is in effect part of an *interface* network which integrates the producer into his/her immediate farming environment composed of a series of other actors involved in input and output service activities. Such interface networks take many different forms: some are built upon personal ties and commitments, whilst others entail membership of officially recognised organisations such as cooperatives, farmers' associations or water-users' organisations (see Long 1989 and Hawkins 1991). Hence the ways in which the producer and his/her counterpart actors construct these social arrangements will vary significantly, thus shaping the organising practices of the farmer and his/her farm enterprise. Systematic study of interface networks within particular farming populations affords a better understanding of the differentiated nature of particular agrarian structures. This will provide additional insights into the heterogeneity of farming styles and economic practice.

Food chains contain within them many other arenas within which commodity and non-commodity values are contested, negotiated and realised. Although often remote from the site of production, these arenas are also important for understanding farming styles, interface networks and agrarian structure. Shifts in consumer tastes, technology development and transnational or supermarket strategies set off a whole series of repercussions that can significantly affect farm decision-making. They may also have a disequilibrating effect on existing agrarian social relations, even to the extent of contributing to the downfall of key political groups and alliances within a region.

It is crucial, therefore, that the analysis of agrarian or rural structures includes not only those forms of organisation that emerge from the struggles that take place between different interest groups within regional settings, but also those framing, ordering and organising processes that arise from the ways in which different farmers and other actors are bound into more global networks. The concept of agrarian structure is essentially a simplifying device for coming to grips with these multiple practices of rural life. Agrarian change evolves in the context of particular types of regional settings and identities, and it is important to develop an analytical framework for understanding the patterns that emerge. But in so doing, one must avoid accepting uncritically the regional definitions and assumptions of administrators, planners and politicians. The lifeworlds of farmers and other actors are not confined to the spatial and strategic options promoted by policy-makers, even when these conceptions acquire a 'reality' as powerful instruments for allocating resources and for defining the discourse of policy and analysis.

Technologies and organising practices of government

We also need some concept of government that embraces the multifarious ways in which the various programmes and organisational structures of the state attempt to control territory and people, and how this relates to non-state modes of control and regulation at both local, regional and even supranational levels. Although there is a burgeoning theoretical literature on social regulation in market, quasi-market, state and other institutional domains, the need remains for detailed empirical studies exploring issues of 'governability' and what is now often called 'governance', by which we mean 'the patterns that emerge from governing activities of social, political and administrative actors', both public and private (Kooiman 1993: 2). Recently Marsden (2000) has underlined the need to apply this to the reorganisation of power and authority relations relating to 'new patterns of food governance' where issues such as food scares, and anxieties surrounding biotechnology and genetic engineering, generate new political groupings and alternative food networks to contest the regulatory frameworks set up by the state.

Another contribution to the question of governability is that of Miller and Rose (1990). They draw on Foucault's notion of 'technologies of government' to emphasise that we need to give more attention to the indirect mechanisms and discourses that link the conduct of individuals and organisations to the political projects of others through 'action at a distance'. Miller and Rose illustrate this by reference to the kinds of discursive control exercised by 'experts' concerned with economic planning or accounting practices that render certain things and people amenable to inscription and calculation. These new 'technologies', along with various other management, marketing, advertising and communication methods and discourses, make up a concerted programme for promoting state policies geared to 'educating citizens in techniques for governing themselves'. Hence political authorities no longer seek to govern directly by putting as many of their own people on the ground as possible – everywhere state bureaucracies have been cut back – but rather to reinforce self-regulating processes among their subjects. Self-regulation, of course, constitutes a key objective of neo-liberal policies, which are sometimes mistakenly presented in terms of the need for 'deregulation'.

The role played by these 'technologies' could be fruitfully extended to cover the activities of non-state bodies such as the World Bank and the IMF, which draw upon a large pool of experts to assist in the promotion of programmes of structural adjustment and 'good governance', as well as various private enterprise initiatives aimed at encouraging competitiveness and entrepreneurship. We might also apply these insights to the field of rural development when studying the strategies and impact of agricultural supply systems and research and technology development programmes.

One shortcoming of this approach, however, is its lack of attention to the ways in which multiple discourses intersect in situated social practice. While the language and discourse of experts may assume an important role in shaping people's reactions to interventions and circumstance, lay opinions and alternative discourses and rationalisations also play a part. Hence we need to complement the discussion of 'external' and hegemonic discourses by examining how other discourses come into play in particular social arenas, thus giving rise to strategic language games. Clearly the meaning and impact of particular arguments or images depend heavily on who is communicating to whom and on how the message is conveyed and received or transformed (see Hilhorst 2000).

These dimensions can only be adequately explored by developing appropriate ethnographic methods for doing so. We need, that is, to document carefully how particular government officials, experts and professionals draw upon different conceptions of the functions of the state to legitimise their activities and task definitions, creating, for instance, images of the state as 'protector', 'arbitrator', 'facilitator', 'investor', 'judge' or 'cajoler'. Attention must also be directed towards understanding how government policy concretely affects the lives and life-chances of populations (rural and urban) and how, in turn, the character of the government and its policies are affected, and sometimes transformed, by people's actions. We must at all costs avoid a reification of state institutions and actions, in the sense of attributing to them an 'internal logic' or a fixed rationality. Likewise, we need to acknowledge that, in some cases, rural populations have devised a 'civilised art of living without a state' at all (Bayart 1993: 135, quoting Lonsdale 1981). Having said this, we must also recognise that images and ideologies of the state clearly shape the attitudes and guide the actions of all those individuals involved in or affected (directly or indirectly) by the activities (or in some cases, the neglect) of state organisations.

Understanding issues of intervention and regulatory practice entails developing a methodology for studying administrative processes and the work and strategies of bureaucrats, especially in respect to the 'bottom-ends' of bureaucratic institutions. Such an analysis should look at problems of access to and rationing of services, as well as the types of labelling (e.g., of target groups, or of state 'functions' etc.) practised by administrative, planning and technical personnel. We also need to refine our understanding of organisational styles and the transformation of policy that occurs during implementation. As shown in Chapters 4 and 9, these dimensions can be usefully integrated into a framework of analysis that deals with the social interfaces of development.

Social differentiation, cultural identifications and commoditisation processes

Another important area of research requiring new analytical insights is that of social differentiation. Unlike much previous work on this topic that concentrates largely on class dimensions, greater attention must be accorded to issues of age, gender, ethnicity and other identity relations. This implies highlighting negotiations and struggles over self-images and modes of identification[23] as well as analysing the interplay of discursive practices through which, for example, women and men are defined in terms of specific roles and meanings are attributed or disowned. Here it is crucial to examine power relations between men and women and how such relations are framed normatively and legitimated by certain social mores and concepts of authority. As with other social and economic relations, aspects of gender need to be re-explored in the context of both global and local processes (see, e.g., Hondagneu-Sotelo's 1994 study of how gender differences have shaped Mexican immigration to the US; and Wolf (1992) who analyses the impact of rural industrialisation on women and their families in Java).

These dimensions of differentiation and identity also relate to broader theoretical issues concerning the character and significance of commoditisation and externalisation (i.e., the delegation of production and reproduction functions of households and enterprises to external bodies). According to this line of argument, increased levels of commoditisation and externalisation are assumed to affect the scale and specialisation of production, the degrees of capitalisation and styles of enterprise management. Thus, as Buttel predicts,

> ...the sphere of household production in agriculture will become progressively smaller and of less and less consequence to the character of the agro-food system. Increased competition will place a premium on technological innovation that can reduce average costs, reduce short-term risks, or rationalise ever-larger enterprises.
>
> (Buttel 1997: 346)

While seemingly valid, these interrelations need more careful explication. For example, as agribusiness and food industries compete for increased shares of new and specialised (niche) markets, so they become more sensitive to the demand for a diverse range of commodities of different quality and tastes. This has led to the promotion of specific localised forms of production in different global production sites of 'comparative advantage'. Many of these sites are characterised by the persistence of smallholder family farms tied to various systems of temporary wage labour (often involving women in the processing and packaging of products) and to contract farming – not always large-scale. This strategy can involve less risk to the agro-industrial entrepreneur than investment in large-scale modernised production systems, and is less likely to bring social disapprobation for taking over land and despoiling rural environments.

These patterns of change have often opened up 'action spaces' for women and closed down spaces for men. They have provided new opportunities for farmers and peasant producers, and in some cases have led to an increasing tendency for them to 'opt out' of certain types of farming. All this can have a major restructuring effect on rural livelihoods, labour and relations with markets.

This brings to the fore the issue of the commoditised and non-commoditised components of global change, which I discussed in Chapters 5 and 6. Many earlier theories of agrarian development assumed that the autonomy and functioning of the peasant farm was undermined by the extension of commodity relations, though the empirical evidence indicated a much more complex and diverse situation. The matter was, I argued, further compounded by the fact that commoditisation and externalisation only become real in their consequences when introduced and translated by specific actors (including here not only farmers but also others such as migrants, traders, bureaucrats and politicians). It is necessary, therefore, to analyse closely how commodity and non-commodity forms enter into the pragmatics of everyday life and shape the organisation of production and consumption. Only in this way can one establish their precise practical and symbolic significance. This applies equally to the affluent agro-industrial entrepreneur and his enterprise as it does to the poor peasant producer and his family.

As I have highlighted in various chapters of this volume, the issue of interpreting commodity relations and values remains contentious, especially in light of global shifts in markets, consumption patterns, attitudes and values towards the environment, the need to include human rights and fair trade issues in production and consumption decisions, and the baffling phenomenon of so-called 'virtual' economies in the digital age. Throughout the commodity chain and the network of relations between producers, processors, transporters, traders, wholesalers, retailers and the consumer, there exist multifarious sets of transactions during which various values are negotiated. As I demonstrated in Chapter 6, although exchange value and added value are clearly relevant, the network of social relations and the room for manoeuvre involved in assigning meanings and values to particular goods and relationships are defined not only by the institutions of the market but also by a range of other cultural and organisational factors. These latter create or constrain choice and play a role in the fixing and/or contesting of value. A better understanding of the interweaving of these complex elements presents a major challenge for future research.

Contests of knowledge: interfaces and the issue of agency

Over the past decade, the sociology of knowledge has embraced a more robust social constructionist perspective, providing fresh insights into how 'expert' and everyday forms of knowledge relate to processes of development and social change (see Chapters 8 and 9). This perspective aims to take full cognisance of social actors, their values and understandings, and their social and material engagements in the construction of knowledge. Linked to this is the concern for analysing competing 'designs for living' in the form of policies or programmes of development as well as less formalised actors' 'projects', ideologies and orientations to change. Although these different bodies of knowledge and understanding may be epistemologically distinct, one should not separate ontologically science from everyday knowledge and practice. Indeed, actor-oriented/social constructionist analysis is particularly interested in analysing situations and embattled arenas where conventional science and other forms of 'received wisdom' are challenged, intellectually and politically, by citing various types of alternative lay or other knowledge constructions. These contests often arise in the context of growing controversies over the role and efficacy of science and modern technology in resolving the many problems generated by the 'failures' of modernity and the repercussions of global change. Such struggles sometimes escalate to become a major focus of media attention and public concern, as is the case with the food scares and crises in agricultural production that have erupted in the UK and other European countries over the last decade or so.

This suggests that the characterisation and analysis of different (and possibly conflicting) forms of knowledge are best explored through a systematic understanding of the critical interfaces involved. Although it is the task of the field researcher to develop appropriate strategies for conceptualising and identifying these interfaces, a few words of warning are perhaps in order. Interactions between government or outside agencies involved in implementing particular development programmes and their so-called 'beneficiaries' cannot adequately be understood through the use of generalised conceptions such as 'state–civil society relations' or by resorting to normative concepts such as 'local participation'. Nor should one assume that certain policy messages unproblematically reach and impact upon target populations. As I have argued throughout this book, an understanding of these processes and modes of communication must be situated within a framework which allows for the detailed analysis of the ongoing 'transfers' and transformations of meaning that take place between actors located within specific social arenas and intersecting institutional domains. Interface analysis concentrates upon analysing critical junctures entailing differences of normative value and social interest. It aims to depict not only the struggles and power differentials that emerge but also seeks to understand the cultural meanings, accommodations and compromises that underpin the interactions and transactions that evolve. Even those interfaces characterised by strong hegemonic tendencies – and therefore symbolically and organisationally geared to the enforcement and reaffirmation of authoritative knowledge and forms of domination – show evidence of counter-tendencies and 'counterwork' which exploit the inherent ambiguities and partial connections of interface phenomena (Arce and Long 2000: 3, 8–9, 19–20). As the many examples reveal, there are myriad ways in which so-called 'subordinate' or 'weaker' actors can create space for themselves, defend their own worldviews and standpoints, and subvert the best-laid plans and discourses of 'dominant' actors, while at the same time continuing to live in a world full of inequalities and vulnerabilities. The advent of global communication technologies has clearly been of considerable logistical benefit to many counter-development actions and movements, including those involving indigenous groups. Although geographically remote from 'centres' of global power, the latter are able to keep abreast of world events and organise crucial resources via satellite TV, cellular phones and now the Internet. Hence, being at a physical distance from certain points of critical decision-making and negotiation may no longer be so much of a handicap as it was in the past. The ever-widening and changing repertoires of cultural choices and organising capacities generated through exposure to global systems of communication, combined with the exponential growth of transnational flows and networks of goods and people, have undoubtedly contributed to the strengthening of the capacities of diverse social groups to carve out their own room for manoeuvre and to define and pursue their own life projects. Even those resource-poor households who continue to eke out a living in the cities and villages of the Andes and elsewhere now face a dramatically changed scenario – in part more risk-prone and vulnerable, and in part more hopeful and challenging – so long as they re-position themselves *vis-à-vis* the global dimensions of their lives, instead of clinging sentimentally to long-since lost and now imagined 'traditional' pasts.

The implications of the present global era for questions of knowledge generation and transformation, the organisation of power, and for issues of agency and counter-development are, then, immense and raise a number of critical questions for further research, which extend far beyond what has been possible in this book. We are now in fact at the point of having to propose yet another agenda for research – namely one that would take us well beyond the rather simplistic categorical or stereotypical ways of talking about 'state', 'market' and 'community' relations, or of distinguishing between planned intervention 'from above' and 'from below', etc. We also need to invent new ways of talking about rural scenarios and change – ways that would give much more serious treatment to the transnational, 're-terri-torialised' and global dimensions of multiple lifeworlds, livelihoods, enterprises, commodities, policy interventions, knowledge processes and organised counter-develop-ment struggles. Perhaps the biggest challenge for an actor-oriented/social constructionist approach to the study of development and social change concerns how to re-conceptualise the relations between knowledge, power and social agency within this global informa-tional world.

APPENDIX

Cornerstones of an actor-oriented approach

Some methodological guidelines

An actor-oriented approach entails:

1 Adopting as a point of departure actor-defined issues or critical events.
2 Taking into account issues of social heterogeneity with a view to understanding the differential interpretations and responses to circumstances (i.e. we have to deal with 'multiple realities').
3 Identifying the actors relevant to the specific arenas of action and contestation, bearing in mind that neither actor categories nor relevance are uniformly defined.
4 Documenting ethnographically the situated social practices of actors, and the ways in which social relationships, technologies, material and other resources, discourses and texts (such as policy documents and arguments – normative or otherwise) are deployed.
5 Focusing on the organising and ordering processes (rather than 'order' *per se*) that are relevant to the different arenas and institutional domains.
6 Tracing the critical sets of social relationships and networks, as well as the meanings and values, generated and negotiated within the different arenas and scenarios.
7 Exploring the critical interfaces that depict the points of contradiction or discontinuity between the different (and often incompatible) actors' lifeworlds, including not only 'local' actors but also 'intervening' institutional actors or other stakeholders.
8 Elucidating the processes of knowledge/power construction entailed in the arenas and interfaces of contestation and negotiation, giving special attention to the reconfiguration of patterns of authority and control.
9 Analysing how matters of scale and complexity shape organising practices and are themselves the product of them.
10 Identifying analytically the discursive and practical underpinnings of newly emergent social forms and connectivities.

Key concepts

Agency refers to the knowledgeability, capability and social embeddedness associated with acts of doing (and reflecting) that impact upon or shape one's own and others' actions and interpretations. Agency is usually recognised *ex post facto* through its acknowledged or presumed effects. Persons or networks of persons have agency. In addition, they may attribute agency to various objects and ideas, which, in turn, can shape actors' perceptions of what is possible. Agency is composed, therefore, of a complex mix of social, cultural and material elements. *Strategic agency* signifies the enrolment of many actors in the 'project' of some other person or persons.

Social actors are all those social entities that can be said to have agency in that they possess the knowledgeability and capability to assess problematic situations and organise 'appropriate' responses. Social actors appear in a variety of forms: individual persons, informal groups or interpersonal networks, organisations, collective groupings, and what are sometimes called 'macro' actors (e.g., a particular national government, church or international organisation). But care must always be taken to avoid reification; that is, one should not assume that organisations or collectivities such as social movements act in unison or with one voice. In fact 'collective' and 'organisational' endeavours are better depicted in terms of 'coalitions of actors', 'interlocking actor projects' and 'the interplay of discourses'.

Lifeworlds are 'lived-in' and largely 'taken-for-granted' social worlds centring on particular individuals. Such worlds should not be viewed as 'cultural backcloths' that frame how individuals act, but instead as the product of an individual's own constant self-assembling and re-evaluating of relationships and experiences. Lifeworlds embrace actions, interactions and meanings, and are identified with specific socio-geographical spaces and life histories.

Livelihoods are made up of practices by which individuals and groups strive to make a living, meet their consumption necessities, cope with adversities and uncertainties, engage with new opportunities, protect existing or pursue new lifestyles and cultural identifications, and fulfil their social obligations.

Organising processes span a wide spectrum of practices that involve cooperation and competition between individuals and groups in and across different social domains. In addition to livelihoods, these practices form part of the activities inherent in both 'informal' and 'formal' types of organisation. They also include practices that mediate or perform brokerage functions between organisations, levels of authority and spheres of control.

Social fields constitute 'open spaces' composed of distributions of heterogeneous elements (material resources, information, technologies, institutional components, discourses and sets of social relationships of various kinds) wherein no single ordering principle prevails. While the pattern of social relationships and the availability and distribution of resources allow for certain organisational possibilities, any order that does emerge within a social field is the result of the struggles, negotiations and accommodations that have taken place between the competing parties. In certain instances, especially in socio-ecological scenarios, the competing parties must also, of course, include animal and plant populations.

Domains represent the loci of rules, norms and values that become central to this process of social ordering and to the establishment of certain pragmatic rules of governance. The idea of domain is also important for understanding how social and symbolic boundaries are defined and upheld, though precisely which normative or strategic principles will prevail situationally or over the longer term remains an open question. Domains should *not* be conceptualised as 'cultural givens' but as being produced and transformed through actors' shared experiences and struggles.

Arenas are spaces in which contests over issues, claims, resources, values, meanings and representations take place; that is, they are sites of struggle within and across domains.

Networks are made up of sets of direct and indirect relationships and exchanges (interpersonal, inter-organisational and socio-technical). They usually transcend institutional domains and link together a variety of arenas. Networks are characterised by flows, content, span, density and multiplicity.

Discourse refers to sets of meanings, metaphors, representations, images, narratives and statements that advance a particular version of 'the truth' about specific objects, persons and events. Discourses produce 'texts' – written and spoken, or even non-verbal such as the meanings embodied in architectural styles (e.g., buildings such as the town halls that 'speak' of civic pride, and factories that 'represent' a bygone industrial age) or dress fashions (e.g., styles associated with class, status, gender, age or ethnicity).

Cultural repertoires characterise the differentiated stock of cultural components that relate to differences in lifestyles, social values and rationales for living.

Identification is the process by which people make and attribute self definitions (some more fixed and continuous and others more fleeting and highly situational) to themselves and others. By studying identification processes one gains insights into people's cultural and socio-political orientations and commitments. It also helps to avoid assuming, as many studies do, that 'collective' action is congruent with 'collective' identity.

Knowledge processes constitute the ways in which actors come to grips with the world around them cognitively, emotionally and organisationally. They do this on the basis of their own and others' experiences and understandings, thus generating new bases for understanding (i.e., knowledge construction). Although the basis for their 'truth-claims' and 'authority' will vary, this applies to 'scientific' as well as to 'non-scientific', 'everyday' forms of knowledge. Knowledge construction is, at one and the same time, 'constructive' in the sense that it is the outcome of many decisions and selective incorporations of previous ideas, beliefs and values, and 'destructive' in the sense of transforming, disassembling or ignoring other existing frames of conceptualisation and understanding, and 'localised' in specific institutional domains and arenas whether of global or local scope.

Power configurations are depicted in terms of the idea of interlocking actors' projects made up of heterogeneous sets of social relations imbued with values, meanings and notions of authority and control, domination and subordination, and sustained by specific patterns of resource distribution and competition (i.e., power construction). Power cannot simply be possessed or accumulated. Nor can it be precisely measured in terms of quantity or quality. It emerges out of social processes and is better considered a 'product' rather than a 'given'. Having power does not entail that others are without it:

there is no zero-sum game. However, power may become reified in social life; that is, people often think of it as a unitary coercive force wielded by 'the ruling class', 'agents of the state' or 'the establishment'.

The notion of social interface

Definition

A social interface is a critical point of intersection between lifeworlds, social fields or levels of social organisation where *social discontinuities*, based upon discrepancies in values, interests, knowledge and power, are most likely to be located.

Implications

- Such discontinuities characterise social situations in which the interactions between actors become oriented around the problem of devising ways of bridging, accommodating to, or struggling against each others' different social and cognitive worlds.
- Interface analysis aims to elucidate the types of social discontinuities present in such situations, and to characterise the different kinds of organisational and cultural forms that reproduce or transform them.
- Although the word 'interface' tends to convey the image of some kind of two-sided articulation or confrontation, interface situations are complex and multiple in nature.
- Interfaces must be analysed as part of ongoing processes of negotiation, adaptation and transformation of meaning.

Knowledge interface

- Involves *discontinuity* rather than *linkage*.
- *Transformation* rather than *transfer* of meaning.
- Knowledge is a *product* of dialogue and negotiation.
- It is *multi-layered* and often *fragmentary* and *diffuse*, not *unitary* and *systematised*.

Epistemic communities

- Composed of those sharing roughly the same sources and modes of knowledge.
- Differentiated internally in terms of knowledge repertoires and application.
- Engineering the creation of a *single* knowledge system within an epistemic community is unwise and unattainable.
- Innovativeness and adaptability to change depends upon the *diversity* and *fluidity* of knowledge rather than on *integration* and *systematisation*.

NOTES

Introduction

1 See my 1975 paper on 'Structural dependency, modes of production and economic brokerage', my 1977 book *An Introduction to the Sociology of Rural Development*, and my 1988 critical review of 'Sociological perspectives on agrarian development and state intervention'.

2 See my two papers on planned intervention co-authored with Jan Douwe van der Ploeg: 'Demythologising planned intervention' (1989) and 'New challenges in the sociology of rural development: a rejoinder to Peter Vandergeest' (1988).

3 In a later paper (1994) Corbridge makes clear what he means by post-Marxism: '[P]ost Marxism...would seek to build into the basic Marxist "metanarrative" (if there is such a thing) a greater sensitivity to the conditions of existence through which capitalist relations of production are secured at particular times and in particular places. It would further insist that the process of securing such relations is always contingent and is often contested...', which, as he points out, takes us back to the work of Weber and Nietzsche, and to our contemporaries – Giddens, Habermas and Mann.

4 Schuurman (1993) and Booth (1994) are edited collections that explore new directions in development theory, and Preston (1996) is a single-authored critical overview of development theory and new analyses of complex change.

5 And is sometimes misconstrued or co-opted through the substitution of the term 'stakeholder' for 'social actor'.

6 In professional and everyday usage the terms 'constructionism' and 'constructivism' are often used interchangeably, which can lead to confusion. Strictly speaking constructivism is applied to learning theory and epistemology; that is, to how people learn and the nature of knowledge. It has therefore a cognitivist ring to it. Constructionism is a more general term and embraces the cognitive as well as the social dimensions of behaviour and social practice.

7 The psychologist Burr (1995: 4) synthesises the social constructionist view thus:

> The goings-on between people in the course of their everyday lives are seen as the practices during which our shared versions of knowledge are constructed. Therefore what we regard as 'truth' (which of course varies historically and culturally), i.e. our currently accepted ways of understanding the world, is a product not of objective observation of the world, but of the social processes and interactions in which people are constantly engaged with each other.

8 Social constructionism has, of course, generated many heated debates, especially in respect to issues concerning the social construction of science and nature. One extreme view is that the term itself is redundant, since anything located in a social setting is necessarily socially constructed; though scientists might argue that, although science is conducted in social and technical settings, its findings or products result fundamentally from the application of scientific, not social, principles. Another difficulty arises because it is all too easy to slip deceptively from talking about social construction as an idea (e.g., relating to gender, delinquency or quarks) to making assumptions about actual social components and relations. Hacking (1999) notes that

those who frequently employ the concept, especially in the titles of their books, have an axe to grind or at any rate are pressing for some change in cultural attitudes, legislation or socio-administrative arrangements (e.g., relating to child abuse or atomic energy power stations). Hacking's discussion is a thorough and entertaining explication and critique of social constructionist arguments. He makes the point, however, that his key concern is with 'local claims' (i.e., those that relate to the social construction of a specific X) and not with more general methodological claims (i.e., that assert 'that a great deal (or all) of our lived experience, and of the world we inhabit, is to be conceived of as socially constructed'; 1999: 6). Elsewhere he also underlines the usefulness of the notion for exposing 'how categories of knowledge are used in power relationships' (1999: 58) and applauds Danziger's (1990) *Constructing the Subject*, a social constructionist history of experimental psychology which analyses the historical 'building' of psychological 'subjects', methods, institutions, and a body of knowledge.

Following from this brief glimpse of the many critiques that can haunt those using the terms 'social construction' and 'social constructionism', I wish to make clear that throughout this book I deploy these terms for conceptual/theoretical reasons but also strategically to challenge certain orthodoxies in development research and policy. Aware of the tedium of over-use, I have tried to use the terms sparingly.

Chapter 1

1 This chapter, which has been revised for this book, was originally written as the keynote lecture for the congress on *Pluraliteit in de Latijns Amerika Studies* (Amsterdam, 21 March 1990), organised by the Werkgemeenschap van Latijns Amerika en Het Caraibisch Gebied. It was subsequently published by CEDLA (Centre for Latin American Research and Documentation), see Long 1990. David Slater (1990) offers a useful commentary on the paper in the same issue of the journal.

2 When I wrote the first version of this text in the late 1980s there was much talk about a crisis in sociological theories of development. This was brought home to me in February 1989 when I gave a lecture at the Rural Studies Centre, University College, London University, on 'The Continuing Quest for a Sociology of Rural Development'. Immediately following the end of the lecture, a lively debate broke out in which several participants expressed their sense of being adrift from their theoretical moorings, their cherished faiths shattered, with nowhere to turn for help. One discussant even suggested that my wish to ground analysis in actor concepts, apparently at the expense of political economy, could easily be misread as an argument in support of entrepreneurial market principles. All of this I found difficult to comprehend because, for me, the 1980s had been liberating in the best sense of the word: theoretical orthodoxies of various types were now challenged, some even totally discarded by their former devotees, and there was space for more innovative and hybrid forms of research and theorisation. This was exciting, not depressing or threatening.

3 Like Hewitt, my use of the term 'paradigm' is broad and does not imply allegiance to physical and natural science models as the exemplary case. Ritzer (1975) agrees with the idea that sociology has never been a unified field with a dominant paradigm or central theory. He adds that sociology consists of multiple paradigms that 'are engaged in political efforts to gain hegemony within the discipline as a whole as well as within virtually every sub-area in sociology' (1975: 12). He distinguishes between three principal paradigms: the 'social facts' paradigm deriving from Durkheimian theory; the 'social definition' paradigm built upon Weber's social action approach; and the 'social behaviour' paradigm, which applies the principles of behavioural psychology to sociological issues.

4 Several papers have revealed major conceptual weaknesses of mainstream development sociology. See, for example, Booth (1985), Foster-Carter (1987), Long (1984b, 1988), and Mouzelis (1988).

5 For example, Bernstein (1986: 19) considers the understanding of variations in commoditisation patterns as a matter of 'concrete investigation' and therefore not intrinsic to developing a more adequate theory of commoditisation. This seems misguided since such a theory must also address itself to the theorisation of structural variance.

6　This simple distinction between macro and micro often blurs a number of important dimensions and issues. For example the difference between 'aggregate' forms based upon number, time and space, and 'emergent' structures which result in part from the unintended consequences of social action. It is also necessary to recognise that so-called macro processes and elements are embedded in the micro-situations of everyday social life. To understand this one needs to 'unpack' macro-sociological metaphors, such as the notion of 'state centralisation' or 'commoditisation', in order to reveal how precisely they shape the lives of particular individuals and social groups. For further discussion of these points, see Collins (1981), Knorr-Cetina (1981b), Giddens (1984: 132–44) and Long (1989: 226–31).

7　The following studies, to mention only a few personal favourites, stand out as being particularly good in this respect: Pahl (1984), Moore (1986), Larson (1988), and Smith (1989). My own work with Bryan Roberts (Long and Roberts 1978 and 1984) attempts to do likewise.

8　I am skating rapidly, here, over all the complexities involved in distinguishing between different structuralist, dependency and neo-Marxist positions. Latin America is an especially interesting case since it has, from the early 1950s onwards, spawned a rich 'indigenous' tradition of development theory. This includes the structuralist school of Prebisch and others who challenged existing neo-classical economics, various dependency writers ('reformist' and 'Marxist' *dependentistas*), as well as more orthodox Marxist theorists. Indeed, as Kay (1989: 126) comments, covering the dependency literature – let alone the rest – 'is like being confronted with a Tower of Babel. Any attempt to give a fair account is fraught with difficulties as one is forced to be selective with respect to both issues and authors'. Kay's book on *Latin American Theories of Development and Underdevelopment* (1989) provides a thorough account of this work 'from the periphery' and shows how theory and policy interrelate.

9　No doubt this will be seen by some as an injudicious and far-sweeping statement, since some works may be cited that avoid at least some of these shortcomings. For example, the best neo-Marxist or dependency studies stress the importance of internal patterns of exploitation and class or ethnic relations, give attention to actual (rather than idealised) historical processes, and try to avoid functionalist or determinist formulations. Yet, while recognising such caveats, the general picture remains, I believe, as I have described it. This view is supported by the sympathetic critical assessment of dependency analysis by Kay (1989: 194–6), who emphasises its 'overdetermination of the external', its 'distorted historical picture of conditions in the pre-dependence period', and its insufficient treatment of 'the internal causes of underdevelopment'. See Long (1977a: 9–104) for a detailed documentation of the differences and similarities of modernisation and neo-Marxist analysis.

10　Slater offers a succinct overview of a number of important contemporary texts (e.g. Baudrillard 1981, Lash and Urry 1987, 1994, Hall and Jacques 1989).

11　See de Janvry 1981 for an early recognition of how the state (underpinned by 'dominant class interests') sets about reforming its development policies in order to resolve crises of capital accumulation.

12　See also Mouzelis 1994 for a theoretical account of the notion of macro institutional actors, Lockie 1996 for a critical assessment of global structuralism, and Goodman and Watts 1997 for a reassessment of theoretical approaches to global agro-food networks.

13　Although one should perhaps avoid writing of 'external' and 'internal' factors, it is difficult when discussing 'intervention' to expunge completely from one's conceptualisation such a dichotomised view, since intervention itself rests upon this kind of distinction. For further elaboration of this point, see Long and van der Ploeg (1989) and Chapter 2 of this book.

14　For a critical appraisal of de Janvry's 'logic of capital' approach and his argument that the state acts as an instrument to resolve the crises of capitalist accumulation, see Long (1988: 108–14); see also Chapter 2 of this book.

15　This position has been sharply criticised, especially by Marxist writers (see Alavi 1973, and Foster-Carter 1978: 244).

16　See Coleman 1990 and 1994, and Elster 1985, 1986 and 1989a, for two of the most cogent applications of rational choice theory in sociology.

17　A new journal called *New Political Economy* was launched in 1996. Its Editorial Policy Statement published in the first issue draws a clear line between what one might call the 'old style' political economy whose central concern was to analyse the relationship between the public (state) and private (market) spheres, and the 'new style' political economy which aims at a more integrated and global analysis of variations in the wealth and poverty of regions, sectors, classes and states. It also underlines the importance of examining 'the responses by individuals and groups to the constraints and opportunities created by new global economic structures, and by rapidly changing identities and roles; the strategic networks of regional production and political and economic regulations; and the new social divisions that cut across territories and national boundaries'. This statement clearly signals some significant connections between political-economic, institutional and actor-oriented modes of analysis.

18 Giddens's attempt to develop a theory of structuration (1979 and 1984) offers a number of important insights into the notion of agency, but in the end tends towards a Durkheimian functionalist view. According to Cohen, Giddens 'treats society (rather than self) as an ontology, which somehow becomes independent of its own members, and assumes that the self is required continuously to adjust to it. It fails to see society adequately as informed by – created by – selves, and by implication, therefore, fails to accord creativity to selves. The "agency" which he allows to individuals gives them the power of reflexivity but not of motivation. They seem doomed to be perpetrators rather than architects of action: "agency refers not to the intentions people have in doing things but to their capability of doing those things in the first place" (Giddens 1984: 9)' (Cohen 1994: 21).

19 Compare this with what is termed the 'ecological fallacy' whereby statements based on aggregate data concerning geographical areas are extended to make inferences about the characteristics of individuals living in them. For an account of how this can misguide development policy decisions, see Bulmer (1982: 64–6).

20 For these reasons, the kind of actor-oriented analysis promoted here must be distanced from those writers who equate the notion of social actor with the dramaturgical sense of acting out roles on a stage – whether 'frontstage', 'backstage' or 'offstage' (see Goffman 1961, 1983), from symbolic interactionists who focus primarily on how the self and social meaning are reproduced (see Mead 1934, Blumer 1969), and from Touraine (1973, 1981) whose 'sociology of action' is founded upon the idea of 'historical subjects' that are framed by and emerge in specific socio-historical circumstances, engaging in 'collective projects' (e.g. the great working class movements of the nineteenth and early twentieth centuries) aimed at transforming the social order.

21 Turner offers a highly perceptive emendation to theories of social action by demonstrating the necessity of incorporating a sociology of the body, which he contends would be 'a non-trivial corrective to mainstream sociological theory' and of critical significance for current research on 'the interpenetration of the technological, biological and social worlds [which] has given rise to a new entity (the cyborg) which cross-cuts the organic and the inorganic' (Turner 1992: 95).

22 These terms are taken from Foucault's work; see especially his *Archaeology of Knowledge* (1972) where he also writes of 'discursive formations' and 'discursive objects'. As Hirst (1985: 173) points out, 'Foucault is concerned to remove the concepts of "statement" and "discourse" from the ghetto of ideas, to demonstrate that discursive formations may be regarded as complex structures of discourse-practice, in which objects, entities and activities are defined and constructed within the domain of a discursive formation'.

23 However, the locus of agency frequently shifts during ongoing social encounters and dialogues. Also in public performances it is often not obvious whose agency is at stake, since the 'speaker' may not be the 'author', and the author may not be the 'legitimate authority'. For a detailed ethnographic analysis of these points, see Keane (1997: 138–75).

24 Then we have the extremely difficult epistemological problem, identified by Fardon (1985: 129–30, 184), of imposing our own analytical ('universal') model of agency on our research data, even if we wish to 'encompass the reflexive awareness and agency of the subjects' themselves. Thus, in explaining or translating social action, we may displace the agency or intentionalities of those we study by our own 'folk' notions or theoretical concepts. Indeed it is probable that the contrast drawn by Strathern for Africa and Melanesia reflects the theoretical difference between early structural-functionalism in Africa and later exchange models as applied to Melanesia, not simply a broad cultural distinction between these two types of society.

25 The following account of my Latin America work derives from an earlier, so far unpublished, lecture given at Harvard University in December 1986 entitled 'Reflections on a Latin

American Journey: Actors, Structures and Intervention'. Slightly different versions of this original lecture have been published in Dutch and German.

26 For a fuller overview of the research see Long (1972b, 1977, 1979); and Long and Roberts (1984: 176–97).

27 Apart from myself and Ann, my wife, the research team consisted of Alberto Arce, who specialised in the study of the agricultural bureaucracy; Dorien Brunt, who focused upon household, gender and *ejido* organisation in an area of sugar production; Humberto Gonzalez, who investigated the role of Mexican agricultural entrepreneurs and companies in export agriculture; Elsa Guzman, who examined the organisation of sugar production and the struggles that occurred between the sugar producers, the mill and government; Gabriel Torres, who studied the social organisation and culture of agricultural labourers; Magda Villarreal, who studied three types of women's groups and the issue of 'countervailing power' in an *ejido* community; and Pieter van Zaag, who was responsible for the technical and organisational analysis of the irrigation system. After an initial period of fieldwork, Lex Hoefsloot joined us to undertake detailed socio-agronomic studies in a central area of the main irrigation system. In addition, several Dutch and Mexican students contributed to the project. The work was financed bilaterally by WOTRO (the Netherlands Foundation for the Advancement of Tropical Research) and the Ford Foundation, to whom we are most grateful.

28 See Roderic Camp's (1985) fascinating account of *Intellectuals and the State in Twentieth-Century Mexico*, which traces their origins, cultures, careers, institutional bases and relationships to the state; see also Bourdieu's 1988 study of the French higher education system.

Chapter 2

1 The chapter is based partly on an article co-authored with Jan Douwe van der Ploeg (1989), and partly on Long 1988.

2 Throughout the text I mainly have in mind institutional forms of intervention involving the setting up of development projects or coordinated programmes of development. Other less direct forms of intervention, such as the use of price and taxation mechanisms or other fiscal and legal measures, are not considered.

3 Development, of course, may be defined in various ways: in terms of increases in productivity or levels of production, income redistribution, increased equity or general welfare, the assault on poverty, or as a political process wherein 'disadvantaged' groups attempt to improve their life chances.

4 The interplay of theoretical and policy (or normative) models is well illustrated by the collection of papers edited by Eicher and Staatz (1984) on *Agricultural Development in the Third World*; see especially their historical overview of theories and policies covering the 1950s up to the early 1980s.

5 In discussing policy implementation, Warwick differentiates between 'planning and control', 'games', 'evolutionary' and 'transactional' models, while Pressman and Wildavsky (1983) conceptualise it as a form of explorative behaviour. An excellent collection of extracts from major texts on policy-making and implementation is that of Hill (1993). See also Marinetto's (1999) introductory overview of policy perspectives, where he traces the growing significance of issues of human agency and organising processes in policy studies. The case study illustrations in the second part of his book explore the 'interdependent coupling' of 'the emergent properties of social and political systems, and the dynamic qualities of human activity' (Marinetto 1999: 60).

6 The argument pursued here converges in important respects with recent anthropological work on development projects and intervention processes in Africa (see Olivier de Sardan 1985, 1988; Chauveau 1985, Elwert and Bierschenk 1988, and Geschiere 1989). It also coincides with some of the critical points elaborated by Schaffer (1984) in his essay 'Towards responsibility: Public policy in concept and practice'. Schaffer's essay, together with his other writings on the politics of administration and policy, remains a fertile source of ideas for developing a more systematic and critical analysis of policy processes.

7 Conyers (1982: 80), herself a researcher and planner, makes this quite explicit in her characterisation of the meaning of 'project':

...a project is normally planned and implemented as a single identifiable activity, or set of related activities. It may have many component parts or involve many different agencies or individuals; but these components are interrelated and it is therefore important that the project is planned and implemented as a whole. Consequently, a project often has its own plan document, a special project manager or management committee, its own budget allocation, and so on. The other important characteristic of a project is that it is normally located in a specific geographical area. The area may vary in size from a project such as a factory which occupies a very limited area to a regional development project covering the whole of an administrative region; but in each case the area covered by the project can be specifically defined. This characteristic [size] is often used to distinguish a 'project' from a 'programme'.

Cernea (1985: 4–5) recognises some of the practical and research limitations of the project approach:

...projects are only segmented units of intervention; they often bypass overall structures, develop atypically, and are subject to the hothouse syndrome. Projects are also criticised because they tend to create enclaves, siphon resources from parallel non-project activities, and may not generate sustainable development beyond their limited time frame.

But, in the end, his discussion simply reinforces project thinking by seeking to identify 'the sociological variables embedded in rural development projects', and by 'learning how to make operational contributions within this planned approach to development'. For a full assessment of the pros and cons of the project approach to development planning, see the debate between Rondinelli and Morgan, and a synthesis of the major points by Honadle and Rosengard in *Public Administration and Development*, vol. 3, 1983.

8 As this quotation clearly brings out, and evident earlier in his book where he sets out his general views on intervention through extension (1988: 39–42), Röling's discussion uses a mixture of pseudo-technical and medical language and analogy. Thus his account of the nature and importance of extension work relies far too heavily upon the notion that society manifests certain pathological traits that must somehow be cured through 'premeditated', 'planned', 'programmed', and usually 'professional' or 'para-professional' intervention from outside (1988: 39–41). Another shortcoming of Röling's account is the way in which he slips into a top-down, externalist and managerialist view of intervention, which he describes as follows:

A systematic effort to strategically apply resources to manipulate seemingly causal elements in an ongoing social process, so as to permanently reorient that process in directions deemed desirable by the intervening party.

(Röling 1988: 144)

Such a vision runs counter to other parts of Röling's discussion of extension strategies where he emphasises the importance of farmers as 'active in developing and adapting information and in asking for the kinds of information which they find useful. They form an active constituency which exerts countervailing clout over the whole system'.

9 If one accepts the view that so-called 'target' groups are also active strategisers, then of course the converse is also true, namely that the members of the target population may likewise use the same conceptual and administrative weapons to block the actions of intervening parties. See Scott (1985) for a discussion of the various forms that everyday resistance can take.

10 I do not, of course, exclude the possibility that intervention practices may significantly affect the social organisation of time and space of those involved. This is illustrated by irrigation projects in the Andes which, in order to cope with their own goals, introduce wage labour for the construction of canals and other infrastructure, when such work is normally organised by communities through the mobilisation of *faenas* (cooperative labour groups). Since the latter mode of organisation often entails longer time spans than the typical project cycle of five years, the organisation of time, space, labour and material resources is forced into a new and much

shorter time frame, with major social implications. For a general discussion of this problem, see van der Ploeg 1987: 155–8.

11 For a full analysis of the meaning of the 'cargo' and the nature of the esoteric knowledge sought by Melanesian cult members, see Lawrence (1964).

12 Röling (1988: 40–41) singles out communication methods and skills as the critical 'leverage instrument' for promoting behavioural change. He goes on to argue that '[c]ommunication requires shared meaning, otherwise the encoding of the message by the sender and its decoding by the receiver would not lead to the intended effect on the receiver'.

13 Apthorpe (1984) takes the argument a step further by analysing three contrasting types of development discourse ('physicalist', 'institutionalist' and 'distributionalist') used to talk about intervention programmes and policy analysis. Apthorpe and Gasper (1996) have since brought together an important collection of papers devoted to the analysis of the representations and discourses of development policy. For further exploration of issues of development discourse, see Cooper and Packard (1997), Grillo and Stirrat (1997) and Arce and Long (2000).

14 See Chapter 9 of this volume for a case illustrating this process.

15 This situation can fruitfully be compared with the increased zeal shown by members of a flying saucer cult in the United States when their prophecy failed. In *When Prophecy Fails*, Festinger, Rieken and Schachter (1964) document how, on the appointed day and hour, the believers gathered on the top of a hill where they expected to be picked up by a flying saucer and transported to the 'New World'. They had already given up their jobs and sold off most of their material possessions. However, the space vehicle failed to arrive, leaving the members of the sect with the almost impossible task of picking up where they had left off with their previous lives. While some despaired and quit the cult, in the end the majority decided to struggle on and to prepare for the next prophesied visitation. They rationalised the crisis by arguing that somehow they must have misread the signs, and perhaps this was to test their religious faith and commitment. So many decided to try again by throwing themselves enthusiastically into proselytising among the population at large. This led to a burst of renewed cult activity, although gradually over time disillusionment began to set in.

16 The term 'objectification' is used here in essentially the same way as Berger (1967: 4–15) describes 'objectivation'. Berger links the latter concept to 'externalisation' or the process by which people build the worlds around them through both physical and mental action. An externalised product acquires a distinctiveness from the person who produces it, and thus 'comes to confront him as a facticity outside of himself' – something 'out there' – that acquires the character of an 'external' and 'objective' reality that is experienced in common with others. The activity of evaluating a development project establishes it as an objectified, delimited part of social reality with its own rationale. Evaluation procedures thereby legitimate project-based activities and reinforce interventionists' conceptions of development.

17 Guda and Lincoln (1987: 207–8) provide an overview of the history of evaluation approaches. They distinguish between (1) the technical approach; (2) the descriptive approach which characterises patterns, strengths and weaknesses with respect to certain stated objectives (i.e. seeing the evaluator as 'describer'); (3) the approach which focuses upon reaching judgements and in which the evaluator assumes the role of judge while retaining the earlier technical and descriptive functions as well; and (4) the new, emerging approach which takes as its point of focus not objectives, decisions, effects or organisers but *'claims, concerns and issues'* put forth by members of a *'variety of stakeholding audiences'*, that is, audiences who are in some sense involved with the evaluation (e.g. development agents, funding bodies, beneficiaries, target groups, and 'marginalised' groups). Guda and Lincoln conclude that even with the new approach the evaluator remains a negotiator entrenched in the policy process itself.

18 As Quarles van Ufford (1988) argues, it is crucial for ensuring the inflow of money for development agencies; and may (as in the case of private Dutch donors) become the focus of intra-organisational conflict between different groups of actors within the organisation, namely between evaluators and desk officers who are charged with making allocative decisions.

19 'Rural development is concerned with the modernisation and *monetisation* of rural society, and with its transition from traditional isolation to integration with the national economy' (World Bank 1975: 3; my italics). It is on the basis of these assumptions that many intervening agencies

indeed were designated as the driving forces of commoditisation (i.e. monetarisation) and institutionalisation (i.e. integration).

20 A succinct overview of theories of the state and bureaucracy by means of selected key texts is provided by Hill (1993: 47–152).

21 Compare de Vries's 1992/1997 ethnography of the interfaces between frontline government officials and peasants in the Atlantic region of Costa Rica. De Vries distinguishes between several contrasting operational styles among implementers: an 'authoritarian' style among politically motivated *agraristas* aimed at social control, a 'propositional attitude' of extensionists geared towards establishing trust relationships with clients, and a 'negotiatory and intermediational' style of social workers (De Vries 1997: 96–134).

22 See also Alonso 1994 and Joseph and Nugent 1994.

Chapter 3

1 This chapter draws upon two earlier publications that explore methodological issues: see Long 1989 and 1997.

2 Throughout the text I use the term 'practices' to stress the concreteness of social action rather than the more abstract notion of *praxis*, which, as Bourdieu (1990: 22) rightly points out, 'tends to create the impression of something pompously theoretical...and makes one think of trendy Marxism, the young Marx, the Frankfurt School, Yugoslav Marxism'.

3 In biology, polymorphism denotes situations in which two or more variants of a species co-exist. An intriguing example is that of the African *Papilio dardanus* butterfly, whose females mimic in colour and wing pattern several other species. This heterogeneity protects them from certain predators who mistake them for other, nasty-tasting, butterflies, giving them a better chance of survival.

4 In formulating the concept of lifeworld I stress the processes by which individuals actively construct or reconfigure their lifeworlds. This contrasts with Habermas's view that lifeworlds constitute 'cultural backdrops' to communicative action.

5 Over the last few years the UK government's Department for International Development (DFID) has re-oriented its aid programme around the issue of sustainable livelihoods. A useful overview of the origins, conceptual framework and policy implications of this livelihood focus is provided by Ashley and Carney (1999). The framework developed by DFID owes much to a network of UK-based researchers but especially to the work of Ian Scoones (1998) and others at the Institute of Development Studies (IDS). Recent contributions have combined the discussion of sustainable livelihoods with the specification of five types of capital assets: human, natural, financial, social and physical.

6 Thus, as both Latour (1987) and Appadurai (1986) argue – though from different theoretical standpoints – a sociology of social action necessitates also a sociology and epistemology of things (see also Miller 1987).

7 The level of abstraction in my use of the term 'social domain' differs strikingly from that of Layder (1996: 1–28), who has recently proposed a 'theory of social domains'. The social domains identified by him are psychobiography, situated activities, social settings and contextual resources. In my view, these are far too general and lacking in specification to be useful for analytical purposes.

8 In fairness to Turner, we should note that he applies a more wide-ranging and historical approach to the analysis of social dramas in his later studies of political and religious movements (see Turner 1974, also Moore 1986).

9 The uprising was timed to coincide with the inauguration of the North American Free Trade Agreement (NAFTA) between the United States and Mexico, which was the linchpin of the new package of neoliberal measures introduced by the Salinas government.

10 That is, 'structured social practices that have a broad spatial and temporal extension: that are structured in what the historian Braudel calls the *longue durée* of time, and which are followed or acknowledged by the majority of the members of society' (Giddens 1981: 164).

11 Marx puts the point strongly by arguing that there exists a 'fetishism of commodities' whereby the 'true' nature and value of commodity exchange is concealed through 'mystification'.

12 See Blau (1964, especially 1–32 and 46–50) for a discussion of the significance of emergent forms and properties in interactional settings, and Kapferer (1972) for a systematic empirical exploration of Blau's ideas using social network and extended case methods. Prigogine (1976: 112–14) illustrates the importance of emergent structures by analysing how termites construct their mounds, a process that begins with uncoordinated and random behaviour but becomes coordinated and structured.

13 There exist a number of interesting anthropological studies on frontline government actors. See, for example, Worsley (1965) on government officers in Saskatchewan, Canada, and Raby (1978) on Sri Lankan district administrators.

14 For an interesting example of this see Gonzalez's (1972) study of the interactions between USAID officials and members of the industrial elite in the Dominican Republic.

15 See Baumann 1996, for further insight into these processes in a multi-ethnic area of London; see also Arce and Long 2000.

Chapter 4

1 The discussion that follows focuses on the studies of Pieter van der Zaag (1992), Alberto Arce (1993), Magdalena Villarreal (1994) and Monique Nuijten (1998), and draws extensively on their arguments.

2 That is, smallholder peasants with access to *ejido* land.

3 The engineers and water guards are mostly, though not exclusively, male. For this reason 'he' is used in the text when engineer or water guard are used in the singular.

4 At the time of the study (late 1980s), the latter was of great benefit since the interest rate on loans was generally 15 per cent or more per month.

5 A socio-legal entity concerned with the administration of (state-owned) land and other collective properties.

6 This is a short summary of the case. The full case study is given in Chapter 9.

7 The furthering of participation goals is not, of course, new to models of planned development (van Dusseldorp 1990). See also Frerks (1991) for a critical overview of participation in relation to planned intervention programmes.

Chapter 5

1 This chapter derives from a keynote lecture given at the XVI Colloquium on 'Las Disputas por el México Rural: Transformaciones de Practicas, Identidades y Proyectos', organised by El Colegio de Michoacán, Mexico, 16–18 November 1994, and contains extracts from Chapters 1 and 2 of *The Commoditisation Debate* (Long et al. 1986).

2 By 'commoditisation' we mean the processes by which the notion of 'exchange-value' – not necessarily at the expense of 'use-value' – comes to assume an increasingly important evaluative and normative role in the discourse and economic life of a given social unit (e.g., household, village, region or national economy). Unlike the notion of commercialisation, which addresses itself to the processes by which products acquire exchange-value through market relations, commoditisation is broader in scope since it applies to all the different phases of production and reproduction. Hence commoditisation covers not only the processes by which goods are valued in the market, but also how commodity values and relations shape consumption, production, distribution, exchange, circulation and investment patterns, cultural values and behaviour. For an analytical appraisal of the commercialisation perspective (based on modernisation theory) and the commoditisation model (based on a political economy/simple commodity model), see Vandergeest 1988, and Long and van der Ploeg 1988.

3 For a fuller theoretical and empirical treatment of the contradictory dynamics of the domains of family/kinship and the market, see de Haan's (1994) analysis of the intersection and cultural management of commodity and non-commodity values on Dutch family farms.

4 See Pieter van der Zaag's (1992) interpretation of irrigation organisation in western Mexico as a negotiated outcome of conflicting social interests and economic values; Pieter de Vries's (1992) interface analysis of the clash of lifeworlds and livelihood commitments between Costa Rican

land reform officials and their 'unruly' peasant clients; Alberto Arce's (1993) similar study of the entanglements of Mexican agricultural bureaucrats and local peasants in which he highlights critical encounters between external 'scientific' models of agricultural development and local people's knowledge and practice; Gabriel Torres's (1994) depiction of the strategic use of irony and other 'subversive' devices by Mexican tomato workers for challenging company notions of 'efficiency' and 'expert knowledge' in the production of commodities for the US market; and Magdalena Villarreal's (1994) analysis of struggles among a group of women involved in a government-initiated bee-keeping enterprise over its economic and personal value to them as individuals and as a group.

5   For a discussion of the 'double-edged' nature of discourse and practice on 'peasant cooperation' and 'collective action', which serve not only to promote sentiments of local solidarity but also to advance the interests of private entrepreneurs and an interventionist state, see Long and Roberts 1978: 297–328.

6   *Mezcal* is an alcoholic drink, like *tequila*, made from a type of *agave* cactus plant.

7   The 'externalisation' of agricultural tasks entails the increasing role of external institutions (e.g., credit banks and agencies of technical assistance and extension) and private enterprises (such as transnational companies) in shaping the farm production process. 'Scientification' refers to the process by which modern science and technology are increasingly used in agriculture.

Chapter 6

1   This chapter is co-authored with Magdalena Villarreal. An earlier draft was presented at a work-shop held in Amsterdam, June 1999, on 'Commodification and Identities: Social Life of Things Revisited', organised and funded by WOTRO (Netherlands Foundation for the Advancement of Tropical Research).

2   In a previous article (Long and Villarreal 1998) on Mexico–US cross-border commodity networks we outlined the trajectory of maize husks from production to consumption and analysed the contestation of social values entailed.

3   See Kopytoff (1986), who stresses the fluctuating nature of the meanings attached to goods and their exchange; A. Long (1992), who uses the example of local beer in Zambia to explore the multiplicity of values surrounding a specific good; and Vijfhuizen (1998: 103–32), who examines how women cultivators (*vis-à-vis* individual buyers, a food processing company and male household members) valorise and thereby shape the exchange value of particular agricultural commodities in an irrigation scheme in eastern Zimbabwe.

4   Ramirez further argues that '[i]n the standard "value chain" account, value is created by producers and destroyed by consumers. But…this idea is becoming meaningless in a world in which companies, suppliers and customers are intimately linked in a global business web with constantly changing relationships. The traditional economic units of analysis break down in such an environment. Distinctions between customers and suppliers and goods and services need to be conceived more fluidly' (1999: 132).

5   For a critique of this position as espoused by the so-called 'new' internationalisation of agriculture literature, see Marsden and Arce 1995, and Arce 1999.

6   In addition to the usual non-market values and relations associated with the domains of family and community, one should also take into account national and international interventions and discourses concerning health, pollution and the illegal trading of drugs and weapons, as well as black-market pricing, which embrace ethical, welfare and political issues that go beyond strict market criteria.

7   Money is generally considered to have five functions: a means of payment, a standard of value, a unit of account, a medium of exchange, and a store of wealth. The latter 'represents the future potential of money for making payments', although 'the assurance that the payee has, that he is under no immediate pressure to make a further payment, is decisive for the success of any monetary system' (Crump 1981: 11). This apparent paradox is pertinent to the cases of credit and delayed payment we describe in this paper. See also Hart's excellent account of the history of money and the rise of non-materialised forms of money leading to electronic digital forms in the age of the Internet (2000: 233–326). The latter marks a major shift from 'real' to 'virtual' money.

8 Here, and in Chapter 5, I use the term *commoditisation* instead of commodification because the latter focuses on the creation or reproduction of monetised or exchange value, while the former *also* takes account of the ongoing historical processes by which commodity and non-commodity relations evolve, though not necessarily in a linear or cyclical form. This depiction of commoditisation rejects those interpretations, especially prevalent in neo-Marxist political economy and commodity-chain analyses, which assume, implicitly or explicitly, a linear process of transformation.

9 This term is used in the US to refer to people living in the US who originate from one of the Latin American countries, regardless of whether or not they have legal residence.

10 Tamales consist of rolls of maize dough stuffed with meat and savouries, or mixed with cinnamon, sugar, raisins, nuts, etc., and wrapped in maize husks for steaming.

11 Magdalena Barros Nock formed part of a joint research project with the authors on 'transnational commoditisation, livelihoods and contests of value', funded by the WOTRO (Netherlands Foundation for the Advancement of Tropical Research) programme on 'Globalization and the Construction of Communal Identities' (1997–99).

12 The term 'Chicano' is sometimes used almost synonymously for Mexican-American. Both terms refer to people of Mexican origin who live permanently in the US. However, the former usually applies to someone who shows a more militant stance towards the furtherance of the rights of Mexican-Americans. For an overview of the economic, political and cultural dimensions of Mexican-American identities, see de la Garza *et al*. 1985.

13 See, for example, Alexander (1992) for an interesting discussion of price setting and the role of cultural values in Indonesian and other trading contexts.

14 See Magdalena Barros Nock (forthcoming) 'Dando y dando. Deuda, préstamos, crédito y pagos diferidos en el mercado de abastos de la calle siete en Los Angeles, California', in M. Villarreal (ed.) *Prácticas de Compensación Social y la Economía de la Deuda*. Guadalajara: CIESAS.

15 They have strong links with owners of packing plants in El Grullo – close to our main Jalisco research site – which is why we followed them up.

16 *Parceleros* is the term used by the packing plant owners to refer to maize producers (whatever their land status – private, communal or rented) who allow them to harvest the maize in exchange for the husks. Packing plant owners consider *themselves* to be the producers of the husks.

17 Maize husks have become an important product in the Autlán–El Grullo Valley, South Jalisco, although they are also produced in other Mexican regions. The valley has a long history of tomato, melon and sugar cane production, as well as maize.

18 This was maize from irrigated plots, which had been harvested in spring.

19 This issue has been quite salient in Latin American history, where debt has been used by large landowners and *hacendados* to create a forced labour system, thus trapping peons (tied labourers) and smallholders in endless cycles of loans and restitutions. Similar ordeals are presently faced by tomato pickers and sugar cane cutters in western Mexico. This labour force is composed mainly of indigenous people from other Mexican regions and is organised by squad leaders who advance them payment for their work and transport them in lorries to the region, where they are lodged in cramped, collective and barrack-like dwellings. They must continue working for the same squad leader, not only because of the debt they have acquired, but also because they have very few alternative options for work. They are billeted within an unfamiliar environment where even the language is a problem. They also depend on the squad leader for providing the lorries to return them home.

20 This earmarking bears some relation to the idea put forward by Bohannan (1955) of different spheres of exchange where there exist barriers to the conversion of goods between the spheres. Such systems he denotes as 'multicentric' as against those that are 'unicentric' with few such barriers.

21 Lave's book *Cognition in Practice* (1998) focuses upon the general issue of how standardised, 'universal' forms of knowledge are transformed into situationally specific forms and categories of quantification. More specifically it explores arithmetic use and its socio-cultural locus in time and space. Chapter six contains a section on money management practices, in which she provides a number of short case-studies of earmarking money among US families. As she reports, the participants in the study 'gave the impression that a universal standard of value and medium of exchange was *not* an advantage, and that effort went into creating

paths and flows of money which both produced and reflected the specific character of different value-expressing activities'. The examples given range from family stashes designed for specific expenditures, such as paying the mortgage, contributing to Christmas clubs, 'petty cash' funds in a teapot or sock equivalent, children's allowances, and husband's and wife's accounts to cover their personal needs. Each use was circumscribed by restrictions on ease of access and purpose of use, and only the contents of certain stashes could be transferred to other uses.

22 Although it is common practice in many countries, in some, like the Netherlands, there exists legislation that treats this as malpractice.

23 For a more detailed elucidation of the many types of earmarking and their social, economic, political and moral implications, see Zelizer's (1994) book on *The Social Meaning of Money*.

24 For example, to make the money used for Christmas gifts special, people have resorted to Christmas savings clubs where they pay money each month until December, when it is withdrawn to buy gifts. Money that is saved through a Christmas savings club is accorded different meanings by the users and by the savings institutions. When banks became involved in this they were not prepared to view such special accounts as warranting the same interest rates as general savings accounts. They did not regard them as investments, though they tried to get people to use the banking system by offering a rate of 2 per cent interest on their Christmas savings, hoping that they would then open regular savings accounts. Linked to this was the effect of gift wrapping by the shops (and later by the factories) in 'decontaminating' selected items of their market values (Waits 1993: 16–49).

25 Linked to this, as Barbara Ward (1960: 151) argues, is the fact that 'the creditor parties to such arrangements themselves have very little capital, and the number of debtors they can serve is therefore closely restricted. Furthermore, these are nearly always arrangements of personal trust made between individuals who are well acquainted with each other, and there is a limit to the number of individuals any one creditor can know well enough to trust in this way, even if he has (as he usually has not) a relatively large stock of capital'. Hence we would normally expect to find (and this is probably also true for trading maize husks) a multiplicity of traders and middlemen, each extending credit to a limited number of trustworthy debtors.

Chapter 7

1 The field material on which this chapter is based was collected in 1971–72 and updated in 1998–99 by Ulla Dalum Berg. The original material formed part of a larger project, 'Regional Structure and Entrepreneurship in a Peruvian Valley'. This project was directed by Bryan Roberts (now of the University of Texas, Austin) and myself, and was funded by grants from the Ford Foundation and from the Social Science Research Council of the United Kingdom.

2 In 1971–72, four Peruvian *soles* were roughly equivalent to one US dollar. The Church sold about 140 hectares in Matahuasi. There was no valuation of land, no public auction, and the land was sold below the market value. The price per hectare varied considerably: early purchasers like Eustaquio paid about 500 *soles*, whereas three years later the price had risen to 1,500 *soles* or more.

3 The inheritance system is bilateral with equal division of property among children of both sexes; how far the rules are followed, though, depends on the family circumstances and whether or not the property is formally registered.

4 Regional associations are organisations whose main function is to bring together migrants from the same village or region. They vary considerably in their activities, some catering primarily to the recreational needs of their members and others combining this with fundraising and lobbying activities in order to promote the development of home communities. Associations of this type are common in the mine towns and in Lima-Callao. For details, see Doughty (1970), Long (1973) and Altamirano (1984).

5 See Aubey, Kyle and Strickon (1974), who distinguish between formal groups and informal, extended networks; Epstein (1963), who differentiates between 'effective' and 'extended' networks among miners on the Zambian Copperbelt; and Leeds (1964), who draws attention to what he calls dispersed networks and organised cliques among members of the Brazilian elite.

6 Other entrepreneurs exhibit a slightly different pattern. For example, transporters in Matahuasi in the 1970s had developed close bonds of friendship with one another and with market traders through their joint membership and control of a fiesta club. This provided a flexible associational framework in which social and economic exchanges took place and acquired symbolic meaning (Long and Roberts 1984: 181–95).

7 Granovetter (1973) does not explicitly define what he means by 'weak ties', but from his definition of 'strong ties' (1973: 1361) we can conclude that the term refers to relationships where no pronounced mutual investment occurs but where there is some mutual acknowledgement of the relationship beyond merely being acquainted. Weak ties, then, are more than nodding relationships.

8 Indeed so apparent was – and still is – the prevalence of small-scale economic activities that one is tempted to compare the situation with the Indonesian bazaar-type economy described by Geertz (1963a and b). This, however, would fail to appreciate the many complex and profound ways in which the Mantaro Valley region, like most Andean locations, is now an integral part of the global commodity economy. If anything, rather than destroying local initiatives, this has dynamised the inventiveness and organisational capacities of a greater variety of small-scale entrepreneurs.

Even though, in the contemporary context, Huancayo can boast of a sector of larger-scale retail businesses and commercial and transport companies, as well as a string of banks and hotels, most of them are financed from outside as branches of national companies, and some even have transnational connections. In addition, the city and its hinterland villages (including some remote highland pastoral settlements that export labour to work on sheep ranches in the US) are becoming increasingly dollarised due to the massive flow of remittances from family members working in the US and Europe; and probably also due to money laundering associated with drugs and other illegal forms of trade. This generalised presence of dollars has not only brought onto the streets a multitude of small-scale money-changers who vie with each other for clients, but has also been a factor in injecting new life into small-scale enterprise generally.

9 Mutuality here does not exclude the possibility of hierarchical relationships, since subordinates within a network also stand to gain from the patterns of transactions that evolve. See Blau's *Exchange and Power in Social Life* (1964) for a systematic analysis of the internal dynamics and interplay of both balanced and unequal exchange relationships.

10 This is the part of the chapter that draws upon data collected in 1998–99 by Ulla Dalum Berg. She has written fieldwork reports on the organisation of the fiesta of San Sebastian and on migration and changing social identities in Matahuasi, and is presently completing a thesis on globalisation issues. She was affiliated during her work to a research project dealing with patterns of migration, globalisation and changing cultural identities, organised by Wageningen University. She had access to my original fieldwork data collected in the 1970s as a baseline for her research. The postscript is based on an original text provided by Ulla.

Chapter 8

1 The main body of this chapter consists of a revised version of a paper co-authored with Magdalena Villarreal (Long and Villarreal 1993). It also includes some material taken from Arce and Long (1994).

2 Though differing theoretically, the following works profile the growing interest in knowledge issues and development during the 1990s: Arce 1993, Escobar 1995, Ferguson 1990, Grillo and Stirrat 1997, Hobart 1993, Long and Long 1992, Long and Villarreal 1993, Marglin and Marglin 1990, Olivier de Sardan 1995, Scoones and Thompson 1994, Sillitoe 1998, Warren, Slikkeveer and Brokensha 1995. A distinctive feature of this work is that it draws insights (sometimes eclectically) from Foucauldian discourse analysis, various genres of postmodernist writings, and social constructionism.

3 Robert Merton (1973) is often cited as one of the few sociologists of this earlier generation to address the issue of the role of science in modern life. However, his views rested upon the notion that scientific practices were by and large guided by an image of science as the yardstick for 'objective', 'disinterested', 'organised questioning' that leads eventually to legislating claims to

universal 'truths' or defined 'falsehoods'. Although Merton gave attention to social institutional factors, in the end he seriously underrated the extent to which 'scientific discoveries' were an outcome of actors' social and political projects and their ideological standpoints. It was in fact C. Wright Mills (1953) who opened Pandora's box when he argued, some ten years earlier, that science and therefore mainstream sociology were driven by social and political *interests* that used knowledge not to create the 'good society' and thereby enrich and modernise people's lives, but rather to control and oppress them. Hence science was not the ideal path to democracy but instead an instrument of power relations.

4　See also Scott and Shore (1979) who explore these issues – in my opinion somewhat unconvincingly – by dichotomising 'knowledge for understanding' as against 'knowledge for action'.

5　Richards (1994: 166) further argues that, to be useful for development purposes, local knowledge must conform 'with general scientific principles, but … because it embodies place-specific experiences, allows better assessments of risk factors in production decisions'.

6　This dichotomised view can be traced back to the lively anthropological and philosophical debate on the rationality of 'modern' versus 'traditional' societies (see Horton 1967, Horton and Finnegan 1973, Hallpike 1976). In this process anthropologists rediscovered the value of relativism and what it means to break with Western philosophical conceptions. This led to the exploration of alternative cultural understandings of fundamental natural, cultural and institutional phenomena (Douglas 1975).

7　Discourse frames our understanding of life experiences by providing taken-for-granted representations of 'reality' and, in this manner, it is said to constitute the significant (and essential) objects, persons and events of our world. Building upon Foucault's perspective on discourse and knowledge/power, several recent works have explored the hegemonic nature of narratives, images and discourses rooted in international and national development institutions and ideologies (see, e.g., Ferguson 1990, Hobart 1993, and Escobar 1995). In contrast, my focus here and in Chapter 9 is on the issue of the interplay of different discourses, what Baumann (1996) calls 'dominant' and 'counter' discourses, embedded in knowledge interfaces.

8　Here it is illuminating to compare Evans-Pritchard's (1937) treatment of the situational logic of Azande witchcraft, oracles and magic with Knorr-Cetina's (1988) study on the social construction of science in a high-tech laboratory of California's Silicon Valley.

9　In addition one may distinguish between what are called 'hard' and 'soft' systems models. While the former adopts a deductive approach, the latter involves a more inductive method through first exploring the complexities of 'particular problematic situation' (see Checkland 1981).

10　For further discussion of the limitations and rigidities of a systems approach as applied to the study of farming practice (farming systems analysis) see Gatter 1993. Gatter, who worked in Zambia as a member of a farming systems team, suggests that while it may seem valid to regard agricultural activities as related in a system oriented to the achievement of specific goals, there is a danger of reading systematicity into what is being observed. In this way farmer's activities are assumed to be systematically related to form a regular and consistent body of local agricultural knowledge. There is also a tendency to work with fixed categories (e.g., subsistence cultivator, peasant farmer, and 'emergent' farmer), or with defined homogeneous farming domains, thus disregarding the essentially fluid, diverse and changing nature of farm knowledge. Fairhead (1992) applies a similar critique to research on indigenous technical knowledge, arguing that the focus on technical knowledge *per se* isolates agriculture from its social context and fails to explore the numerous ways in which non-agricultural elements shape farming practice. It also reinforces social distance between researchers and farmers, since the former apply models that dichotomise farmers' and scientists' knowledge and lead to an over-systematisation of knowledge itself.

11　More recent research by Leeuwis (1993), Engel (1995) and Salomon and Engel (1997) has used a social constructionist approach in the attempt to reconcile soft systems and social actor concepts.

12　Personal communications from Gabriel Torres and Magda Villarreal, who worked with various peasant groups in Tomatlán during the 1980s.

13　'Thus the interface might be too heterophilous to allow an effective linkage mechanism. The term linkage mechanism is reserved for the operational device which actualises the interface' (Röling 1988: 43).

14　A more detailed case of the kind of knowledge dicontinuities concerned with agriculture provides the core of Chapter 9.

15 In order to advance such work it is necessary to emphasise that '[n]etwork analysts are concerned with explanations of behaviour connected with the patterned interconnections of members, rather than the independent effects of personal dispositions or dyadic relationships. They avoid explanations of behaviour based upon normative beliefs or categorical relationships like gender, race or class, because such explanations are inherently a-structural' (Milardo 1988: 15).

16 According to Checkland 1985, adequate models must meet two criteria: namely they must be 'systematically desirable and culturally feasible in the particular situation in question', but how exactly one establishes these conditions is unclear.

17 See Long and van der Ploeg 1989 for a discussion of the 'trade of images' that takes place within intervention situations.

18 James Scott describes these issues beautifully in his book *Weapons of the Weak* (1985). His analysis falls somewhat short, however, in its reliance upon prefabricated class categories, which is his way of making the pieces (i.e., countervailing strategies) fit the puzzle (i.e., the persistence of hegemonic forms).

19 The furthering of participation goals is not, of course, new to models of planned development (van Dusseldorp 1990). See also Frerks (1991) for a critical overview of participation in relation to planned intervention programmes.

20 Pieter de Vries (1992) suggests that, with respect to development situations, the various actors advance their own interpretations of agency. Thus for experts it entails the right to 'represent' other people such as peasants and 'recipients' of state services as 'traditional', rationally risk averse, marginalised or exploited. For frontline workers, it means the capacity to create room for manoeuvre by increasing discretion while negotiating the extent to which they are accountable to superiors or to beneficiaries. Agency to farmers means the capability to choose not to become recipients of state services, to confront the authorities or adapt to them if necessary to penetrate and manipulate state bureaucracies.

21 Marglin and Marglin's analysis focuses upon the ideological dominance of Western systems of knowledge and their subordination and devaluation of other cultures and forms of knowledge. He distinguishes in ideal-typical terms between two kinds of knowledge, which he calls *techne* and *episteme*. The former represents a practical type and is the product of a personalised social order (i.e., what modernisation theorists might term a 'traditional' society), and the latter the kind that might be associated with Western science and logical reasoning (i.e., 'modern' society) while making a number of powerful criticisms of existing development theories and policies. Marglin and Marglin's argument founders, I believe, on the rocks of dichotomisation, since, like many previous writers, they posit a sharp distinction between a dominant Western knowledge system and other knowledge systems.

Chapter 9

1 This chapter is co-authored with Alberto Arce. An earlier version was published in *Boletin de Estudios Latinoamericanos y del Caribe* (Arce and Long 1987).

2 See Okely 1981: 77f. Gypsies often absorb from the wider society various symbols, rituals and myths. However, as Okely points out, this is a 'systematic, not random, selection and rejection. Some aspects in fact have been transformed or given an inverted meaning'.

3 This is not to deny, of course, that one can legitimately examine the grounds and means of reproduction for particular assumptions, beliefs and knowledge-claims.

4 The case data for this paper were collected during fieldwork in Jalisco, western Mexico, during 1983–84. The research was supported by the Economic and Social Research Council of Great Britain and affiliated to El Colegio de Jalisco, Guadalajara. Assistance was provided by students of the ITESO (*Instituto Tecnologico*) and the University of Guadalajara. Special thanks are due to the main participants of this case for letting the researchers into their lives with such *confianza* (trust).

5 Lopez Portillo had, some years earlier (1965–70) as *secretaria de la Presidencia* [Ministry of the President], initiated a project aimed at reforming the bureaucracy. It appears that he wished to use the SAM programme as a test case for developing a more efficient and rational public administration.

6 This word comes from *la grilla*, meaning the process of politicking and manipulating people for personal or small-group gain. It is likened to the monotonous and strident noise that a cricket makes when rubbing its legs. Here Roberto is perceived by his superiors as an expert in this activity. The term *grilloso*, instead of *grillo*, implies that one has this expertise.

7 In Mexico there is a well-known saying that runs: 'Con tal de barbear el jefe va quedar bien con el, son capaces de empenar el alina al diablo' (Those that crawl to the boss to keep in well with him are capable of selling their soul to the devil) (Mejia 1985: 23). This saying and the use of *chupa barba* in this administrative context highlight the fact that this behaviour is institutionalised around a set of cultural notions concerning the relations between juniors and seniors in Mexican social life.

8 The verb *zorrear* was used. This comes from the word *zorro* (fox), an animal known for its cunning. Here the implication is that the Mexican government is always devising ways of tricking people.

9 This assessment is sustained by an analysis of the number of *técnicos* and other personnel allocated to different municipalities in Rainfed District No. 1. The distributions are highly skewed, with a majority of fieldworkers being concentrated in more developed areas of the District. For details see Arce 1986: 53–8.

10 Producers exchange maize seed amongst themselves, even if the seed is exactly the same type. They maintain that this 'tricks' the soil into thinking that the seed is different from that of last year.

11 *Coamil* is a 'traditional' method of maize cultivation. It is carried out on the less productive land of the *ejido*, usually on the slopes of hills where it is impossible to use animals for ploughing. The producer digs holes for sowing with an instrument called an *azadón*. The system is highly labour intensive but, because no fertilisers are used, the inputs are relatively cheap. The plot will be used only once, after which new land will be opened up.

12 The same strategy has been noted for peasant producers in the highlands of Peru by Figueroa (1978: 33–5) who argues that insecticides are the first items of modern technology to be absorbed into existing farming systems.

13 *Convivencias* are important social gatherings, usually organised by the Head of Unit or his deputy and financed by contributions from the office staff. They take place every one or two weeks in the different *ejidos* that fall under the jurisdiction of the Unit. The invitations are extended to all personnel of the unit and sometimes staff from the District office are also invited. The secretaries and other female employees are responsible for the preparation of food and are often chivvied by the males to hurry up with the meal. At these gatherings the gender divide is very sharp: the women sit preparing the salads (with their eyes streaming from the peeling of onions) and the other dishes, whilst the men stand on the veranda of the *ejido* 'country house', drinking tequila with ice and lemon, gossiping at length about events in the District. These gatherings are crucial for consolidating links and loyalty among and between the different status groups and for the development of networks of political support. As the men become more inebriated, they engage in 'rituals of rebellion', whereby they challenge their superiors by criticising administrative procedures, etc.

Chapter 10

1 This chapter is a revised version of a keynote lecture given in Tasco, Mexico, in *Seminario Internacional: Nuevos Procesos Rurales en México: teorias, estudios de caso y perspectivas*, May–June 1994, and subsequently published in English in Moore 1996.

2 One of the most fervent protagonists of the idea that globalisation is not at all new is Wallerstein (2000), who argues that the present-day situation is no more than the latest crisis of the capitalist world economy that was born around about 1450 and has now entered its 'terminal crisis'.

3 Cf. Rhodes and Sawday (2001) for a similar exploration of the invention of printing and how in certain respects it foreshadowed the conditions of the present digital age.

4 Waters (1995: 7–8) identifies three similar 'arenas' of global change (the economic, the political and the cultural) and provides an excellent overview of the types of transformation taking place. His book is also notable for its treatment of the relations between globalisation approaches and precursor theories, focusing on notions of structural convergence, world capi-

talism, post-industrialism and postmodernity. However, somewhat surprisingly, he gives hardly any attention to the global issues of science and technology. This is clearly an important missing dimension that I specifically include in my discussion, preferring instead to deal with 'cultural change' as intrinsic to all three fields.

5 Sayer and Walker (1992) provide a detailed analysis of the reworking of divisions of labour, production systems and service and other economic activities in the late twentieth century. Marsden *et al.* (1993) and Goodman and Watts (1997) offer interpretations of post-Fordist/post-productivist tendencies in agriculture; and Smith (1999: 167–92) discusses the importance of adopting an ethnographic approach to the study of 'informalised' livelihoods and regional economies in western Europe.

6 Sassen (2000) and Held (2000) provide two recent interesting contributions to how national state politics, territoriality and forms of governance are shaped by global processes. Held points out that 'it makes more sense to talk about the transformation of state power in the context of globalisation – rather than simply to refer to what has happened as a decline…The entitlement of states to rule within circumscribed territories (sovereignty) is far from on the edge of collapse, although the practical nature of the engagement – the actual capacity of states to rule – is changing its shape' (2000: 397). Castells (1997: 243–4) takes a somewhat more radical view, arguing that 'the growing challenge to states' sovereignty around the world seems to originate in the inability of the modern nation-state to navigate the uncharted, stormy waters between the power of global networks and the challenge of singular identities'. He also shows how the global-isation of crime (through drug trafficking and the movement of other illicit items such as weapons, radioactive materials, illegal immigrants, art treasures and human organs) plays a significant part in this.

7 On the other hand, one must also note the rapid growth in the number and influence of inter-state organisations dealing with issues such as finance and trade, environmental protection and wildlife conservation; as well as the established multilateral institutions such as the World Trade Organisation (WTO), the International Monetary Fund (IMF), World Health Organisation (WHO) and the forum of G8 countries. In addition, we have witnessed the expansion of many new advocacy and protest groups organised on a transnational basis and brought together through the Internet.

8 See Castells (1996: 29–147) for a historical account of how advances in information technology interacted with shifts in the organisation, management and networking of firms to give rise to a 'globalised' informational economy 'in which information generation, processing, and transmis-sion become the fundamental sources of productivity and power' (p. 21). Compare this with Lash and Urry (1994) who characterise contemporary societies as made up of 'economies of signs and space' in which new aesthetic/expressive (as well as cognitive) forms of reflexivity become coupled to the accelerated, ever-widening global movement of goods, people, ideas and images. According to Lash and Urry, the 'structural basis for today's reflexive individuals' is the 'pervasion of *information and communication structures*'. Later they illustrate this point compara-tively: 'the thick interweaving of information structures makes the institutionally regulated Japanese and German production systems more "modern" than market-regulated Anglo-American production' (1994: 6, 108). This observation clearly points to the need for more detailed work on how information flows and communication networks actually shape the organ-ising practices and social identifications of 'global' producers, traders, distributors and consumers – an especially intriguing topic for food studies. A final point of interest concerns the fact that both Castells and Lash and Urry adopt a common notion of 'global' relations and processes. As Bartelson (2000: 189) indicates, they focus on 'networks' and 'flows' rather than on newly defined or preconstituted categories of social agents or kinds of organisations. This connects with my attempt in Chapters 1 to 3 to develop a more process- and actor-oriented framework of analysis.

9 The question of time–space compression signifies 'the intrusion of distant events into everyday consciousness' (Giddens 1991: 27). These events may concern tragic circumstances of a personal or collective nature, or they may relate to some special social occasion or celebration with which an individual or group can empathise. In this way, people are 'transported' instanta-neously from one scene to another, and thus entangled in memories of the past, visions of the future (of what could be), as well as the predicaments or commitments of the present. Although

this process is intrinsic to human experience and consciousness at all times and places, global electronic and satellite communications and media clearly facilitate and heighten the process; they also generate a more 'global' sense of self and one's location within global networks. Time–space compression and the various other ways in which time and space are interrelated (see Lash and Urry 1994: 241–51, for a full treatment of these topics) therefore have a bearing on issues of social consciousness in a global era. See Robertson (1992) for an interpretation of the notion of 'global consciousness', and Arce (1997) for a critique of his approach. Arce focuses on a topic that is germane to the present book, namely the ways in which global objects – in this case food – are incorporated into people's everyday lives.

10 A striking example of this is the website devoted to 'Global Issues That Affect Everyone', with its large database on human rights, trade and environmental issues, and questions of geopolitics. Under the sub-heading 'Free Trade and Globalisation', we find a number of informative and at times combative overviews and discussions devoted to the following topics: A Primer on Neoliberalism, WTO and Free Trade, Deregulation or Protectionism?, Some Regional Free Trade Agreements, Public Protests Around the World, WTO Protests in Seattle, etc., and a new one dealing with the Prague protests in September 2000 directed against the policies of the IMF and the World Bank. In addition, there exist other websites that offer advice for organising specific types of protest and for dealing with the media, etc. Like the Seattle protests, the Prague demonstrations involved a heterogeneous and 'unholy' mixture of interest groups: students, church groups, radical environmentalists, farmer and trade union activists, human rights and disarmament workers and extreme right-wing elements. A recent hard-hitting survey of the mounting opposition to transnational corporations traces how anti-corporate activism increasingly focuses on revealing the points of origin of brand-name goods such as the Nike sneakers sweatshops of Vietnam, the Barbie doll child labourers of Sumatra, and Shell's oil coming from the poor and polluted Ongoni villages of Nigeria (Klein 2000). The account shows how, in certain cases, citizens' groups have succeeded in forcing brand-name corporations to take measures to outlaw these and similar abusive practices at the sites of production, though much vigilance is required to ensure that more humane codes of practice are in fact effectively implemented. Klein concludes:

> When this resistance began to take shape in the mid-nineties, it seemed to be a collection of protectionists getting together out of necessity to fight everything and anything global. But as connections formed across national lines, a different agenda has taken hold, one that embraces globalisation but seeks to wrest it from the grasp of multinationals. Ethical shareholders, culture jammers, street reclaimers, McUnion organisers, human-rights hacktivists, school-logo fighters and Internet corporate watchdogs are at the early stages of demanding a citizen-centred alternative to the international rule of the brands. That demand, still sometimes in some areas of the world whispered for fear of a jinx, is to build a resistance – both high-tech and grass-roots, both focused and fragmented – that is global, and as capable of co-ordinated action, as the multinational corporations it seeks to subvert.
>
> (Klein 2000: 445–6)

11 Castells (1997) builds his theoretical interpretation of the similarities and differences of these movements on Touraine's (1965) typology of social movements based on three principles: the movement's identity, the movement's adversary and the movement's vision or social model – or what Castells calls societal goal. For a broader assessment of theories of social movements and their usefulness for the study of local and regional responses to development interventions, see Hilhorst, who emphasises the importance of social constructivist and discourse perspectives (2000: 44–72).

12 Much environmental discourse combines technical/ecological, economic, participatory and management elements. Yet the manner in which the arguments are constructed often serves to de-contextualise local issues, thus preventing local people from participating in the process of defining precisely which problems are to be considered as 'environmental'. This approach has sometimes been justified by stressing the urgent need to save an ever-diminishing domain of natural resources within a world in constant crisis. Hence environmental conservation schemes

are, it seems, frequently geared to satisfy 'global' audiences rather than the needs of local people, the so-called beneficiaries of these schemes. This process takes place within a scientific discourse where authority is accorded to 'experts'. Such expert knowledge – wrapped up in environmental policies and actions – may make little sense to those who daily have to interact with the natural environment in pursuit of their livelihoods.

13 Hoefle (2000: 495–6) makes the important distinction between riverine peasants and recent colonists of the Central Amazon, where there is a lack of wide-scale mobilisation, and the groups of Amerindians of the Amazon who have formed a coordinating indigenous organisation for the Brazilian Amazon underpinned by strong alliances with Brazilian and foreign anthropologists, environmentalists and religious organisations. 'This political movement, together with the work of their national and foreign allies, has put effective pressure on foreign governments and funding agencies who in turn have pressured the Brazilian federal government into setting aside huge areas for Amerindian's reservations and ecological reserves. The latter in turn infuriate regional politicians who favour development and the military who fear that large reservations located along [and across] national borders could be declared independent from Brazil.'

14 For a historical synopsis of changing conceptions of citizenship in Latin America, see Roberts 1995.

15 Mango (personal communication, Ph.D in progress, Wageningen University) provides a detailed analysis of the 'rediscovery' of indigenous maize varieties among Luo households of western Kenya. Hybrid maize was introduced in the 1970s, but the unfavourable man–land and cost–benefit ratios now make it much less attractive to grow. There are also fewer prospects of finding urban work to supplement household incomes. This has led to a strategic distancing from hybrid varieties and a consequent re-cultivation and experimentation with local varieties. Mango's data demonstrate that the yields for indigenous varieties can rival those of hybrid maize. Local maize is also valued for the many symbolic meanings it carries for Luo history and culture.

16 See, for example, Han Seur's (1992) impressive re-study of my original Zambian research (Long 1968). His study traces out meticulously, for one rural district of the Central Province, the introduction of ox ploughing and its interaction with existing methods of hoe and axe cultivation. This reveals a highly variegated pattern of technology use and cropping, which matches the different trajectories and situational dynamics of farm development that have evolved over the twenty- to thirty-year period. For a summary of some of his findings, see also Seur 1994.

17 In their Preface, Braun and Castree provide a mad example of the kinds of contradictory processes that can arise when environmentalists challenge development plans on the grounds that they threaten the destruction of 'natural habitat'. The case concerns the struggle that took place over the proposed extension of Manchester airport, which, it was claimed, would necessitate the clearing of an ancient area of woodland. The environmentalists took direct action by occupying the woodland and constructing tunnels and living spaces from which to defend the habitat. There followed a lot of public support for the cause and eventually the airport authorities agreed, at great extra cost, to implement an environmental preservation programme. Later, however, the professional ecologists hired by the airport authorities to implement this plan issued a report that documented the irreparable damage inflicted on this 'natural habitat' by the environmentalists themselves, and so the preservation plan was finally abandoned.

18 As Schuurman (1997) documents, decentralisation discourses are rampant and receive positive support from all quarters – international finance agents, governments, the political left, NGOs and people's organisations as well as planners and applied social scientists. The issue remains, however, as to how far such policies effectively empower local groups and strengthen local forms of governance. Or are they, as Schuurman is inclined to conclude, a part of neo-liberal discourse that contributes to the 'hollowing out of the state' and to the furtherance of global forms of capitalist exploitation? The same questions need to be carefully researched in relation to community wildlife conservation programmes and the creation of relatively autonomous national parks that cater for safari tourism.

19 Lowe et al. (1997) provide an interesting discussion of how discourses on nature, rural living and morality in the British countryside intersect at the interfaces between dairy farmers, pollution inspectors, agricultural advisors and environmentalists. The study is essentially actor-oriented in its use of interface and actor-network concepts. It concludes by elucidating how confrontations between pollution regulators and conservative, productivist farmers are avoided through the

negotiation of a new moral order based on environmentally responsible agricultural practice, which at the same time makes it possible for locally labelled 'rogue' farmers to be prosecuted for serious environmental pollution.

20 This theme has been explored in several Ph.D and postdoctoral research projects directed by myself, Alberto Arce and Magdalena Villarreal.

21 A project on this theme is presently being undertaken in respect to the central highlands of Peru under the coordination of myself and Pieter de Vries (Wageningen, the Netherlands), Teófilo Altamirano (Catholic University, Lima, Peru) and Moshe Shokheid (Tel-Aviv University, Israel).

22 See Paerregaard's (1997) detailed and insightful migration ethnography exploring the interconnections and cultural universes of rural and urban families originating from one southern Andean Peruvian community, and his continuing research on the Peruvian diaspora to other Latin American countries and to the US, Europe and Japan.

23 I prefer the concept of modes of identification to that of collective or individual social identity, since it allows one to consider a wide range of self and collective definitions, some more fixed and continuous, others more fleeting and highly situational. How people construct and attribute identifications to themselves and others offers a key to understanding cultural and socio-political orientations and commitments. How to approach the meshing of personal and collective identities, however, is a thorny issue, and one which is central to analysing both social differentiation processes and 'the collectivity' issue in social movements (cf. Gamson 1992).

BIBLIOGRAPHY

Adams, R. N. (1959) *A Community in the Andes: Problems and Progress in Muquiyauyo.* Seattle and London: University of Washington Press.
—— (1970) 'Brokers and Career Mobility Systems in the Structure of Complex Societies', *Southwestern Journal of Anthropology*, 26, 4: 315–27.
—— (1975) *Energy and Structure: A Theory of Social Power.* Austin and London: University of Texas Press.
Alavi, H. (1973) 'Peasant Classes and Primordial Loyalties', *Journal of Peasant Studies*, 1, 1: 26–62.
Albrow, M. (1996) *The Global Age.* Cambridge: Polity Press.
Alexander, J. C. (1995) *Fin de Siècle Social Theory: Relativism, Reduction, and the Problem of Reason.* London and New York: Verso.
Alexander, P. (1992) 'What's in a Price? Trade Practices in Peasant (and other) Markets', in R. Dilley (ed.) *Contesting Markets: Analyses of Ideology, Discourse and Practice.* Edinburgh: Edinburgh University Press.
Allen, T. J. and Cohen, S. T. (1969) 'Information Flow in Research and Development Laboratories', *Administrative Science Quarterly*, 14: 12–15.
Alonso, A. (1994) 'The Politics of Space, Time and Substance: State Formation, Nationalism and Ethnicity', *Annual Review of Anthropology*, 23: 379–405.
Altamirano, T. (1984) 'Regional Commitment among Central Highlands Migrants in Lima', in N. Long and B. Roberts (eds) *Miners, Peasants and Entrepreneurs: Regional Development in the Central Highlands of Peru.* Cambridge Latin American Studies, No. 48. Cambridge: Cambridge University Press.
—— (1991) 'Pastores Quechuas en el Oeste Norteamericano', *América Indígena*, 50: 2/3. Mexico: Instituto Indigenista Interamericano.
Anderson, M. (1971) *Family Structure in Nineteenth Century Lancashire.* Cambridge: Cambridge University Press.
Anderson, P. (1989) *Imagined Communities.* London: Verso.
Ansoff, H. I. (1965) *Corporate Strategy.* Harmondsworth: Penguin Books.
Appadurai, A. (ed.) (1986) *The Social Life of Things. Commodities in Cultural Perspective.* Cambridge: Cambridge University Press.
—— (1990) 'Disjuncture and Difference in Global Cultural Economy', *Public Culture*, 2: 1–24. Reprinted in A. Appadurai (1996) *Modernity at Large: Cultural Dimensions of Globalisation.* Minneapolis and London: University of Minnesota Press.
Appadurai, A. and Breckenridge, C. A. (1988) 'Why Public Culture?' *Public Culture*, 1, 1: 5–9.
Apthorpe, R. (1984) 'Agriculture and Strategies: The Language of Development Policy', in E. J. Clay and B. B. Schaffer (eds) *Room for Manoeuvre: An Exploration of Public Policy in Agriculture and Rural Development.* London: Heinemann Educational Books.
Apthorpe, R. and Gasper, D. (eds) (1996) *Arguing Development Policy: Frames and Discourses.* London: Frank Cass.
Arce, A. (1986) *Agricultural Policy Administration in a Less Developed Country: The Case of SAM in Mexico.* Ph.D. thesis, University of Manchester.
—— (1989) 'The Social Construction of Agrarian Development: A Case Study of Producer–Bureaucrat Relations in an Irrigation Unit in Western Mexico', in N. Long (ed.)

Encounters at the Interface: A Perspective on Social Discontinuities in Rural Development.
Wageningen: Wageningen Agricultural University.

—— (1993) *Negotiating Agricultural Development: Entanglements of Bureaucrats and Rural Producers in Western Mexico.* Wageningen Studies in Sociology, Wageningen: PUDOC.

—— (1997) 'Globalisation and Food Objects', in H. de Haan and N. Long (eds) *Images and Realities of Rural Life. Wageningen Perspectives on Rural Transformations.* Assen: van Gorcum.

—— (1999) 'Globalisation and Agrarian Transformations in Latin America'. Paper presented to CEDLA/WAU Workshop on 'Land in Latin America: New Context, New Claims, New Concepts' held at the Royal Tropical Institute, Amsterdam.

Arce, A. and Long, N. (1987) 'The Dynamics of Knowledge Interfaces between Mexican Agricultural Bureaucrats and Peasants: A Case from Jalisco', *Boletin de Estudios Latinoamericanos y del Caribe.* CEDLA 43, December: 5–30. Reprinted in N. and A. Long (eds) (1992) *Battlefields of Knowledge: The Interlocking of Theory and Practice in Social Research and Development.* London and New York: Routledge.

—— (1994) 'Repositioning Knowledge in Rural Development', in A. J. Jansen and D. Symes (eds.) (1994) *Agricultural Restructuring and Rural Change in Europe.* Wageningen: Wageningen Agricultural University

—— (eds) (2000) *Anthropology, Development and Modernity: Exploring Discourses, Counter-tendencies and Violence.* London and New York: Routledge.

Arce, A. and Marsden, T. (eds) (1993) 'The Social Construction of International Food: A New Research Agenda', *Economic Geography,* 69: 293–311.

Ashley, C. and Carney, D. (1999) 'Sustainable Livelihoods: Lessons from Early Experience'. DFID Paper. London: Department for International Development.

Assadourian, C. S. (1982) *El Systema de la Economia Colonial: Mercado Interno, Regiones y Espacio Económico.* Lima: Instituto de Estudios Peruanos.

Aubey, R. T., Kyle, J. and Strickon, A. (1974) 'Investment Behaviour and Elite Social Structure in Latin America', *Journal of Interamerican Studies and World Affairs,* 16: 71–95.

Barnes, J. A. (1954) 'Class and Committees in a Norwegian Island Parish', *Human Relations,* 7, 1: 39–58.

Bartelson, J. (2000) 'Three Concepts of Globalisation', *International Sociology,* 15, 2: (June): 180–96.

Basch, L., Glick Schiller, N. and Szanton Blanc, C. (1994) *Nations Unbound: Transnational Projects, Post Colonial Predicaments and Deterritorialised Nations.* Basel: Gordon and Breach.

Basu, A. and McGrory, C. V. E. (eds) (1995) *The Challenge of Local Feminisms. Women's Movements in Global Perspective.* Boulder, San Francisco and Oxford: Westview Press.

Bates, R. H. (1983) *Essays on the Political Economy of Rural Africa.* Cambridge: Cambridge University Press.

Batley, R. (1983) *Power through Bureaucracy: Urban Political Analysis in Brazil.* Aldershot: Gower.

Baudrillard, J. (1981) *For a Critique of the Political Economy of Signs.* Originally published in 1972. St Louis, MO.: Telos.

Baumann, G. (1996) *Contesting Culture: Discourses of Identity in Multi-Ethnic London.* Cambridge University Press.

Bayart, J.-F. (1993) *The State in Africa: The Politics of the Belly.* London and New York: Longman.

Beal, G. M., Dissanayake, W. and Konoshima, S. (eds) (1986) *Knowledge Generation, Exchange and Utilization.* Boulder, CO.: Westview Press.

Benedict, B. (1964) 'Capital, Savings and Credit among Mauritian Indians', in R. Firth and B. S. Yamey (eds) *Capital Savings and Credit in Peasant Societies.* London: George Allen and Unwin.

—— (1968) 'Family Firms and Economic Development', *Southwestern Journal of Anthropology,* 24: 1–19.

Bennett, J. (1968) 'Reciprocal Exchanges among North American Agricultural Operators', *Southwestern Journal of Anthropology,* 24: 276–309.

—— (1981) *Of Time and Enterprise: North American Family Farm Management in the Context of Resource Marginality.* Minneapolis: University of Minnesota Press.

Bennholdt-Thomsen, V. (1981) 'Subsistence Production and Extended Reproduction', in K. Young *et al. Of Marriage and the Market.* London: SCE Books.

Benvenuti, B. (1975) 'General Systems Theory and Entrepreneurial Autonomy in Farming: Towards a New Feudalism or Towards Democratic Planning?', *Sociologia Ruralis*, XV, 1/2: 47–62.

—— (1985) 'On the Dualism between Sociology and Rural Sociology: Some Hints from the Case of Modernization', *Sociologia Ruralis*, XXV, 3/4: 214–30.

—— (1987) 'E Ancora Valido il Concetto di Struttura? Che Cosa Cambia nelle Strutture Ambientali dell'Azienda Agraria?', in *La Struttura Productiva Agricola: Analisi, Rilevazione, Evoluzione*. Rome: INEA.

—— (1991) 'Towards the Formalisation of Professional Knowledge in Farming. Growing Problems for Agricultural Extension', in *Proceedings of the International Workshop on Agricultural Knowledge Systems and the Role of Extension*, Hohenheim, Germany: 34–50.

Benvenuti, B. and Mommaas, L. (1985) *De Technologisch-Administratieve Taakomgeving van Landbouw Bouwbedrijven: een Onderzoeksprogramma op het Terrein van de Economische Sociologie van de Landbouw*. Wageningen: Wageningen Agricultural University.

Berger, P. (1967) *The Sacred Canopy*. New York: Doubleday.

Berger, P. and Luckmann, T. (1967) *The Social Construction of Reality*. New York: Doubleday.

Bernstein, H. (1977) 'Notes on Capital and the Peasantry', *Review of African Political Economy*, 10: 50–73.

—— (1979) 'African Peasantries: A Theoretical Framework', *Journal of Peasant Studies*, 6: 421–43.

—— (1981) 'Notes on State and Peasantry: The Tanzanian Case', *Review of African Political Economy*, 21: 44–62.

—— (1985) 'The Agrarian Crisis and Commoditisation in Africa', Lecture given in Wageningen, Congress on *Technologie en Landbouwonderontwikkeling in de Derde Wereld*.

—— (1986) 'Capitalism and Petty Commodity Production', Special Issue on Social Analysis, *Journal of Cultural and Social Practice*, 20, December.

Binsbergen, W. M. J. van and Geschiere, P. L. (eds) (1985) *Old Modes of Production and Capitalist Encroachment*. London and Boston: Kegan Paul International.

Blau, P. (1964) *Exchange and Power in Social Life*. New York: John Wiley and Sons.

Blumer, H. (1969) *Symbolic Interactionism: Perspective and Method*. Berkeley: University of California Press.

Bohannan, P. (1955) 'Some Principles of Exchange and Investment among the Tiv', *American Anthropologist*, 57: 60–70.

Boiral, P., Lanteri, J.-F. and Olivier de Sardan, J.-P. (eds) (1985) *Paysans, Experts et Chercheurs en Afrique Noire. Sciences Sociales et Développement Rural*. Paris: Karthala.

Boissevain, J. (1974) *Friends of Friends. Networks, Manipulators and Coalitions*. Oxford: Basil Blackwell.

Bolhuis, E. E. and van der Ploeg, J. D. (1985) *Boerenarbeid en Stijlen van Landbouwbeoefening*. Leiden: Leiden Development Studies.

Bonnano, A., Busch, L. and Friedland, W. (1994) *From Colombus to Conagra: The Globalisation of Agriculture and Food*. Lawrence: University Press of Kansas.

Booth, D. (1985) 'Marxism and Development Sociology: Interpreting the Impasse', *World Development*, XIII, 7: 761–87.

—— (ed.) (1994) *Rethinking Social Development: Theory, Research and Practice*. Burnt Hill and Harlow: Longman Scientific and Technical.

Bott, E. (1957) *Family and Social Network*. London: Tavistock.

Bourdieu, P. (1977) *Outline of a Theory of Practice*. Cambridge: Cambridge University Press.

—— (1980) 'Le Capital Social. Notes Provisoires', *Actes de la Recherche En Sciences Sociales*, 31: 2–3.

—— (1981) 'Men and Machines', in K. Knorr-Cetina and A. V. Cicourel (eds) *Advances in Social Theory and Methodology: Toward an Integration of Micro and Macro Theories*. Boston, London and Henley: Routledge and Kegan Paul.

—— (1984) *Distinction: a Social Critique of the Judgement of Taste*. London: Routledge and Kegan Paul.

—— (1986) 'The Forms of Capital', in J. G. Richardson (ed.) *Handbook of Theory and Research for the Sociology of Education*. Westport, CT: Greenwood Press.

—— (1988) *Homo Academicus*. Cambridge: Polity Press.

—— (1990) *The Logic of Practice*. Oxford: Basil Blackwell.

Bourdieu, P. and Wacquant, L. J. D. (1992) *An Invitation to Reflexive Sociology*. Cambridge: Polity Press.

Box, L. de la Rive (1984) 'Cassava Cultivators and their Cultivars: Preliminary Results of Case Studies in the Sierra Region of the Dominican Republic', in *Proceedings of 6th Symposium of the International Society for Tropical Root Crops*. Lima: International Potato Centre.

—— (1986) 'Commoditization and the Social Organisation of Crop Reproduction: Conceptualisation and Cases', in N. Long, J.-D. van der Ploeg and C. Curtin (eds) *The Commoditization Debate: Labour Process, Strategy and Social Network*. Wageningen: Agricultural University.

—— (1987) 'Experimenting Cultivators: A Methodology for Adaptive Agricultural Research', *ODI Agricultural Administration (Research and Extension) Network Discussion Paper* 23. London: Overseas Development Institute.

—— (1989) 'Knowledge, Networks and Cultivators: Cassava in the Dominican Republic', in N. Long (ed.) *Encounters at the Interface: A Perspective on Social Discontinuities in Rural Development*. Wageningen Studies in Sociology, no. 27, Wageningen: Wageningen Agricultural University.

Braun, B and Castree, N. (1998) Remaking Reality: Nature at the Millenium. London and New York: Routledge

Bruner, J. S., Goodnow, J. J. and Austin, G. A. (1956) *A Study of Thinking*. New York: Prentice-Hall.

Brush, S. B. (1986) 'Basic and Applied Research in Farming Systems: An Anthropologist's Appraisal', *Human Organization*, 45, 3: 220–8.

Bulmer, M. (1982) *The Uses of Social Research: Social Investigation in Public Policymaking*. London: Allen and Unwin.

Burawoy, M. (1985) *The Politics of Production: Factory Regimes under Capitalism and Socialism*. London: Verso Press, New Left Books.

Burr, V. (1995) *An Introduction to Social Constructionism*. London and New York: Routledge.

Buttel, F. H. (1994) 'Agricultural Change, Rural Society, and the State in the Late Twentieth Century: Some Theoretical Observations', in D. Symes and A. J. Jansen (eds) *Agricultural Restructuring and Rural Change in Europe*. Wageningen: Wageningen Agricultural University.

—— (1997) 'Nature's Place in the Technological Transformation of Agriculture: Some Reflections on the Recombinant BST Controversy in the USA', *Environment and Planning*, A. 30: 1151–63.

Callon, M. (1986) 'Some Elements of a Sociology of Translation: Domestication of the Scallops and the Fishermen of St. Brieu Bay', in J. Law (ed.) *Power, Action and Belief: A New Sociology of Knowledge?* London, Boston and Henley: Routledge and Kegan Paul.

Callon, M. and Law, J. (1995) 'Agency and the Hybrid *Collectif*', *South Atlantic Quarterly*, 94: 481–507.

Camp, R. A. (1985) *Intellectuals and the State in Twentieth-Century Mexico*. Austin: University of Texas Press.

Cancian, F. (1966) 'Maximization as Norm, Strategy, and Theory: A Comment on Programmatic Statements in Economic Anthropology', *American Anthropologist*, 68: 465–70.

—— (1972) *Change and Uncertainty in a Peasant Economy. The Maya Corn Farmers of Zinacantan*. Stanford: Stanford University Press.

Carlos, M. (1981) *State Policies, State Penetration and Ecology: A Comparative Analysis of Uneven Development and Underdevelopment in Mexico's Micro-agrarian Regions*. La Jolla: University of California.

Carlos, M. L. and Anderson, B. (1981) 'Political Brokerage and Network Politics in Mexico: The Case of the Dominance System', in D. Willer and B. Anderson (eds) *Networks, Exchange and Coercion*. New York and London: Elsevier.

Castells, M. (1996) *The Rise of the Network Society*. Vol. 1 of *The Information Age: Economy, Society and Culture*. Oxford: Blackwell Publishers.

—— (1997) *The Power of Identity*. Vol. 2 of *The Information Age: Economy, Society and Culture*. Oxford: Blackwell Publishers.

Cernea, M. M. (ed.) (1985) *Putting People First: Sociological Variables in Rural Development*. New York and London: Oxford University Press.

Chambers, R. (1983) *Rural Development: Putting the Last First*. London, Lagos and New York: Longman.

—— (1993) *Challenging the Professions: Frontiers of Rural Development*. London: Intermediate Technology Publications.

Chambers, R., Pacey, A. and Thrupp, L. A. (1989) *Farmer First: Farmer Innovation and Agricultural Research*. London: Intermediate Technology Publications.

Chapa, J. (1978–1979) 'The Creation of Wage Labour in a Colonial Society: Silver Mining in Mexico, 1520–1771', *Berkeley Journal of Sociology*, XXIII: 99–128.

Chauveau, J. P. (1985) 'Mise en Valeur Coloniale et Développement. Perspective Historique sur Deux Exemples Ouest-Africains', in P. Boiral, J.-F. Lanteri and J.-P. Olivier de Sardan (eds) *Paysans, Experts et Chercheurs en Afrique Noire. Sciences Sociales et Développement Rural*. Paris: Karthala.

Chayanov, A. V. (1925, 1966) *The Theory of Peasant Economy*. London: Irwin.

Cheater, A. (1984) *Idioms of Accumulation: Rural Development and Class Formation among Freeholders in Zimbabwe*. Gweru: Mambo Press.

Checkland, P. (1981, second Edition 1988) *Systems Thinking, Systems Practice*. Chichester: John Wiley.

—— (1985) 'From Optimizing to Learning: A Development of Systems Thinking for the 1990s', *Journal of the Operational Research Society*, 36, 9: 757–67.

—— (1988) 'Soft Systems Methodology: An Overview', *Journal of Applied Systems Analysis*, 15: 27–30.

Chevalier, J. (1982) *Civilisation and the Stolen Gift: Capital, Kin, and Cult in Eastern Peru*. Toronto and London: University of Toronto Press.

Clammer, J. (ed.) (1978) *Towards a New Economic Anthropology*. London: Macmillan.

Clay, E. J. and Schaffer, B. B. (eds) (1984) *Room for Manoeuvre: An Exploration of Public Policy in Agriculture and Rural Development*. London: Heinemann Educational.

Clegg, S. R. (1989) *Frameworks of Power*. London: Sage.

Cochrane, A. and Pain, K. (2000) 'A Globalising Society?', in D. Held (ed.) *A Globalising World? Culture, Economics, Politics*. London and New York: Routledge and The Open University.

Cohen, A. (1994) *Self Consciousness: An Alternative Anthropology of Identity*. London and New York: Routledge.

Cohen, A. P. (1985) *The Symbolic Construction of Community*, London and New York: Tavistock and Ellis Horwood.

—— (1987) *Whalsay: Symbol, Segment and Boundary in a Shetland Island Community*. Manchester: Manchester University Press.

Coleman, J. (1990) *Foundations of Social Theory*. Cambridge, MA: Harvard University Press.

Coleman, J. S. (1988) 'Social Capital in the Creation of Human Capital', *American Journal of Sociology*, 94: S95–S120.

—— (1994) 'A Rational Choice Perspective on Economic Sociology', in N. J. Smelser and R. Swedberg (eds) *The Handbook of Economic Sociology*. Princeton, NJ and New York: Princeton University Press and Russell Sage Foundation.

Collins, R. (1981) 'Micro-Translation as a Theory-Building Strategy', in K. Knorr-Cetina and A. V. Cicourel (eds) *Advances in Social Theory and Methodology: Toward an Integration of Micro- and Macro-Sociologies*. Boston, London and Henley: Routledge and Kegan Paul.

Collinson, M. (1982) 'Farming Systems Research in Eastern Africa: The Experience of CIMMYT and Some National Agricultural Services, 1976–1981', MSU International Development Paper 3, East Lansing: Michigan State University.

Conyers, D. (1982) *An Introduction to Social Planning in the Third World*. Chichester and New York: John Wiley and Sons.

Cook, I. (1994) 'New Fruits and Vanity: Symbolic Production in the Global Food Economy', in A. Bonanno, L. Busch and B. Friedland (eds) *From Colombus to Conagra: The Globalisation of Agriculture and Food*. Lawrence: University Press of Kansas.

Cook, S. (1975) 'Economic Anthropology: Problems in Theory, Method and Analysis', in J. J. Honigman (ed.) *Handbook of Social and Cultural Anthropology*. Chicago: Rand McNally.

Cooper, F. and Packard, R. (1997) (eds) *International Development and the Social Sciences: Essays on the History and Politics of Knowledge*. Berkeley, Los Angeles and London: University of California Press.

268

Corbridge, S. (1990) 'Post-Marxism and Development Studies: Beyond the Impasse', *World Development*, 18, 5: 623–39.

—— (1994) 'Post Marxism and Post-colonialism: The Needs and Rights of Distant Strangers', in D. Booth (ed.) *Rethinking Social Development. Theory, Research and Practice.* Harlow: Longman Scientific and Technical.

Cornelius, W. A., Craig, A. L. and Fox, J. (eds) (1994) *Transforming State–Society Relations in Mexico: The National Solidarity Strategy.* La Jolla: Center of US–Mexican Studies, University of California, San Diego.

Cotler, J. (1967–1968) 'The Mechanics of Internal Domination and Social Change in Peru',. *Studies in Comparative International Development*, III 12: 229–46.

—— (1970) 'Haciendas y Comunidades Tradicionales en un Contexto de Movilizacion Politica', in R. Keith (ed.) *El Campesino en El Peru.* Lima: Instituto de Estudios Peruanos.

Crespi, F. (1992) *Social Action and Power.* Oxford and Cambridge, MA: Blackwell. (First edition in Italian, 1989.)

Croll, E. and D. Parkin (1992) 'Anthropology, the Environment and Development', in E. Croll and D. Parkin (eds) *Bush Base: Forest Farm*, London: Routledge.

Crump, T. (1981) *The Phenomenon of Money.* London: Routledge and Kegan Paul

Cyert, R. M. and March, J. G. (1963) *A Behavioural Theory of the Firm.* Englewood Cliffs, NJ: Prentice-Hall.

Dahl, R. (1961) *Who Governs? Democracy and Power in an American City.* New Haven, CT: Yale University Press.

Dalton, G. (1961) 'Economic Theory and Primitive Society', *American Anthropologist*, 62: 483–90.

Das, V. (1995) *Critical Events: An Anthropological Perspective on Contemporary India.* Delhi and Oxford: Oxford University Press.

Dissanayake, W. (1986) 'Communication Models in Knowledge Generation, Dissemination and Utilisation Activities', in G. M. Beal, W. Dissanayake and D. S. Konoshima (eds) *Knowledge Generation, Exchange and Utilisation.* Boulder, CO: Westview Press.

—— (1996) 'Introduction: Agency and Cultural Understanding. Some Preliminary Remarks', in W. Dissanayake (ed.) *Narrative of Agency: Self-making in China, India and Japan.* Minneapolis and London: University of Minnesota Press.

Doughty, P. L. (1970) 'Behind the Back of the City: "Provincial" Life in Lima, Peru?', in W. Mangin (ed.) *Peasants in Cities.* Boston: Houghton Mifflin.

Douglas, M. (1975) *Implicit Meanings: Essays in Anthropology.* London: Routledge and Kegan Paul.

Dusseldorp, D. B. W. M. van (1990) 'Planned Development via Projects: Its Necessity, Limitations and Possible Improvements', *Sociologia Ruralis*, XXX, 3/4: 336–52.

Edwards, M. (1989) 'The Irrelevance of Development Studies', *Third World Quarterly*, 11, 1 (January): 116–35.

Eicher, C. K. and Staatz, J. M. (eds) (1984) *Agricultural Development in The Third World.* Baltimore and London: Johns Hopkins University Press.

Eisenstadt, S. N. (1963) 'Need for Achievement', *Economic Development and Cultural Change*, XI, July: 420–31.

Ekeh, P. P. (1974) *Social Exchange Theory: The Two Traditions.* London: Heinemann.

Ellen, R. F. (1996) 'Introduction: 1990 Debate. Human Worlds are Culturally Constructed', in T. Ingold (ed.) *Key Debates in Anthropology.* London and New York: Routledge.

Ellen, R. F. and Fukui, K. (eds) (1996) *Redefining Nature: Ecology, Culture and Domestication.* Oxford and Washington, DC: Berg.

Elster, J. (1985) *The Multiple Self.* Cambridge: Cambridge University Press.

—— (1986) *Rational Choice.* Oxford: Basil Blackwell.

—— (1989a) *Nuts and Bolts for the Social Sciences.* Cambridge: Cambridge University Press.

—— (1989b) *The Cement of Society: A Study of Social Order.* New York and Cambridge: Cambridge University Press.

Elwert, G. and Bierschenk, T. (1988) 'Development Aid as an Intervention in Dynamic Systems', *Sociologia Ruralis*, XXVIII, 2/3, Special issue on Aid and Development: 99–113.

Engel, P. G. H. (1990) 'Knowledge Management in Agriculture: Building upon Diversity', *Knowledge in Society. The International Journal for Knowledge Transfer*, 3, 3: 28–35.

—— (1995) *Facilitating Innovation: an Action-Oriented Approach and Participatory Methodology to Improve Innovative Social Practice in Agriculture*. Ph.D thesis, Wageningen Agricultural University.

Engel, P. G. H. and Salomon, M. L. (1997) *Facilitating Innovation for Development: A RAAKS Resource Box*. Amsterdam: Royal Tropical Institute.

Epstein, A. L. (1958) *Politics in an Urban African Community*. Manchester: Manchester University Press.

—— (1963) 'The Network and Urban Social Organisation', *Rhodes-Livingstone Journal*, 29: 29–62.

Epstein, T. S. (1962) *Economic Development and Social Change in South India*. Manchester: Manchester University Press.

Escobar, A. (1995) *Encountering Development: The Making and the Unmaking of the Third World*. Princeton: Princeton University Press.

Esman, M. J. and Uphoff, N. T. (1984) *Local Organisation: Intermediaries in Rural Development*. Ithaca and London: Cornell University Press.

Evans, P. (1996a) 'Introduction: Development Strategies across the Public-Private Divide', *World Development*, 246: 1033–7.

—— (1996b) 'Government Action, Social Capital and Development: Reviewing the Evidence on Synergy', *World Development*, 246: 1119–32.

Evans-Pritchard, E. E. (1937) *Witchcraft, Oracles and Magic among The Azande*. Oxford: Clarendon Press.

Fairclough, N. (1989) *Language and Power*. London and New York: Longman.

Fairhead, J. (1992) 'Indigenous Technical Knowledge and Natural Resources Management in Sub-Saharan Africa: A Critical Overview'. Paper presented to Social Science Research Council on Project on African Agriculture Conference, Dakar, Senegal.

Fairhead, J. and Leach, M. (1995) 'False Forest History, Complicit Social Analysis: Rethinking Some West African Environmental Narratives', *World Development*, 23, 6: 1023–35.

Fals-Borda, F. (1981) *Sciencia Propria y Colonialismo Intelectual*. Bogota: Carlos Valencia.

Fardon, R. (ed.) (1985) *Power and Knowledge. Anthropological and Sociological Approaches*. Edinburgh: Scottish Academic Press.

Featherstone, M. (ed.) (1990a) *Global Culture*. London, Newbury Park, New Delhi: Sage.

—— (1990b) 'Global Culture: An Introduction', *Theory, Culture and Society*, 7, 2 and 3.

Ferguson, J. (1990) *The Anti-Politics Machine: Development, Depoliticization, and Bureaucratic Power in Lesotho*. Cambridge and New York: Cambridge University Press.

Festinger, L. H., Rieken, H. and Schachter, S. (1964) *When Prophecy Fails*. New York: Harper Torch.

Figueroa, A. (1978) 'La Economía de Las Comunidades Campesinas: El Caso de la Sierra Sur del Perú', *Publicaiones CISEPA*, 36. Lima: Universidad Católica del Perú. Dpto de Economía.

—— (1982) 'Production and Market Exchange in Peasant Economies: The Case of the Southern Highlands of Peru', in D. Lehman (ed.) *Ecology and Exchange in the Andes*. Cambridge: Cambridge University Press.

—— (1984) *Capitalist Development and the Peasant Economy in Peru*. Cambridge: Cambridge University Press.

Foster-Carter, A. (1978) 'Can We Articulate "Articulation"?', in J. Clammer (ed.) *The New Economic Anthropology*. London: Macmillan.

—— (1987) 'Knowing What They Mean: Or Why is There No Phenomenology in the Sociology of Development?', in J. Clammer (ed.) *Beyond the New Economic Anthropology*. London: Macmillan.

Foucault, M. (1972) *Archaeology of Knowledge*. London: Tavistock.

—— (1981) *The History of Sexuality. Volume 1: An Introduction*. Harmondsworth: Penguin.

Fox, B. (1980) (ed.) *Hidden in the Household: Women's Domestic Labour under Capitalism*. Ontario: The Women's Press.

Freire, P. (1970) *The Pedagogy of the Oppressed*. New York: Herder and Herder.

Frerks, G. (1991) 'Participation in Development Activities at the Local Level: Case Studies from a Sri Lankan Village'. Ph.D thesis, Wageningen Agricultural University.

Fresco, L. O. (1986) *Cassava and Shifting Cultivation. A Systems Approach to Agricultural Technology Development in Africa*. Ph.D thesis, Wageningen/Amsterdam: Wageningen Agricultural University and Royal Tropical Institute.

Fresco, L. O. and Westphal, E. (1988) 'A Hierarchical Classification of Farm Systems', *Experimental Agriculture*, 24: 399–419.

Friedmann, H. (1980) 'Household Production and the National Economy: Concepts for the Analysis of Agrarian Formations', *Journal of Peasant Studies*, 7: 158–84.

—— (1981) 'The Family Farm in Advanced Capitalism: Outline of a Theory of Simple Commodity Production in Agriculture', in F. H. Buttel and T. Murphy (eds) *The Political Economy of Agriculture in Advanced Industrial Societies*. New York: University Press of America.

Fukuyama, F. (1989) 'The End of History', *The National Interest*, 16 (Summer).

—— (1995) 'Social Capital and the Global Economy', *Foreign Affairs*, 74, 5: 89–103.

Galjart, B. (1980) 'Counterdevelopment', *Community Development Journal*, XVI: 88–96.

Galtung, J. (1982) *Development, Environment and Technology: Towards a Technology for Self-reliance*. New York: United Nations.

Gamson, W. A. (1992) 'Social Psychology of Collective Action', in A. D. Morris and C. M. Mueller (eds) *Frontiers in Social Movement Theory*. New Haven and London: Yale University Press.

Garbett, K. and Kapferer, B. (1970) 'Theoretical Orientations in the Study of Labour Migration', *The New Atlantis*, 2, 1: 179–97.

Garfinkel, H. (1967) *Studies in Ethnomethodology*. Englewood Cliffs, NJ: Prentice-Hall.

Garza, R. O. de la, Bean, F. D. and Bonjean, C. M. (eds) (1985) *The Mexican American Experience*. Austin: University of Texas.

Gasper, D. (1997) 'Logical Frameworks: A Critical Assessment'. Working Paper No. 278. The Hague: Institute of Social Studies.

Gatter, P. (1993) 'Anthropology in Farming Systems Research: A Participant Observer in Zambia', in J. Pottier (ed.) *Practising Development: Social Science Perspectives*. London and New York: Routledge.

Geertz, C. (1963a) *Peddlers and Princes: Social Change and Economic Modernization in Two Indonesian Towns*. Chicago: University of Chicago Press.

—— (1963b) 'Religious Belief and Economic Behaviour in a Central Javanese Town', *Economic Development and Cultural Change*, IV, 2: 134–58.

Gereffi, J. and Korzeniewics, T. (1994) *Global Commodity Chains*. Boulder, CO: Westview Press.

Gergen, K. J. and Gergen, M. M. (1984) 'The Social Construction of Narrative Accounts', in K. J. Gergen and M. M. Gergen (eds) *Historical Social Psychology*. Hillsdale, NJ: Lawrence Erlbaum Associates.

Gerschenkron, A. (1962) *Economic Backwardness in Historical Perspective*. New York: Harvard University Press.

Geschiere, P. L. (1989) 'Moderne Mythen: Cultuur en Ontwikkeling in Afrika'. Inaugural lecture, Leiden: University of Leiden.

Gibbon, P. and Neocosmos, M. (1985) 'Some Problems of Political Economy of "African Socialism"', in H. Bernstein (ed.) *Contradictions of Accumulation in Africa*. London: Sage.

Giddens, A. (1976) *New Rules of Sociological Method: A Positive Critique of Interpretive Sociology*. London: Hutchinson.

—— (1979) *Central Problems in Social Theory: Action, Structure and Contradiction in Social Analysis*. London: Macmillan.

—— (1981) *A Contemporary Critique of Historical Materialism*. London: Macmillan.

—— (1984) *The Constitution of Society: An Outline of the Theory of Structuration*. Cambridge: Polity Press.

—— (1987) *Social Theory and Modern Sociology*. Cambridge: Polity Press.

—— (1991) *Modernity and Self-Identity*. Cambridge: Polity Press.

Glade, W. P. (1967) 'Approaches to a Theory of Entrepreneurial Formation', *Explorations in Entrepreneurial History*, Second Series, 4, 3.

Glavanis, K. R. G (1984) 'Aspects of Non-Capitalist Social Relations in Rural Egypt: The Small Peasant Household in an Egyptian Delta Village', in N. Long (ed.) *Family and Work in Rural Societies: Perspectives on Non-wage Labour*. London and New York: Tavistock.

Gluckman, M. (1958) 'Analysis of a Social Situation in Modern Zululand', *Rhodes-Livingstone Paper*, 28. Originally published in 1940 in *Bantu Studies*, 14: 1–30, 147–74.

—— (1968) 'The Utility of the Equilibrium Model in the Study of Social Change', *American Anthropologist*, 70: 219–37.

Gluckman, M., Mitchell, J. C. and Barnes, J. (1949) 'The Village Headman in British Central Africa', *Africa*, XIX, 2: 89–106.

Godelier, M. (1972) *Rationality and Irrationality in Economics*. Translated from French by B. Pearce. London: New Left Books.

Goffman, E. (1959) *The Presentation of Self in Everyday Life*. Garden City, NY: Doubleday.

—— (1961) *Encounters: Two Studies in the Sociology of Interaction*. Harmondsworth: Penguin.

—— (1983) 'The Interaction Order'. The 1982 American Sociological Association Presidential Address. Reprinted in K. Plummer (ed.) *Symbolic Interactionism*. Vol. 2: *Contemporary Issues*. Aldershot: Edward Elgar.

Gonzalez Chavez, H. (1994) *El Empresario Agricola: En El Jugoso Negocio de las Frutas y Hortalizas de Mexico*. Ph.D thesis, Wageningen Agricultural University.

Gonzalez, N. L. (1972) 'Patron–Client Relationships at the International Level', in A. Strickon and S. M. Greenfield (eds) *Structure and Process in Latin America*. Albuquerque: University of New Mexico Press.

Goodin, R. E. (1992) *Green Political Theory*. Cambridge: Polity Press.

Goodman, D. and Redclift, M. (1981) *From Peasant to Proletarian: Capitalist Development and Agrarian Transitions*. Oxford: Blackwell.

—— (1985) 'Capitalism, Petty Commodity Production and the Farm Enterprise', *Sociologia Ruralis*, XXV, 3/4: 231–47.

Goodman, D. and Watts, M. J. (eds) (1997) *Globalising Food: Agrarian Questions and Global Restructuring*. London and New York: Routledge.

Gordon, C. (ed.) (1980) *Power, Knowledge: Selected Interviews and Other Writings 1972–1977 by Michel Foucault*. New York: Pantheon Press.

Gould, J. (1997) *Localising Modernity: Action, Interests and Association in Rural Zambia*. Helsinki: The Finnish Anthropological Society.

Gouveria, L. (1997) 'Reopening Totalities: Venezuela's Restructuring and Globalisation Debate', in D. Goodman and M. J. Watts (eds) *Globalising Food: Agrarian Questions and Global Restructuring*. London and New York: Routledge.

Grammig, T. (2001) *Observing Technical Assistance*. London and New York: Routledge

Granovetter, M. (1973) 'The Strength of Weak Ties', *American Journal of Sociology*, 78: 1360–80. Reprinted 1983 in R. Collins (ed.) *Sociological Theory*. San Francisco: Jossey-Bass.

—— (1985) 'Economic Action and Social Structure: The Problem of Embeddedness', *American Journal of Sociology*, 91: 481–510.

Gregory, C. (1982) *Gifts and Commodities*. London: Academic Press.

Grillo, D. R. and Stirrat, R. L. (eds) (1997) *Discourses of Development: Anthropological Perspectives*. Oxford and New York: Berg.

Grindle, M. (1977) *Bureaucrats, Peasants and Politicians in Mexico: A Case Study in Policy*. Berkeley and Los Angeles: University of California Press.

—— (ed.) (1980) *Politics and Policy Implementation in the Third World*. Princeton, NJ: Princeton University Press.

—— (1985) *State and Countryside: Development Policy and Agrarian Politics in Latin America*. Baltimore and London: Johns Hopkins University Press.

Guda, E. G. and Lincoln, Y. S. (1987) 'The Countenances of Fourth Generation Evaluation', in D. J. Palumbo (ed.) *The Politics of Program Evaluation*. Newbury Park, CA: Sage.

Gudeman, S. (1986) *Economics as Culture: Models and Metaphors of Livelihood*. London and New York: Routledge and Kegan Paul.

Gupta, A. (1992) 'The Song of the Non-Aligned World: Transnational Identities and Re-Inscription of Space in Late Capitalism'. *Current Anthropology*, 7, 1: 63–77.

Guyer, J. (1981) 'Household and Community in African Studies', *African Studies Review*, 24, 2/3: 86–137.

Haan, H. J. de (1994) *In the Shadow of the Tree: Kinship, Property and Inheritance among Farm Families*. Amsterdam: Het Spinhuis.

Habermas, J. (1987) *The Theory of Communicative Action: Critique of Functionalist Reason, II*. Translated by T. McCarthy. Boston: Beacon Press.

Hacking, I. (1999) *The Social Construction of What?* Cambridge, MA. and London: Harvard University Press.

Hagen, E. (1962) *On the Theory of Social Change*. Homewood, IL: Dorsey Press.

Hall, A. and Midgley, J. (eds) (1988) *Development Policies: Sociological Perspectives*. Manchester: Manchester University Press.

Hall, S. and Jacques, M. (eds) (1989) *New Times: The Changing Face of Politics in the 1990s*. London: Laurence and Wishart.

Hallpike, R. (1976) 'Is There A Primitive Mentality?', Man, New Series, II: 253–70.

Hamilton, N. (1982) *The Limits of State Autonomy: Post-Revolutionary Mexico*. Princeton: Princeton University Press.

Handelman, D. (1976) 'Bureaucratic Transactions: The Development of Official–Client Relationships in Israel', in B. Kapferer. (ed.) *Transaction and Meaning*. Philadelphia: ISHI.

—— (1978) 'Introduction: A Recognition of Bureaucracy', in D. Handelman and E. Leyton (eds) *Bureaucracy and World View: Studies in the Logic of Official Interpretation*. St John's, Newfoundland: Institute of Social and Economic Research, Memorial University of Newfoundland.

Handelman, D. and Leyton, E. (eds) (1978) *Bureaucracy and World View: Studies in the Logic of Official Interpretation*. St. John's, Newfoundland: Institute of Social and Economic Research, Memorial University of Newfoundland.

Hannerz, U. (1990) 'Cosmopolitans and Locals in World Culture', Theory, Culture and Society, 7, 2–3: 237–51.

Harriss, B. (1978) 'Access and the Co-operative: A Study of an Intermedium in Structural Change in Sri Lankan Dry Zone Paddy Production', Development and Change, 9: 277–98.

Harriss, J. (ed.) (1982) *Rural Development: Theories of Peasant Economy and Agrarian Change*. London: Hutchinson.

Harriss, J. and Renzio, P. de (1997) '"Missing Link" or Analytically Missing? The Concept of Social Capital. An Introductory Bibilographic Essay', Journal of International Development, 9, 7: 919–37.

Hart, K. (2000) *The Memory Bank: Money in an Unequal World*. London: Profile.

Harvey, N. (1998) *The Chiapas Rebellion: The Struggle for Land and Democracy*. Durham and London: Duke University Press.

Hasler, R. (1996) *Agriculture, Foraging and Wildlife Resource Use in Africa*. London: Kegan Paul International.

Havelock, R. G. (1969) *Planning for Innovation through Dissemination and Utilization of Knowledge*. Ann Arbor: Institute of Social Research, University of Michigan.

—— (1986) 'Linkage: Key to Understanding the Knowledge System', in G. M. Beal, W. Dissanayake and S. Konoshima (eds) *Knowledge Generation, Exchange and Utilization*. Boulder, CO: Westview Press.

Hawkins, E. (1991) *Changing Technologies: Negotiating Autonomy on Cheshire Farms*. Ph.D thesis, London: South Bank Polytechnic.

Hayami, Y. and Ruttan, V. (1985) *Agricultural Development: An International Perspective*. Baltimore: Johns Hopkins University Press.

Hebinck, P. and van der Ploeg, J. D. (1997) 'The Dynamics of Agricultural Production. An Analysis of Micro–macro Linkages', in N. Long and H. de Haan (eds) *Images and Realities of Rural Life: Wageningen Perspectives on Rural Transformations*. Assen: Van Gorcum.

Held, D. (1991) 'Democracy, the Nation-State and the Global System', in D. Held (ed.) *Political Theory Today*. Cambridge: Polity Press.

—— (2000) 'Regulating Globalisation? The Reinvention of Politics', International Sociology, 15, 2 (June): 394–408.

Hewitt, C. de Alcántara (1982) *Boundaries and Paradigms: The Anthropological Study of Rural Life in Post-Revolutionary Mexico*. Leiden: Leiden Development Studies 4. Revised 1984, *Anthropological Perspectives on Rural Mexico*. London: Routledge and Kegan Paul.

Higgins, B. (1968, first edition 1959) *Economic Development: Problems, Principles and Policies*. New York: Norton.

Hildebrand, P. E. (1981) 'Combining Disciplines in Rapid Appraisal: The Sondeo Approach', Agricultural Administration, 8, 6: 423–32.

Hilhorst, D. (2000) *Records and Reputations. Everyday Politics of a Philippine Development NGO*. Ph.D thesis, Wageningen University.

Hill, M. (1993) *The Policy Process. A Reader*. London and New York: Harvester Wheatsheaf.

Hindess, B. (1986) 'Actors and Social Relations', in M. I. Wadell and S. P. Turner (eds) *Sociological Theory in Transition*. Boston: Allen and Unwin.

Hirst, P. Q. (1985) 'Constructed Social Space', in R. Fardon (ed.) *Power and Knowledge. Anthropological and Sociological Approaches*. Edinburgh: Scottish Academic Press.

Hobart, M. (ed.) (1993) *An Anthropological Critique of Development: The Growth of Ignorance*. London and New York: Routledge.

Hoefle, S. W. (2000) 'Patronage and Empowerment in the Central Amazon', *Bulletin of Latin American Research*, 19, 4: 479–500.

Hondagneu-Sotelo, P. (1994) *Gendered Transitions. Mexican Experience of Immigration*. Berkeley, Los Angeles and London: University of California Press.

Horton, R. (1967) 'African Traditional Thought and Western Science', *Africa*, XXXVII: 50–71.

Horton, R. and Finnegan, R. (eds) (1973) *Modes of Thought*. London: Faber and Faber.

Hoselitz, B. F. (1964) 'A Sociological Approach to Economic Development', in D. Novack and R. Lekachman (eds) *Development and Society*. New York: St Martin's Press.

Howard, A. (1963) 'Land, Activity Systems, and Decision-Making Models in Rotuma', *Ethnology*, 2: 407–40.

Huizer, G. (1979) 'Research-through-Action: Experiences with Peasant Organisations', in G. Huizer and B. Mannheim (eds) *The Politics of Anthropology: From Colonialism and Sexism towards a View from Below*. The Hague: Mouton.

Hutchinson. S. E. (1996) 'Blood, Cattle, and Cash: The Commodification of Nuer Values', in S. E. Hutchinson *Nuer Dilemmas: Coping with Money, War, and the State*. Berkeley, Los Angeles and London: University of California Press.

Ingold, T. (1986) *The Appropriation of Nature: Essays on Human Ecology and Social Relations*. Manchester: Manchester University Press.

—— (ed.) (1996) *Key Debates in Anthropology*. London and New York: Routledge.

Isbell, B. J. (1978) *To Defend Ourselves: Ecology and Ritual in an Andean Village*. Austin: University of Texas Press.

Jamison, A. (1996) 'The Shaping of the Global Environmental Agenda: The Role of Non-Government Organisations', in S. Lash, B. Szerszynski and B. Wynne (eds) *Risk, Environment and Modernity. Towards a New Ecology*. London, Thousand Oaks, and New Delhi: Sage.

Janvry, A. de (1981) *The Agrarian Question and Reformism in Latin America*. Baltimore and London: Johns Hopkins University Press.

Jessop, B. (1982) *The Capitalist State*. Oxford: Martin Robertson.

—— (1988) 'Regulation Theory, Post Fordism and the State: More than a Reply to Werner Bonefield', *Capital and Class*, 34: 147–68.

Jones, A. D. (1966) 'Social Networks of Farmers among the Plateau Tonga', in D. Forde (ed.) *The New Elites of Tropical Africa*. Oxford: Oxford University Press.

Joseph, G. and Nugent, D. (1994) (eds) *Everyday Forms of State Formation: Revolution and the Negotiation of Rule in Modern Mexico*. Durham and London: Duke University Press.

Kapferer, B. (1972) Strategy and Transaction in an African Factory: African Workers and Indian Management in a Zambian Town. Manchester: Manchester University Press.

—— (1976) Transaction and Meaning: Directions in the Anthropology of Exchange and Symbolic Behaviour. Philadelphia: ISHI.

Kasdan, L. (1965) 'Family Structure, Migration, and the Entrepreneur', *Comparative Studies in Society and History*, VII, 4: 345–57. Reprinted 1971 in P. Kilby (ed.) *Entrepreneurship and Economic Development*. New York: The Free Press.

Kautsky, K. (1899, English reprinted version 1988) *The Agrarian Question*. London: Zwan Publications.

Kay, C. (1989) *Latin American Theories of Development and Underdevelopment*. London: Routledge.

Keane, W. (1997) *Signs of Recognition: Powers and Hazards of Representation in an Indonesian Society*. Berkeley, Los Angeles and London: University of California Press.

Kearney, M. (1988) 'Mixtec Political Consciousness: From Passive to Active Resistance', in D. Nugent (ed.) *Rural Revolt in Mexico and U.S. Intervention*. San Diego: Center for US–Mexican Studies.

—— (1991) 'Borders and Boundaries of State and Self at the End of the Empire', *Journal of Historical Sociology*, 4, 1: 53–74.

Kelly, G. (1955) *The Psychology of Personal Constructs*. New York: Norton.

Kilby, P. (ed.) (1971) *Entrepreneurship and Economic Development*. New York: The Free Press.

Kitching, G. (1985) 'Politics, Method, and Evidence in "The Kenya Debate"', in H. Bernstein and B. K. Campbell (eds) *Contradictions of Accumulation in Africa: Studies in Economy and State*. Beverly Hills: Sage.

Klein, N. (2000) *No Logo. Taking Aim at the Brand Bullies*. London: Flamingo.

Knorr-Cetina, K. D. (1981a) *The Manufacture of Knowledge: An Essay on the Constructivist and Contextual Nature of Science*. Oxford: Pergamon Press.

—— (1981b) 'The Micro-Sociological Challenge of the Macro-Sociological: Towards a Reconstruction of Social Theory and Methodology', in K. D. Knorr-Cetina and A. V. Cicourel (eds) *Advances in Social Theory and Methodology: Toward an Integration of Micro- and Macro-Sociologies*. Boston, London and Henley: Routledge and Kegan Paul.

—— (1988) 'The Micro-Social Order: Towards a Reconception', in N. G. Fielding *Actions and Structure*. London and Beverly Hills: Sage.

Knorr-Cetina, K. D. and Cicourel, A. V. (eds) (1981) *Advances in Social Theory and Methodology: Toward an Integration of Micro- and Macro-Sociologies*. Boston, London and Henley: Routledge and Kegan Paul.

Knorr-Cetina, K. D. and Mulkay, M. (eds) (1983) *Science Observed: Perspectives on the Social Study of Science*. London: Sage.

Kooiman, J. (ed.) (1993) *Modern Governance. New Government–Society Interactions*. London, Newbury Park and New Delhi: Sage.

Kopytoff, I. (1986) 'The Cultural Biography of Things: Commoditisation as Process', in A. Appadurai (ed.) *The Social Life of Things. Commodities in Cultural Perspective*. Cambridge: Cambridge University Press.

Korten, D. C. (1987) 'Introduction: Community Based Resource Management', in D. C. Korten (ed.) *Community Management: Asian Experiences and Perspectives*, West Hartford, CT: Kumarian Press.

Kosik, K. (1976) *Dialectics of the Concrete: A Study on Problems of Man and World*. Dordrecht: Reidel.

Kronenburg, J. B. M. (1986) *Empowerment of the Poor, A Comparative Analysis of Two Development Endeavours in Kenya*. Amsterdam: Royal Tropical Institute.

Kuhn, T. S. (1962) *The Structure of Scientific Revolutions*. Chicago: University of Chicago Press.

Kuiper, D and Röling, N. G. (1991) *The Edited Proceedings of the European Seminar on Knowledge Management and Information Technology*, Department of Communication and Innovation Studies, Wageningen Agricultural University.

Kunkel, J. H. (1965) 'Values and Behaviour in Economic Development', *Economic Development and Cultural Change*, 13: 257–77. Reprinted 1971 in P. Kilby (ed.) *Entrepreneurship and Economic Development*. New York: The Free Press.

Lévi-Strauss, C. (1949) *Les Structures Élémentaires de la Parenté*. Paris: Presses Universitaires de France. English translation 1969, London: Eyre and Spottiswoode.

Lacroix, A. (1981) *Transformations du Procés de Travail Agricole: Incidence de l'Industrialisation sur les Conditions de Travail Paysannes*. Grenoble: INRA-IREP.

Laguna, P. (2000) 'The Global Production of Quinoa in Bolivia', unpublished paper, Wageningen University.

Laite, J. and Long, N. (1987) 'Fiestas and Uneven Capitalist Development in Central Peru', *Bulletin of Latin American Research*, 6, 1: 27–53.

Larson, B. (1988) *Colonialism and Agrarian Transformation in Bolivia: Cochabamba, 1550–1900*. Princeton, NJ: Princeton University Press.

Lash, S. and Urry, J. (1987) *The End of Organised Capitalism*. Cambridge: Polity.

—— (1994) *Economies of Signs and Space*. London, Thousand Oaks and New Delhi: Sage.

Latour, B. (1983) 'Give Me a Laboratory and I Will Raise the World', in K. D. Knorr-Cetina and M. Mulkay (eds) *Science Observed: Perspectives on the Social Study of Science*. London: Sage.

—— (1986) 'The Powers of Association', in J. Law (ed.) *Power, Action and Belief: A New Sociology of Knowledge?* London, Boston and Henley: Routledge and Kegan Paul.

—— (1987) *Science in Action: How to Follow Scientists and Engineers through Society*. Cambridge, MA.: Harvard University Press.

—— (1993) *We Have Never Been Modern*. Cambridge, MA.: Harvard University Press.

—— (1994) 'On Technical Mediation – Philosophy, Sociology, Genealogy', *Common Knowledge*, 34: 29–64.

Lave, J. (1988) *Cognition in Practice*. Cambridge: Cambridge University Press.

Law, J. (ed.) (1986) *Power, Action and Belief: A New Sociology of Knowledge?* London, Boston and Henley: Routledge and Kegan Paul.

—— (1994) *Organising Modernity*. Oxford: Blackwell.

Lawrence, P. (1964) *Road Belong Cargo*. Manchester: Manchester University Press.

Layder, D. (1996) *Modern Social Theory: Key Debates and New Directions*. London: UCL Press.

Leeds, A. (1964) 'Brazilian Careers and Social Structure: An Evolutionary Model and Case History, *American Anthropologist*, 66: 1321–47.

Leeuwis, C. (1993) *Of Computers, Myths and Modelling: The Social Construction of Diversity, Knowledge, Information and Communication Technologies in Dutch Horticulture and Agricultural Extension*. Ph.D thesis, Wageningen Agricultural University.

Lenin, V. I. (1899, revised 1908, English edition 1977) *The Development of Capital in Russia*. Moscow: Progress.

Lindbolm, C. (1980), *The Policy-Making Process*, 2nd edition. Englewood Cliffs, NJ: Prentice-Hall.

Lionberger, H. (1960) *Adoption of New Ideas and Practices*. Ames, Io: Iowa State University Press.

Lipsky, M. (1980) *Street-Level Bureaucracy: Dilemmas of the Individual in Public Service*. New York: Russell Sage.

Lipton, M. (1968) 'The Theory of the Optimizing Peasants', *The Journal of Development Studies*, 4, 3: 327–51.

Lockie, S. D. (1996) *Sociocultural Dynamics and the Development of the Landcare Movement in Australia*. Ph.D thesis, Charles Sturt University, Australia.

Lomnitz, L. (1977) *Networks and Marginality: Life in a Mexican Shanty Town*. New York and London: Academic Press.

Lomnitz, L. and Perez-Lizuar, M. P. (1987) *A Mexican Elite Family: 1820–1980*. Princeton, NJ: Princeton University Press.

Long, A. (1992) 'Goods, Knowledge and Beer: The Methodological Significance of Situational Analysis and Discourse', in N. Long and A. Long (eds) *Battlefields of Knowledge: The Interlocking of Theory and Practice in Social Research and Development*. London and New York: Routledge.

—— (1998) 'Contested Values: Livelihoods and Wildlife Management Intervention in the Central Luangwa Valley of Zambia', unpublished paper, London School of Economics.

Long, A. and Ploeg, J. D. van der (1995) 'Reflections on Agency, Ordering the Future and Planning', in G. E. Frerks and J. H. D. den Ouden (eds) *In Search of the Middle Ground: Essays on the Sociology of Planned Development*. Wageningen: Wageningen Agricultural University.

Long, N. (1968) *Social Change and the Individual: Social and Religious Responses to Innovation in a Zambian Rural Community*. Manchester: Manchester University Press.

—— (1972) 'Kinship and Associational Networks among Transporters in Rural Peru: The Problem of the "Local" and the "Cosmopolitan" Entrepreneur, Paper in seminar series on Kinship and Social Networks. London: Institute of Latin American Studies, University of London.

—— (1973) 'The Role of Regional Associations in Peru', in M. Drake *et al.* (eds) *The Process of Urbanization*. Bletchley: The Open University.

—— (1977a) *An Introduction to the Sociology of Rural Development*. London: Tavistock.

—— (1977b) 'Commerce and Kinship in Highland Peru', in R. Bolton and E. Mayer (eds) *Andean Kinship and Marriage*, Washington, DC: American Anthropological Association.

—— (1979) 'Multiple Enterprise in the Central Highlands of Peru', in S. N. Greenfield *et al.* (eds) *Entrepreneurs in Cultural Context*. Alberquerque: University of New Mexico Press.

—— (ed.) (1984a) *Family and Work in Rural Societies: Perspectives on Non-wage Labour*. London: Tavistock.

—— (1984b) 'Creating Space for Change: A Perspective on the Sociology of Development'. Inaugural lecture, Wageningen: Agricultural University. Revised version in *Sociologia Ruralis*, XXIV, 3–4: 168–84.

—— (1988) 'Sociological Perspectives on Agrarian Development and State Intervention', in A. Hall and J. Midgley (eds) *Development Policies: Sociological Perspectives*. Manchester: Manchester University Press.

—— (ed.) (1989) *Encounters at the Interface: A Perspective on Social Discontinuities in Rural Develop-ment.* Wageningen Studies in Sociology, No. 27, Wageningen: Wageningen Agricultural University.

—— (1990) 'From Paradigm Lost to Paradigm Regained: The Case for an Actor Oriented Sociology of Development', *European Review of Latin American and Caribbean Studies*, 49: 3–24.

—— (1992) 'From Paradigm Lost to Paradigm Regained: The Case for an Actor-oriented Sociology of Development', in Long and Long (eds.) 1992.

—— (1997) 'Constraints and Agency, Precepts and Practice: A Theoretical Position', in H. de Haan and N. Long (eds.) (1997) *Images and Realities of Rural Life*: Wageningen Perspectives on Rural Transformations. Assen: Van Gorcum.

Long, N., J. D. van der Ploeg, and Curtin, C. (1986) *The Commoditisation Debate: Labour Process, Strategy and Social Networks*, Wageningen: Wageningen Agricultural University.

Long, N. and Long, A. (eds) (1992) *Battlefields of Knowledge: The Interlocking of Theory and Practice in Social Research and Development.* London and New York: Routledge.

Long, N. and Ploeg, J. D. van der (1988) 'New Challenges in the Sociology of Rural Development: A Rejoinder to Peter Vandergeest', *Sociologia Ruralis*, XXVIII, 1: 30–41.

—— (1989) 'Demythologising Planned Intervention: An Actor Perspective', *Sociologia Ruralis*, XXIX, 3/4: 226–49.

—— (1994) 'Heterogeneity, Actor and Structure: Towards a Reconstitution of the Concept of Structure', in D. Booth (ed.) *New Directions in Social Development: Relevance, Realism and Choice.* London: Longmans.

Long, N. and Richardson, P. (1978) 'Informal Sector, Petty Commodity Production and Social Rela-tions of Small-Scale Enterprise', in J. Clammer (ed.) *Towards a New Economic Anthropology.* London: Macmillan.

Long, N. and Roberts, B. (eds) (1978) *Peasant Cooperation and Capitalist Expansion in Central Peru.* Austin, TX: University of Texas Press.

—— (1984) *Miners, Peasants and Entrepreneurs: Regional Development in the Central Highlands of Peru.* Cambridge Latin American Studies, No. 48. Cambridge: Cambridge University Press.

Long, N. and Villarreal, M. (1989) 'The Changing Lifeworlds of Women in a Mexican Ejido: The Case of the Beekeepers of Ayuquila and the Issue of Intervention', in N. Long (ed.) *Encounters at the Interface: A Perspective on Social Discontinuities in Rural Development.* Wageningen Studies in Sociology, No. 27, Wageningen: Wageningen Agricultural University.

—— (1993) 'Exploring Development Interfaces: From the Transfer of Knowledge to the Transfor-mation of Meaning', in F. J. Schuurman (ed.) *Beyond the Impasse: New Directions in Development Theory.* London: Zed Books.

—— (1998) 'Small Product, Big Issues: Value Contestations and Cultural Identities in Cross-Border Commodity Networks', *Development and Change*, 29 (4), October 1988: 725–50.

Long, N. and Winder, D. (1975) 'From Peasant Community to Production Cooperative: An Anal-ysis of Recent Government Policy in Peru', *Journal of Development Studies*, 12: 75–94.

Lonsdale, J. (1981) 'States and Social Processes in Africa: An Historical Survey', *African Studies Review*, XXIV: 2–3.

Lowe, P., Clark, J. and Seymour, S. (1997) *Moralising the Environment. Countryside Change, Farming and Pollution.* London: UCL Press.

Mackay, H. (2000) 'The Globalisation of Culture' in D. Held (ed.) *A Globalising World? Culture, Economics, Politics.* London and New York: Routledge and The Open University

McClelland, D. C. (1961) *The Achieving Society.* New York: The Free Press.

McCrone, D. (1992) *Understanding Scotland: The Sociology of a Stateless Nation.* London: Routledge.

McMichael, P. (ed.) (1994) *The Global Restructuring of Agro-Food Systems.* Ithaca: Cornell Univer-sity Press.

Malkki, L. H. (1995) *Purity and Exile. Violence, Memory and National Cosmology among Hutu Refugees in Tanzania.* Chicago and London: University of Chicago Press.

Mannheim, K. (1936) *Ideology and Utopia: An Introduction to the Sociology of Knowledge.* New York: Harcourt Brace and World.

Marglin, F. A. and Marglin, S. A. (eds) (1990) *Dominating Knowledge: Development Culture and Resis-tance.* WIDER Studies in Development Economics. Oxford: Clarendon.

Marglin, S. A. (1990) 'Towards the Decolonisation of the Mind', in F. A. Marglin and S. A. Marglin (eds) *Dominating Knowledge: Development Culture and Resistance*. WIDER Studies in Development Economics. Oxford: Clarendon.

Mariátegui, J. C. (1928) *Siete Ensayos de Interpretación de la Realidad Peruana*. Lima: Amauta.

Marinetto, M. (1999) *Studies of the Policy Process: A Case Analysis*. London and New York: Prentice-Hall.

Marsden, T. (2000) 'Food Matters and the Matter of Food: Towards a New Food Governance?', *Sociologia Ruralis*, 40, 1: 20–9.

Marsden, T., Murdoch, J. and Lowe, P. (1993) *Constructing the Countryside*. Restructuring Rural Areas 1. London: UCL Press.

Marsden, T. K. and Arce, A. (1993) 'Constructing Quality: Globalisation, the State and Food Circuits', *Globalisation of Agriculture and Food*, Working Paper No.1, The University of Hull and Wageningen Agricultural University.

—— (1995) 'Constructing Quality: Emerging Food Networks in the Rural Transition', *Environment and Planning A*, 27: 1261–79.

Marsden, T. K., Lowe, P. and Whatmore, S. (1992) *Labour and Locality: Uneven Development and the Rural Labour Process*. London: Fulton.

Martinez, S. T. (1983) *Los Campesinos y el Estado en Mexico*. Ph.D thesis, Mexico: Universidad Iberoamericana.

Marx, K. (1852, English edition 1962) 'The Eighteenth Brumaire of Louis Bonaparte', *Selected Works* (2 vols). Moscow: Foreign Languages Publishing House.

—— (1867, English edition 1979) *Capital*. Vol. 1. London: Wishart.

Masterman, M. (1970) 'The Nature of a Paradigm', in I. Lakatos and M. Musgrave (eds) *Criticism and the Growth of Knowledge*. Cambridge: Cambridge University Press.

Mead, G. H. (1934) 'Mind, Self and Society', in W. Morris (ed.) *Mind, Self and Society*. Chicago: Chicago University Press.

Meillassoux, C. (1972) 'From Reproduction to Production', *Economy and Society*, 1, 1: 93–105.

Mejía, J. P. (1985) *Así Habla el Mexicano: Diccionario Básico de Mexicanismos*. Mexico City: Panorama Editorial, S. A.

Merton, R. K. (1973) *The Sociology of Science: Theoretical and Empirical Investigations*. Chicago: Chicago University Press.

Mey, M. de (1982) *The Cognitive Paradigm*. Dordrecht, Boston and Lancaster: Reidel.

Miele, M. (2001) *Creating Sustainability: The Social Construction of the Market for Organic Products*, Ph.D thesis, Wageningen University.

Milardo, R. M. (ed.) (1988) *Families and Social Networks*. London: Sage.

Millar, D. (1994) 'Experimenting Farmers in Northern Ghana', in I. Scoones and J. Thompson (eds) *Beyond Farmer First: Rural People's Knowledge, Agricultural Research and Extension Practice*. London: Intermediate Technology Publications.

Miller, D. (1987) *Material Culture and Mass Consumption*. Oxford: Blackwell.

Miller, P. and Rose, N. (1990). 'Governing Economic Life', *Economy and Society*, 19, 1: 1–31.

Milliband, R. (1969) *The State in Capitalist Society*. New York: Basic Books.

Mitchell, J. C. (1969) *Social Networks in Urban Situations: An Analysis of Personal Relationships in Central African Towns*. Manchester: Manchester University Press.

Monberg, T. (1970) 'Determinants of Choice in Adoption and Fosterage on Bellona Island', *Ethnology*, 9: 99–136.

Mongbo, R. L. (1995) *The Appropriation and Dismembering of Development Intervention: Policy, Discourse and Practice in the Field of Rural Development in Benin*. Ph.D thesis, Wageningen Agricultural University.

Montoya, R. (1970) *A Propósito de Caracter Predominantemente Capitalista de la Economía Peruana Actual*. Lima: Ediciones Teoria y Realidad.

Moore, H. L. (ed.) (1996) *The Future of Anthropological Knowledge*. London and New York: Routledge.

Moore, S. F. (1973) 'Law and Social Change: The Semi-Autonomous Social Field as an Appropriate Subject of Study', *Law and Society Review*, Summer: 719–46.

—— (1986) *Social Facts and Fabrications: 'Customary' Law on Kilimanjaro, 1880–1980*. Cambridge: Cambridge University Press.

Moser, C. (1996) *Confronting Crisis: A Comparative Study of Household Responses to Poverty and Vulnerability in Four Poor Urban Communities*. Environmentally Sustainable Studies and Monograph Series No. 8. Washington, DC: World Bank.

Moser, C. and Holland, J. (1997) *Urban Poverty and Violence in Jamaica*. World Bank Latin American and Caribbean Studies. Washington, DC: World Bank.

Mouzelis, N. P. (1988) 'Sociology of Development: Reflections on the Present Crisis', *Sociology*, 22, 1: 23–44.

—— (1994) *Back to Sociological Theory: The Construction of Social Orders*. London and New York: Routledge

Nelson, N. and Wright, S. (eds) (1995) *Power and Participatory Development: Theory and Practice*. London: Intermediate Technology Publications.

Njonjo, A. L. (1981) 'The Kenya Peasantry: A Re-Assessment', *Review of African Political Economy*, 20: 27–40.

Normann, R. and Ramirez, R. (1993) 'From Value Chain to Value Constellation', *Harvard Business Review*, July–August: 65–7.

—— (1994) *Designing Interactive Strategy*. New York and Chichester: John Wiley and Sons.

Nuijten, M. (1998) 'History, Story Telling, and the Construction of Community', in M. Nuijten *In the Name of the Land: Organisation, Transnationalism and the Culture of the State in a Mexican Ejido*. Ph.D thesis, Wageningen University.

—— (1998) *In the Name of the Land: Organisation, Transnationalism and the Culture of the State in a Mexican Ejido*. Ph.D thesis, Wageningen University.

Okali, C., Sumberg, J. and Farrington, J. (1994) *Farmer Participatory Research: Rhetoric and Reality*. London: Intermediate Technology Publications.

Okely, J. (1981) *The Traveller-Gypsies*. Cambridge: Cambridge University Press.

Olivier de Sardan, J. P. (1985) 'Sciences Sociales Africanistes et Faits de Developpement', in P. Boiral *et al.* (eds) *Paysans, Experts et Chercheurs en Afrique Noire. Sciences Sociales et Développement Rural*. Paris: Karthala.

—— (1988) 'Peasant Logics and Development Project Logics', *Sociologia Ruralis*, XXVIII, 2/3: 216–27.

—— (1995) *Anthropologie et Développement: Essai en Socio-anthropologie du Changement Social*. Marseille and Paris: APAD and Karthala.

Oppenheimer, A. (1996) *Bordering on Chaos: Guerrillas, Stockbrokers, Politicians, and Mexico's Road to Prosperity*. Boston, New York, Toronto and London: Little, Brown.

Orlove, B. and Custred, G. (1980) 'The Alternative Model of Agrarian Society in the Andes: Households, Networks and Corporate Groups', in B. Orlove and G. Custred (eds) *Land and Power in Latin America: Agrarian Economics and Social Process in the Andes*. New York: Holmes and Meier.

Ortiz, S. (1967) 'The Structure of Decision-Making', in R. Firth (ed.) *Themes in Economic Anthropology*. London: Tavistock.

—— (1973) *Uncertainties in Peasant Farming: A Colombian Case*. London: Athlone Press.

Ouden, J. den (1995) 'Who's for Work? The Management of Labour in the Process of Accumulation in Three Adja Villages, Bénin', *Africa*, 65, 1: 1–35.

Paerregaard, K. (1997) *Linking Separate Worlds. Urban Migration and Rural Lives in Peru*. Oxford: Berg.

Pahl, R. E. (1984) *Divisions of Labour*. Oxford and New York: Basil Blackwell.

Palumbo, D. J. (ed.) (1987) *The Politics of Program Evaluation*. Beverley Hills and London: Sage.

Palumbo, D. J. and Nachmias, D. (1983) 'The Pre-Conditions for Successful Evaluation. Is there an ideal type?', *Policy Sciences*, 16: 67–79.

Parker, I. (1992) *Discourse Dynamics: Critical Analysis for Social and Individual Psychology*. London: Routledge.

Parkin, D. (1972) *Palms, Wines, and Witnesses: Public Spirit and Private Gain in an African Farming Community*. London: Intertext Books.

Patnaik, U. (1979) 'Neo-Populism and Marxism: The Chayanovian View of the Agrarian Question and its Fundamental Fallacy', *Journal of Peasant Studies*, 6, 4: 375–420.

Peña, G. de la (1986) 'Poder Local, Poder Regional: Perspectivas Socioantropológicas', in J. Padua and A. Vanneph (eds) *Poder Local, Poder Regional*. Mexico City: El Colegio de Mexico/CEMCA.

—— (1994) 'Rural Mobilisations in Latin America since c. 1920', in L. Bethell (ed.) *The Cambridge History of Latin America*, Vol. VI, Part II, *Latin America since 1930. Economy, Society and Politics*. Cambridge and New York: Cambridge University Press.

Peluso, N. L. (1993) 'Coercing Conservation: The Politics of State Resource Control', in Lipschutz and K. Conca (eds) *The State and Social Power in Global Environmental Politics*. New York: Columbia University Press.

Perri 6 (1994) 'Trust, Social Theory and Public Policy: Directions for Research'. Working paper, Social Policy Unit, University of Bath.

Pigg, S. (1992) 'Inventing Social Categories through Place: Social Representations and Development in Nepal', *Comparative Studies in Society and History*, 34: 491–513.

Pile, S. (1990) *The Private Farmer: Transformation and Legitimation in Advanced Capitalist Agriculture*. Aldershot: Dartmouth.

Ploeg, J. D. van der (1977) *De Gestolen Toekomst, Imperialisme, Landhervorming en Boerenstrijd in Peru*. Wageningen: Uitbuit.

—— (1986) 'The Agricultural Labour Process and Commoditization', in N. Long, Ploeg, J. D. van der and Curtin, C. *The Commoditisation Debate: Labour Process, Strategy and Social Networks*. Wageningen: Wageningen Agricultural University

—— (1987) *De Verwetenschappelijking van de Landbouwbeoefening*. Wageningen: Wageningen Agricultural University.

—— (1989) 'Knowledge Systems, Metaphor and Interface: The Case of Potatoes in the Peruvian Highlands', in N. Long (ed.) *Encounters at the Interface: A Perspective on Social Discontinuities in Rural Development*. Wageningen Studies in Sociology, No. 27, Wageningen: Wageningen Agricultural University.

—— (1990) *Labour, Markets and Agricultural Development*. Boulder, San Francisco and Oxford: Westview Press.

—— (1992) 'The Reconstitution of Locality: Technology and Labour in Modern Agriculture', in T. K. Marsden, P. Lowe and S. Whatmore, *Labour and Locality: Uneven Development and the Rural Labour Process*. London: Fulton.

—— (1999) *De Virtuele Boer*. Assen: Van Gorcum.

Plummer, K. (ed.) (1991) *Symbolic Interactionism*. Vol. 2: *Contemporary Issues*. Aldershot: Edward Elgar.

Polanyi, K. (1944) *The Great Transformation*. Boston: Beacon Press.

Pollack, D. C. and Reiken, R. E. van (1999) *The Third Culture Kid Experience: Growing Up among Worlds*. Yarmouth: Intercultural Press.

Portes, A. (ed.) (1995) *The Economic Sociology of Immigration*. New York: Russell Sage.

Portes, A. and Landolt, P. (1996) 'The Downside of Social Capital', *The American Prospect*, 26: 18–22.

Potter, J. and Wetherel, M. (1987) *Discourse and Social Psychology: Beyond Attitudes and Behaviour*. London: Sage.

Pottier, J. (1988) *Migrants No More: Settlement and Survival in Mambwe Villages, Zambia*. Manchester: Manchester University Press.

—— (ed.) (1993) *Practising Development: Social Science Perspectives*. London and New York: Routledge.

—— (1997) 'Towards an Ethnography of Participatory Appraisal and Research', in R. D. Grillo and R. L. Stirrat (eds) *Discourses of Development: Anthropological Perspectives*. Oxford and New York: Berg.

—— (1999) *Anthropology of Food. The Social Dynamics of Food Security*. Cambridge and Oxford: Polity Press.

Powell, W. W. and Smith-Doerr, L. (1994) 'Network in Economic Life', in N. J. Smelser and R. Swedberg (eds) *The Handbook of Economic Sociology*. Princeton, NJ and New York: Princeton University Press and Russell Sage Foundation.

Prattis, J. I. (1973) 'Competing Paradigms and False Polemics in Economic Anthropology', *Anthropological Quarterly*, 46, 4: 278–96.

Pressman, J. L. and Wildavsky, A. (1983), *Implementation*. Berkeley, Los Angeles and London: University of California Press.

Preston, P. (1996) *Development Theory. An Introduction*. Oxford: Blackwell.

Prigogine, I. (1976) 'Order Through Fluctuation: Self-Organisation and Social System', in E. Jantsch and C. H. Waddington *Evolution and Consciousness. Human Systems in Transition*. Reading, MA. and London: Addison-Wesley.

Putman, R. (1993) *Making Democracy Work: Civic Traditions in Modern Italy*. Princeton, NJ: Princeton University Press.

—— (1995) 'Bowling Alone: America's Declining Social Capital', *Journal of Democracy*, 6, 1: 65–78.

Putzel, J. (1997) 'Accounting for the "Dark Side" of Social Capital: Reading Robert Putnam on Democracy', *Journal of International Development*, 9, 7: 939–49.

Quarles van Ufford, P. (1988) 'The Myth of Rational Development Policy: Evaluation versus Policy-Making in Dutch Private Donor Agencies', in P. Quarles van Ufford, D. Kruijt and T. Downing (eds) *The Hidden Crisis in Development: Development Bureaucracies*. Amsterdam: Free University Press.

Quarles van Ufford, P., Kruijt, D. and Downing, T. (eds) (1988) *The Hidden Crisis in Development: Development Bureaucracies*. Amsterdam: Free University Press.

Röling, N. G. (1988) *Extension Science: Information Systems in Agricultural Development*. Cambridge: Cambridge University Press.

—— (1990) 'The Agricultural Research-Technology Transfer Interface: A Knowledge Systems Perspective', in D. Kaimowitz (ed.) *Making the Link. Agricultural Research and Technology Transfer in Developing Countries*. Boulder, Colorado: Westview Press.

Röling, N. G. and Engel, P. G. H. (1990) 'Information Technology from a Knowledge Systems Perspective: Concepts and Issues', *Knowledge in Society: The International Journal of Knowledge Transfer*, 3, 3: 6–18.

Raby, A. N. (1978) *Bureaucracy, Politics, and Society in a Provincial Town in Sri Lanka*. Ph.D thesis. San Diego: University of California.

Radin, N. J. (1996) *Contested Commodities*. Cambridge, MA. and London: Harvard University Press.

Ramirez, R. (1999) 'Unchaining Value in a New Economic Age', in *Mastering Global Business*. London: Financial Times and Pitman Publishing.

Ranger, T. (1985) *Peasant Consciousness and Guerrilla War in Zimbabwe*. London: James Currey.

Redclift, N. (1985) 'The Contested Domain: Gender, Accumulation and the Labour Process', in N. Redclift and E. Mingione (eds) *Beyond Employment: Household, Gender and Subsistence*. Oxford: Basil Blackwell.

Rees, S. (1978) *Social Work Face to Face: Clients' and Social Workers' Perceptions of the Content and Outcomes of their Meetings*. London: Edward Arnold.

Rey, P.-P. (1975) 'The Lineage Mode of Production', *Critique of Anthropology*, 3: 27–79.

Rhoades, R. E. (1984) *Breaking New Ground: Agricultural Anthropology*. Lima: International Potato Centre.

Rhoades, R. E. and Bebbington, A. J. (1988) *Farmers Who Experiment: An Untapped Resource for Agricultural Development*. Lima: International Potato Centre.

—— (1990) 'Mixing it up. Traditional Farmer Rationales for Mixed Cropping Practices in Peru', *Field Crops*, 25: 145–56.

Rhodes, N. and Sawday, J. (2001) *The Renaissance Computer. Knowledge in the First Age of Print*. London and New York: Routledge.

Richards, P. (1985) *Indigenous Agricultural Revolution*. London: Hutchinson.

—— (1994) 'Local Knowledge Formation and Validation: The Case of Rice Production in Central Sierra Leone', in I. Scoones and J. Thompson (eds) *Beyond Farmer First: Rural People's Knowledge, Agricultural Research and Extension Practice*. London: Intermediate Technology Publications.

Ritzer, G. (1975) *Sociology. A Multiple Paradigm Science*. Boston: Allyn and Bacon.

Roberts, B. and Spener, D. (1994) 'Social Networks and Trade on the Texas Mexico Border: The Role of Small-Scale Enterprise in the Integration of Transnational Space', Paper presented at the Latin American Studies Association XVIIIth International Congress, Atlanta, Georgia, March.

Roberts, B. R. (1995) 'The Development of Citizenship', in B. R. Roberts *The Making of Citizens. Cities of Peasants Revisited*. London and New York: Arnold and Halsted Press.

Robertson, A. (1984) *People and the State: The Anthropology of Planning*. Cambridge: Cambridge University Press.

Robertson, R. (1992) *Globalisation: Social Theory and Global Culture*. London: Sage.

Robinson, J. A. and Majak, R. R. (1967) 'The Theory of Decision-Making', in J. C. Charlesworth (ed.) *Contemporary Political Analysis*. New York: The Free Press.

Rocco, R. (1997) 'Citizenship, Culture and Community: Restructuring in Southeast Los Angeles', in W. V. Flores and R. Benmayor (eds) *Latino Cultural Citizenship: Claiming Identity, Space and Rights*. Boston: Beacon Books.

Roe, E. (1991) 'Development Narratives, Making the Best of Blueprint Development', *World Development*, 19, 4: 287–300.

Roest, K. de (2000) *The Production of Parmiggiano-Reggiano Cheese. The Force of an Artisinal System in an Indistrialised World*. Assen: Van Gorcum.

Rogers, E. M. (1962, third edition 1983) *Diffusion of Innovation*. Glencoe, IL: The Free Press.

Rogers, E. M. and Shoemaker, F. F. (1971) *Communication of Innovations: A Cross-Cultural Approach*. New York: Free Press.

Rosaldo, R. and Flores, W. V. (1997) 'Identity, Conflict, and Evolving Latino Communities: Cultural Citizenship in San Jose, California', in W. V. Flores and R. Benmayor (eds) *Latino Cultural Citizenship: Claiming Identity, Space and Rights*. Boston: Beacon Books.

Rosenau, J. N. (1967) 'The Premises and Promises of Decision-Making Analysis', in J. C. Charlesworth (ed.) *Contemporary Political Analysis*. New York: The Free Press.

Rouse, R. (1991) 'Mexican Migration and the Social Space of Post-Modernism', *Diaspora*, 1, 1: 8–23.

Rubin, I. I. (1973, originally published 1886) *Essays on Marx's Theory of Value*. Montreal: Black Rose Books.

Said, E. W. (1978) *Orientalism*. New York: Random House.

Salomon, M. L. and Engel, P. G. H. (1997) *Networking for Innovation: A Participatory Actor-Oriented Methodology*. Amsterdam: The Royal Tropical Institute.

S.A.M. (1980) *Systema Alimentario Mexicano*. Mexico City: Mexican Government Publication.

Samaniego, C. (1978) 'Peasant Movements at the Turn of the Century and the Rise of the Independent Farmer', in N. Long and B. Roberts (eds) *Peasant Cooperation and Capitalist Expansion in Central Peru*. Austin, TX: University of Texas Press.

Sanderson, S. E. (1986) *The Transformation of Mexican Agriculture: International Structure and the Politics of Rural Change*. Princeton, NJ: Princeton University Press.

Sarbin, T. R. and Kitsuse, J. I. (eds) (1994) *Constructing the Social*. London, Thousand Oaks, New Delhi: Sage.

Sassen, S. (2000) 'Territory and Territoriality in the Global Economy', *International Sociology*, 15, 2 (June): 372–93.

Sayer, A. and Walker, R. (1992) *The New Social Economy: Reworking the Division of Labour*. Cambridge, MA. and Oxford: Blackwell.

Schaffer, B. (1984) 'Towards Responsibility: Public Policy in Concept and Practice', in E. J. Clay and B. Schaffer (eds) *Room for Manoeuvre: An Exploration of Public Policy in Agriculture and Rural Development*. London: Heinemann Educational.

Schaffer, B. and Lamb, G. (1976) 'Exit, Voice and Access', *Social Science Information*, 13, 6: 73–90.

Schatz, S. P. (1965) 'Achievement and Economic Growth: A Critical Appraisal', *Quarterly Journal of Economics*, 79, 2: 234–41.

Schneider, H. K. (1974) *Economic Man: The Anthropology of Economics*. New York: The Free Press.

Schuthof, P. (1989) 'Common Wisdom and Shared Knowledge: Knowledge Networks among the Tonga of Mola Chiefdom in Zimbabwe'. Unpublished Report of the Centre of Applied Social Studies, University of Zimbabwe, and Department of Rural Extension and Adult Education, Wageningen Agricultural University.

Schutz, A. (1962) *The Problem of Social Reality*. The Hague: Mijhoff.

—— (1967) *Phenomenology of the Social World*. Evanston, IL: Northwestern University Press.

Schutz, A. and Luckmann, T. (1973) *The Structures of the Life-world*. Evanston, IL: Northwestern University Press.

Schuurman, F. J. (ed.) (1993) Beyond the Impasse: New Directions in Development Theory. London: Zed Press.

—— (1997) 'The Decentralisation Discourse: Post-Fordist Paradigm or Neo-Liberal Cul-de-Sac?', *The European Journal of Development Research*, 9, 1: 150–66.

Scoones, I. (1998) 'Sustainable Rural Livelihoods: A Framework for Analysis'. Working Paper No 72. Brighton: Institute of Development Studies.

Scoones, I. and Thompson, J. (eds) (1994) *Beyond Farmer First: Rural People's Knowledge, Agricultural Research and Extension Practice*. London: Intermediate Technology Publications.

Scott, J. C. (1985) *Weapons of the Weak: Everyday Forms of Peasant Resistance*. New Haven and London: Yale University Press.

Scott, R. A. and Shore, A. R. (1979) *Why Sociology does not Apply: A Study of the Use of Sociology in Public Policy*. New York: Elsevier.

Seur, H. (1992) *Sowing the Good Seed: The Interweaving of Agricultural Change, Gender Relations and Religion in Serenje District, Zambia*. Ph.D thesis, Wageningen Agricultural University.

—— (1994) 'Peasants, Policy and the Plough: The Introduction, Adoption and Transformation of Agricultural Innovations in Chibale Chiefdom, Central Province', in K. Crehan and A. von Oppen (eds) *Planners and History. Negotiating Development in Rural Zambia*. Lusaka: Multi-Media Press.

Shirley, R. W. (1971) *The End of a Tradition: Culture Change and Development in the Municipio of Cunha, São Paulo, Brazil*. New York: Columbia University Press.

Sik, E. (1984) 'Reciprocal Exchange of Labour in Contemporary Hungary', *Papers on Labour Economics*, No. 5, Department of Labour and Education Economics. Budapest: Karl Marx University of Economics.

Sillitoe, P. (1998) 'What Know Natives? Local Knowledge in Development', *Social Anthropology: The Journal of the European Association of Social Anthropologists*, 6, 2: 203–20.

Simon, H. A. (1959) 'Theories of Decision-Making in Economics and Behavioural Science', *American Economic Review*, 49, 3: 253–83.

Siriwardena, S. S. A. L. (1989) *From Planned Intervention to Negotiated Development. The Struggle of Bureaucrats, Farmers and Traders in the Mahaweli Irrigation Scheme in Sri Lanka*. Ph.D thesis, Wageningen Agricultural University.

Skar, H. O. (1982) *The Warm Valley People: Duality and Land Reform among Quechua Indians of Highland Peru*. Oslo-Bergen-Tromso: Universitets-forgalet.

Skar, S. L. (1984) 'Interhousehold Co-operation in Peru's Southern Andes: A Case of Multiple Sibling-Group Marriage', in N. Long (ed.)(1984a).

Sklair, L. (1991) *Sociology of the Global System*. New York/London: Harvester Wheatsheaf.

Skocpol, T. (1979) *States and Social Revolution: A Comparative Analysis of France, Russia and China*. Cambridge: Cambridge University Press.

—— (1985) 'Bringing the State Back In. Strategies of Analysis in Current Research', in P. Evans, S. Rueschemeyer and T. Skocpol (eds) *Bringing the State Back In*. Cambridge: Cambridge University Press.

Slater, D. (1990) 'Fading Paradigms and New Agendas – Crisis and Controversy in Development Studies', *European Review of Latin American and Caribbean Studies*, 49: 25–32.

—— (1997) *Consumer Culture and Modernity*. Cambridge: Polity Press.

Slicher van Bath, B. (1985) 'In Acculturatie-Processen is het Allernieuwste niet steeds het Allerbeste'. Paper presented at International Agricultural Centre Meeting on Studiekring voor Ontwikkelingsvraagstukken.

Smelser, N. J. and Swedberg, R. (eds) (1994) *The Handbook of Economic Sociology*. Princeton, NJ and New York: Princeton University Press and Russell Sage Foundation.

Smith, G. (1984) 'Confederations of Households: Extended Domestic Enterprises in City and Country', in N. Long and B. Roberts (eds) *Miners, Peasants and Entrepreneurs: Regional Development in the Central Highlands of Peru*. Cambridge and New York: Cambridge University Press.

—— (1989) *Livelihood and Resistance: Peasants and the Politics of Land Reform in Peru*. Berkeley: University of California Press.

—— (1999) *Confronting the Present: Towards a Politically Engaged Anthropology*. Oxford and New York: Berg.

Smith, G. A. (1986) 'Reflections on the Social Relations of Simple Commodity Production', *Journal of Peasant Studies*, 13: 99–108.

Spahr van der Hoek, J. J. and Postma, O. (1952) *Geschiedenis van der Friese Landbouw*, Deel 1. Leeuwarden: Friesche Maatschappij van Landbouw.

Spradley, J. P. (1972) 'Adaptive Strategies in Urban Nomads: The Ethnoscience of Tramp Culture', in T. Weaver and D. White (eds) *The Anthropology of Urban Environments*. Washington, DC: The Society for Applied Anthropology Monograph Series 11.

Srinivas, M. N. (1969) *Social Change in Modern India*. Berkeley and Los Angeles: University of California Press.

Standage, T. (1998) *The Victorian Internet*. London: Weidenfeld and Nicolson.

Stephen, L. (1997) *Women and Social Movements in Latin America. Power from Below*. Austin: University of Texas Press.

Stepputat, F. (2000) 'At the Frontiers of the Modern State in Post-War Guatemala', in A. Arce and N. Long (eds) *Anthropology, Development and Modernity: Exploring Discourses, Counter-tendencies and Violence*. London and New York: Routledge.

Stern, S. J. (ed.) (1987) *Resistance, Rebellion and Consciousness in the Andean Peasant World, 18th to 20th Centuries*. Madison: University of Wisconsin Press.

Stolzenbach, A. (1994) 'Learning by Improvisation: Farmers' Experimentation in Mali', in I. Scoones and J. Thompson (eds) *Beyond Farmer First: Rural People's Knowledge, Agricultural Research and Extension Practice*. London: Intermediate Technology Publications.

Strathern, M. (1985) 'Knowing Power and being Equivocal: Three Melanesian Contexts', in R. Fardon (ed.) *Power and Knowledge. Anthropological and Sociological Approaches*. Edinburgh: Scottish Academic Press.

—— (1988) *The Gender of the Gift: Problems with Women and Problems with Society in Melanesia*. Berkeley and Los Angeles: University of California Press.

Strickon, A. (1972) 'Carlos Felipe: Kinsman, Patron and Friend', in A. Strickon and S. M. Greenfield (eds) *Structure and Process in Latin America*. Albuquerque: University of New Mexico Press.

Sutherland, A. (1987) *Sociology in Farming Systems Research*. Occasional Paper 6, Agricultural Administration Unit, London: Overseas Development Institute.

Taussig, M. T. (1980) *The Devil and Commodity Fetishism in South America*. Chapel Hill: University of North Carolina Press.

Terray, E. (1972) *Marxism and 'Primitive' Societies*. London and New York: Monthly Review Press. (Original French edition 1969.)

Thibaut, J. W. and Kelley, H. H. (1959) *The Social Psychology of Groups*. New York: John Wiley.

Thomas, N. (1991) *Entangled Objects: Exchange, Material Culture, and Colonialism in the Pacific*. Cambridge, MA.: Harvard University Press.

Thompson, J. (1990) *Ideology and Modern Culture*. Cambridge: Polity Press.

Torres, G. (1994) *The Force of Irony: Studying the Everyday Life of Tomato Workers in Western Mexico*. Ph.D thesis, Wageningen Agricultural University. Revised version 1997, Oxford and New York: Berg.

Touraine, A. (1965) *Sociologie de l'Action*. Paris: Editions du Seuil.

—— (1973) *Production de la Société*. Paris: Editions du Seuil. (English translation 1977, *The Self-Production of Society*. Chicago: University of Chicago Press.)

—— (1981) 'The Historical Actors', in *The Voice and the Eye. An Analysis of Social Movements*. Cambridge and Paris: Cambridge University Press/Editions de la Maison des Sciences de L'homme.

—— (1984) 'Is Sociology Still the Study of Society?', *thesis Eleven*, 23.

—— (1989) 'The Waning Sociological Image of Social Life', *International Journal of Comparative Sociology*, 25, 1 and 2.

Turnbull, B. (1998) *Street Children and their Helpers: A Social Interface Analysis*. D.Phil. thesis, Brighton, University of Sussex.

Turner, B. (1992) 'Regulating Bodies: The Sociology of the Body', in B. S. Turner *Regulating Bodies: Essays in Medical Sociology*. London and New York: Routledge.

Turner, V. W. (1957) *Schism and Continuity in an African Society*. Manchester: Manchester University Press.

—— (1974) *Dramas, Fields and Metaphors: Symbolic Action in Human Society*. Ithaca and London: Cornell University Press.

Uphoff, N. (2000) 'Understanding Social Capital: Learning from the Analysis and Experience of Participation'. Presentation given at Wageningen University, October.

Vanclay, F. (1994) *The Sociology of the Australian Agricultural Environment*. Ph.D thesis, Wageningen Agricultural University.

Vandergeest, P. (1988) 'Commercialisation and Commoditisation: A Dialogue between Perspectives', *Sociologia Ruralis*, XXVIII, 1: 7–29.

Velsen, J. van (1964) *The Politics of Kinship.* Manchester, Manchester University Press.

—— (1967) 'Situational Analysis and the Extended Case Method', in A. L. Epstein (ed.) *The Craft of Anthropology.* London: Tavistock.

Velzen, T. van (1973) 'Robinson Crusoe and Friday: Strengths and Weakness of the Big Man Paradigm', *Man*, 8, 4: 592–612.

Verschoor, G. M. (1997) *Tacos, Tiendas and Mezcal: An Actor-Network Perspective on Small-Scale Entrepreneurial Projects in Western Mexico.* Ph.D thesis, Wageningen University.

Vijfhuizen, C. (1998) *The People We Live With: Gender Identities and Social Practices, Beliefs and Power in the Livelihoods of Ndau Women and Men in a Village with an Irrigation Scheme in Zimbabwe.* Ph.D thesis, Wageningen Agricultural University.

Villarreal, M. (1990) *A Struggle over Images: Issues of Power, Gender and Intervention in a Mexican Village.* M.Sc. thesis, Wageningen Agricultural University.

—— (1992) 'The Poverty of Practice: Power, Gender and Intervention from an Actor-Oriented Perspective', in N. Long and A. Long (eds) *Battlefields of Knowledge: The Interlocking of Theory and Practice in Social Research and Development.* London and New York: Routledge.

—— (1994) *Wielding and Yielding: Power, Subordination and Gender Identity in the Context of a Mexican Development Project.* Ph.D thesis, Wageningen Agricultural University.

—— (2000) 'Deudas, Drogas, Fiado y Prestado en las Tiendas de Abarrotes Rurales', *Revista Desacatos*, 3. México D.F.: CIESAS.

Vries, P. de, (1992)*Unruly Clients: A Study of How Bureaucrats Try and Fail to Transform Gatekeepers, Communists and Preachers into Ideal Beneficiaries.* Ph.D thesis, Wageningen Agricultural University. Reprinted in revised form by CEDLA, Amsterdam (1997).

Waits, W. B. (1993) *The Modern Christmas in America: A Cultural History of Gift Giving.* New York and London: New York University Press.

Waldinger, R. D. (1986) *Through the Eye of the Needle: Immigrants and Enterprise. New York's Garment Trades.* New York: New York University Press.

—— (1996) *Still the Promised City? African-Americans and New Immigrants in Post-Industrial New York.* Cambridge, MA.: Harvard University Press.

Wall, R. (ed.) (1983) *Family Forms in Historic Europe.* Cambridge: Cambridge University Press.

Wallerstein, I. (1990) 'Societal Development, or Development of the World-System?', in M. Albrow and E. King (eds) *Globalisation, Knowledge and Society.* London: Sage.

—— (2000) 'Globalisation or the Age of Transition? A Long-term View of the Trajectory of the World System', *International Sociology*, 15, 2 (June): 249–65.

Wallman, S. and associates (1982) *Living in South London: Perspectives on Battersea 1871–1981.* Aldershot: Gower, for the London School of Economics and Political Science.

Walton, J. (1985) 'Review of Miners, Peasants and Entrepreneurs', *Contemporary Sociology*, 14, 4: 471–2.

Ward, B. (1960) 'Cash or Credit Crops?', *Economic Development and Cultural Change*, 8: 148–63.

Warren, D. M., Slikkeveer, L. J. and Brokensha, D. (1995) *The Cultural Dimension of Development Indigenous Knowledge Systems.* London: Intermediate Technology Publications.

Warwick, D. (1982) *Bitter Pills: Population Policies and their Implementation in Developing Countries.* Cambridge: Cambridge University Press.

Waters, M. (1995) *Globalisation.* London and New York: Routledge.

Watson, W. (1958) *Tribal Cohesion in a Money Economy: A Study of the Mambwe People of Zambia.* Manchester: Manchester University Press.

Wikan, U. (1990) *Managing Turbulent Hearts: A Balinese Formula for Living.* Chicago and London: University of Chicago Press.

Willems, S. (2001) 'Knowledge Differences and Social Diversity among Global Pineapple Producers in the Ivory Coast', unpublished paper, Wageningen University.

Wilson, F. (ed.) (1999) *Violencia y Espacio Social: Estudio sobre Conflicto y Recuperacin.* Lima: Traducoras Asociadas.

Winder, D. (1974) *The Effect of the 1970 Reform on the 'Peasant Communities' and on the Community Development Process in an Area of Peru.* M.Ed. thesis, Manchester University.

Winkler, J. (1976) 'Corporatism', *European Journal of Sociology*, XVII: 100–36.

INDEX

access theory 67–9
actor-oriented approach 1, 2, 9–29, 191, 224–5,
    227; advantages 13, 14–15, 49, 57; and
    agency *see* agency; and agrarian structure 40;
    arguments against and shortcomings 4, 14,
    15, 62; central significance of starting from
    'lived experience' 14–15; and
    commoditisation 107–9; and concern for
    discourse 53; cornerstones of 49–50, 240–3;
    criticised for being 'methodologically
    individualist' 4; criticism of emphasis on
    discursive rationality of individuals 15; and
    exploring intervention processes in western
    Mexico 26–8; farmer responses and strategies
    44–5; fundamental principle of 90; and
    knowledge 170, 182; reasons for central
    theoretical importance 20; and social
    constructionism 3–4, 18; and state
    intervention 45–8
actors' projects, interlocking of 61–2, 89
actors, social 13, 53, 91, 238, 241; and agency
    16–17, 50–1, 90, 112–13, 182; 'collective' 56–7
Adams, R.N. 56
Africa 98, 101; bride payments 104; colonialism
    99; and notion of personhood 19; role of
    headman 66
agency 4, 12–13, 16–19, 24, 48, 49, 50–1, 56,
    62, 89, 90, 112–13, 182, 240–1 agrarian
    development/change 43, 44–5, 46, 48, 107;
    commoditisation approach 11, 98–9, 101,
    236–7; and heterogeneity 39, 44, 224;
    interface and clash of cultural paradigms 70;
    and intervention 38–9, 46; *see also* farmers
agrarian movements 219–20
agrarian structure(s): actor-oriented approach to
    40; and interface actor networks 233–4; and
    processes of institutionalisation 39–41
agricultural export quotas: European Union 219
agricultural extension: systems model in 171–2
agricultural knowledge 173, 179–80
agriculture: globalisation and localisation 224–6
aid, development 52

Alejandrina 163
Alfredo (Eric Hutton) (Jiménez family) 148,
    151, 162–3, 166
'alternative development' associations 218
Althuserian structuralism 28
Amazonian groups 219
American 'Patriot' movement 218
Andes: small-scale producers 182–3
Ansoff, H.I. 134
Antonio (Jiménez family) 147, 162
Appadurai, A. 108, 221, 229
APRA (*Alianza Popular Revolucionaria
    Americana*) 145
Arce, Alberto 47, 51, 67, 91
areas de castigo ('punishment zones') 47
arenas *see* social arenas
Atilio (Jiménez family) 142, 147, 148, 162
Aum Shinrikyo millenarian cult 218
Autlán-El Grullo irrigation scheme (Mexico)
    73–9

Balinese 14
Bangladesh: floods in 84
Battlefields of Knowledge (Long and Long) 107
bee-keeping enterprise (Mexico) 79–81, 178,
    183
Benedict, B. 146
Bennett, J. 44–5
Benvenuti, B. 43, 61
Benvenuti, B. *et al* 179
Bernstein, H. 40, 43, 97, 98, 99, 101, 104
Bhopal chemical plant disaster (1984) 60–1, 84
'blackboxing' 19–20, 84, 92
Bolhuis, E.E. and van der Ploeg, J.D. 44
Bolivia 219
Booth, David 3, 22
Bourdieu, P. 14, 58, 130, 132
Bourdieu, P. and Wacquant, L.J.D. 58
Box, Louk 179, 180
Brazil: Leeds' work on social careers 135–6
bribes 127, 128
bricolage 51